THEY FOUGHT on the wettest wildest beachheads and under the hottest fire this side of hell.

And now the men who were there tell about it. Here are their blazing firsthand reports of the War in Europe—of Dunkirk, Tobruk, Dieppe, Sicily and Salerno.

And here are special maps and commentaries to give complete, authentic background for each report and put it in the larger context of the War in Europe.

This is a companion volume to COMBAT: THE WAR WITH JAPAN.

COMBAT
THE WAR WITH GERMANY

WORLD WAR II

Edited by DON CONGDON
Introduction by Herbert Mitgang

A DELL BOOK / an original edition

Published by DELL PUBLISHING CO., INC.
750 Third Avenue, New York 17, N.Y.
© Copyright, 1963, by Don Congdon
Dell ® TM 681510, Dell Publishing Co., Inc.
First printing—September, 1963
Second printing—December, 1963

Printed in U.S.A.

Contents

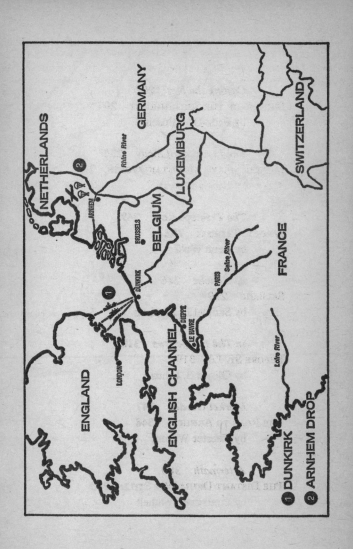

NETHERLANDS

GERMANY

Rhine River

LUXEMBURG

BELGIUM

BRUSSELS

ARNHEM

SWITZERLAND

FRANCE

Seine River

PARIS

DUNKIRK

DIEPPE

LE HAVRE

Loire River

ENGLAND

LONDON

ENGLISH CHANNEL

1 DUNKIRK

2 ARNHEM DROP

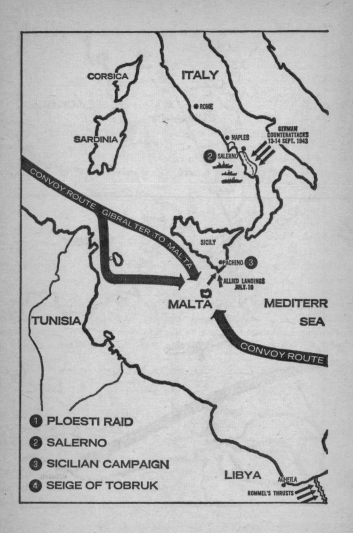

CORSICA

ITALY

SARDINIA

ROME

NAPLES

② SALERNO

GERMAN
COUNTERATTACKS
13-14 SEPT. 1943

CONVOY ROUTE - GIBRALTER TO MALTA

SICILY

PACHINO ③

ALLIED LANDINGS
JULY. 10

MALTA

MEDITERR

SEA

TUNISIA

CONVOY ROUTE

LIBYA

① PLOESTI RAID

② SALERNO

③ SICILIAN CAMPAIGN

④ SEIGE OF TOBRUK

AGHEILA

ROMMEL'S THRUSTS

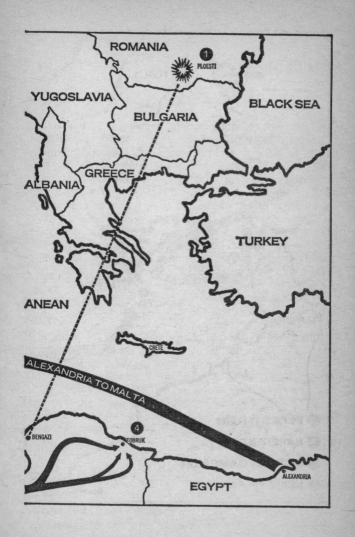

INTRODUCTION

Two decades after the stirring events recalled so vividly here—from defeat at Dunkirk to victory inside Germany—a reader (especially a young one) has a right, indeed an obligation, to demand: Why dredge up particulars about battles that are only names out of a rapidly dimming past? What glories of war are you talking about? With the cold war's megatons clicking loudly over the heads of us all, why stir the ashes of World War II?

I think that the answers to these questions are essential if for no other reason than we cannot escape history. There is a historic background to these stories of man engaged in combat and crisis. The reader unaware of that background will be reading merely war stories instead of the story of an epoch with great terrors and even greater moral responses.

All of us, however engaged, in whatever theater of war, saw in Hitler's Germany an enemy more than worthy of our hatred. Yes, it was moral to hate, to sacrifice, to strike back furiously and bravely.

Be aware of the indignities suffered by all manner of people in the countries of occupied Europe. Be aware of the deaths efficiently engineered by the Storm Troopers and, still more, the hundreds of thousands of aware but unprotesting Germans stoking the ovens of Dachau, Buchenwald and other concentration and slave labor camps. Be aware of what it meant to live in London during the blitz when the glorious Luftwaffe hurled incendiary bombs on your home. Then read these stories of combat with a deeper understanding of what was being fought for.

There were glorious moments in the great roll call of place names mentioned in these pages: for the seaman who sailed from the cold Atlantic ports zigzagging through U-boat waters on the way to Malta down the long and perilous Mediterranean Sea; for the airman who climbed into a thin-skinned, propeller-slow, heavy bomber and flew over a flak alley to a place called Ploesti; for the rifleman who clambered up the beaches of Salerno (or name your favorite beachhead) and learned what it felt like to be nakedly exposed under the efficient machinery of war manufactured by Krupp and other German industrial giants.

This past summer I found myself searching for the mood and meaning of the Furious Forties. I was driving in a remote mountain region of Sicily. Frankly, I was feeling a little low because I had run into several people who seemingly had erased the wartime liberation from their minds. To me, Sicily had been a steppingstone to the European mainland in that July of '43, when it was not merely an island controlled by Fascists goaded by Nazis but an operation named Husky. Then, something happened that cheered me. A farmer noticed an American's car and his face lit up. He yelled, "Hey, Joe!" As I grinned a return greeting, he raised his fingers in a V-for-Victory sign, and so did I. Not many Americans had come through these mountains over the years. The important ones were those anonymous Joes (some of whose lives ended in these once-numbered hills) who, with British Tommies, had brought freedom and kindnesses to Sicily.

That "V," and all it signified, stirred the ashes of memory and deepened understanding of what this biggest, next-to-the-last war meant.

The next war *will be* the last one. That is why we must look for the residue of goodwill from the past and tilt our consciences to the human level, twenty years later and in our remaining future. The Second World War multiplied battles and ideals all over the globe. Its explosive energy still encircles the continents. Those who were caught up in the events do have a need to sit upon the ground and talk of the death of dictators and of comrades; of the blacks and whites of conscience peering through the smoke of that war. My thought is this: We must still multiply the ideals but not the battles.

—Herbert Mitgang
New York, N. Y.
March 10, 1963

With Their Backs to the Sea

In May 1940, the German Panzer (armored) divisions plunged into France through the Ardennes Forest, cutting through the weakest sector of the French front near Sedan, just north of the Maginot Line. Before the Allied armies could recover from the blow, the Germans gathered momentum and drove straight for the Channel coast. The British forces were north of this thrust and, as their right flank to the south gave way, they withdrew. Had the French army commanders ordered a general withdrawal earlier, a line might have been established between the French and British armies at the Somme River. But, on May 28, the British left flank was suddenly exposed when the Belgian armies capitulated.

In the event a retreat proved necessary, the British had selected Dunkirk as the debarkation port. Now, as the troops began to retreat toward the coast, a corridor was formed by establishing defense positions along each flank. Troops began to pour down along this corridor to the port area. As the last allied troops were taken in, the end of the corridor was collapsed and defense positions were assumed a few miles closer to the coast.

By May 30, all British troops had arrived within the defense perimeter in front of Dunkirk. In Britain, meanwhile, Operation Dynamo had been set in motion. Masses of small ships gathered in the British Channel ports from all over the coast—lifeboats, pleasure boats, tugs, yachts, fighting craft were all commandeered, anything that could carry men across the channel. On the evening of May 27, this great fleet of small boats set sail for the beaches of Dunkirk.

There, the troops were formed up on the approaches to the harbor and on the beaches. While they waited, they drew heavy fire from German planes strafing and bombing. A British officer describes the scene as he arrived with his men:

"We were now in the region of the dunes, which rose like humps of a deeper darkness. And these in their turn were dotted with the still blacker shapes of abandoned vehicles, half-sunk in the sand, fantastic twisted shapes of burned-out skeletons, and crazy-looking wreckage that had been heaped up in extraordinary piles by the explosions of bombs. All these black shapes were silhouetted against the angry red glare in the sky which reflected down on us the agony of burning Dunkirk.

"Slowly, we picked our way between the wreckage, sinking ankle-deep in the loose sand, until we reached the gaunt skeletons of what had once been the houses on the promenade. The whole front was one long continuous line of blazing buildings, a high wall of fire roaring and darting in tongues of flame, with the smoke pouring upwards and disappearing in the blackness of the sky above the roof-tops. Out seawards, the darkness was as thick and smooth as black velvet, except for now and again when the shape of a sunken destroyer or paddle-steamer made a slight thickening on its impenetrable surface. Facing us, the great black wall of the Mole stretched from the beach far out into sea, the end of it almost invisible to us. The Mole had an astounding, terrifying background of giant flames leaping a hundred feet into the air from blazing oil tanks. At the shore end of the Mole stood an obelisk, and the high explosive shells burst around it with monotonous regularity. Along the promenade, in parties of fifty, the remnants of practically all the last regiments were wearily trudging along. There was no singing, and very little talk. Everyone was far too exhausted to waste breath.

"From the margin of the sea, at fairly wide intervals, three long, thin, black lines protruded into the water, conveying the effect of low wooden breakwaters. These were lines of men, standing in pairs behind one another far out into the water, waiting in queues till boats arrived to transport them, a score or so at a time, to the steamers and warships that were filling up with the last survivors. The queues stood there, fixed and almost as regular as if ruled. No bunching, no pushing. Nothing like the mix-up to be seen at the turnstiles when a crowd is going into a football match. Much more orderly, even, than a waiting theatre queue.

"About this time, afraid that some of our men might be tailing off, I began shouting, '2004th Field Regiment . . . 2004th Field Regiment. . . .'

"A group of dead and dying soldiers on the path in front of us quickened our desire to quit the promenade. Stepping over the bodies we marched down the slope to the dark beach. Dunkirk front was now a lurid study in red and black; flames, smoke, and the night itself all mingling together to compose a frightful panorama of death and destruction. Red and black all the time, except for an occasional flash of white, low in the sky, miles away to the left and right where big shells from coastal defence guns at Calais and Nieuport were being hurled into the town.

"Down on the beach you immediately felt yourself surrounded by a deadly evil atmosphere. A horrible stench of blood and mutilated flesh pervaded the place. There was no escape from it. Not a breath of air was blowing to dissipate the appalling odour that arose from the dead bodies that had been lying on the sand, in some cases for several days. We might have been walking through a slaughterhouse on a hot day. The darkness, which hid some of the sights of horror from our eyes, seemed to thicken this dreadful stench. It created the impression that death was hovering around, very near at hand.

"We set our faces in the direction of the sea, quickening our pace to pass through the belt of this nauseating miasma as soon as possible.

" 'Water . . . Water. . . .' groaned a voice from the ground just in front of us.

"It was a wounded infantryman. He had been hit so badly that there was no hope for him. Our water bottles had long been empty, but by carefully draining them all into one, we managed to collect a mouthful or two. A sergeant knelt down beside the dying man and held the bottle to his lips. Then we proceeded on our way, leaving the bottle with the last few drains in it near the poor fellow's hand so that he could moisten his lips from time to time.

"On either side, scattered over the sand in all sorts of positions, were the dark shapes of dead and dying men, sometimes alone, sometimes in twos and threes. Every now and then we had to pull ourselves up sharply in the darkness to avoid falling over a wooden cross erected by comrades on the spot where some soldier had been buried. No assistance that availed anything could be given to these dying men. The living themselves had nothing to offer them. They just pressed forward to the sea, hoping that the same fate would not be theirs. And still it remained a gamble all the time whether that sea, close though it was, would be reached in safety. Splinters from bursting shells were continually whizzing through the air, and occasionally a man in one of the plodding groups would fall with a groan." *

By June 1, about 200,000 British, French and Belgian troops had been landed safely in England, but the battle was just reaching its climax.

DUNKIRK: JUNE 1ST AND 2ND**

by David Divine

Swiftly, the drama of Dunkirk moved to its climax on the 1st of June. In the morning hours the Royal Navy was to suffer losses as heavy and as significant as those of some of the great sea battles of the past. There is in one of the accounts of the opening of this disaster a phrase that establishes its continuity with history, that links it irrevocably with tradition.

"We were setting our topsail to carry out this operation when a large number of German planes appeared overhead and immediately started bombing and machine-gunning us."

This was the beginning of the heaviest air attack of the operation. Skipper H. Miller of the barge *Royalty* had been ordered to beach his ship opposite the first houses of Malo-les-Bains. "We were setting our topsail" when the whole weight of two air fleets was unleashed for the second time against the crowded anchorage.

Up to this moment, the embarkations of the first hours of the day had achieved new records. The paddle mine sweeper *Whippingham* had started loading, under shellfire, about ten o'clock the previous evening. By 1:30 A.M. she

Return Via Dunkirk, by Gun Buster, published by Hodder & Stoughton.

** This is a condensed version of two chapters from *The Nine Days of Dunkirk.*

estimated that she had loaded 2,700 men and, with her sponsons only about twelve inches above the water, she cast off from the Mole, worked her way out between the wrecks that now, more thickly than ever, studded the narrow channel, and got clear. Her commander, Lieutenant Eric Reed, R.N.R., says that her passage back was slow because she was "very much overloaded." Again this is a classic example of understatement.

Royal Sovereign had been picking up off La Panne. She sailed at 2:30 A.M. with a heavy load, and her master, usually very spare of words, wrote that the beach had come under "terrific bombarding and shelling."

One of the best accounts of the abandonment of La Panne is that of Captain R. P. Pim, R.N.V.R., formerly Assistant Secretary to the Ministry of Home Affairs in the Government of Northern Ireland and, at this time, keeper of Winston Churchill's Map Room. Captain Pim had been on leave at the beginning of the evacuation. He volunteered and crossed with one of the tows. The report of his work says:

"By midnight all the troops which he could find were embarked and placed in ships which sailed for England. Just before midnight he went along some of the beaches to look for stragglers and was told by a staff officer that no more troops would embark from those beaches, but that it was anticipated that the beaches would be shelled and would probably be in German hands the following day. This was a correct forecast.

"He estimates that, from the pontoons and beaches, about 5,000 were embarked. He was impressed by the kindness that was shown to the tired soldiery in the various ships in which they were embarked and also by the fact that the military chaplains were always among the last of their respective parties to leave the beach.

"Anchorage had to be shifted during the night as shells meant for the beaches were ricocheting over H.M.S. *Hilda* [which had towed them over] . . ."

Another tow of small craft was operating nearer to Malo-les-Bains.

The Belgian fishing boats were over again in this period.

The *Anna Marguerite* lifted 120 French soldiers and, on her return journey, picked up thirty survivors of a French cargo ship which had been sunk by a magnetic mine. The *Georges Edouard*, which was commanded by a Merchant Marine officer, picked up nearly 500 men this day and, with an earlier trip, carried a total altogether of 1007. The *Guido Gazelle* carried 403 on two trips.

The destroyers *Icarus*, *Vanquisher* and *Windsor* carried 3000 men between them. Despite the difficulties of the beaches, the loads throughout were tremendously heavy. Mine sweepers, Dutch skoots, trawlers, drifters, paddle-steamers—they all carried enormous numbers of men.

The sun rose and still they loaded. Through this night the Germans had bombed the harbour area intermittently, using brilliant flares. Now, with the sun, the raids re-doubled. At five o'clock heavy bombing attacks developed over the whole area from La Panne to Dunkirk, and fighters began to make almost incessant strafing runs along the beaches. The first R.A.F. patrol had been ordered to be over the area soon after 5 A.M. It was heavily engaged on arrival. A second patrol followed at 6 A.M. and again met exceptionally strong opposition. Thereafter there was a gap until nine o'clock, and in this gap the Luftwaffe pounced.

The barge *Royalty*, as has been recorded, set her topsail under fire and ran herself ashore. She was loaded with food, water, and ammunition, and her job was to beach herself as high up the sands as possible so that the troops could unload her as the tide turned. Having carried out his operation im-maculately, Skipper Miller rowed out to the tug *Cervia*, which had towed him across. On the way he picked up a launch, with twenty-five soldiers on board, that had broken down. When he joined her, *Cervia* closed the barge *Tolles-bury*, which had picked up 180 men.

"At 7:20 A.M.," said W. H. Simmons, *Cervia's* master, "we dropped our anchor and watched the barge. Soldiers began to run down the beach towards her, but guns started to bang away on the outskirts of Dunkirk, and an air-raid siren blew and the soldiers went back to shelter."

The wail of that siren ushered in the attack which, had it been made earlier, might have been decisive in the history of Dunkirk. It is possible that this devastating raid was synchronized with the German's first assault of the day on the perimeter line. At 7:20 A.M. a very heavy force of enemy bombers—predominantly Junkers 87 dive bombers, but with the support of twin-engined Junkers 88s, elaborately escorted by fighters—made its appearance. There were no Allied aircraft in the air at the time; there was no escort for the ships in that narrow channel of destruction. The destroyers themselves, fighting against attack through almost every hour of the past days, were desperately short of ammunition. Many of them had had no time to re-ammunition in the brief spells at Dover. There was only time to discharge their troops, to take on fresh oil, to slip and put to sea again. *Keith,* after fighting all the previous day, had thirty rounds of A.A. ammunition left.

At once the attacks developed on the nearest ships. There is an appalling grandeur in that scene. From behind the beaches, from the harbour, from those ships whose guns could still answer the challenge of the air, the sky was filled with the pock-marks of bursting shells, with the thin trails of tracer bullets, with the whistle and roar of projectiles. Below the sea was flecked with small plumes as the splinters of the shells sang down into the water, between them lifted the monstrous, swirling fountains of the bombs.

Keith was heavily attacked by the first wave. Twisting, turning, at the utmost speed that she could manage in the narrow waters of the roadstead, she eluded the bombs. The account by the master of *Cervia* of these moments—cool, almost dour in its absence of emotion—conveys a graphic picture.

"A British destroyer outside of us began to fire at the enemy planes and bombs began to fall near her as she steamed about. At full speed with her helm hard to port nine bombs fell in a line in the water, along her starboard side, and they exploded under water, heeling the destroyer over on her beam ends, but she was righted again and a sloop joined in the gunfire, also shore batteries, and as the raiders made off over towards the land they machinegunned us and we returned the fire with our Lewis gun."

To avoid being rammed, *Cervia* weighed anchor and got

under way. She made toward the damaged *Keith* but, as she was doing so, a further air attack took place and the destroyer was again straddled by a stick of bombs. The tug *St. Abbs* and a sloop were also going to the help of *Keith*, so *Cervia* turned round and picked up a motorboat full of soldiers.

Actually *Keith* was damaged in the first attack, though she did not suffer a direct hit. A near miss jammed her rudder, and she turned in small circles for some time. In the second attack she was hit almost at once down her after-funnel and very near misses damaged her side severely. She was moving at high speed and turning at the moment of impact, and she at once listed heavily to port. Enormous clouds of steam came up through the after-funnel and boiler room casings. Still turning, she lost speed rapidly as the steam went, and in a little her commander was compelled to bring his ship to anchor. Captain E. L. Berthon (he had won his D.S.C. at Zeebrugge during the great attack on St. George's Day, 1918) had taken the place of Captain D. J. R. Simson, Captain (D) of the 19th Flotilla, who had been killed at Boulogne on May 24. By the time the anchor took hold, *Keith* was listing almost 20 degrees to port and had no more than two feet of freeboard on that side. At this point, however, she seemed to steady up and sank no farther for the time being.

Though *Keith* was still afloat, she was clearly out of action. Admiral Wake-Walker, with his staff, disembarked into M.T.B. 102, which had closed the destroyer immediately after she was damaged the second time, and headed down the roadstead to call up tugs. But the tugs had already turned towards the battered ship—the Admiralty tug *St. Abbs*, the tug *Vincia*, and the tug *Cervia*. Captain Pim, in H.M. Skoot *Hilda*, was also making his best speed towards the wreck. Before they could reach her she was hit in a third attack. This time the bombs dropped under the bridge, and she heeled right over and sank almost instantly. *Hilda* picked up fifty survivors from the water, including Lieutenant General W. G. Lindsell, the Quartermaster General, and other staff officers. The tug *Vincia* picked up 108 officers and ratings, including staff officers from both British and French headquarters, and *St. Abbs,* which closed her just before she sank, took off Captain Berthon and more than 100 survivors.

All the while there was no cessation in the fury of the Luftwaffe's attack. Farther down the water the dive bombers were peeling off at 10,000 feet and coming down with a terrifying snarl of their motors to within a few hundred feet of the water. While the work of rescue was in progress the destroyer *Basilisk,* which had been held ready to give supporting fire in the event of enemy attack along the beach, was bombed. *St. Abbs,* under the orders of Captain Berthon, turned towards the spot to rescue survivors. Aircraft were flying overhead continuously and a Junkers 88, at high level, let go a single bomb. By a thousand-to-one chance it hit the hurrying tug amidships. She disintegrated and sank, leaving Captain Berthon and the comparatively small number of men who now survived, a second time in the water.

Shortly after, the destroyer *Whitehall* on her first trip—she made two trips this day—found the still-floating hulk of H.M.S. *Basilisk* and sank it. She was herself dive-bombed and suffered damage from near misses. H.M.S. *Worcester* was also damaged by bombing and was to be in collision as she struggled back to Dover.

The gunboat *Mosquito,* which had done magnificent work now for many days, was hit in the same period, badly damaged, set on fire, and had to be abandoned. The Fleet minesweeper *Salamander* was damaged and tugs were sent in search of her. There were other naval casualties, other ships damaged in this period. Admiral Wake-Walker, hurrying to Dunkirk itself in the M.T.B. which had picked him up, was dive-bombed but not hit. All up and down the long, narrow channel of the roadstead there was havoc and the thunder of the bombs. All up and down the roadstead were the long and lamentable pools of oil which marked the new ship graves; and with them, floating on the tide, was the pitiful wreckage of smashed boats and empty rafts, of battered furnishings and splintered planks.

Within little more than an hour the Royal Navy had lost three destroyers, a Fleet minesweeper and a gunboat, and four destroyers had been damaged.

Nor was this the end of disaster. At 1 P.M. the French destroyer *Foudroyant,* the last surviving ship of the 2nd Destroyer Flotilla, came in through Route X. Four miles from the West Mole she was "submerged in a cloud of Stukas," according to a French account. The channel at that point was narrow and manœuvring was impossible. In less than a minute she was hit by a number of bombs and capsized instantly. Small craft and the minesweeper *Sainte-Bernadette-de-Lourdes,* herself damaged by splinters from near misses and listing heavily, picked up her survivors.

The naval losses were desperately serious but the personnel ships suffered almost equally heavy loss in the same period. *Prague,* coming in by Route X, reached Dunkirk at the very height of the first attacks. Her armament was one Lewis gun and one Bren gun, but she closed the entrance and went inside. She berthed at the western side of the outer harbour, close outside the locks, and loaded about 3000 French troops. On the return voyage towards the Downs, the ship was shelled off Gravelines and dive-bombed off No. 5 buoy. Although not actually hit on either occasion, she suffered severe internal damage and the starboard engine was put out of action. Captain Baxter reported:

"From the time of the explosion (10:25) the ship was kept going ahead as fast as it was possible to do on the port engine which was the only one left in service, craft in the vicinity were warned and several naval auxiliaries agreed to stand by us and the ship slowly progressed homewards. It was evident, however, that the water was gaining, and such measures as getting as many troops as possible forward to ease the weight on the after part of the ship were giving only temporary respite, so I decided to try to transfer the troops while the ship was still under way so as to lose as little time as possible. H.M. Destroyer *Shikari* and a sloop and a paddle-minesweeper whose names I was unable to obtain came alongside in turn and very skilfully managed to transfer all except a handful of troops while the ship was steaming as fast as possible towards the Downs. . . ."

H.M.S. *Shikari* transferred under way 500 men. She then called the *Queen of Thanet* to come alongside in her turn. Commander S. P. Herival, R.N.V.R., asked how many troops were left on board and was told, 2000. He embarked most of these—remember both ships were moving at the best speed *Prague* could make all the time—and took them in to Margate. The corvette *Shearwater* then transferred approximately 200 of the remainder and took them to Sheerness.

It was a rescue that in time of peace would have held the attention of the world. There is a tremendous drama, a tension, in the race to beach the ship before she sank under them. There is a desperate excitement in the transfer of those 3000 exhausted men.

As *Prague* came out from the Dunkirk roadstead through the bombing, another railway steamer, the *Scotia*, went in. She was a coal burner, and in addition to the exhaustion and difficulty of the work that she was doing was the necessity to ship coal. There were no proper facilities. For the oil burning ships there were tankers from which they could take their oil direct by pipe line. *Scotia* and the other coal burners had to be supplied with bags and shovels and work their own coal aboard from colliers or hulks. She herself shipped ninety tons from the coal hulk *Agincourt*, then moved to Margate roads and fiinished bunkering from the coaster *Jolly Days*. Her whole crew took part in the work, filling bags and manhandling them to the bunkers. On the way across a homeward-bound destroyer signaled to her: "Windy off No. 6 buoy." The humour was grim. Off No. 6 buoy she was attacked. In the course of the attack British aircraft came in and the enemy disappeared, to re-appear again as soon as the R.A.F. patrol had gone.

Scotia returned to Dunkirk under air attack, being near missed off the entrance. She berthed at the West Mole. "We found Dunkirk quiet except for a few rounds fired from shore batteries," wrote Captain Hughes, and she embarked about 2,000 French troops. As she reached No. 6 buoy on the return voyage she was attacked by three formations of enemy aircraft in groups of four. The ship was hit abaft the engine-room on the starboard side and on the poop deck, and in the final attack one bomb went down the after-funnel. *Scotia* was heavily damaged and began to sink by the stern, heeling steadily over to starboard.

"We carried ten boats, but three of them had been smashed by the bombs. The troops, being French, could not understand orders and they were rushing the boats, which made it very difficult to man the falls—the port boats being most difficult as the vessel was heeling over to starboard. The chief officer had been given a revolver to use by a French officer, threatening to use this helped matters a little. However, they obeyed my mouth whistle and hand signs and so stood aside while the boats were being lowered.

"Commander Couch of H.M.S. *Esk* had received our S.O.S. He was lying at Dunkirk at the time; he came at full speed to the rescue. By now the boat deck starboard side was in the water and the vessel was still going over. He very skilfully put the bow of his ship close to the forecastle head, taking off a large number of troops and picking up hundreds out of the sea. Backing his ship out again, he came amidships on the starboard side, his stem being now against the boat deck, and continued to pick up survivors.

"The *Scotia* had by now gone over until her forward funnel and mast were in the water. Two enemy bombers again approached us dropping four bombs and machine gunning those swimming and clinging to wreckage. The *Esk* kept firing and drove the enemy away. Commander Couch again skilfully manœuvered his ship around to the port side, the *Scotia* having gone over until the port bilge keel was out of the water. Hundreds of the soldiers were huddled on the bilge and some of them swam to the *Esk*, while others were pulled up by ropes and rafts."

While the work of rescue was in progress a fresh bombing attack developed, but the aircraft were driven off by gunfire and the rescue continued uninterrupted until finally only three men were left lying against the bilge keel of the *Scotia*. Captain Hughes fastened ropes round each of these men in turn, they were hauled up to the deck of the *Esk*, and eventually he himself reached the rescue ship. Thirty of *Scotia's* crew were killed or died subsequently, and Captain Hughes estimated that between two and three hundred

Frenchmen were lost. The sinking of the *Scotia* was a tragedy: but for the coolness of Captain Hughes and the brilliant work of the rescue ship it might have been a very great disaster.

H.M.M. *Brighton Queen,* one of the paddle-minesweepers of the 7th Flotilla, which had come down from the Firth of Forth in reinforcement the previous day, made her second trip in the early afternoon. She picked up 700 French and Moroccan troops, and stood out on the homeward passage. At the end of the narrows she was made the target of a concentrated attack by dive bombers. For some while she dodged the rain of bombs, but eventually she was hit in the stern and badly holed. The minesweeper *Saltash* was the first ship to reach her. She reported that "the French troops behaved steadily and intelligently though nearly half of them were killed by the explosion."

Four destroyers had been sunk in a matter of a few hours, four had been seriously damaged. Two of the largest of the cross-Channel steamers and a paddle-minesweeper had been lost. Up and down the roads small ships were on fire and sinking. New wrecks studded the narrow waters of the Channel from No. 6 buoy across the banks. The time had come for a change of plan.

At noon the Commander-in-Chief, Nore, signaled the Admiralty to suggest the "discontinuation of the use of destroyers by day off the French coast." At 6 P.M. a signal from Dunkirk to Admiral Ramsay said:

"Things are getting very hot for ships; over 100 bombers on ships here since 0530, many casualties. Have directed that no ships sail during daylight. Evacuation by transports therefore ceases at 0300. If perimeter holds will complete evacuation tomorrow, Sunday night, including most French. General concurs."

The Admiralty made up its mind. Independently Admiral Ramsay came to similar conclusions. Signals from London and from Dover crossed. The Admiralty directed the suspension of evacuation from Dunkirk at seven o'clock the following morning. Admiral Ramsay's message stated that he had ordered all ships to withdraw from Dunkirk before daylight—the ships could no longer accept the danger of the day. As Admiral Ramsay, considering the problem, wrote:

"In these circumstances, it was apparent that continuation of the operation by day must cause losses of ships and personnel out of all proportion to the number of troops evacuated, and if persisted in, the momentum of evacuation would automatically and rapidly decrease."

But at dusk the ships would go in again—this was not yet the end.

This day criticism of the R.A.F. reached its height. It is not easy to balance the scales in this matter. On June 1 the R.A.F. was asked to provide patrols from 5 A.M. onward. Eight fighter sweeps were made in the course of the day, varying in strength from three to four squadrons. Smaller sweeps had been found impracticable early in the operation. On May 27 twenty-three sweeps had been flown, but the weakness of small patrols invited strong enemy reaction. On this Saturday a second sweep followed at 6 A.M. There was then a three-hour gap until nine. There was another gap through the middle of the day. It was in these two gaps that the heaviest loss took place.

In addition to these fighter operations, Coastal Command and the Fleet Air Arm flew patrols over the approach channels and the open sea, and an astonishing variety of planes was used—Hurricanes, Spitfires, Defiants, Ansons, Hudsons and Swordfish. Three Ansons, reconnaissance aircraft of Coastal Command, engaged nine Messerschmitt fighters at one period of the day, flying almost at water level. They shot down two of them, possibly two more, and drove the rest away. Three Hudsons found "a patch of sky black with Jerrys"—Junkers 87s and 88s ready to dive on transports, with a dense screen of Messerschmitts above them. In thirteen minutes three dive bombers had been shot down, two had dived out of control, and the formation had been driven off. Spitfires claimed twelve German bombers and fighters during a morning patrol, and in the afternoon went up again and claimed another six.

At the end of the day the R.A.F. claimed seventy-eight

enemy aircraft destroyed. It was believed that a new record for the war had been established. A more sober analysis of claims brought the figure down to forty-three. In actual fact, German returns examined since the war show that ten fighters and nineteen bombers in all were lost in the course of the day's operations. Of this total, a number must be credited to ships. Naval vessels claimed thirteen 'kills' during daylight hours. On the other side of the ledger, thirty-one British aircraft were lost this Saturday. The legend of qualitative superiority that was built up over Dunkirk rested on perilously slender foundations.

At sea and in the air the battle had reached points of crisis. What was the position on the land?

At 8 A.M., while the Luftwaffe attack against the ships was at its height, General Alexander met Admiral Abrial and General Fagalde again. It was obvious by now that there was no question of a successful completion of the evacuation by the dawn of Sunday. General Alexander agreed to a modification of the original plan. The line was to be held as before until midnight. Thereafter it was proposed that he should withdraw to what is described as "a bridgehead round Dunkirk with all available anti-aircraft and anti-tank guns and with such troops as had not yet embarked."

Already heavy German attacks were developing against the "Canal Line." At Bergues, the 1st Loyals were forced out of the town and took up new defensive positions on the canal bank on its outskirts. At Hoymille, a little to the east, the enemy penetrated a position held by the Warwickshires and secured a foothold across the canal. The position was restored late in the afternoon by the Loyals in a vigorous counterattack. The Border Regiment was also pushed back, and, at dark, the last of the British troops were withdrawn through the French on the intermediate line, which ran through Uxem and Ghyvelde. The Canal des Chats at Uxem was less than four miles from the beaches. The end was very close.

Thirty-one ships in all were lost and eleven were seriously

26

damaged between midnight and midnight. It was a major disaster, and yet such is the strange quality of Dunkirk that through it all the loading went on, hardly losing its rhythm. Though it was interrupted as the Stukas raided the open beaches, though ships withdrew under attack or were turned back from the approach channels, though the Mole was almost incessantly under fire now, it never ceased. Through it all the small craft worked, pausing sometimes to rescue drowning men from the water, helping to tow a damaged ship, standing by a sinking one.

At dawn from Ramsgate a convoy of eight boats, including *Westerly, Naiad Errant* and *White Heather,* moved off for Dunkirk. The description of Able Seaman Palmer is perhaps the best individual account by any member of the lower deck who took part in the beach work through this time. Palmer was a "Westoe". He came to Ramsgate with a draft from the Royal Naval Barracks, Devonport, where he had been serving for some time past as a member of the Plymouth City Patrol. He was a "stripey," a three-badge man, and held the Long Service and Good Conduct medals, but he was still an Able Seaman. His narrative is simple and graphic with the simplicity of the "Old Navy."

"The adventure began with a sudden draft from Devonport to Ramsgate. For one night at Ramsgate I was billeted with other seamen in the Fun Fair Ballroom, and the next day action began. I was told off with another seaman, two ordinary seamen, and two stokers, to take over two motor yachts, the *Naiad Errant* and the *Westerly.* Being the senior hand, I detailed one seaman, an ordinary seaman, and one stoker to take charge of the *Westerly* and took the remainder on board the *Naiad Errant* with me. I thought she looked the better of the two boats. . . .

"About three miles outside Dunkirk I saw a French destroyer doing about twenty-four to thirty knots, [this was the *Foudroyant*] making her way into Dunkirk. I took my eyes off her for a minute or two and then glanced back, but there was nothing there. She must have had a direct hit from a bomb and sunk within a few minutes. I made my course over to where she had gone and picked up her survivors, which altogether numbered only about twenty.

Those I picked up I put on board a French tug which happened to be in the vicinity, and once more carried on into Dunkirk.

"Eventually I arrived off the beach where the swarms of soldiers were gathered, and at the same time one of our big ships came and anchored close inshore. Three of our little convoy of eight had arrived. The first immediately filled with soldiers and carried on back to England. The second went aground. My first job was to ferry soldiers from the beach to the big ship, and I made a number of trips. Then I tried to tow the boat that had run aground off the beach but the young seaman with me got the tow rope around my propellers, the result being that I had to give the job up and that my own ship ran aground. All around there was ceaseless activity and, jumping over the side, I gave a hand carrying the wounded soldiers to the big ship's skiff which had been launched. . . ."

Naiad Errant's crew was ordered aboard the "big ship," but in turn she ran aground. In the interval soldiers got *Naiad Errant* clear again, and Palmer, after securing enough petrol for the return journey, started back. Shortly after *Naiad Errant's* engines failed.

"With no engineer on board, and me without the slightest knowledge of engines, I had to hope that the soldiers could get her going again. The engineers among them got to work. The others I ordered to break up both the cabin doors and use the pieces as paddles in order to keep a little way on the boat and prevent her from running on to the pier. Although they were dead tired they put all they knew into it and so we managed to keep a little way on the boat and keep her in a safe position. About this time I began to shiver and got very cold as it got dark, for I had on the same togs that I had been swimming in. I was still wet through. Then one of the soldiers tapped me on the shoulder. He handed over a flask, asking me to drink. I did. It was rum, and it certainly put warmth and fresh life into me.

"The soldiers tinkered with the engine in the darkness and it must have been between ten and eleven o'clock at night when there was a clamour of excitement. They had got the starboard engine going! I told them to 'drop everything' and leave the port engine and I would get them over to England all right on the one engine, which gave me about five to six knots. I counteracted the pull of the one engine with the wheel. . . .

"Just after dawn I struck Dover dead centre and then followed the coast up to Ramsgate, arriving there at eleven and I put the soldiers ashore on the pier."

White Heather was abandoned. *Westerly* was damaged and her people were rescued later.

Another convoy left Ramsgate about 9:30 A.M. Between the two there were a number of individual sailings. In the convoy were the tugs *Prince, Princess* and *Duke* with the Isle of Wight ferry *Fishbourne* in tow. The *Sun III* had four barges astern of her—*Ada Mary, Haste Away, Burton* and *Shannon*. She had great trouble with barges breaking adrift, and *Duke* was detached from *Fishbourne* to pick up *Haste Away* and *Ada Mary*. By 2:30 P.M. they were close in to Dunkirk. Air attacks were heavy again at this time, and it was eventually decided that *Fishbourne* should return to Ramsgate. The barge tows, meanwhile, had got well ahead of her and in the middle of the afternoon reached position a little north of Dunkirk during the inevitable air attack. The master of *Duke*, B. P. Mansfield, records, however, that this attack was split up by our own fighter aircraft.

Half an hour after they had left Ramsgate the yacht *Sundowner* began her crossing. *Sundowner* belonged to Commander C. H. Lightoller, R.N.R. (Retd.), who, as senior surviving officer of the *Titanic*, had been the principal witness at the inquiry into the disaster. She was a biggish craft, approximately sixty feet with a speed of ten knots and, with the assistance of his son and a Sea Scout, Commander Lightoller had taken her out of Cubitt's Yacht Basin at Chiswick on May 31 and had dropped down the river to Southend as part of a big convoy of forty boats which had mustered at Westminster. At dawn on June 1 he left Southend with five others and, reaching Ramsgate, was instructed in the casual manner of those days to "proceed to Dunkirk for further orders." His charts were somewhat antiquated, and he was fortunate enough to be able to obtain a new set. At ten o'clock he left by the route laid down.

On the way across Commander Lightoller picked up the crew of *Westerly*, originally one of Able Seaman Palmer's flotilla. She was broken down and on fire. Finding no more men on the beaches, and successfully dodging several air attacks, he headed up for Dunkirk harbour, where he berthed alongside a destroyer and started to load troops. With great foresight every bit of unnecessary gear had been removed from *Sundowner* before leaving Cubitt's Yacht Basin. Commander Lightoller wrote:

"My son, as previously arranged, was to pack the men in and use every available inch of space—which I'll say he carried out to some purpose. On deck I detailed a naval rating to tally the troops aboard. At fifty I called below, 'How are you getting on?' getting the cheery reply, 'Oh, plenty of room yet.' At seventy-five my son admitted they were getting pretty tight—all equipment and arms being left on deck.

"I now started to pack them on deck, having passed word below for every man to lie down and keep down; the same applied on deck. By the time we had fifty on deck, I could feel her getting distinctly tender, so took no more. Actually we had exactly 130 on board, including three *Sundowners* and five *Westerlys*.

"During the whole embarkation we had quite a lot of attention from enemy planes, but derived an amazing degree of comfort from the fact that the *Worcester's* A.A. guns kept up an everlasting bark overhead. . . .

"Arriving off the harbour I was at first told to 'lie off'. But when I informed them that I had 130 on board, permission was at once given to 'come in' (I don't think the authorities believed for a minute that I had 130), and I put her alongside a trawler lying at the quay. Whilst entering, the men started to get to their feet and she promptly went over to a terrific angle. I got them down again in time and told those below to remain below and lying down till I gave the word. The impression ashore was that the fifty-odd lying on deck plus the mass of equipment was my full load.

30

"After I had got rid of those on deck I gave the order 'Come up from below,' and the look on the official face was amusing to behold as troops vomited up through the forward companionway, the after companionway, and the doors either side of the wheelhouse. As a stoker P.O., helping them over the bulwarks, said, 'God's truth, mate! Where did you put them?' He might well ask. . . ."

The old stagers were still carrying on. H.M.M. *Medway Queen* was over again, having left for Dunkirk at 9:30 A.M. With the ships' boats which she towed again was Mr. R. B. Brett. Writing subsequently, he said that he saw one of the crew of the *Medway Queen*, a Royal Naval pensioner, calmly fishing over the stern while the *Medway Queen* was lying off the Mole waiting for her turn to go in.

"When told that there were no fish about and that, if there were, they were dead, he sang out, 'You never can tell, sir. I might catch a bloody Boche helmet.' "

Brett took his boat in until she had almost grounded and then, being the tallest man on board, he waded ashore, calling out, "I want sixty men!" For some time he received no reply. Then, he wrote:

"I sighted a causeway about eight feet wide heading out into the water. To my surprise I found it to be a perfectly ordered straight column of men about six abreast, standing as if on parade. When I reached them a sergeant stepped up to me and said, 'Yes, sir. Sixty men, sir?' He then walked along the column, which remained in perfect formation, and detailed the required number to follow me."

A footnote to the stoicism of Mr. Brett's "human pier" is his account of a blinded man. His hand was placed in Mr. Brett's and he was led to the boat and told that he was being taken to safety. He said simply, "Thanks, mate," and followed patiently and wordlessly into the deep water.

Admiral Wake-Walker, after the bombing of *Keith,* ordered M.T.B. 102, which had picked him up, to proceed into Dunkirk. Landing near the naval dug-out headquarters at the base of the Mole, he was informed of General Alexander's intention to continue the evacuation during the night from the western beaches and Dunkirk, the rear guard retiring at dawn on Dunkirk itself. Fearing the results of a second attack such as the one that had just been experienced, Admiral Wake-Walker returned to Dover for direct contact with Admiral Ramsay. He crossed in the M.T. B., bombed and machine-gunned on the way. At 7:45 P.M. he was off Dunkirk again to take charge of the embarkation operations for the night, and at a conference at Bastion 32 with General Alexander and Captain Tennant the last details of the night's operations were agreed. At that conference he was informed that the French were holding a line in rear of the British positions through which the British rear guard would withdraw.

The whole emphasis had been changed to night loading. Admiral Ramsay's plan provided for all minesweepers, paddle-steamers, skoots, and small craft to work the Malo beach for a mile and a half from Dunkirk. The harbour itself was to be served by eight destroyers and seven personnel ships. Drifters and smaller craft from Ramsgate were to go up into the inner harbour. French ships were to use the guiding jetty and the West Mole, and very small ships the Quai Félix Faure. French fishing craft and drifters were to work with the British on the Malo beach.

The night was very dark. At times as many as six or seven ships were attempting to use the wreck-studded entrance to the harbour at once. Collisions and obstruction were incessant. The confusion of other days seemed to be redoubled, yet again the confusion was apparent rather than real. The sense of individual masters, the seamanship of their crews, the determination of everyone concerned in the operation was such that this vast concentration of ships moved in and out with astonishingly small loss.

Yet loss there was. *Maid of Orleans* was one of the earliest of the personnel ships of the night flight to leave. In six trips she had lifted 5319 men. The utter disregard that this unarmed vessel showed for the almost intolerable dangers of the work and the limitless endurance of her people give her a high place in the record of famous ships.

At 8:30 P.M. she moved out from the Admiralty Pier and within ten minutes was in collision with the destroyer *Worcester*. *Worcester* had been damaged by bombs earlier

32

in the day. She had been towed most of the way across the Channel and then engineers, working in the crippled engine room, had managed to get her under her own steam again. She was slipping thankfully into port now when the two ships met with a tremendous crash. There were many tugs and small craft available; men thrown into the water were picked up, and both ships were towed into harbour. *Maid of Orleans,* however, was so damaged as to be unable to continue her voyage. She had done most gallant work. *Worcester* also was finished as far as Dunkirk was concerned, and she too had matched the very highest traditions of her Service. In the six trips which she had made, two of them under very heavy attack from the enemy, she had brought back 4350 men.

Even endurance has its inevitable limits. The personnel ships had been working now, some of them, for a full week. They were civilian ships—before everything this must be remembered. They were not trained to the necessities of war, they were not moulded to its disciplines. Now, as their weariness grew, there were failures. *Tynwald* should have sailed from Folkestone at this time. She had completed three hard voyages, bringing away 4500 men, but on this evening she failed to sail. Her master stated that his men had been continually on their feet for a week, that his officers were completely exhausted, and that he himself had had only four hours' rest in the whole course of the week and was unfit for further duty. *Malines* and *Ben-My-Chree* were in the same condition.

Exhaustion was beginning to show amongst the naval vessels as well. It was found possible in certain instances to put fresh captains on board. With the personnel ships Admiral Ramsay now took the necessary step of putting a naval commander or lieutenant commander on board with a party of ten seamen. Relief crews were ordered up for *Ben-My-Chree* and *Tynwald.*

As this night went on what was left of the 46th Division, the 1st Division and the 126th Infantry Brigade were taken aboard the ships.

The destroyers still were lifting the greater share of the

total. H.M.S. *Whitshed* had made good the damage that she had received at Boulogne. This night she came back to service. She berthed at one o'clock against the concrete of the outer nose of the Mole.

As she made fast her ropes the Mole was empty. Commander Conder left his ship and walked along the Mole. A little way down it he found a bicycle lying up against a post and on this he rode down to the town. There was damage at various points. At one place the decking of the Mole had gone completely and the gap was bridged by a ship's gangway. At other points there were shell holes patched with any material available. At the far end there was another area of damage, and he had to dismount to circumvent it. Just beyond this he met a naval pier party and was told that troops would be coming at any moment. He went on past the pier party and in a warehouse a few hundred yards farther down found a number of exhausted French and Belgian troops. These he stirred into wakefulness and sent down the pier. There was an air attack on at the time but he was busy hunting. A little farther he found a party of British troops in command of a sergeant—their officers had brought them down as far as the pier and gone back to round up more men. These he took back with him.

The destroyers were taking incredible risks in stowing the vast quantities of men they lifted. It is recorded that *Whitshed* had first unshipped her mess tables and cleared all possible movable gear on the lower deck; now she opened compartments that normally were shut in danger areas, leaving the watertight doors open throughout the ship in order to make "living spaces." Having taken approximately 1000 men on board by these heroic measures, *Whitshed* sent a berthing party to take the ropes of the succeeding destroyers as they came in and, as soon as these were berthed, pulled out stern first between the breakwaters, listing heavily with the weight of men, and got clear.

Her commanding officer's search is typical of many of the efforts made by naval officers at this time. Whenever there was a break in the flow a party from the ships would search. *Malcolm's* navigator marched through the streets of Dunkirk playing a set of bagpipes as a summons to the weary men—there is no evidence on record as to the skill with which he played them.

At 2 A.M. a signal from Dunkirk read:

"C.-in-C. says it is essential that rear guard B.E.F. embarks from the beaches east of Mole on account of French congestion on Mole. Considerable number British troops still on Mole. Military are expecting further arrivals there. Rear guard expects to arrive at beach at 0230."

This was an hour and a half after *Whitshed* had restarted the flow. It seemed obvious that large numbers would not arrive until after the time set for the close of operations. The reaction of Dover was immediate and forthright. It is embodied in a signal which said: "Endeavour to embark rear guard from beach remaining after 3 A.M. if necessary." The wording is simple. It was, however, the acceptance of a challenge. The events of the previous morning were still very vivid in the minds of Admiral Ramsay and the Dover Command. Yet, if the men could not be got down to the beach before dawn, the Navy was still prepared to wait until after dawn to take them.

Through this period the small boats worked steadily. They worked in circumstances of rapidly increasing difficulty. The language problem, now that the French predominated along the beaches, was almost impossible. Amongst certain units discipline had broken down, and it was equally hard without an absolute command of the language to stop men from rushing the boats and settling them firmly into the sand. Latecomers could not be prevented from jumping into overloaded boats. There were not a few cases of small craft that left the beach and sank as soon as they reached deep water and the tumultuous wash of the destroyers.

The great bulk of those of the small boats that still floated and were still capable of progressing under their own steam left in accordance with orders at zero hour. The French continued loading a little later than the British ships. A battalion of the B.E.F., which had marched from Bergues through the night, reached the end of the Mole as the last of the British personnel ships, already fully loaded, cast off for home. The battalion turned and marched off the

Mole against the line of the French who still marched down to their own ships. In a little that line ceased also. Those who were left dug themselves into the canal banks and the dunes on the outskirts of the town and lay there till night.

The last ships had held on until sun-up. In full daylight they pulled out to join the end of the long stream that was headed back to the English coast. Over the waters of Dunkirk channel a silence fell. At midnight, when the list for June 1 closed, 64,429 men had been brought safe to the English shore. With all the destruction, with all the loss, this was another Glorious First of June.

A little after sunrise on June 2 a chaplain of the British Expeditionary Force celebrated Holy Communion in the Dunkirk dunes. John Masefield, who tells the story, says that five times before the service ended the congregation of men of the weary rear guard was scattered by low-flying aircraft.

Between 3000 and 4000 of the B.E.F. remained ashore this day. Detachments of these men, with seven anti-aircraft and twelve anti-tank guns, worked with the French throughout the day on the "intermediate line." The French figures were still uncertain. At Dover Admiral Ramsay recorded that the estimate as to "the number of French troops remaining was increasing from the 25,000 quoted the previous evening to figures in the region of 50,000 to 60,000." This uncertainty made planning almost unbelievably difficult. One factor harshly simplified it—the capacity of the embarkation facilities that remained. There was left now only the harbour—almost continuously under shell fire— and a bare mile and a half of beach—equally within range of the German guns.

It was estimated that 25,000 men could be moved during the hours of darkness provided a rapid flow of troops to the embarkation points could be maintained. The night's operation was, therefore, planned on the basis of a lifting of 25,000. Thirteen personnel vessels, two large store carriers, eleven destroyers, five paddle-minesweepers, nine Fleet sweepers, one special service vessel, nine drifters, six skoots, two armed yachts, one gunboat, and a number of tugs towing small craft and free-lance motor-boats were ordered to sail from five o'clock onwards. The French sent altogether forty-three ships, including the Breton fishermen who had worked well the previous day. It was possible for most of the ships' companies this day to get some rest.

There was, however, one aspect of the evacuation for which at this time no provision could be made. The outward flow of wounded virtually ceased this morning. One Casualty Clearing Station remained—12 C.C.S. at Rosendaël. The difficulties which had faced the hospital ships and the accumulating disaster of the morning of June 1 had stopped the movement of stretcher cases. The staff of 12 C.C.S. had abandoned all hope of returning to England.

Late in the morning, however, orders came from I Corps H.Q. to say that one officer and ten men were to be left for every hundred casualties and that the remainder of the medical personnel of 12 C.C.S. was to proceed to the Mole for evacuation. The order led to one of the most remarkable ballots in army history. At two o'clock in the afternoon the names of all medical personnel remaining were placed in a hat. There were by now 230 stretcher cases at Rosendaël, and three officers and thirty men had to be chosen to stay with them. It was decided that "first out of the hat" was first to go, and there were left at the end an officer who had been separated from his field ambulance, another who had been sent over from England for beach duties at Dunkirk, and the surgical specialist of the unit. At ten o'clock at night the remainder of the personnel of 12 C.C.S. moved to the Mole and after an interminable journey reached three destroyers at the end of it.

The wounded, however, were not yet abandoned. The authorities in England decided, shortly after the arrival at Dover of the first of the returning members of the unit, to make a direct appeal to the Germans. At 10:30 A.M. a signal was made by wireless *en clair* to the German Command. It read:

"Wounded situation acute and hospital ships should enter during day. Geneva Convention will be honourably observed and it is felt that the enemy will refrain from attacking."

The Southern Railway steamer *Worthing,* which had been taken over at the beginning of the war for service as a hospital carrier, was lying in the Downs. Two hours after the broadcast she received her orders and at 12:55 P.M. she left for Dunkirk at twenty knots. At 2:32 P.M. she was attacked by twelve enemy aircraft. Nine bombs were dropped, two of which fell within three or four feet of her despite drastic avoiding action. This attack was carried out in good visibility and regardless of the fact that the ship was carrying all the marks and signs of a hospital ship as required by the Geneva Convention. The Convention had been repeatedly flouted throughout the evacuation as it had been flouted on countless occasions before. On this day, however, the attack was more despicable even than upon these earlier occasions. It was made in flagrant, open contempt of the appeal that had been sent out.

While these attacks were taking place the Navy also suffered loss. Though all movements in the area of Dunkirk itself had ceased, the patrols on the approaches had to be maintained. Destroyers, anti-submarine trawlers, drifters, and minesweepers worked throughout the day to safeguard the channels for the night flow.

The diminished perimeter about Dunkirk held. To the west of the town no serious attack had been made on the sector of the line which ran down to the sea in the vicinity of Mardyck, though a number of batteries had been positioned in the vicinity to harass shipping. From Mardyck it held firm along the course of the old Mardyck Canal to Spycker, then along the main canal to Bergues, and from Bergues diagonally across through Uxem and Ghyvelde to the old fortifications on the Franco-Belgian frontier and so back to the sea.

The normal approach to Dunkirk from the south, as has been said, is by the main road which passes through Bergues and, running parallel with the broad Bergues-Dunkirk Canal, moves almost due north into the suburbs of the town. The successful defence of the junction of this canal with the Bergues-Nieuport Canal had so far held the Germans from any attempt at a direct assault, but attacks to the eastward of this road over the level ground which led towards the village of Teteghem had placed the new line there in jeopardy.

At six o'clock in the morning, therefore, the French launched a counterattack in this area. Though it began vigorously, it was brought to a halt by two successive air attacks, each by more than fifty aircraft, and it was finally stopped at the hamlet of Notre Dame des Neiges. At 9 A.M. it was decided to fall back on the Canal des Moëres opposite Teteghem. Throughout the day this position was maintained.

On the other side of the main approach road pressure now increased steadily in the area of Spycker and, as evening fell, the line was penetrated there and a general withdrawal took place. The strength of the holding position in the complicated junction between the canals and roads which led to Dunkirk from the outskirts of Bergues had evidently dissuaded the Germans from a direct frontal assault, and they were plainly endeavouring to find an indirect approach. At nightfall, however, they suspended operations.

Throughout the defence of the perimeter night attacks were rare and hardly ever strongly maintained. The explanation of this lies almost certainly in the nature of the terrain, cut up, as it was, by a complex of navigable canals with, between them, an endless succession of large and small drainage dykes.

As the ships of the night flow approached Dunkirk the position was, therefore, that the perimeter had fallen in but that the line, threatened on either side of the main approach road, still held.

At 3:30 in the afternoon Commander Clouston, who had returned to Dover for a brief rest, left with an augmented pier party in two R.A.F. motor-boats, Nos. 243 and 270, to make the necessary arrangements at the Mole to receive the first ships of the night. Off Gravelines the boats were attacked by eight Junkers 87. No. 243, in which Commander Clouston had sailed, was near-missed early in the attack and became waterlogged. As the attacks continued, both with small bombs and with machine-guns, the crew of 243, with Commander Clouston, took to the water. No. 270 was also damaged but managed, by zigzagging and high speed, to avoid the worst of the attack. Ten minutes after 243 had been hit she returned to the waterlogged wreck. Commander Clouston, who was in the water, waved to her to get clear. Some of his crew had been killed, but with one officer and some of the survivors he set out to swim to a boat that could be seen about two miles away, while the R.A.F. men endeavoured to swim to shore. The water was cold. Commander Clouston, who had for the past week worked almost without sleep and without rest, rapidly became exhausted. He decided finally that he could not make the distance and turned to swim back to the waterlogged wreck of 243. He was not seen again.

The officer with him, after swimming for nearly three hours, reached the boat and found her deserted. With great difficulty he boarded her and was eventually picked up by a French trawler, which had lost her way and which he navigated back to Ramsgate. One of the aircraftmen also turned back to the wreck, reached it and was picked up eight hours later by H.M.S. *Whitshed*.

This is one of the great tragedies of Dunkirk. Commander Clouston was responsible for the traffic of the Mole from the beginning of the operation. Under his guidance 200,000 men had passed down its narrow plankway to safety. It is impossible to exaggerate the importance of his achievement. It was carried out under conditions that could have been surmounted only by a strong spirit. Darkness, wind, sea, enemy shellfire, and incessant bombing conspired always against those who tried to control the traffic of the Mole. The plankway itself was wrecked by direct hits. The loading berths were blocked by sunken ships. The flow of troops was irregular, and the difficulties of dealing with men unaccustomed to the sea and heavy with the exhaustion of defeat were indescribable. Throughout it all Commander Clouston maintained the very highest traditions of the Royal Navy. His service to the B.E.F. and to his country is not to be measured in words.

No. 270 followed her orders and went on to Dunkirk. It had been intended that she should police the fairways and direct traffic. She was, however, so damaged that this was now impossible. Sub-Lieutenant Wake, who commanded her, landed at the Mole and, in the tradition of the Navy, took over the task which Commander Clouston had set out to perform. The inherent difficulty of persuading the inland *poilu* to embark upon an unfamiliar element now reached its height. Coupled with the ordinary language difficulty and the macabre setting of the Mole at night under shellfire and air attack the problem of maintaining the flow was enough to daunt much older men. Sub-Lieutenant Wake kept it going by methods that were at times empirical.

The motor-boat *Blue Bird* crossed under the command of Lieutenant-Colonel H. T. B. Barnard, who had made two previous attempts to get across. This day, however, he left Sheerness with a mixed crew of yachtsmen and ratings. *Blue Bird* closed the eastern end of the beaches but found no troops and, moving down the beach towards the base of the Mole, discovered that water had been put in the petrol tank. This last mishap was a common one through the greater part of the evacuation. Water, as has been described, was being taken over for the use of the Army. The available water cans of the Southern Command—and indeed of the south of England—were used up early, and as a substitute petrol cans were filled and taken over. The petrol for the small craft was also stored in ordinary two-gallon cans. These were appropriately marked, but dumps got mixed on occasion—especially when refuelling was done at night—and the mixture proved disastrous to many ships. *Blue Bird* was towed home by H.M. Skoot *Hilda*.

Sea Roamer, a 40-foot motor cruiser owned and commanded by Mr. J. E. W. Wheatley, also crossed this Sunday evening, with a naval party on board. They towed over a boat to work the beaches and made an independent course across the shallows of the off-lying banks. Outside the harbour they were told to investigate the beaches but, though they closed to within fifty yards of the shore, they could see no signs of life in any part of the area which they examined. While they were doing this the Casino and the Kursaal were hit by incendiary bombs and went up in flames. They searched to two and a half miles north-east of Dunkirk and then, abandoning hopes of picking up anybody from the sands, decided to inspect the wrecks offshore. Circling the first one and shouting, they were rewarded by a head popping up over the side and demanding, *"Etes-vous Allemands ou Français?"* They replied that they were English, and picked up a number of French soldiers who had reached the wreck the day before. These men said that they had seen nobody on the beach for the past twenty-four hours. As she was nearing the next wreck, *Sea Roamer's* people sighted a low, fast-looking vessel carrying, apparently, a heavy gun. There was for some little while considerable exchange of anxiety between the two ships until the new-comer turned out to be the *Massey Shaw* with her powerful fire-fighting monitor on the foredeck. Continuing the search, they worked finally down to the Dunkirk entrance, where they were in collision with a destroyer. *Sea Roamer* herself was slightly damaged, but the boat she was towing was reduced to splinters and the towrope, suddenly freed, fouled her propeller. She was able to move slowly with the auxiliary engine, but she was eventually picked up and towed home by a paddle-steamer.

Sea Roamer, incidentally, recorded one of the better stories of the operation. Discussing the difficulty of persuading French troops to entrust themselves to small boats, her owner said:

"The French, it seems, were not always prepared to wade out and clamber into the dinghies in the surf. A story was told me of a French officer who steadfastly refused to do this. Finally he sent a note to the anxious yacht skipper. It read, 'I have just eaten and am therefore unable to enter the water.'"

The *Massey Shaw* had left Ramsgate at 6:40 P.M. under the command of Lieutenant G. Walker, R.N.V.R., but with eight of her own crew still on board. She found no troops on the beach and Walker took her up the harbour, leaving finally at 3:15 A.M.

Admiral Taylor, having dispatched from Sheerness everything that would float and move, went to Ramsgate in the middle of Sunday afternoon. Discussing the conditions with military officers who had just arrived, he was informed that a pocket of men who had not been able to get into Dunkirk was holding out near Malo-les-Bains, and a special party was organised to get these men away. Three skoots and a dozen fast motor-boats were selected, and sailed late in the afternoon. Commandant Anduse-Faru of the French Navy undertook to arrange for a paddle-steamer and a French ship to be off the beach, and for a number of French fishing vessels to co-operate with Admiral Taylor's boats and ferry off troops to them and to the skoots. He was taken out to the fishing vessels to make arrangements. They had lovely names: *Ciel de France, Ave Maria Gratia Plena, Jeanne Antoine, Arc en Ciel*. They had done good work already and they were very tired but, after argument in the French fashion, they went over again.

Admiral Taylor, who had completed his work ashore, decided to proceed to Dunkirk to supervise the lifting of the pocket from Malo-les-Bains in person. I had at that time stolen a small twin-screw Thames motor cruiser and was ordered to stand by to take the Admiral over. Her name was *White Wing*, she was about thirty foot in length and she had a speed of approximately twelve knots but, owing to trouble with the starboard engine, did not make this speed all the way across. We reached Dunkirk with only minor difficulties and our work for the night is covered in an account that I wrote at the time.

"Having the Admiral on board, we were not actually working the beaches but were in control of small boat operations. We moved about as necessary and, after we had spent some time putting boats in touch with their towing ships, the 5.9 battery off Nieuport way began to drop shells on us. It seemed pure spite. The nearest salvo was about twenty yards astern, which was close enough.

"We stayed there until everybody else had been sent back

and then went pottering about looking for stragglers. While we were doing that, a salvo of shells got one of the ships alongside the Mole. She was hit clean in the boilers and exploded in one terrific crash. There were then, I suppose, about 1000 Frenchmen on the Mole. We had seen them crowding along its narrow crest, outlined against the flames. They had gone out under shellfire to board the boat, and now they had to go back again, still being shelled. It was quite the most tragic thing I ever have seen in my life. We could do nothing with our little dinghy."

The rate of flow through this early part of the night was admirable. Steadily the last of the British element of the rear-guard was marched to the Mole and embarked. French troops came down in a continuous stream, and the prospects for the night looked excellent.

One important mishap marred the proceedings. The French cross-Channel steamer *Rouen,* with a number of men on board, stranded on the mud inside the harbour as she was turning. The tug *Foremost* 22 went to her assistance, but ran aground herself and only just got clear. The tide was ebbing fast, and she left the area so that a tug of lesser draught could make the attempt. The *Sun X* then closed the *Rouen,* but 200 feet away she found only ten feet of water and it was obvious that it would be impossible to move her until the next high tide. Both tugs loaded with men, some of them from the *Rouen.*

General Alexander, with his staff, was picked up by Admiral Wake-Walker in M.A./S.B. 10. He was subsequently transferred to a destroyer which was attacked and machine-gunned when close to Dover.

By eleven o'clock the last of the British Expeditionary Force was moving on to the ships. *St. Helier* claims the honour of the final lifting, and appropriate finish to a great record. At about 11:30 P.M., fully loaded, she slipped her ropes for the last time and felt her way out of the harbour, down by the head and leaking badly in her forepeak.

So ended a chapter in the story of the British Army, a story that had begun a bare three weeks before, as the British Expeditionary Force moved through the barriers of the

Belgian frontier and raced into Belgium with lilac on their hats. So ended the story of a great retreat, one of the greatest in military history. So ended, though no man knew it on that day, Hitler's opportunity to break the power of Britain.

At 11:30 P.M. Captain Tennant, Senior Naval Officer, Dunkirk, made the simple signal: "B.E.F. evacuated."

The Battle of Britain

After Dunkirk, the British rushed defense preparations for the expected German invasion. Hitler, who was inclined to believe the British would now surrender, had not reckoned with the new spirit exemplified by Winston Churchill, whose speeches to the British Parliament and to the public had infused everyone with new hope. When evidence of this change was brought to Hitler, he ordered the German Luftwaffe to bomb England to her knees and to destroy the Royal Air Force, preparatory to launching the German Armies across the Channel. Until now, the very threat of bombing from the German air fleets had struck terror in the hearts of Europeans. But the British Fighter Command and its Spitfire and Hurricane pilots were ready for the onslaught.

Churchill said, "Our fate now depended upon victory in the air," and in speaking to Parliament on June 4, he added, "The great French Army was very largely, for the time being, cast back and disturbed by the onrush of a few thousand armored vehicles. May it also be that the cause of civilization itself will be defended by the skill and devotion of a few thousand airmen?" *

Hitler gave the Luftwaffe two primary tasks in the beginning of the Battle of Britain: to drive British shipping out of the Channel, and to crush the R.A.F. if it were thrown over the Channel as a protective umbrella. Throughout July, the Germans flew sortie after sortie over the Channel and the Channel ports. They achieved a partial victory. "After July 4, all big ship convoys on world routes in and out of the port of London had been driven from the Channel; after July 25, all coastal convoys had been stopped; on July 28, the withdrawal of the Dover destroyers had been forced; after July 29, the use of destroyers in the Channel by day had been prohibited." **

*Their Finest Hour, by W. S. Churchill, p. 274.

** Strike from the Sky, by Alexander McKee, p. 54.

But still, the destroyers could operate at night and were a threat against any invasion fleet. While the British fighters had suffered some losses, not all the squadrons had been committed and there were still 708 fighters and some 1400 pilots available to throw against the Luftwaffe.

Now the battle moved inland. The new objective was the destruction of the R.A.F. in direct combat to achieve the supremacy necessary for the invasion which Hitler and his generals had agreed could take place no later in 1940 than September 20.

"British fighter pilots had no fear whatsoever of the German bombers which were easy prey for the Hurricanes and Spitfires. The He-111s, Do-17s and 215s and the Ju-88s were not fast enough, particularly when operating in formation. Moreover, they were indifferently armed. They could rarely bring more than one gun to bear on an attacking fighter.

"The attitude towards the Me-109 was different. This type was very effective and accounted for most of the losses suffered by Fighter Command during the battle. It was as fast as the Spitfire, considerably faster than the Hurricane, and it would out-dive and out-climb either. Its armament was formidable. Half a dozen explosive shells from its cannon could do far more damage than the equivalent length of burst of Browning rounds. On the other hand, the firing rate of the Brownings was much higher, which gave the British pilots a better chance of scoring with a short burst.

"In one vital respect the Me-109 was at a disadvantage. It could be out-turned by the Spitfire and the Hurricane. This was a serious handicap to the Luftwaffe pilots assigned to escorting bombers. Their freedom of action was curtailed. They were, therefore, unable to pursue the tactics best suited to their aircraft. They never found a way around this problem and their difficulties were aggravated when Goering, infuriated by the losses inflicted on his bombers, ordered the fighters to stay closer still to their charges.

"At the beginning of the battle the German fighters used their speed to advantage which, coupled with their more recently evolved tactics, played havoc with the antiquated practices of Fighter Command.

"British tactics were completely wrong when the Battle began, but steadily improved. Fighter Command squadrons at the outset flew in tidy tight formations so close that only the leader could see where he was going and what was going on. The other members of the formation concentrated on keeping station.

47

"This was a handover from peacetime. It looked good at an air display but in combat a close formation of aircraft is easier to see. The result was that many unsuspecting pilots were 'bounced.'

"Since the Battle, the importance of the Hurricane to victory has been slowly undermined. The Spitfire tends to hold pride of place to the extent that a fallacy runs the risk of becoming accepted as historical fact.

"There were more Hurricanes in the Battle of Britain than Spitfires. The Hurricane Mk. 1, with a constant-speed propeller, was a fine fighting aircraft, an excellent gun platform and magnificently maneuverable up to 20,000 feet. It was extremely strong and could take an extraordinary amount of punishment." *

Alexander McKee, author of *Strike from the Sky*, says:

"The limiting factor on the British side was pilots and not aircraft; had another 100 pilots been available, there were sufficient machines for them. The production problem had already been solved; partly because of the planned expansion programme controlled by Air Marshal Sir Wilfrid Freeman, partly by the impact of Lord Beaverbrook's personality, and partly because of the crisis atmosphere after Dunkirk. There was a shortage of A.A. guns, particularly of the lighter type most useful for airfield defence; and here the limiting factor was production—but a number of substitutes were found. This, then, was the force which the Germans had to destroy if they were to win the battle. It was to be found largely in the air, but it was dependent on airfields and aircraft factories for its existence, and for its efficiency on the radar stations located along the coast, and the Sector Operations Rooms located at the main base airfield in each Sector. The controlling headquarters for the whole force was deep underground and beyond the reach of bombers.

"It was a problem quite unlike any other which the Germans had previously faced—fast, well-armed fighters which could not be evaded, a long-range radar warning of the bombers' approach, a radio control system to direct the fighters onto the bombers before they even reached the target, and no possibility of going forward effectively by leaps and bounds, with the tanks driving on to take advantage of the confusion created by the raids before the effect evaporated. Nevertheless, the advance, 'by leaps and bounds,' was the solution adopted, because the Luftwaffe was limited by a technical factor—the

*The Narrow Margin, by Wood and Dempster, pp. 414-415.

48

short range of their only effective fighter, the Messerschmitt 109. There was not the slightest possibility of unleashing an air attack which could surge at once over the whole of the United Kingdom, striking at the most vital parts of the British war machine, and at the same time confusing the defence by coming in simultaneously from all points of the compass." *

Throughout August the German Luftwaffe bombed targets selected by Goering. British radar installations, airfields, and some factories were hit. Until the end of the month, the Spitfire and Hurricane pilots gave better than they got. Then, for a few days, the Germans intensified their attack on the British airfields. The rate of loss of planes was so severe that the British Fighter Command could not have survived had the attacks continued. But, luckily, on September 7, Goering ordered the major part of the Luftwaffe to begin bombing London. Fighter Command was saved; it could now bind its wounds and be ready to fight another day.

THE CRISIS OF FIGHTER COMMAND**
31 AUGUST-6 SEPTEMBER

by Alexander McKee

In the first week of September the German plan came near to fulfilment. The concentration of German fighters in Pas de Calais swept repeatedly across Kent, shooting to pieces the handful of squadrons sent up against them and carrying the bombers again and again to Sector Stations, laying them in ruins and putting out of action vital parts of the control system. In the air, the British lost

* *Strike from the Sky*, p. 75.

** A slightly condensed version of the above chapter from *Strike from the Sky*.

more fighters than did the Germans, indeed their losses were higher than the total German losses of both fighters and bombers; and on the ground, they lost more fighters, so that the reserve of machines became seriously depleted. If the process was continued, there could be only one end for Fighter Command.

The strain on the outnumbered British pilots was intense. "It was no picnic," said Colin Gray, "despite what anyone might say later. I've seen Al Deere and others push away their breakfast when told to go up. Most of us were pretty scared all the bloody time; you only felt happy when the battle was over and you were on your way home. Then you were safe for a bit, anyway."

The strain on the Germans was equally terrible. Unlike the British, they were not being taken out of the line for rest. Every fighter pilot in the Luftwaffe, apart from those in a small unit held back to guard Wilhelmshaven against possible attacks by Bomber Command, was on the Channel coast and flying two or three sorties a day over England.

The atmosphere on the German fighter airfields can best be gauged by the photographs taken at the time. The pilots are demonstrating with their hands how they shot down that Spitfire or Hurricane, but the faces are tense with strain and at the same time drained of emotion and nervous strength. For the leaders, especially, there was the burden of responsibility. As soon as a *gruppe* commander landed, he had to worry about his losses. How many shot down—or missing? And who? How many aircraft serviceable? How long to repair the damaged aircraft? And then the order for the next take-off. And the crossing, once more, of what the German pilots, with fury, called the, "Shite Kanal," that "sewer," that "bit of dirty water." "I emphasise," said Galland,* "that this fear of coming down in the water did as much damage to our morale as the British fighters." This sentiment, surprising as it is to an Englishman accustomed to regard salt water, and espe-

*German air ace and group leader.

cially the Channel, as basically friendly, was echoed by all the German airmen who fought in the battle, whether in fighters or bombers, but more especially in the single-engined fighters. When the battle was on, they were too excited to feel fear of the enemy, but the nagging thought of that merciless sea waiting for the man whose engine failed either from enemy bullets or a mechanical fault, was continually with them.

On 31 August the Germans struck at three Sector Stations in 11 Group—Biggin Hill, Hornchurch, and Debden —and one Sector Station in 12 Group—Duxford. The 12 Group squadrons, held back to guard the Midlands and to act as flank guard and reserve to 11 Group, were, through no fault of their own, seeing very little action; consequently, they were fit and rested. The Duxford attack, the first of the day, failed.

At 7:30 a.m. the Spitfires of 19 Squadron scrambled from Fowlmere, a satellite field in the Duxford Sector. There were nine of them, led by Flight Lieutenant W. G. Clouston; the second section was led by J. B. Coward, the third section by Flight Lieutenant F. N. Brinsden. Coward had seen action over Dunkirk, but he had been away having his tonsils removed, and had rejoined only two days before, so this was his first action in the Battle of Britain. All nine Spitfires were fitted with two cannon instead of the normal armament of eight machine guns.

With adequate warning of the raid, they climbed away to the east and ten miles from Duxford sighted the enemy —about fifteen Dorniers escorted by perhaps sixty fighters. 25,000 feet below them, at Little Shelford, was Coward's home. The nine fighters pressed on in loose line astern, then Brinsden led his section of three up toward the escort while Clouston took the other six Spitfires into the bombers in a "copybook" pre-war formation attack.

Coward chose the number two Dornier in the second kette, the other two pilots of his section aiming at its companions. Diving in from the beam, Coward aimed at the nose of the bomber and opened fire. "The whole experience was an exhilarating one," said Coward, "for we were fighting over our own homes." His cannons thundered briefly, "boom-boom"—and then stopped. Almost instantly, there was a thud as something hit the Spitfire. Coward felt no pain, but saw his bare foot lying on the floor of the cockpit, almost severed from the leg. The Spitfire went out of control, the nose falling violently in the beginning of an outside loop, which forces the pilot forward against his straps, out of the cockpit.

With the "g" behind him, Coward got out quite easily, but his parachute became caught on the fuselage, his gloves were ripped off by the screaming slipstream and his nearly severed foot was banged repeatedly against the falling Spitfire. He had intended to do a delayed drop, but the pain in his foot caused him to pull the ripcord.

The opening parachute pulled him clear at 20,000 feet and, looking down, he saw the blood pumping out of his leg and dropping away far below. His bare hands, numbed by the cold, were unable to force aside the straps of the parachute harness so that he could get at the first aid kit and handkerchief in his pockets, but if he was to survive, he had to improvise a tourniquet quickly. Frantically, feeling his strength ebbing away and aware that his life depended on it, he struggled with half-frozen fingers to undo the strap and buckle of his helmet, to which was attached a wireless lead.

Once the helmet was off, Coward wound the lead round his thigh, just above the knee, pulling it as tightly as he could to choke off the supply of blood, and at the same time holding his leg almost up to his chin. By these means, he managed to reduce the flow of blood to a trickle. In this position he drifted slowly across Duxford airfield, where the rest of the squadron were now landing. Then the wind changed and he sailed back over Duxford again and came down in a field near the roundabout on the Royston/Newmarket road. The impact was hard and painful and, worried about infection of the wound, Coward tried to keep his leg off the ground.

"A youth came running up with a pitchfork at the charge, obviously thinking I was a German (I was wearing a black flying overall). He stood looking at me, speechless with horror at the sight of the blood. This maddened me because I was hoping for some help. My language was a bit coarse and he departed without saying anything at all."

Years later, when Coward was instructing at a Fighter Operational Training Unit, he met the boy again—now a Pilot Officer. He remembered their previous meeting in the field by the Newmarket road, and told Coward that he had actually run to find a doctor and that the first car he had stopped had contained one. Within half an hour an ambulance had driven him away to hospital in charge of Squadron Leader Brown, an R.A.F. doctor.

Brown had then driven on to Little Shelford to break the news gently to Coward's wife. As he was knocking at the front door, the baker was round at the back, telling the kitchen staff that he had just passed the wreck of Coward's Spitfire; he thought the pilot had been killed. So, when this story reached Mrs. Coward, she already knew that her husband had been operated on and that he had lost one leg below the knee. When he recovered, Coward was posted to Chequers to take charge of the Prime Minister's roof spotters.

The bombers had jettisoned their load before reaching the airfield and 19 Squadron claimed three victories. But they were certain that they would have got more if their cannons had not packed up after firing only a few rounds. Cannon armed Spitfires had been successful in combat against reconnaissance machines off the northeast coast, but in dogfights there occurred these exasperating and inexplicable jams. They caused such fury among the baulked pilots that it was suggested to Lord Beaverbrook that the armament should revert to machine guns. Instead, he ordered an immediate enquiry. Consequently, a few days later, when the attack had begun to switch to aircraft factories, Mr. E. L. Cooper, of the Supermarine factory at Southampton, was to find himself solving the practical aspects of this problem under fire.

Shortly after the Duxford fight had ended, Teddy Morris, leading six Hurricanes of 79 Squadron, was vectored down the Thames Estuary to intercept what was probably the raid on Hornchurch coming in—half a hundred Dorniers with a large escort. The Hurricanes were still climbing, too low to put in a fast attack, but Morris engaged. He passed under the bombers, firing as he went, and then turned to attack the rearmost bombers. He was knocking pieces off a Dornier when he saw a 109 nose up alongside him about twenty yards away. Just time enough to finish off the Dornier, he thought, wrongly. Cannon shells and machine-gun bullets ripped into the Hurricane; Morris, struck by several bullets, his legs sprayed with shell fragments, took violent evasive action and limped back to Biggin Hill where he crash-landed on the airfield. Lying doped in Station Sick Quarters, he was vaguely conscious of bomb explosions and of other casualties being brought in.

Before Morris had even reached Biggin Hill, the raiders were over Hornchurch. Below them, the Spitfires of 54 Squadron were racing across the airfield in a belated attempt to get airborne. Colin Gray, who was flying with them, noted in his diary, "Red Section blown to blazes but no one hurt. Miraculous."

This is probably the most famous single incident of the Battle of Britain. The official *Fight at Odds* prints the Station diary; Richard Hillary, a Hornchurch pilot who saw the affair from the ground, described it in *The Last Enemy* (Macmillan); and Al Deere, the leader of the section "blown to blazes," has given his own account in *Nine Lives,* as it was an occasion on which he lost one of them.

After several false alarms, the engines of the squadron's Spitfires had been started and stopped so many times that they were overheated and difficult to start again when the agitated Controller screamed, "Take off! Take off!" Colin Gray, one of the first eventually to get away, climbing up under the raid, saw Hornchurch disappear in smoke and dust. Al Deere had swung into the wind, to find his take-off blocked by a Spitfire from his own section. "Get to hell out of the way, Red Two!" he bellowed. Deere had got his tail up and was bumping over the grass when he saw the first bomb exploding, ahead and to the left; then the bumping stopped and he was airborne, his section close behind him. The bombs were still falling.

"Out of the corner of my eye," wrote Richard Hillary, "I saw the three Spitfires. One moment they were about twenty feet up in close formation; the next, catapulted apart as though on elastic. The leader went over on his back and ploughed along the runway with a rending crash of tearing fabric; number two put a wing in and spun round on his airscrew, while the plane on the left was blasted wingless into the next field. I remember thinking, stupidly, 'That's the shortest flight he's ever taken,' and then my feet were nearly knocked from under me, my mouth was full of dirt, and Bubble, gesticulating like a madman from the shelter entrance, was yelling, 'Run, you bloody fool, run!' I ran."

When Gray landed after the action, he saw Deere's KL-B over on its back, a sorry mess; he thought, "Poor old Al's had it." But no, he found Deere had lost only his helmet and a streak of skin and hair torn off the top of his head. His Spitfire had skated along the ground, upside down, at over 100 m.p.h., dirt and stones battering at his face, and the top of his head virtually in contact with the earth over which the fighter was careering, close enough, anyway, nearly to scalp him. When the wreck wrenched to a halt, he was trapped upside down in the tiny cockpit, with a sea of petrol soaking into the grass around the crash, and no possibility of getting out.

His number three, Pilot Officer Edsell, who had crashed right way up but had hurt his legs so badly that he could not walk, then began to crawl over the aerodrome, which was still being bombed, towards KL-B. While he wrenched from outside and Deere pushed from inside, they got the cockpit door open. Deere wriggled out and, as Edsell could not stand, helped his rescuer to Station Sick Quarters.

Of Sergeant Davies, Deere's number two, there was no sign, although his aircraft could be seen, minus its tail, lying just beyond the boundary fence. His fate was a mystery for some time. He turned up hours later, carrying his parachute—there was no gap in the boundary fence, and he had had to walk several miles around it to get onto the aerodrome again.

The airfield was a mass of craters, in which lay the three

wrecked Spitfires of Red Section, and in the dispersal area four of their reserve aircraft had been destroyed, but not a great deal of damage had been done to hangars and workshops. Hornchurch was bombed again that day and the next morning Deere, Edsell and Davies were in action again; Deere, in particular, had bailed out or crash landed many times before, a split-second escape being involved in each case. Later in the war, the qualifications for the V.C. were amended, in the case of Group Captain Cheshire, to recognise the fact that unremitting performance and endurance may rank as highly as the single exceptional act of courage. Had this been so in 1940, there might have been more than merely a single V.C. awarded to Fighter Command.

In the evening, Biggin Hill, bombed already three times in two days, was the target. Worrall, Frankland and Igoe were in the Operations Room as the raid came in. Frankland was controlling, with Worrall helping him. The W.A.A.F.s continued to plot the steadily approaching bombers as Frankland and Worrall passed the orders to the fighters. "The W.A.A.F.s may have been scared to death," said Frankland, "but if so, they certainly didn't show it and their work wasn't affected." With the bombers right on top, the W.A.A.F.s were ordered under the table. Corporal Henderson, however, remained at her post. The telephone connection with 11 Group, and Sergeant Turner had to be forcibly dragged from the switchboard. Frankland felt as a crunch, rather than heard, the bomb which came through the roof and struck the top of a safe fifteen feet away in the Signal Officer's office. The Operations Room was plunged into darkness as the lights failed, a substantial part of the roof fell in, and choking clouds of dust filled the air.

Desmond Sheen had moved in that morning, from Acklington, with 72 Squadron, which was relieving 612 Squadron at Biggin Hill; he had hardly settled in before he was airborne again on the interception being controlled by Frankland at the time of the bombing. When he landed, most of the remaining hangars and workshops had either been destroyed or were so full of holes that they could not be blacked out for use at night. A W.A.A.F Armament

Sergeant was having the time of her life going round the bomb craters and marking with red flags the small significant holes which indicated delayed action bombs. The W.A.A.F. who drove Sheen across the wrecked airfield with a nonchalant disregard of the D.A. bombs had lost her husband and many of her friends in a previous raid; it was the attitude of this girl and some of the others which impressed Sheen most of all.

Meanwhile, the severe fighting had caused significant attrition among many squadrons. 56 Squadron, for instance, had virtually ceased to exist as an effective fighting unit; in the space of only a few days it had lost most of its leaders and a number of other pilots—dead, burned, wounded, or just badly shaken. The gallant "Jumbo" Gracie —"a fat chap, full of fun, full of life, a most positive cavalier character," Sutton called him—had been shot down and crash-landed on the 30th. He flew again on the 31st, joking about the stiff neck he had got in the crash, then bounced into Epping Hospital for a quick X-ray, cheerfully exaggerating (he thought) with, "I've got a broken neck!" He returned after X-ray, rather white— "It really is broken." Three pilots were in the hospital with severe burns, one of them Barry Sutton.

He was shot down, he always thought, by a Spitfire. At any rate, when returning alone from an attack on a bomber formation, he was "bounced" and the aircraft that circled his parachute was a Spitfire, presumably exulting over the demise of a 109. Just previously, he had been with the squadron, had sighted the German formation, which looked like a "great swarming mass of flies," had reported them, but presumably not been heard, for when he streaked off in their direction he found himself alone, with no sign of the rest of the squadron. His first instinct was to run, but suspecting that the Germans had not seen him and that a quick dive into the middle of them could hardly fail to get one, he went straight through them, spraying bullets. "Looking back on it afterwards with the experience of years, I am quite certain I shot well up out of range and I doubt whether I did much damage."

Grateful still to be alive, Sutton flew back over the Thames Estuary towards Hornchurch, gradually losing height. It was a beautiful evening, so he slid back the hood, raised the seat for a better view—and began to sing.

"Absolutely reprehensible," he commented afterwards. "One should never do this . . . but I thought I was well away from the battle area. Then the instrument panel suddenly began to break up and there was a great explosion, rather like a bang from an oven door." The hood was already open and Sutton got out so fast that all he remembered of it was the tail plane going past his face, very close. He pulled the ripcord, but could not hold on to the shroud lines because the flames which had blown back into the cockpit had raised large blisters on his hands.

"So I just swung about helplessly and listened to the birds, and saw the Spitfire coming round, and finally I began to see the trees and telegraph wires coming up very closely, and a road, and then people running. The people running turned out to be women and I actually landed in the middle of the street in a village near Canterbury, and these old dames came running out, I am not absolutely certain, but I think with rolling pins in their hands—they were very hostile-looking and quite certain I was a German. Then, there arrived an ambulance and a Wolseley 14 car with a soldier in it, and I was not going to get into the ambulance and insisted on the car. I was very rude to the ambulance driver, but he must have won; he put me back in the ambulance—this shows the power of one's will in conditions of shock, which is what I had. Next morning, the Sister produced a 'T' piece from my badly burned tunic, as she thought it might be of value. She didn't know what it was, and I couldn't identify it for a moment, until I realised it was the door-piece of the ambulance, which I had pocketed out of spite because they had insisted that I went in this bumpy old thing instead of the nice Wolseley."

After these losses, 56 Squadron were taken out of the line and sent to Boscombe Down where the few surviving experienced pilots would train the reinforcements. A few days later, 54 Squadron were also to be taken out of the line; but on the 31st Colin Gray got a 109 near Maidstone, which gradually slowed down, spewing glycol, and landed in a field. Circling the crash, Gray saw the pilot get out of the wreckage and three men advancing on him. Each time the Spitfire whistled over the three men, they went down flat on their faces, so that it took some minutes to reach the German; he, meanwhile, took off his parachute and jumped on it. Gray assumed he was an "ace" whose vanity was hurt.

Sunday, 1 September, was the last day of Biggin Hill's "Bad Weekend." Colin Gray attacked a Heinkel formation while they were actually bombing it, and was hit by just one bullet from some German gunner—which severed both elevator control wires. He could turn and bank but not dive or climb, so he turned onto the bearing for Hornchurch, intending to use his trimming tabs to get the nose down. This he did, and brought off a successful landing in the middle of a new rash of bomb craters.

During the day, Desmond Sheen took off from Biggin with 72 Squadron and engaged an escorted Dornier formation coming in south of the Thames; he was brushed off a bomber by the 109s, had to mix it with six of them, collected a cannon shell in his engine—and finally got away. Then he climbed up after the bombers once more. And his engine promptly burst into flames. He slid back the hood, turned the Spitfire onto its back, pulled the harness-release pin—and shoved the stick hard forward, so that the fighter tried to do an outside loop. Out he went, "clean as a whistle," and fell free, somersaulting, until he had counted ten and pulled the ripcord.

"The parachute opened smoothly and there was a reassuring jolt as it took effect," he recalled. "I found myself swaying gently some twelve to fifteen thousand feet above the ground. The descent took some time and was very pleasant; moreover, it gave me a, perhaps, unusual opportunity to survey the battle. It was a clear cloudless day, in fact, a beautiful Sunday morning.

"But, on my right, I could see bombs bursting in the Dover area with the answering fire of the A.A. defences. The A.A. were also very active in the London area on my left, and in between, a series of running fights was taking place. Above all could be heard the crump of bombs and A.A. shells, the roar of bomber engines and the distinctive whine of climbing, diving fighters. There was a smell of cordite in the air. Quite close to me a 109 went down vertically in flames. I think it was the pilot of this one who bailed out but had a faulty harness—he parted company with his parachute. Another 109 turned towards me, but a Spitfire turned onto his tail and both quickly disappeared.

"I landed in the middle of a field with nothing but a slight jar. I got out of my harness and began to roll up the parachute. A young girl came up and eyed me shyly and a few minutes later a young Army Lieutenant appeared, doubtfully waving his revolver in my general direction. I was wearing my old Australian Air Force uniform, which was then a generally unfamiliar sight, and there was no doubt that he wondered whether I was a German. However, I ignored the revolver, continued to pick up my parachute, and started as normal a conversation as possible under the circumstances."

Since Friday morning some seventy people had been killed or wounded at Biggin Hill and every hangar had been destroyed, although the shell of one was still standing. To keep a fighter fit to fly under normal conditions required a team of about five men, who had to carry out daily more than 150 inspections on the aircraft, its airframe, engine, instruments, electrics, radio, and armament. Many of the aircraft were now coming back shot to pieces and if the squadrons were to keep flying at full strength most of the repairs would have to be done on the spot. The sheer pressure of work on the ground crews was tremendous; they slaved to keep the fighters airworthy and suffered casualties while they did it. "Pilots who were on the ground when there was a raid couldn't get into the air quick enough," said Jackson, the Engineer Officer. "When you can hit back it's a build to morale. But to sit on the ground, without a gun, unable to hit back, and just get blasted, is a terrifying experience."

Biggin Hill was the worst hit of the Sector Stations, but what happened there during this climax of the battle against Fighter Command was different only in degree from what happened to most of the other Sector Stations. All except Northolt suffered a similar experience, and the cumulative effect of the attacks was becoming serious.

The attack on the Sector Stations continued without intermission; Hornchurch was raided on 2 September, North Weald on 3 September. The Germans were getting their thrusts home with distressing frequency, partly because of the enormous concentration of fighters in Pas de Calais, partly because they were becoming more expert in protecting their bombers. But the 109s, flying to the limit of their fuel, were vulnerable on the return; they could not fight, but only dive for home. On the 2nd, J. Feric of 303 Squadron pursued a 109 with such enthusiasm that he was still firing at it over France. Park mildly rebuked the Poles, saying that although he appreciated their fine offensive spirit, "this practice is not economical or sound now that there is such good shooting within sight of London." On the 3rd, Colin Gray met a 109 returning from the big raid on North Weald and chased it all the way to the French coast; it was streaming glycol but very determined to get home. As it was steadily slowing down and he was low on ammunition, he waited to fire until he had crept up to 150 yards. It promptly turned over, pretending to be dead, flipped right way up again, and carried gamely on, the propeller slowly ticking over. There, Gray had to leave it, "because its chums were coming out." The Germans were forced to include yet one more refinement in their escort technique—"Fighter Reception"—groups of 109s waiting over the Channel to greet the bomber formations, possibly broken up and certainly with "lame ducks" lagging behind, and possibly separated now from their escort, which would be low on fuel and unable to fight.

4 September marked the introduction of a new type of target for the German bombers on the western flank, those largely under command of *Luftflotte* 3. Whereas in the last week of August they had been employed against targets which had direct connection with the invasion—the bombing of naval bases, particularly Portsmouth—they now began a systematic series of raids on aircraft factories, but without discriminating between those making bombers and those engaged in fighter production. What might have happened if they had concentrated on the fighter factories and done so earlier, in mid-August, is an interesting speculation; possibly, it might have been fatal.

At midday on the 4th, Mr. C. F. Andrews, who is now Public Relations Officer of Vickers-Armstrong at Weybridge, was arguing with a colleague in a bank at Woking, where he was then employed, as to the possibilities of recognising enemy aircraft by the sound of their engines. He maintained that it was not only possible, but easy; his colleague scoffed. "Well now, it's a most extraordinary thing," replied Andrews, "but there's a formation of aircraft coming straight up over the railway line now. And I'll take a small bet that that is a hostile formation, probably Ju-88's." Before they could even reach the door, the guns were firing. When they looked out, the bombers were scattering and they counted at least six parachutes. The man in command of the battery, which had brought down two bombers with its first salvo, was a Sergeant—the officers were away at lunch. He had seen about fourteen aircraft flying low and fast up the main railway line from Portsmouth to London, taken one look at them, roared, "Bloody Ju-88s! Take post! Fire!" (or words to that effect), and the first shell had burst between two of them, bringing both down.

This was most extraordinary. Everything in this case had depended on quick and accurate recognition of the aircraft as German, and most A.A. gunners (the Navy were particularly notorious) had no grasp whatever of this subject. The Army gunners relied on the warnings passed to them by Fighter Command, with which they were integrated. This situation, and the poor quality of the recognition material had caused a group of aviation enthusiasts, mainly whole-time or part-time members of the Observer Corps in nearby Guildford, to form the Hearkers Club. A purely private organisation—it met in a café—it received help from the Technical Editor of *The Aeroplane*, Peter Masefield, and Leonard Taylor, of the Air League, and set such a standard, that it was eventually taken over officially. Andrews was a member and so was the Sergeant who had put his knowledge to such good use.

But he had not stopped the bombers; the remainder, rather scattered, pressed on to their target. This was the Vickers-Armstrong factory, producing Wellington bombers, at Brooklands aerodrome near Weybridge. It was 1:25 p.m., so that large crowds of men and women were leaving the canteen and washrooms or were clocking in; there were not many actually on the factory floor among the machinery, which afforded good protection from blast. Mr. C. Pipe, who had been delayed, had not even reached the building. He had got as far as number three gate, where an old man was standing, leaning on the gate and looking up at a segment of sky across which came four bombers, roaring in low and fast. "Now I don't think I've seen any of those before," observed the old man. There were women and girls passing through, but the sight of the black crosses on the wings of the bombers temporarily distracted Mr. Pipe. "Don't stand there—get down, for flip's sake!" he bellowed, and set the example. One of the four planes banked steeply and a bomb fell away from it, plunging through the roof of the factory.

Watching from the door of the machine shop at that moment was an assistant foreman, Mr. J. Hilyard. His segment of sky contained two planes, from which bombs fell at the exact moment someone exclaimed, "Look at those Spitfires!"

Mr. F. W. Hackney, a storekeeper, had had lunch in the canteen and was just leaving the adjoining washroom; both were on the upper floor with a "well" in the centre. On the floor below was the clocking-in area. Canteen, washrooms, the stairs leading down, and the clocking-in area were crowded with men and girls. The roof above was of glass. One heavy bomb detonated here with maximum effect. It went down through the "well"—passing Mr. Hackney on the way—and exploded, actually underneath him, on the top of a large rubber die-forming press. He heard no explosion. The place just started crumbling away, falling to pieces around him, dissolving, and filling the air with dust. He ran down the stairs, saw the body of a girl, and after a moment's hesitation, took her to the First Aid Post. Because of the dust, smoke, and ruin, every man's view was, for the moment, localised.

Mr. A. G. Bugden, an assistant foreman, had stopped for perhaps one minute later than he usually did, to buy a bar of chocolate in the canteen; so he was coming down the stairs when he heard aeroplanes and was abruptly blown some distance by the bomb. He recovered consciousness, saw a man who was blood-stained, wiped the blood off him —and discovered that he himself was similarly streaming blood. He went into the machine shop, through dense clouds of dust, and saw that the glass from the roof was hanging down in slices, held up by the wire underneath. Two men were lying under the wreckage of the stores, but part of the roof girders had come down on top of it all, and there was nothing that could be done for them. He went to his own desk and found it crushed by a roof support—buying the bar of chocolate had saved his life. Many of the men went home to tell their wives that they were all right, then came back to help.

It was fairly quiet, except for a low, persistent moaning which seemed to come from everywhere. One girl was sitting on her stool, quite lifelike, and quite dead. Of another girl, only the legs were left—with not a crease or crinkle in the stockings. Many other bodies had been wholly or partially stripped of their clothing by the blast, but there was little blood, often none at all, except among the people cut down by the flying slivers of glass. The blast had killed, apparently, without a wound. A.R.P. precautions had familiarised everyone with gas, but not with the effects of large amounts of high explosive inside a thin covering of steel. They were freakish, streams of blast streaking out as unpredictably as water from a running tap when a thumb is placed under it, and striking anything in its path with a force equal to collision with a fast motor car. The delicate internal organs—lungs, liver, spleen—were crushed or ruptured by the blow; the wounded were shocked and bleeding internally. Ordinary First Aid was useless; morphia, not bandages, was required.

Mr. Hackney, anxious to see if his brother was all right, searched for him without result, and then began to help in the work of carrying out the dead. When the supply of stretchers ran out, they piled the bodies on the completed wings of Wellington bombers, and carried them out that way. He saw a man's foot sticking out from under wreckage, but decided to leave him. The general feeling about this was, "They're gone. Leave it." Over one body, he had an argument with another man as to how to move it; they decided to turn the corpse over, and Mr. Hackney got hold of an arm—but it came right out of the body, which had been broken by the blast.

Mr. Pipe saw a removal van drive up to where he, also, was engaged on this task. The driver asked casually, "Can I help?" So they unloaded its cargo of shiny new bicycles, and put in the wounded and the dead as they were brought out from the factory. After three or four trips to the hospital, there seemed to be an end to the job, so the driver calmly took a broom, swept out the thickly caked blood from the floor of the van, reloaded his shiny bicycles, and drove off without even giving his name.

First casualty lists were put up in Sub-Post Offices throughout the district at 6 p.m. One list alone contained 132 names, but the total was not known for several days—88 killed and more than 600 wounded.

"It was eerie walking round the works that night," said a Fire Officer. "Bits of glass kept tinkling as they fell from the roof. Then there was the rubble covering the big press, and you knew, as you went past, that there were people under there. Next day, I remember, there was a chap with a concrete breaker working to uncover the bodies; hat pushed back on his head, he was singing away quite cheerfully."

On 5 September, as 72 Squadron were climbing up over Kent to get height over a raid reported coming in from the east, Desmond Sheen was "bounced" from the rear. He heard a warning shout from one of the "weavers," and almost instantaneously, the Spitfire shuddered from what must have been an accurate and heavy burst from astern. He felt sudden pain in the leg and hand, and then passed out. Possibly, his oxygen bottle had been hit and exploded.

The Spitfire went whining down, vertically, with large pieces missing from the port wing; when Sheen recovered consciousness, he had no control over the aircraft, he could not even level out or roll over so that he could drop clear. And the fighter was going straight down at the deck, speed rapidly building up towards the 500 m.p.h. mark. The hood was already open, and when Sheen pulled the harness pin to release himself from his straps, he was sucked out of the cockpit; but his feet were trapped by the top of the windscreen. He lay straddled along the top of the fuselage, struggling to get free, with no idea how much height or time he still had. Not very much, he suspected.

Then, for no apparent reason, his feet were free and, without waiting to slow down or even get clear of the aircraft, he pulled the ripcord. With a snap that jarred every bone in his body, the parachute opened; Sheen had a split-second glimpse of trees under his feet—and then he was down in Maidstone Wood.

He fell between the trees, his parachute caught on the top branches to act as a brake, and he landed as lightly as a feather, barely touching the ground. He crawled to a path and saw a policeman riding a bicycle, followed by spectators. The policeman's first action was to produce a flask, the second to express surprise that Sheen had waited so long before getting out of his aircraft. His wounds were not serious, but they kept him out of the air for about a month.

When they were jumped, the squadron had been flying in the old tight formation of vics of three, instead of the loose pairs used by the Germans; to offset the difficulties of look-out which made this formation vulnerable, the two rear machines of the last section had been "weaving" but this method was not satisfactory and the "weavers" had seen the Germans too late to avoid the "bounce." Superior numbers and the holding of the initiative, combined with the rigid and inflexible thinking of their opponents, enabled the Germans to inflict heavier losses than they themselves suffered; the Hurricanes particularly, with their comparatively low ceiling and poor performance above 18,000 feet, suffered from the "bounce." Malinowski was three times with formations which were jumped on from the top: the first time, he was shot down; the second time, the attackers consisted only of six 109s, but they got two Hurricanes as they dived through; the third time, there was only one 109, but he also shot down two Hurricanes. These were ambush tactics pure and simple, which, rather than dogfighting, were the essence of fighter v. fighter combat.

On the morning of the 5th, the staff of Vickers-Armstrong had reported for work as usual, but most were not allowed inside the factory because the structure was unsafe. What work there was consisted largely of moving out the machine tools and stacking them for dispersal; this took four days. Lord Beaverbrook's Ministry of Aircraft Production ruled that buildings in the neighbourhood should be requisitioned to house the machine tools as, in effect, small aircraft factories, and that the main factory should do only assembly work, so that never again should such a concentrated, vulnerable target be presented to the enemy. A bookbinding works, a cable works, a timber stores, many garages, and one film studio—which proved ideal for building main wings—were taken over.

The Company had been producing 134 Wellingtons a month, nearly two-thirds at Brooklands, the rest at Chester, out of range of day bombing. Production never actually stopped—the lowest weekly figure following the raid was four Wellingtons—but it was not until eight months later that production again reached peak. Coming three weeks after the raid on Shorts, Bomber Command had been struck a substantial blow. Two important factories in the area were intact, both producing fighters—Hawkers, on the opposite side of Brooklands aerodrome to Vickers-Armstrong, and Supermarine at Southampton. No sooner had Park been relieved of the responsibility for escorting convoys, than he was directed by Dowding, as a result of the Weybridge raid, to give "maximum fighter cover" to the remaining factories, thus imposing maximum strain on his already inadequate forces, whose bases were largely in ruins. Nevertheless, those factories were vital and had to be protected—and they were on the Luftwaffe target list.

On 6 September the debris was being cleared at Weybridge and unsafe parts of the structure brought down. Canadian troops, brought in to do this job, were walking the girders, high above the ground, or sitting on them and knocking out broken glass, singing to their hearts' content. When the whistles blew to signal another raid, and they were told to shelter, they shouted back, "Aw, hell! We came here to work and no goddam Jerry's going to stop us." At midday the raid came in, directed at Hawkers on the far side of the aerodrome. A bomb hit the banked racing car track which encircled the landing ground, bounced along the concrete like a football and ended up at the bottom, unexploded. The Engineering Division was hit and, also, the Home Guard armory, from which rifles showered out: and cannon shells and bullets punched holes in the parked cars of the Directors. But the effect was much less devastating than that caused at the Vickers factory.

The Home Guards—most factories provided their own battalions from members of the staff—worked the unexploded bomb by the banking onto a sheet of corrugated iron and then lifted it onto a truck driven by a Canadian. With one man sitting on the bomb to keep it steady, they drove across the airfield to the nearest bomb crater, lowered the bomb into it—and exploded it there.

While Weybridge was being bombed, the main effort was being made over the eastern outskirts of London; the vapor trails of the dogfight could be clearly seen from the centre of the capital. The target, the oil storage tanks at Thameshaven, was set on fire and burned furiously. Below the battle, busy betting on the dogs at a greyhound racing stadium, were a dozen tired pilots from 66 Squadron who had been flying four and five sorties a day, and had been given the day off. "There was a terrific dogfight going on overhead," recalled Oxspring, who was betting with Rupert Leigh. "He appeared to take no notice, borrowed ten bob off me to put on a dog, then looked up and said, 'You know, I can't help feeling this is a case of Nero fiddling while Rome is burning.' "

Oberst Carl Viek, Chief of Staff to the JAFU 2, had in the beginning been able to do the same thing for his pilots, giving them the day off, by squadrons, to go down to the beach and have a swim, and also, on his own responsibility, grounding the leaders who appeared to be on the point of cracking under the strain. This now was no longer possible; he had been accused of "softness" and nearly lost his job because of it. Nevertheless, in his opinion, greater than the physical strain was the psychological effect of their being told by the high command that, according to arithmetical calculations, there were no British fighters left. "But when they went up they found lots of them—and that caused doubts about the Government."

However, on this day the British defences were torn apart by the improved escort methods of the Germans. The radar system helped the British to offset their disparity in numbers—but only up to a point. Park was trying to engage with as many squadrons as possible—but usually there was insufficient time to assemble more than two squadrons together. The Poles of 303 Squadron, successful the previous day, failed on this day with heavy losses. Squadron Leader R. G. Kellett, who was leading them, saw that the rearguard of 109s was already being engaged by a Spitfire squadron and took his Hurricanes down on the bombers. He alone reached them, setting the engine of a Dornier on fire, before being hit and slightly wounded by cannon fire from a 109. Two of the Polish pilots were wounded and the Polish C.O., Major Z. Krasnodebski, was so badly burned that he was in hospital for a year. Four Hurricanes were lost and two damaged. The new Polish C.O. was Flying Officer W. Urbanowicz, who was to take over the squadron when Kellett left. Later, he became a Wing Commander and Polish Air Attache in the U.S.A., during which appointment he managed, somehow, to visit the Japanese battlefront and to shoot down two "Zero" fighters. His combat report of 6 September contained much pertinent comment.

"Only two of our squadrons in the area—and a hundred Germans," he wrote. "The Germans had now developed a new principle of covering the whole length of the approach to London—a sort of blanket of fighters—under which the bombers had free passage. That made it very difficult to get at them because, invariably, we had to engage the fighters first, and in view of their superiority in numbers, there was no chance to deal with them in time to catch the bombers. So—heavy fighting, considerable losses, where pilots had to engage one Messerschmitt after another and only Kellett was lucky enough to get to the bombers. The English are a bit too cautious in restricting interception to one or two squadrons, which cannot be effective, instead of, on such occasions, putting everything in the air and sweeping it clean." He added, as an afterthought, "I was lucky enough to shoot down a 109. Gave it a very short burst; to my surprise it went straight down in flames; the pilot did not jump."

In the week beginning on 31 August and ending on 6 September, Fighter Command lost 161 fighters in air battles alone, against a German loss of 154 bombers and fighters. The battle in the air—of fighter versus fighter—was being decisively won by the Luftwaffe. If this continued, there really would be no British fighters left, or at any rate, not enough to put up an effective defence. Then the whole of the German bomber force could sweep over southern England, destroy the aircraft factories to make their victory complete, and turn, finally, to the essential bombing of targets connected with the invasion. And that afternoon, from the cliffs of Dover, part of the German invasion fleet was sighted, steaming west past Cap Gris Nez to its embarkation ports in the Channel.

The Polish comment, "the English are too cautious," found its echo later on the German side. The R.A.F. had almost as many fighters as the Germans, certainly enough to sweep that carpet of German fighters and roll it up by squadrons passing across from east to west. In the German view, the British could have brought the German onslaught to a dead stop within three days, instead of being on the verge of defeat, if only they had matched the German concentration of fighters in Pas de Calais with an equivalent concentration of their own. Furthermore, why did the British doggedly carry on from the aerodromes on the southern and eastern sides of London, which were just within the range of German operations, instead of withdrawing to aerodromes north and west of London, which were out of range? They had already withdrawn from their exposed forward aerodromes, why not withdraw the target altogether and leave the Germans to beat at the air? They concluded that the British could not fully have understood the weakness of the German position caused by the limited range of the 109.

Unknown to them were the weaknesses of the British position. Firstly, the limited number of squadrons which the control system could handle, and secondly, the fact that the aerodromes were not merely base aerodromes, as the Germans understood them to be, but Sector Stations of the control system which was too complicated to be moved in a hurry and for which in any case emergency alternatives had been provided. The British therefore felt themselves forced to stand and fight where they were, instead of withdrawing. But certainly they could have engaged with greater numbers, if Dowding had taken the risk of stripping other parts of the country of fighter protection in favour of concentration on the main battle. It was not even necessary to control them, merely to get them airborne in time, so that they could indulge in a British "free hunt" across the German fighter "carpet." In the last analysis, it was not even necessary to retain fighters at the Sector Stations, for the control aspect consisted of an Operations Room and its annexes, together with landlines to a transmitter and telephone lines to Group; it was convenient and efficient for the control staff and the fighter pilots to be in personal contact with each other, but it was not strictly necessary. On the other hand, a withdrawal could produce a momentarily critical situation if the Germans landed suddenly on the southeast coast; the British fighters were just as short-ranged as the 109s, and from bases behind London they could not intervene effectively against bombers supporting the troops on the beaches.

The British reaction to the new German tactics was not altogether satisfactory. Instead of bringing the fresh 12 Group squadrons into the battle area, under Park's control, he was merely given to understand that they would relieve him of responsibility—at some time while attacks were in progress—for guarding his bases northeast of London. In practice, they either did not take part in the battle at all, or came in too late. As these squadrons were fully efficient and, indeed, exceedingly impatient for action, the failure to use them fully partly justifies the criticism of undue caution. But it should be remembered that Dowding held the major responsibility in a battle to which he could see no certain end, at a time when the facts could not be fully known, and when a false move could lose the war. What might have happened if the German attacks on the Sector Stations had continued further to disrupt the effectiveness of his command is guesswork.

The Valorous Island

Halfway between Gibraltar and Alexandria, in the middle of the Mediterranean Sea, lies the island of Malta. Before World War II, the British wrote off Malta as too vulnerable to bombing raids from the Italian mainland. When Churchill became Prime Minister, he was quick to recognize Malta's strategic value athwart the North-South supply routes from Italy to North Africa. The Royal Navy was immediately asked to stockpile foodstuffs. The island's defenses would be strengthened with fighters and antiaircraft guns. Before this action could be taken, war broke out.

The garrison, consisting of five battalions of infantry, was pitifully weak to defend an island of 112 square miles and 300,000 people.

To properly supply the island, the British Royal Navy and Merchant Navy would need to sail 40,000 ton convoys to Malta twice a month. Each convoy would need heavy escort protection and would be subjected to fierce attacks from the Axis air forces; the closer a convoy got to Malta the more perilous its position due to the hazards of the Narrows—a narrow passage between North Africa and Malta, replete with shallows, sandbars, enemy submarines and patrol boats. In fact, Malta's defense outlook was so dim that Mussolini announced to the world that within a month after Italy's entry into the war his main fleet would be in Malta's Grand Harbor.

The British Royal Navy would have something to say about this. If Malta fell, "Allied warships and planes would have been unable to operate in the Central Mediterranean; the German and Italian armies in North Africa would have been reinforced quickly and easily; Cairo and Alexandria would certainly have fallen, and the whole of the Middle East (with its vital supplies of oil) might well have been brought under Axis control." *

The early actions in defense of Malta produced the usual sagas of

*Red Duster, White Ensign, by Ian Cameron, published by Doubleday & Co., Inc., p. 16.

courageous sacrifice on the part of a few; "usual" only in that both Britain and the United States earned precious time due to gallant last-ditch stands by those troops caught out on the defense perimeters. The following selection tells of one of the most gallant battles of the early war against fantastically uneven odds.

MALTA

by Ian Cameron

Sixty miles from Malta lay the island of Sicily, its shore line dotted with a series of large modern airdromes—Catania, Augusta, Siracusa, and Pandrino to the east; Comiso, Biscari, Bo Rizzo, Marsala, and Trapani to the south; and, inland, the airstrips of Gela and Gerbini and the great civil airport of Castelvetrano. Based on three dozen airdromes, all of them within fifteen minutes' flying time of Malta, were the cream of the Italian Air Force: some three hundred and fifty bombers (Cants, Savoias, and B.R. 20s) and some two hundred fighters (C.R.42s, Reggiane 2001s, and Macchis); fast modern planes, based on first-class airfields and manned by skilled pilots, many of whom had gained operational experience in the campaigns in Abyssinia and Spain. Only one target was within range of this great armada of aircraft—Malta. Seldom, if ever, had so much strength been ranged against so small and defenseless a target.

Nor was there any doubt about the manner in which, in the event of war, this strength would be used. Giulio Douhet, the high priest of strategic pattern bombing, the man whose theories had been proved in the holocaust of Barcelona, was quite specific on this point. "The guiding principle of bombing," he wrote, "is that the target should be obliterated in one raid. If, however, this is not possible, the target should be 'saturated' by unremitting waves of attackers. A people who are bombed today as they were bombed yesterday, and who know they will be bombed again tomorrow and can see no end to their martyrdom, are bound to call for peace in the end."

Sixty miles away Malta watched and waited. And every day, during the last uneasy weeks of peace, an Italian civil airliner flew openly over the island taking photographs, noting the absence of defending aircraft, pinpointing the dozen or so AA batteries which alone stood between the Maltese people and the acolytes of Giulio Douhet.

Early on the morning of June 11 the expected happened: the sirens started their high-pitched wail; Mussolini had declared war and within a few minutes—to be precise, at 6:57 A.M.—the first wave of Italian bombers were approaching the island.

There were only ten of them in this first wave: ten Savoia 79s, which approached the island at 14,000 feet in two V-shaped formations. The AA that greeted them was spasmodic and ragged, and the Italians, in perfect formation, came steadily on. They dropped their bombs with undisturbed precision; half on Hal Far, half on the dockyard. Then they turned for home.

It had, for the men of the Regia Aeronautica, been as easy as they had expected. They knew Malta hadn't a single defending aircraft; they knew her defenses were pitiably thin. They knew Mussolini had boasted he would be in Grand Harbour within a matter of weeks—and it seemed there was nothing to stop him. In the hindmost Savoia, the rear gunner sang to himself contentedly. *"Vido mare quante bello . . ."* He smiled; for the sea, as they set course for Sicily, really did look beautiful: hushed and very still in the pale half light of dawn.

> *Vido mare quante bello,*
> *Spira tantu sentimente . . .*

And that was as far as he got. For his serenade was cut short by the clatter of machine guns. A neat little row of bullet holes perforated the fuselage not a foot from his head.

He looked back. And—unbelievably—there on his tail was a fighter.

The Air Officer Commanding Malta—Air Commodore Maynard—had been told that the island's official quota of aircraft, in the event of war, was four squadrons of fighters (Hurricane Mk. IIs) and two squadrons of bombers and reconnaissance planes (Wellingtons and Blenheims). But he knew that this was a pipe dream; that there wasn't a chance of the aircraft arriving, for they were needed too desperately elsewhere. In time, the authorities admitted this. "There is no immediate prospect," reads an Air Ministry signal of May 14, "of any aircraft being available for Malta."

Many British commanders, on the eve of war, were faced with the job of making a little go a long way. Maynard's task was more difficult than that. He was faced with the job of making something out of nothing. His efforts to beg, borrow, or steal aircraft from neighboring commands were thwarted. His attempts to convert the island's few civil or nonoperational aircraft were unsuccessful. And it began to look as if the outbreak of war would find Malta without even a single makeshift fighter. Then, at last, Maynard had a stroke of luck.

One day he got to hear that a series of mysterious packing crates were standing on the slipway at Kalafrana. On opening these, he found they contained the component parts of eight naval Sea Gladiators, aircraft which should be embarked on H.M.S. *Glorious* when the carrier sailed for Norway, but which had, in the rush to get her to sea, been overlooked. The aircraft were old, dismantled, and the property of another service. There were no pilots qualified to fly them and no maintenance crews trained to service them. But—of a sort—they were fighters. Maynard went to his opposite number, Rear Admiral Willis, and asked if he could have them.

This request put Willis in a difficult position, for the Admiralty knew all about the Sea Gladiators and had earmarked them for another carrier, H.M.S. *Eagle*. But, fortunately for Malta and the Maltese, Willis was a man who could recognize an emergency. Like Nelson, he turned a blind eye to Admiralty orders, and gave half the Sea Gladiators to Maynard.

Such was the birth of a fighter defense force whose deeds will be honored for as long as the spirit of man is stirred by tales of high endeavor and unflinching sacrifice.

The Gladiators were sturdy little machines, but they were sadly outdated by the planes of the Regia Aeronautica. They were single-bay biplanes, descendants of the Pups, Camels, and S.E.5s that had fought in the First World War. With their fixed undercarriage and one-pitch propellers, their maximum speed was no more than 250 m.p.h. But, on the other hand, they were tough—their compressed-steel lattice ribs making for great internal strength—and they were highly maneuverable—they, if any plane could, could turn on the proverbial sixpence, and, in the Air Display of 1938, three of them had looped the loop, *chained together*. The Gladiators, in fact, though some thing of transition machines between ancient and modern, were not mongrels, but no thoroughbreds either. What they lacked in speed and firepower they made up for in airworthiness. They were the final flower of the sturdy old dogfighting biplanes.

Having got his fighters, Maynard set about finding pilots to fly them and ground crews to maintain them.

There were, on the eve of war, about a dozen pilots in Malta, most of them either in administrative jobs or flying the nonoperational aircraft of Station Flight, Hal Far. Not one of them had been trained as a fighter pilot, but they all volunteered, without exception, to fly the newly acquired Sea Gladiators. In the end, seven were chosen and formed into a Fighter Flight. The names of the seven deserve to be remembered: they were Squadron Leader Martin, Flight Lieutenant Burges, Flight Lieutenant Keeble, Flying Officers Hartley, Waters, and Woods, and Pilot Officer Alexander.

As for the men to service the Gladiators, the Aircraft Repair Section at Kalafrana could boast an experienced and highly efficient team: Maltese ex-dockyard apprentices, Maltese Auxiliary Air Force mechanics, and a nucleus of R.A.F. riggers and fitters. Under the leadership of Flying

Officer Collins, an ex-warrant officer, who had been on the island since 1936, these men had been welded together into a competent, hard-working unit. The fact that they had no experience in handling Gladiators and no spares didn't unduly perturb them. They had faith in their ability to improvise.

So, the Sea Gladiators were taken to Hal Far, assembled, stripped of arrestor hooks and other evidence of their naval ancestry, tested, and flown—though not when the Italian civil airliner was over the island.

The pilots were unanimous about their new machines. They may have been archaic-looking and long in the tooth (officially all operational squadrons had been re-equipped with Hurricanes in 1938), but they were first-class aircraft. As John Waters said, "They could turn on a sixpence and climb like a bat out of hell. Other aircraft all had their nasty little ways, but the Gladiator had no vices at all."

And so, day after day, the seven pilots practiced formation flying, emergency take-offs, interception tactics, and air-to-air firing. They couldn't, of course, help wondering what chance of survival they would have if Italy did enter the war: four planes matched against five hundred and fifty: four obsolescent biplanes facing the cream of a modern air force. But—perhaps luckily—there wasn't much time for thinking. For, a few weeks after their aircraft had been uncrated, the sirens were wailing, Hal Far tannoy was blaring "Scramble the fighters," and the Gladiators were roaring down the take-off strip—and into history.

That first day the Italians, true to the principles of Giulio Douhet, mounted eight raids against Malta. They used well over a hundred and fifty bombers, and in the later raids— as a tribute to the Gladiators—they brought over a fighter screen of Macchis and C.R.42s. When the Italians had a clear run their bombing was unpleasantly accurate. But they didn't like the Gladiators. And the ancient biplanes, whose top speed was actually less than that of the bombers they were trying to intercept, managed again and again to break them up or turn them aside. And they gave the Italian fighters something to think about, too. Here is Timber Woods' report of one of the evening engagements.

"We sighted a formation of Savoia 79s approaching Valletta at approximately 15,000 feet. We climbed until we were slightly above them, then delivered an attack from astern. The enemy turned out to sea. I closed from astern and got in a good burst at a range of about 200 yards. My fire was returned. I broke away and returned to the island.

"While climbing to gain more height, I heard machine-gun fire behind me. I immediately went into a steep left-hand turn and saw a single-engine fighter (a Macchi) diving and firing at me. For quite three minutes we circled each other tightly, then I got him in my sights. I got in a good burst, full deflection, and he went down in a steep dive with black smoke pouring from his tail. He fell into the sea a little to the south of Grand Harbour."

Beneath the bare facts of this report can be seen a story of coolness, resolution, and superior skill. Woods had proved that, contrary to all expectations, the antiquated Gladiators could outfly and outfight their more modern opponents. That, in itself, was heartening.

But more heartening still was the effect on the Maltese of the destruction of an enemy aircraft within full view of hundreds—if not thousands—of onlookers. The sight of the Italian falling like Icarus out of the sky, over which he had so insolently claimed dominion, gave civilian morale a boost at just the right psychological moment. Malta, it seemed, wasn't defenseless, after all. She could hit back.

And from that moment the Gladiators took on, in the eyes of hundreds of thousands of Maltese, a special sort of significance. They became a symbol of the island's spirit of defiance. As long as they stayed in the air, Malta, it was felt, would stay unconquered.

But how long *could* they stay in the air?

That first day all four planes miraculously escaped damage. But such luck was clearly too good to last; and it was decided on the evening of June 11 that from then on one plane (No. N.5524) must be kept permanently in the Aircraft Repair Section at Kalafrana as a source of spare parts: a skeleton which could be stripped to keep the other planes serviceable.

It was decided, too, that new interception tactics were

called for. George Burges put the case very clearly here. In a talk with the A.O.C. after the first day's fighting he said, "The Italian bombers are faster than we are. So our only chance is to scramble and climb as quickly as we can, and hope to get four or five thousand feet above on them by the time they reach the island. Then we must dive on them; but not from astern: from the beam."

And that, in the engagements to come, was just what they did. Day after day. Week after week. Month after month.

The Regia Aeronautica, of course, tried everything they knew to destroy the three little planes which, alone, stood between them and a complete control of the air. They came over in massed formations: fifty to sixty bombers escorted by stepped-up tiers of Macchis and C.R.42s. They sent over decoy planes, with packs of fighters shadowing them, up in the sun. And they deliberately straggled out of formation to try and tempt the Gladiators into dogfights. But somehow the little biplanes, slippery and elusive as eels, always managed to outtwist or outmaneuver them.

But they didn't, of course, escape undamaged. Time and again, in those early days of June and July, a Gladiator landed back on Hal Far so appallingly damaged that it seemed as if nothing short of a miracle would get it back into the air. Three times a plane touched down with its entire tail unit dangling by a single strut and a strand of cable; twice, a wing tip was shredded entirely away; often, the cockpits were ringed with bullet holes, the mainplanes colandered, the landing wheels shot off, the instrument panels shattered. Yet somehow, thanks to the planes' basic toughness and the skill and hard work of the Aircraft Repair Section, the damage was always patched up. Somehow, no matter how often the sirens wailed (and there were, that first month, a total of over a hundred raids), either two or three of the Gladiators always managed to struggle into the air.

And they gave the Italians plenty to think about. Although they scored comparatively few kills, they broke up countless formations, forcing the bombers off their targets, making them bomb quickly, inaccurately, or (in quite a lot of cases) jettison their bombs harmlessly into the sea.

Gradually, in their efforts to avoid the Gladiators, the Savoias and Cants were forced higher and higher: to twenty, twenty-five, and finally to thirty-thousand feet; and from these heights their bombing, of course, was far less accurate. The bombing formations shrank in size, too; to start with, the Italians had sent over, say, thirty Savoias and a dozen Macchis; but soon the ratio was reversed. But the end of June, in an effort to scotch the Gladiators, the Italians were sending over a handful of bombers, escorted by stepped-up tiers of Macchis and C.R.42s. But somehow the little biplanes, against all the odds, still managed to stay in the air.

And so, week after week, the fantastic struggle went on. Three obsolete planes against the might of a modern air force. With the unbelievable happening. The three planes seeming to bear a charmed life, and the air force being reduced to angry impotence.

By the end of June the Gladiators and their pilots had won a niche in history. They had won, too, a unique place in the affections of the Maltese. People showered the pilots with St. Christophers, pasted photographs of them beside their beds, and prayed for them nightly at the shrines in their rock shelters. When the pilots went into the streets, they were followed by admiring crowds; when they took to the air, thousands of people disdained the safety of their shelters and, forgetful of the danger of bomb and shrapnel, stood watching the fantastic dogfights that took place daily over the island. It was history in the making.

One quiet evening in early July, when there hadn't been a raid for several hours, the pilots were sitting on the grass at Hal Far, watching the three Gladiators being refueled.

"You know," Jock Martin said reflectively, "we ought to give them a name."

Someone suggested Pip, Squeak, and Wilfred; but this wasn't received with much enthusiasm. It was John Waters —quiet, good-looking, and technically the most brilliant pilot of the seven—who made the inspired suggestion.

"How about Faith, Hope, and Charity?" he said.

The names caught on. They spread beyond Hal Far, beyond Valletta and the Three Cities, beyond the shore of

Malta itself. Soon, every time the Gladiators took to the air, people would stop, point skyward, and cry:

"Look! There they go. *Faith, Hope,* and *Charity!*"

To most Britishers on the island the names brought no more than a wry, appreciative smile; but to the Maltese they brought something more. For the people of Malta are intensely religious, and it meant a great deal to them that the men and machines which were defending them so valiantly had been christened with the words of St. Paul. Now, more than ever before, the three Gladiators came to epitomize the island's spirit of defiance; they became symbols of a cause which began to take on something of the sanctity of a crusade. As, four centuries earlier, the people of Malta had helped the Knights of St. John to defend their island against the hordes of the Ottoman Empire, so the twentieth-century Maltese now rallied around the British garrison in defense of their island against the forces of another and even greater menace to Christendom. If the British, in spite of the fantastic odds, were willing to make a fight for it, so were the Maltese.

Exactly how many aircraft *Faith, Hope,* and *Charity* shot down will never be known. By the end of a month, each of the pilots could claim at least one kill, and Burges (*"Il Ferocio,"* the Maltese called him) could claim as many as six. And it is now known that many aircraft claimed only as possible did, in fact, fail to make the return journey to their Sicilian bases. In all, in June and July, the Italians probably lost upward of sixty or seventy aircraft in their assault on Malta—about half to the AA and half to the Gladiators. And the island still stood firm. Mussolini wasn't in Grand Harbour yet. Or anywhere near it.

All through June and the first half of July, *Faith, Hope,* and *Charity* kept up their fantastic battle. Then the inevitable happened.

July 16 was a day of heavy raids, and late in the afternoon Burges and Keeble got involved in a dogfight with a mixed formation of Macchis and C.R. 42s. One of the AA gunnery officers has described the combat that followed:

"I watched them twisting and diving and trying to get on

each other's tail. Keeble dived onto a Macchi, but two C.R. 42s followed him down. He managed to shake one of them off, but the other was good—one of the rare ones—and he clung to Keeble's tail. In a desperate effort to elude him, Keeble came down to ground level and flew under the wireless aerials to Pinella, hoping his pursuer would hit one of the cables. But the trap failed. As Keeble dipped under the aerials the Italian followed and shot him down; but he, himself, was so close to the ground that he hadn't time to pull out of his firing dive. The two aircraft crashed in the same field and exploded within a few yards of each other. Both men were brave pilots, and very young."

Peter Keeble's death was felt as a personal loss throughout the island. Normally the death of a pilot in action, though mourned by his friends at the time, is regarded as part of the inevitable price of war. But the outstanding immunity of the little squadron through six weeks of bitter fighting, and in the face of outrageous odds, had lulled everyone into a sense of false security. The Gladiator pilots had seemed to bear a charmed life: to be near immortal. Now it was suddenly brought home how pitiably mortal they were.

But the struggle, of course, still went on. The strain on the pilots was terrific; but the strain on the ground crews (many of whom worked twenty hours out of twenty-four) was even greater. For soon the Gladiators began to crack up.

It was only to be expected, really. They had been flown flat out for a couple of months, and there hadn't been either time or spares for the routine overhauls without which no aircraft can stay airworthy for long. Now, quite suddenly, the engines lost power and began to seep oil; one afternoon when the fitters stripped down *Faith's* engine they found holes, big as florins, in the cylinder heads. They patched the engine up as best they could, working in the open with bombs falling all around them and low-flying Macchis machine-gunning the airstrip, and by the evening *Faith* was airborne again. But everyone knew that the repair was only temporary: that unless something drastic was done the aircraft would soon be grounded for good.

Then Flying Officer Collins had an idea. In the Aircraft Repair Section at Kalafrana were a number of crated Mercury 8 and Mercury 15 engines. These had been intended as spares for the Blenheims; but perhaps, with adaptations, they could be fitted into the Gladiators? At any rate, it was worth a try.

The miracle that followed can be fully appreciated only by those with a knowledge of air engineering. For to fit the engine of one aircraft into the fuselage of another is a stupendous undertaking. In this particular case the Blenheim engines were designed to operate a host of ancillary controls which didn't exist in the Gladiators, and each of these devices had to be laboriously sealed off. Then a number of major components had to be radically adapted—oil sumps, petrol pumps, carburetors, and oil throwers, to mention only a few—and all this the mechanics had to do with improvised tools, *and* in double-quick time and in the midst of near-continuous air raids. Somehow they achieved the impossible: and after forty-eight hours' nonstop work the change-over was made, and the surviving Gladiators took on a new lease of life.

A few days later Collins was responsible for another masterpiece of improvisation. It had been decided to use one Gladiator as a high-level interceptor to break up the Italian bombers and the other as a low-level patrol plane to deal with fighter strafing attacks on the airdromes. In the latter plane, maneuverability was less important than firepower, and it was decided to increase the Gladiator's armament. This was easier said than done. But in the end, Collins hit on the scheme of mounting a pair of .303s, Great War fashion, on top of the upper mainplane. The result was that the silhouette of the low-level Gladiator took on an even more archaic outline than ever. With its biplane wings, outsized engine, makeshift propeller, and upper-mainplane guns, it looked, in the uncertain twilight, like the silhouette of a ghost plane flown straight from the Western Front. Somebody, catching sight of it for the first time, aptly christened it the "Bloodiator." It was certainly a bizarre-looking machine. But at least it could fly. And one afternoon it shot down a Macchi *and* a C.R. 42.

So the days passed: days of raid after raid, with the pair of patchwork biplanes continually taking on odds of anything up to fifty to one. It was the sort of hopelessly heroic struggle that caught at the imagination of the Maltese; and the debt that is owed to *Faith, Hope,* and *Charity* lies, not only in the thirty to forty planes they shot down, not only in the thousands of tons of bombs they caused to miss their target, but also in the inspiration they afforded the people of Malta. For the Maltese never forgot the Gladiator pilots' example of fortitude and self-sacrifice. It was an example they, themselves, were to follow, with equal heroism, in the months to come.

By late August, the end seemed very near. The Gladiators and their pilots had flown themselves to exhaustion. They were reeling about the sky like a pair of punch-drunk boxers, fighting instinctively in a haze of tiredness, sleeplessness, and pain. Then the miracle happened. One morning there was a louder-than-usual roar over the airstrip at Hal Far. The AA guns were silent as four sleek monoplanes came hurtling over the airfield. Burges and Waters, who were standing by, dived instinctively for shelter. Then they looked up.

"By God!" Both spoke as one. "Hurricanes!"

The problem of flying fighter reinforcements to Malta was two-fold. In the first place, every available plane was needed, in the summer of 1940, in the Battle of Britain. In the second, there was no Allied airfield within flying range of the island—even with extra fuel tanks and a following wind neither Spitfires nor Hurricanes had the slightest hope of reaching the island without refueling.

Eventually, a system of embarking fighters on an aircraft carrier, convoying them to within range of the island, and then flying them off was perfected; with the result that, in two years, some three hundred and fifty fighter aircraft were flown to Malta with no more than a dozen casualties. These air-ferry operations, being primarily a Navy commitment, were planned and controlled by Admiral Somerville from his headquarters at Gibraltar; and generally speaking, their history is one of effective co-operation between Navy and Air Force.

The smooth running of the later trips, however, was achieved only at a price—the price of men's lives: lives that were lost in the early star-crossed Operation "White," one of the most poignant tragedies of the war.

The first air-ferry operation had taken place in August, when twelve Hurricanes had flown in to relieve *Faith, Hope,* and *Charity*. This operation had been an unqualified success. But from the moment the planes touched down, the Italians stepped up the tempo of their attacks in an effort to prevent the R.A.F. from gaining a permanent foothold: and by October only four Hurricanes and one Gladiator were left. It was, therefore, decided to repeat the operation, and toward the end of the month twelve tropicalized Hurricanes and twelve specially chosen pilots were embarked on the ancient aircraft carrier *Argus* and taken at short notice to Gibraltar. Here they waited, until the warships of Force H were ready to guard them on their way to a flying-off position somewhere south of Sardinia.

The basic plan of Operation "White" was simple. Admiral Somerville would escort the *Argus* and her Hurricanes to within flying range of Malta; the aircraft would then take off in two subflights of six, each subflight being led by a Fleet Air Arm Skua (in which an observer would plot their best course for the island). It was found that the route followed would take the planes very close to Galita Island (off the Tunisian coast); and as an additional safeguard, Air Officer Commanding Malta agreed to have two of his long-range bombers waiting over the island to meet the Hurricanes and guide them back along the last stage of their journey. As soon as the planes had left *Argus*, Admiral Somerville was to retire to Gibraltar. Nothing, it seemed, could be simpler.

There were, however, two outside factors which had to

be taken into account: the weather and the Italian fleet. Bad weather could, of course, jeopardize the whole operation; while if the Italian fleet put to sea it could, all too easily, interefere decisively, annihiliating both the *Argus* and her comparatively light escort. It was, in the end, an unhappy combination of these two factors which was to prove disastrous.

At 4 A.M. on November 15, 1940, Force H pulled out of Gibraltar. The night was fine, with bright moonlight silhouetting the ships as they moved past the Rock.

Admiral Somerville had managed to muster quite an impressive-looking escort. The *Renown* was there, flying the admiral's flag; so was the *Ark Royal*, together with three cruisers and seven destroyers. The Hurricane pilots, as they watched the massive warships positioning themselves around their carrier, must have reckoned that they were in good hands. Yet, in many respects, Force H was more impressive in appearance than in fact. The *Renown*, for example, was something of a white elephant, being slow, lightly armored, and no match for a modern Italian battleship; the *Ark Royal*, with her unarmored flight deck, was peculiarly vulnerable; while the *Argus* (she was *pre*-First World War!) was unbelievably snail-like. Small wonder that Admiral Somerville, as he surveyed his ships, hoped the Italian fleet would remain in harbor.

And within a few hours of sailing, something happened that added to his already considerable anxiety. At 11:30 that morning a Spanish civil airliner, bound from Tetuán to Melilla, passed almost directly over the fleet; and it was well known that Spanish radio operators were prone to forget international law and broadcast on Italian frequencies.

That evening Somerville's suspicions were confirmed, and his anxiety deepened. For at sunset came news of Italian naval forces concentrating in the Gulf of Sorrento.

A couple of hours later the barometer began to fall.

November 16 dawned dull and overcast, with a blustering westerly wind, low cloud, and poor visibility. By noon the weather was too bad for flying, and *Ark Royal's* anti-submarine patrols had to be withdrawn. Withdrawn, too, were Malta's reconnaissance planes from the Gulf of Sorrento; though not before one of them had reported a battleship, seven cruisers, and an unspecified number of destroyers standing south out of Naples.

Admiral Somerville was now in a difficult position. If he kept on, he might well, in the bad weather, run slap into the Italian fleet. If he turned back, Malta would fail to get her badly needed planes. His own words (in the official report written after the operation) explain his dilemma exactly—and his solution to it.

"It seemed to me" [he wrote]

1. The Italians were probably aware of our departure from Gibraltar.
2. They might well consider engaging Force H with their superior forces in the hope of balancing their recent losses at Taranto.

"In view of this, I deemed it advisable to fly off the Hurricanes from a position as far to the west as weather would permit. In reply to an enquiry, *Argus* informed me that with the wind as at present the Hurricanes could be flown off from Latitude 37° 40′ N, Longtitude 6° 40′ E. Since all available meteorological information indicated a continuation of the westerly winds . . . I decided to accept this as the flying-off position."

Position 37° 40′ N, 6° 40′ E was some forty miles to the west of the flying-off area originally agreed on. But it seemed to Admiral Somerville, and to Captain Rushbrooke of the *Argus*, that this new position still gave the Hurricanes a reasonable margin of safety. For the amended position was rather less than 420 miles from Malta, and the range of the Hurricanes, in still air, was—according to the Air Ministry Handling Notes—521 miles. Bearing in mind the following wind, there seemed not the slightest doubt that the Hurricanes could reach the island without difficulty.

So the new position was unanimously agreed upon.

During the night of November 16-17 the weather started

to clear, but the latest "met." report from Malta (timed 11:30 A.M. on the sixteenth) indicated that the wind in the Malta Channel was still west-southwesterly. And there seemed no reason to believe it would change. On board the *Argus* the first subflight was ranged on deck, ready to take off at dawn.

Force H arrived in position 37° 40′ N, 6° 40′ E at 5:45 A.M. It was still dark. Loath to proceed farther east, Admiral Somerville waited impatiently for dawn. At six o'clock the eastern sky paled imperceptibly; the Hurricanes and the Skua started their engines, and at 6:15 A.M. the first planes roared safely off *Argus'* narrow deck. They circled the carrier several times, climbing to 2000 feet. In the gray uncertain light it took them the better part of fifteen minutes to get into formation and take departure over the center of the fleet. As they left the deck, *Argus'* meteorological officer checked the wind. It was 220° /20 knots. An hour later the second subflight followed the first; and again the meteorological officer checked the wind. It was 250°/16 knots. Veering and falling.

Before the planes were out of sight, Admiral Somerville had reversed course and was heading at top speed for Gibraltar. He thought at first that Operation "White" had been an unqualified success; but toward midday a spate of disturbing signals came streaming in. By sunset he knew the worst. Of the fourteen planes to take off from *Argus,* only five had arrived. Somewhere, in the sea lanes leading to Malta, nine of the aircraft had run out of petrol and crashed.

The leader of the first subflight of Hurricanes was Flying Officer J. A. F. Maclachlan, D.F.C. Though only twenty-one, Maclachlan was an experienced pilot; he had served with 88 Bomber Squadron in France (earning his D.F.C. by blowing up the last bridge over the Marne) and had later transferred to a Hurricane squadron and taken part in the Battle of Britain. Now, he formed up beside the Skua and soon saw the rest of his subflight strung out beside him in loose echelon starboard.

And so, at 150 m.p.h., they headed for Malta. Their height was 2000 feet.

After a while the observer of the Skua noticed something strange. On the surface of the sea, cloud shadows were moving increasingly slowly; and the sea itself was changing its pattern. He dropped smoke floats and found a wind. To his amazement it was east-southeasterly, eleven knots: almost an exact reciprocal of when they had left the carrier. He realized that with the wind now almost dead ahead, they would be hard pressed to reach Malta before they ran out of fuel. Making a slight alteration of course to allow for the new direction of the wind, he kept steadily on. There was nothing more he could do. (All pilots had been briefed to fly at a certain height and speed: the most economic, he assumed, for the Hurricanes.) Soon, to add to their difficulties, visibility worsened; patches of thickening sea mist drifting over the Tunisian shore. By seven o'clock they were flying blind through a baffling patchwork of mist and cloud. But the Skua observer kept his head; he concentrated on his dead-reckoning plot and made an exact landfall—albeit twenty-five minutes late—over the northern tip of Galita Island. Here, much to the pilots' relief, a Malta-based Sunderland was waiting for them, to lead them back on the second stage of their journey.

But this second stage proved even more nerve-racking than the first. For the Hurricane pilots realized now what was happening: realized that with every revolution of their propellers, with the combustion of every drop of their petrol, their expectation of life was draining inexorably away.

Maclachlan—who had recently taken a course on Hurricanes—adjusted his mixture control and his constant-speed airscrew to squeeze the last fraction of a mile out of his dwindling supply of fuel; but several of the other pilots, accustomed to flying older Hurricanes with variable-pitch propellers, were uncertain how to adjust their pitch, mixture, and throttle controls to the most economic setting. They were forty-five miles short of Malta when the engine of the Hurricane next to Maclachlan started to run roughly. For several minutes it spluttered and coughed uneasily. Then it cut. Stone-dead. The Hurricane broke formation. Like a slowly falling leaf she spiraled down: down into the sea. Maclachlan watched her. For a moment he hesitated; then he, too, broke formation. Losing height, he began to circle the spot where the Hurricane had ditched. He could see the pilot struggling in the sea. He called up the Sunderland, and soon the big unwieldly flying boat came down to join him. Maclachlan flew low over the pilot, rocking his wings; and the Sunderland landed on the sea, taxied across to the pilot, and hauled him aboard. Then Sunderland and Hurricane again headed for Malta.

Soon they saw the other planes, away ahead of them: five Hurricanes trailing the single Skua. They disappeared into a veil of cloud. When they emerged there were only four Hurricanes. Another of the fighters had run out of fuel: had fallen helplessly into the sea. The pilot was never found.

Visibility in the Malta Channel was very bad, with a light southeasterly wind drifting a mixture of fog, mist, and cloud over the sea. But both Sunderland and Skua were in radio contact with Luqa, and D.F. bearings enabled the planes to home directly on to the island. Without the radio they would hardly have stood a chance; for Malta lay wreathed in cloud: invisible until they were actually over the land. Then, sudden and unexpected, out of the mist rose the plateau of Mdina Rabat, and two minutes later, the dusty runways of Luqa. The Hurricanes hadn't sufficient fuel for a circuit; they plummeted down, higgledy-piggledy, as quickly as they could. The engine of one cut dead before the plane had taxied clear of the runway; the second plane to touch down had three gallons left in her tank; the third had less than four; and in Maclachlan's tank there wasn't sufficient petrol to cover an upended six-pence! Another five minutes and all four of them would have crashed.

The first subflight had been lucky; it was otherwise with the second.

Exactly what happened to them will never be known,

and it is perhaps kinder not to probe too searchingly. But the basic facts are these.

The second subflight missed Galita Island; they never kept their rendezvous with the bomber from Malta. As soon as he realized they were lost, the Skua observer called up Malta for help. But his radio receiver was faulty, and he couldn't pick up the island's reply. Desperately he cast around the Sicilian Channel, hoping every minute to see the longed-for shore. But no shore came. One by one, the Hurricanes that were with him ran out of fuel and fell helplessly into the sea. At last only the Skua was left. Soon she, too, was very close to the limit of her endurance. Then suddenly, through the curtain of mist, the pilot sighted land: a low, green shore line sweeping the width of the northern horizon. He turned toward it. Crossing the coast, he was still trying to identify his landfall when ack-ack guns barked angrily; and the Skua—seventy-five miles off course—fell blazing off the Sicilian shore.

Of the fourteen aircraft that had that morning taken off from *Argus*, only five were left. It was a tragic loss of vitally needed planes and brave men's lives.

Like every other wartime disaster, Operation "White" was followed by boards of inquiry, top-secret reports, and a spate of official findings. After twenty years the ashes are too cold to be raked over again. Yet it is perhaps easier to assess responsibility now than it was at the time, and certainly today the official findings strike an unbiased observer as being more than a little unjust.

For the board of inquiry ascribed the catastrophe as being "mainly due to a lack of knowledge on the part of the Hurricane pilots as to how to fly their aircraft when fitted with constant-speed airscrews"; while a contributory cause was stated to be "bad navigation on the part of the observor of the second Skua." It is easy to blame air crew; especially when they are dead. A more balanced judgment, made today, would seem to indicate that the tragedy was brought about by four contributory factors.

(1) Inadequate weather forecasting. The significant point here is that when the Hurricanes took off at dawn on

November 17 the latest meteorological report they had received from the area they were flying into was timed 11:30 A.M. on the day before: was, in other words, nineteen hours out of date. In subsequent operations far greater attention was paid to obtaining accurate, last-minute weather reports.

(2) Lack of liaison between Navy and Air Force. The Naval Air Operations officers aboard *Argus* and *Ark Royal* were unaccustomed to dealing with Hurricanes; all their information about them had to be gleaned from the Air Ministry Handling Notes. These Handling Notes state specifically that "the range of a Hurricane Mk. II (tropicalized) in still air, at 130 knots, at 10,000 feet is 521 miles." Yet the pilots were briefed to fly at 2000 feet. Naturally their range in the "heavier" lower air was considerably less than if they had flown at the correct height. An R.A.F. liaison officer, to assist in briefing the pilots, would have prevented such a mistake. In every subsequent air-ferry operation, one was carried.

(3) Excessive caution on the part of Admiral Somerville. Bearing in mind that the safe arrival of the Hurricanes was the sole objective of Operation "White," it is reasonable to argue that greater risk to the fleet ought to have been accepted in order to penetrate far enough east to make the success of the operation beyond doubt. Certainly in subsequent trips the carriers concerned nearly always stood well to the east of 6° 40′ E, and as Sir Winston Churchill put it, "Never again were the margins cut so fine, and though many similar operations took place in the future never did such a catastrophe recur."

(4) Pilots' and observers' errors. That some of the pilots and one of the observers made errors of judgment is undeniable. But, looking back, it would seem that these errors were among the lesser rather than the greater of the factors which contributed to the disaster. For even if no air-crew errors had been made, the fate of the Hurricanes would still have hung precariously in the balance. What happened to Maclachlan proves that. It is interesting to note that when planning subsequent air ferries an attempt

was generally made to give the pilots concerned a certain amount of practice in long-distance sea flying.

And this underlines the heartening factor which goes far toward relieving the tragedy of Operation "White." Its lessons were well learned, were never forgotten; and subsequent air ferries were conducted with a degree of concentrated efficiency which enabled consignment after consignment of fighters to be flown without loss to the island which had such desperate need of them.

Editor's Footnote: By the fall season of 1941 Malta was garrisoned with 30,000 troops, had some eighty Hurricanes and an antiaircraft defense of 1400 guns—"fiercer than London's," said a Luftwaffe pilot who'd been at the shooting end of both—and foodstuffs for five months.

"It was Malta's growing strength that proved her undoing; that, and the winter stalemate on the Eastern front. For in November 1941, Hitler, balked of quick victory in Russia, again turned his attention to the Middle East. And it soon became clear to the German General Staff that no worthwhile scheme could be embarked on in the Mediterranean while Malta remained unconquered. For the island, which only a year ago had seemed so defenseless, was now proving a poisoned thorn in the Axis' side: a stumbling block to their every plan. They couldn't mount an offensive in Africa because Malta's aircraft and ships disrupted their supply line. (In October, for example, over a quarter of Rommel's reinforcements had been sunk en route.) They couldn't prepare an offensive elsewhere, because Malta's reconnaissance planes reported every concentration of troops and shipping. And soon harbors, airfields, and railways on the Italian mainland were feeling the weight of a not inconsiderable air offensive launched from Luqa and Hal Far. There was, Hitler and Mussolini decided, only one thing to do. Malta must have her teeth drawn; she must be first battered to impotence, then captured by assault from the air. Toward the end of November, Ciano made a note of this decision in his diary. "It has been decided," he wrote, "that Malta must be obliterated." *

From January, 1942, to early May, Malta was blasted by Axis bombers. To save the island, squadrons of Spitfires were shipped into the Mediterranean aboard the American aircraft carrier *Wasp* to within flying range of Malta.**

The April delivery ran afoul of quick retaliatory raids on the airfields, while the Spitfires were being refueled. Another group landed in May; these were refueled and were airborne within four minutes of arrival to meet the Axis attackers in headlong battle. Thirty-seven Axis planes were destroyed as against a loss of only three Spitfires. It took only several days' battle at these odds before the Germans and Italians abandoned their efforts to knock out the island.

* *Red Duster, White Ensign,* pp. 123-124.

** Heretofore, no British carriers were available for the task.

The Dagger's Point

The siege of Tobruk was one of the longest in contemporary military history. The seaport's position between Alexandria and Sfax* on the Mediterranean coast of North Africa, with its sizable harbor, made Tobruk immensely important in the strategy of the Desert campaign. When the Axis front lines pushed close to the border of Egypt, the British were able to hold and maintain Tobruk as a dagger pointed in the left flank of the Axis troops; when the British pushed westward beyond Tobruk, the port served them as an advance base.

Before the war, the Italians "had constructed a series of wide defenses enclosing an area around Tobruk of roughly 135 square miles. These consisted of a double ring of concrete emplacements eight or nine miles from the town and harbor covering a frontage of some 35 miles. The eastern and western extremities of this perimeter were well protected by steep wadis, impassable to tanks and mechanized vehicles. But for the greater part of its length, the perimeter ran across a flat featureless plain protected by rusting barbed-wire and an anti-tank ditch." **

The early phases of the Desert campaign have been described in the companion volume *Combat: European Theater*. By the beginning of 1941, the British had pushed the Italians back along the Libyan coast to El Agheila, capturing Tobruk as well as Benghazi. Instead of strengthening the forward units, the British decided instead to send their reinforcements to Greece, while some of the forward units were withdrawn to rest and be refitted in Egypt.

Meanwhile, German General Erwin Rommel had arrived in Tripoli on February 12; in the succeeding weeks German troops reinforced the Italians, and Rommel sent his troops probing into the British lines. On

*Alexandria, Egypt and Sfax, Tunisia.
**From *Tobruk*, by A. Heckstall-Smith, p. 23.

March 21, he launched a solid left jab; the British defenses, now manned by green troops of the Australian 9th Division, suddenly crumbled and Rommel drove their scattered units ahead of him along the Libyan coast toward Egypt.

By April 7, Australian troops began to straggle into the Tobruk fortress. Later that day, General Morshead, the Tobruk commander, announced to his men: "Tobruk will be no Dunkirk; there will be no surrender and no retreat." With these tough words, he hoped to turn the minds of the newly arrived troops away from defeat. Tobruk was to be more than a fortress, the troops should consider it as a "sally-port" as well from which the enemy would be attacked.

On April 9, general reconnaissance was made by General Morshead and his commanders.

"The decision was taken that, until the whole defence system could be put in order and greatly increased in depth, an all-out effort must be made to improve and repair the old Italian perimeter. There, at least, were the series of concrete posts, the barbed-wire, the anti-tank ditch—such as it was—and what remained of the Italian minefields after many of the mines had been lifted or 'deloused' during the January assault.

"For the immediate emergency the perimeter was manned by seven of the garrison's thirteen infantry battalions, each with a reserve company in support dug in about half a mile in the rear. With each company holding a front of more than a mile, Morshead had every reason to warn their commanders to expect penetrations. Nevertheless, every post was to be held to the last man and each foot of ground fought for.

"Later, this defence system was greatly strengthened, and became known as the 'Red Line.' Two miles behind it the garrison constructed a second defence system—the 'Blue Line.' This was composed of a continuous minefield covered by barbed-wire and the fire from anti-tank and machine-guns dug in to well-wired and mined strongpoints. And as the siege went on, so were these positions made stronger, and the area between the Red and the Blue so thickly sown with mines that the sappers themselves could no longer keep track of them.

"But it was many months before this formidable defence system was finally completed, and at the beginning of April the fate of the fortress depended upon the cold courage of its troops rather than the strength of its defences. The garrison's armour at the outset consisted of a regiment of armoured cars, four 'I' tanks, twenty-six cruisers, and fifteen light tanks; these last being useless in an armoured battle. It possessed no medium artillery except a few captured Italian guns. Its field artillery was made up of three 25-pounder regiments from Cyrenaica, and one fresh from Egypt. In addition to these there were two anti-tank regiments, one Australian and the other British, both of which were a battery short. The harbour area was defended by an anti-aircraft brigade with sixteen heavy and fifty-nine light guns.

"For two days while the stifling khamsin lashed the surface of the desert into a raging sandstorm, wearing anti-gas goggles and with handkerchiefs over their mouths, the men of the garrison laboured ceaselessly, preparing the perimeter defences. Day and night the sappers laid minefields, infantry wrestled with rusting barbed-wire and hurled the sand from the concrete posts and the crumbling anti-tank ditch; gunners dug in their 25-pounders; and signallers unwound their miles of wire as they linked the posts one to another. And through the fog of driving sand, thicker than a London 'pea-souper,' struggled the trucks carrying the ammunition and rations up the rocky escarpment to the gun-sites and forward positions.

"Blinded, choking, their sweating half-naked bodies coated with sand, these men had no time to reflect that the very wind they cursed was their staunchest ally. For out in the desert its fury had brought Rommel's armour to a grinding halt and had pinned down his dive-bombers on their airstrips. Under cover of the storm the survivors of the 3rd Australian Anti-Tank Regiment, the 3rd Indian Motor Brigade, and the 3rd Royal Horse Artillery, who had escaped from the hell of Mechili, where they had suffered a hundred casualties, straggled in to the perimeter bringing with them some forty guns to strengthen the lean defences.

"For two days the sandstorm blotted out the sun, filling the water-cans and the dixies, driving into the shallow dugouts and through blankets and ground-sheets. Then, at about noon on April 10, the storm abated. And as the dust cleared, the men in the advanced posts on the western end of the perimeter saw the enemy's tanks and trucks coming down the road from Derna. This was the signal for the sappers to blow the bridge over the road and for a battery of captured Italian 75s and 105s, manned by Australian infantrymen, to fire the first rounds in the garrison's defence.

"By the morning of April 10, Rommel had informed his Staff that the British force in the desert was but a rabble on the run, and had blandly announced that his next objective was the Suez Canal. At the same time he said that on no account must the British be allowed to break out of Tobruk." *

TOBRUK**

by Anthony Heckstall-Smith

The wind that had whipped up the dust-clouds throughout the day had died with the sun. The night was still and the deep blue dome of the sky above the escarpment was bright with stars. The air was cold, and the men in their forward posts sat huddled with their greatcoats over their shoulders watching the young moon rise.

Except for the occasional stutter of a machine-gun, the line was quiet. Too quiet, for all day behind a veil of dust the Australians had watched the enemy's transports, staff cars, and motor-cycles darting about the desert. In the late afternoon German tanks followed by bunches of infantry had moved up towards the perimeter again, but were driven off by our artillery.

Now, the quiet was charged with tension; a tension that caused the men in the forward posts to talk in whispers, nervously fingering the triggers of their rifles and machine-guns. They had been warned to expect an attack that night. But when and where? Sitting waiting for it in the flea-ridden posts behind the rusting wire played hell with a man's nerves. . . .

The mortar barrage which opened up at ten o'clock came almost as a relief to the waiting men, for they knew it was the overture to the night attack. For an hour they crouched in their posts while the mortar shells burst amongst the tangle of barbed-wire in front of them and

*From *Tobruk,* pp. 48, 49, 50.
** This is a condensed version of several chapters of *Tobruk.*

the machine-gun bullets ripped into the sandbags along the parapet. Then, as suddenly as it had started, the barrage stopped.

In Post 33, just west of the El Adem road, Lieutenant Mackell, the platoon commander, looked at his watch. The time was eleven o'clock. Beside him, Corporal Jack Edmonston, a sheep-farmer's son from New South Wales, peered into the darkness and the thinning dust-cloud. He gave a low whistle.

"Jerries! A whole heap of the ——s!"

Mackell's eyes followed the corporal's pointing finger. Vaguely he could see the Germans moving through a gap in the wire to the east of his post; twenty or thirty of them.

"Let 'em have it!"

As the machine-guns opened up, to Mackell's astonishment the Germans replied with mortars and light field-guns, plastering the post with shells.

Dug in about a hundred yards away, it was obvious that the Germans were determined to cover a bridgehead through which their tanks could pass. It was equally obvious that they could not be driven out by small-arms fire.

By midnight the situation was fraught with danger, and it began to look as if the line had been breached and that soon the enemy armour would come rolling through the gap.

Mackell decided to drive them out with bayonets and grenades.

With Edmonston and five others, covered by the fire from the post, he sprinted into the darkness, running in a wide semi-circle so as to approach the Germans from their flank. But almost immediately the enemy spotted them and turned all their guns on them, forcing them to go to ground.

A second dash brought the little party to within fifty yards of their objective. Once again they threw themselves down, and as they lay there panting they pulled the pins from their grenades. Then, with a wild yell, which was taken up by their comrades in the post, they charged.

For a few terrible minutes the seven men came under a deluge of fire. Edmonston took the full blast of a machine-gun in his belly just as he hurled his grenade into the midst of its crew. Another bullet hit him in the throat. But he kept on running and, having thrown his second grenade, he went in amongst the Germans with his bayonet.

In a panic of terror they bolted out of their ditch, running blindly into the wire, to hang there screaming as their attackers bayoneted them.

Soon young Mackell was in difficulties, for as he fought with one German on the ground another came for him with a pistol. He yelled to Edmonston for help. With blood pouring from his throat, the Corporal dashed to his rescue, killing both Germans with his bayonet. In the hand-to-hand fighting which followed, Mackell, having broken his bayonet in a German's chest, clubbed another to death with his rifle-butt, while Edmonston and the five others killed a dozen more. The Corporal went on fighting until the last of the enemy had fled, abandoning their weapons. Then he collapsed, and the others carried him back to the post, where he died soon after dawn. He was awarded the Victoria Cross.

All through the night the battle went on. Although young Mackell's charge had routed the enemy's advance guard, by two in the morning the Germans had established a bridgehead several hundred yards inside the wire. In spite of being heavily shelled by two regiments of the Royal Horse Artillery, they held their ground.

Just after dawn, the first German tanks moved through the gap. By a prearranged plan the forward troops made no attempt to stop them, but lay in wait for the infantry. By 5:45 a.m. some thirty-eight tanks of the 5th Tank Regiment's 2nd Battalion, which had made a name for itself in Poland and France, formed up for attack nearly a mile inside the perimeter wire. At the same time the 1st Battalion's tanks were moving up in the wake of the anti-tank and field-guns and infantry. Indeed, the attack was taking on the familiar pattern of all those other German attacks which had proved so invincible in Europe.

But this time the Panzer troops were in for a rude shock, for without suspecting it they had rolled into a trap. Ahead of them were the 25-pounders of the 1st R.H.A. and the anti-tank guns of the 3rd Australian Regiment. To their left were the mobile anti-tank guns of the 3rd R.H.A., and to the right more mobile guns of the same regiment, as well as tanks of the 1st Royal Tank Regiment dug in, in hull-down positions.

The Germans first came under fire from the 25-pounders, sited just inside what were later to become the Blue Line defences. Our gunners engaged them over open sights at a range of less than 600 yards with devastating effect, one heavy tank having its armoured turret blown sky-high.

Altogether seven tanks were knocked out before the remainder disengaged and turned eastward in an attempt to outflank the batteries. Immediately they came under fire from the guns of the 3rd Australian Anti-Tank Regiment and suffered further casualties.

Baffled and battered, the Germans retired. But as they did so they were heavily shelled from both sides by the mobile guns of the R.H.A., mounted on 30-cwt. trucks, as well as the cruiser tanks.

At 7 a.m. the Germans rallied for a further attack against the thin defences of the Blue Line, but were again driven off, for without their anti-tank and field-guns and the 8th Machine-Gun Battalion they had no support. In fact, these units were still struggling to get beyond the gap. To their confusion, they were being savagely mauled by the Australian infantry, whom they had expected to surrender as soon as the tanks had broken through. Indeed, they had even called on the Australians to throw down their arms. But the Diggers answered them with everything they had got and bayoneted those who took refuge in the anti-tank ditch from the hail of small-arms fire.

A typical example of the fighting happened near Post 32, where before dawn some of the 8th Machine-Gun Battalion had established themselves in a ruined building. Early in the morning, Colonel Crawford, commanding the 2/17th Battalion of the 20th Australian Brigade, sent two platoons forward to clear the house. One section went in with bayonets and grenades, while the others gave them covering fire. The Germans returned their fire until the grenades started bursting amongst them and they saw the glint of the Australians' bayonets. Then half of them surrendered. The rest were already dead.

It was because of this and similar infantry operations that after daylight on the 14th no guns or infantry were able to break through to support the tanks. By seven-thirty that morning what was left of the German armour was fighting desperately to escape through the gap in the wire. Soon this retreat became a rout, as the tanks, gunners, and infantry, in a swirling cloud of dust and smoke from burning tanks, fled for their lives. Into this rabble the defenders fired every weapon they possessed: 25-pounders, mortars, anti-tank guns, Brens, and rifles.

A captured Panzer officer described this ghastly shambles as "a witches' cauldron."

For many hours after the main battle had ended the mopping-up operations went on, and it was not until noon that the last of the enemy were rounded up. Some 250 dazed and bewildered Germans, many of them weeping with shame at their defeat, were marched back to the prisoner-of-war cage.

They referred to that Easter battle as "the Hell of Tobruk," admitting that nothing like it had happened to them before.

"In Poland, Belgium, and France when our tanks broke through the soldiers gave in. They knew they were beaten. But at Tobruk you went on fighting," they said, "and fighting like devils out of hell!"

So certain had they been of success that some units—amongst them the 8th Machine-Gun Regiment—had advanced with their administration trucks ready to set up the headquarters in Tobruk. Undoubtedly, their repulse came as a great shock to those proud Panzer troops, and their morale was severely shaken. They had been assured that the garrison would surrender. Instead, the defenders had steadfastly held their ground, and to them must go the honour of winning the first battle against the Germans in the war.

After this setback, Rommel gave up any further attempts against the southern sector. Two days later, he personally directed an attack from the west, employing troops from the Ariete Division and the 62nd Infantry Regiment of the Trento Division. But, although urged on by German tanks, the Italians had little heart for their task, and when the Australians counter-attacked they surrendered in the hundreds, advancing towards our lines waving white handkerchiefs.

Thus ended the opening rounds of Rommel's battle for Tobruk. But, while the enemy still staggered under these first severe blows, General Morshead sent out small patrols and sorties against them.

These sorties so disturbed Rommel that he sent urgent signals to hasten the arrival of the 15th Panzer Division. He was, however, not the only one who viewed the situation outside Tobruk with concern. For the Italian *Comando Supremo* had sent a despatch to the O.K.W. asking for the latter's agreement to call a halt to the advance into Egypt. Time was needed for the attacking force to be reorganized and for its badly strained supply line to be given a chance to recover.

General Halder, Chief of the General Staff, O.K.H., wrote in his diary that he was disturbed by the news from North Africa.

"Rommel," he recorded angrily, "has not sent in a single clear report, and I have a feeling that things are in a mess. . . . All day long he rushes about between his widely scattered units and stages reconnaissance raids in which he fritters away his strength . . . piecemeal thrusts of weak armoured forces have been costly. . . . His motor vehicles are in poor condition and many of his tank engines need replacing. . . . Air transport cannot meet his senseless demands, primarily because of lack of fuel. . . . It is essential to have this situation cleared up without delay. . . ."

To this end the O.K.W. decided to send General Paulus, a Deputy Chief of the General Staff, to North Africa, whom Halder believed to be "perhaps the only man with enough influence to head off this soldier gone stark mad."

General Paulus arrived at Rommel's headquarters to find the stage set for a further assault against Tobruk. It was planned for April 30. He withheld his permission for two days until he had discussed the situation with General Gariboldi. In the meantime he made it clear to Rommel that there was to be no more "high-falutin'" talk about Suez being the next objective. Thanks to "Barbarossa," * the O.K.H. had no resources from which to supply any more troops or weapons to the Afrika Korps. That force's task was now to take Tobruk, and if, and when, the fortress fell, to secure Cyrenaica by holding a line from Siwa to Sollum. Having given his impetuous junior time to reflect upon all this, Paulus then sanctioned the plans for the attack on Tobruk.

The new attack was to be launched in the south-west in the environs of Ras el Medauar. Rommel's plan was that at 8 p.m. on the night of April 30, two German divisions, the 15th on the left and the 5th on the right, should make the break-through. Assault groups of the Ariete and Brescia Divisions would then advance through the breach to roll back the enemy's defences on both flanks. While this was being done, German troops pushing forward east would make reconnaissances to discover whether a main thrust could be made to the harbour. If this could be done, the flanks would then be held by the Italians, and the Panzer troops would attack again on the following morning.

At the section of the perimeter chosen, the line bulged in a salient. The twenty-two concrete posts to the north and south of Hill 209 were held by three companies of the 2nd Battalion of the 24th Australian Infantry Brigade, with a further company in reserve, approximately a mile east of the hill. During the lull between the attacks, the garrison

*Hitler's attack on Russia.

had worked night and day strengthening the defences, and fortuitously had laid minefields between the Blue and the Red Lines in the southwestern sector.

For the past two weeks the troops in the southwestern salient had watched the dust-clouds rising between Acroma and Hill 209 as the enemy's lorry-loads of infantry, tanks, and guns assembled some two miles beyond the perimeter. But on the morning of April 30 the dust-clouds thickened, and then in the afternoon the posts were heavily shelled, and out of the red sunset a score of Stukas came screaming down to bomb and machine-gun the forward positions. Their ammunition expended, they turned away, to be followed by yet another formation which hurled its bombs on the barbed wire and the infantry positions around Hill 209. Then, as the last Stuka headed for home, its magazines empty, the Germans laid down a deadly barrage of artillery fire on the same positions and, under cover of the dust and growing darkness, the 2nd Machine-Gun Battalion and sappers of the 33rd Panzer Pioneers raced forward to render safe the mines and blast gaps in the wire to left and right of the hill.

The men in the forward posts had been so heavily bombed and shelled that they were unable to prevent the German penetrations between their widely dispersed posts or to stop them setting up machine-gun nests in their rear. Moreover, as a result of the bombing, the signal lines linking the company holding the hill with their H.Q. had been cut, so that their Commanding Officer, Lt.-Colonel Spowers, was without news of them.

Again and again he sent out runners and signalmen to try to make contact with the company through a curtain of machine-gun fire. Some failed to get through; others to get back. So concentrated was the enemy's fire that one signalman took four and a half hours crawling on his belly to cover the mile and a quarter between his company's post and the Battalion H.Q., mending the wire as he went. In the confusion, patrols got lost in their own minefields, and just before dawn the reserve company, a mile to the rear, reported enemy tanks and infantry to the east of the hill.

When daylight came a thick ground mist shrouded the

desert, and since no one seemed to know where the Germans were, Colonel Spowers did not dare order the artillery to shell the hill. At eight o'clock, when the mist cleared, the situation was even worse than had been feared. The Germans had not only established themselves a bridgehead a mile and a half wide, but had overrun seven of the advanced posts around Hill 209, killing or taking prisoner the men holding them.

Soon after seven-thirty the German tanks which were to thrust eastwards to the harbour began forming up on the hill. But because they were still without information our gunners left them alone. Heading east, forty tanks came straight for the 2/24th's reserve company's positions, blazing at them with cannons and machine-guns. But near the Acroma road the first flight met the fire of the 24th Australian Anti-Tank Company, commanded by Captain Norman. One gun managed to knock out and set on fire a Mark III before it was itself set upon by eleven tanks and its crew all wounded. Two other guns were also silenced, and the tanks swept forward to within a few yards of the reserve company's positions where they ran into a minefield.

In a matter of minutes, seventeen tanks were brought to a standstill, most of them with shattered tracks. But although they were sitting targets, all our anti-tank guns within range had been put out of action. Nor did the field-gunners dare to shell them heavily for fear of detonating our own mines and thus clearing a passage for the enemy.

However, after their initial setback the Germans made no further effort to penetrate the minefield, but turned away to the south.

By early that morning both Rommel's tank thrusts had failed. But he still had large reserves, and our reconnaissance aircraft reported a force of some 200 tanks in and around Acroma and Hill 209. Against this force all General Morshead could muster was twelve "I" tanks and nineteen cruisers. So heavily outnumbered, his only chance was to hold his armour in reserve and rely upon his artillery and the minefields to reduce the enemy's strength. In fact, at this stage Morshead was in a dilemma so far as his tanks were concerned. He had been criticized for using his armour in "penny packets" rather than in strength. But this is an injustice. His air reconnaissance was, to say the best of it, scrappy, and so he had no means of foreseeing from which direction Rommel's next thrust would come. Thus, in order to cope with the unexpected, he was obliged to keep some of his pitifully small force in reserve.

Even as it was, he took risks. On the afternoon of May 1, for instance, he sent out a small force, consisting of five "I" tanks and three cruisers, for the purpose of regaining control of the forward posts. This force was repeatedly attacked by superior numbers of German tanks. First, it came up against fifteen of them. Immediately an "I" tank received a direct hit which killed all its crew except the driver, although the tank itself was not destroyed. As the seven others struggled to withdraw, they were set upon by another batch of fourteen Germans, and a further "I" tank was knocked out and one of the cruisers badly damaged. In these two encounters the Germans lost four tanks. Nevertheless, Morshead can hardly be blamed for holding his little force in reserve and depending upon his artillery, as indeed he had done with such marked success in the Easter battle. But Rommel was aware of these tactics and time and again he sent waves of Stukas to dive-bomb and machine-gun our gun sites. But since they were well dug in, he failed to silence them, and before the battle was over they played havoc with his armour.

Although the defenders could not know it, by the end of the first day's fighting General Paulus had advised Rommel to abandon any further attempts to capture Tobruk and to be content with holding Hill 209 and the positions around it. And so, by the night of May 1, the battle had resolved itself into a struggle for this hill. It was, from then on, a battle of attack and counter-attack, in which both sides fought doggedly, neither gaining nor giving ground.

Throughout May 2, in a thick sandstorm, the Germans fought desperately to hold the posts they had captured, suffering severe casualties in both men and tanks. On the night of May 3, General Morshead threw in his reserve brigade—May 18—in an attempt to retake Hill 209. The attack was planned as a converging one by two battalions. But as they assembled the Australians were so heavily shelled from the hill that zero hour had to be put forward until just before nine o'clock at night. In the darkness, the attack quickly became a series of hand-to-hand skirmishes and individual bayonet raids on the enemy's strongpoints.

Typical of the night's fighting was an incident on the Acroma road when some Australians of the 2/9th, led by Lieutenant W. H. Noyes, saw three Italian tanks approaching. With Sergeant Hobson and three men, he crept on to the tanks and, lifting their turrets, dropped hand grenades inside, blowing them up.

In the early hours of the morning General Morshead called off the attack, since he did not wish his troops to be caught in the open after daylight.

Thus ended the second major battle for Tobruk. As a result of it, Rommel's troops had penetrated the perimeter defences to the depth of less than two miles on a front of nearly three miles. They had captured Hill 209, which gave them an excellent observation point. In achieving this the Axis had suffered more than eleven hundred casualties and had lost a large percentage of its armour. Paulus claimed the battle as an important success. Nevertheless, he gave definite orders that the attack on Tobruk was not to be renewed unless the garrison showed signs of evacuating the port.

There can be no doubt that at the time the defenders' courageous resistance to these attacks by vastly superior forces, employing the same blitzkrieg tactics by which they had conquered half Europe, prevented the Axis Armies marching triumphantly on to Suez.

"Omnis Gallia in tres partes divisa est."

The fortress of Tobruk, like Caesar's Gaul, may be said to have been divided into two parts; the perimeter defences and the harbour area. The whole covered an acreage of roughly the size of the Isle of Wight and was inhabited by an exclusively male population of approximately 30,000.

While it is difficult to generalize about the living conditions within the fortress, since they varied from one area to another, it is true to say that every man's comfort depended largely upon his own ingenuity and resourcefulness. The men quartered in the town lived in reasonable comfort by comparison with those in the forward areas. Generally speaking, the nearer a man lived to the perimeter, the worse was his lot and the more he suffered from the violence of the North African climate, the lack of water, the torment of flies and fleas, and the misery of the dust churned up by the wheels of the trucks and tanks. But dust-storms, flies, and fleas were plagues common to all men in Tobruk.

At the end of the siege a sergeant of an anti-aircraft battery, who had spent seven months in the fortress, wrote:

"Almost worse than the bombs as a tribulation to the flesh and the spirit were the fleas. The desert fleas are famous, and ours were obviously in the pay of the enemy. How we cursed them on the nights when the moon was late up and we hoped to catch a couple of hours' sleep before the inevitable procession of night-bombers started. The fleas marched and counter-marched up and down our twitching bodies until we thought we would go crazy. . . . And we needed those hours of sleep, for when the moon was up we would get mighty little rest. Twenty-one alarms in one night was our record; and it was nothing to have half a dozen night after night. . . .

No wonder we looked forward to our periodic 'day off' by the sea. Even then we had to keep an eye open for the bombers and dive into the caves for shelter from swooping Stukas, but it was heaven to wash ourselves and our sweaty clothes in the clear blue water, and lie naked on the sand and dream of home, beauty, and beer. . . .

And we had our 'quiet days' when the wind howled and the dust devils swept over the desert so that one could not venture out without goggles or eyeshields;

and as we lay in our shallow dug-outs dozing and reading some tattered paperback, the dust would settle in a floury yellow veil over face, hands, and blankets. We ate it and breathed the stuff so that in the end we scarcely noticed it. . . . Mostly our grouse was plain boredom—week after week, month after month, the same eternal desert, the same discomforts, the same raids. Danger itself becomes tedious after a while. . . ."

None knew better than General Morshead that boredom could demoralize the spirit of his garrison more rapidly than even Rommel's Stukas. So, living up to the nickname of "Ming the Merciless" which the Diggers had given him, he kept his troops constantly working and in continual contact with their besiegers. His infantry battalions were moved every few weeks from the concrete posts in the Red Line back to the Blue Line where they worked on the fortifications, and then into reserve. After a few days' rest, swimming, sun-bathing, and washing clothes, they were usually sent up to the Salient sector, where a night seldom passed without patrols being sent out across no-man's-land to the enemy strongpoints.

Overlooked by the Germans on Hill 209, conditions in the Salient during the early days of the siege were the hardest of all to endure. The positions, due to the rock beneath a shallow layer of sand, were part weapon-pit and part sangar, and, since they were provided with no sort of cover overhead, their occupants were exposed all day to the heat of the desert sun. The majority of these section posts were not even connected by crawl trenches, so that the men were forced to crouch or lie face downwards in what were little better than open graves.

Throughout the long hours of daylight bully beef and biscuits formed their staple diet, while the bitter, chlorinated water in their bottles became so warm that it no longer eased their burning throats. Only by night was any movement possible, and then under cover of darkness the ration-truck came forward and a hot meal was issued, and a further supply of hard rations left for the following day.

Thus, the men had their breakfast at 9:30 p.m., a hot lunch at about midnight, and dinner before dawn. After a week of such living the troops left their sangars thin and weak and often racked with dysentery.

Rommel clung tenaciously to Hill 209 and the ground he had captured immediately to the east of it, since he looked upon it as a weak spot in the garrison's defence through which a way could be forced when the moment came to renew his offensive. But to hold the Salient he was obliged to use a third of his total infantry strength.

For Morshead, too, this sector of the perimeter was a constant source of anxiety. Before the enemy's attack on May 3–4 the garrison had held three and a half miles of the old perimeter, well mined and wired and covered by fire from the old Italian strongpoints. Now it had to hold a front of nearly five and a half miles without wire or minefields, the whole length of which was overlooked by the enemy. Ten companies of infantry were required to defend a sector which had previously been held by only two.

In spite of the fact that he had been reinforced by the arrival of the 2/23rd Battalion by sea, Morshead was hard put to it to hold the Salient. But since his chief role was to keep the greatest number of German troops pinned down outside Tobruk, he never lost an opportunity of taking aggressive action. Now, he took it to shorten the front in the Salient so that he could hold it with two infantry battalions. But, owing to the enemy's complete air superiority at this time, reinforcements were so slow in arriving that Morshead was obliged to draft men, like the Pioneers and the R.A.S.C. from the docks, into the infantry battalions. He also resorted to cunning. By a series of patrols into no-man's-land by night which came to grips with the enemy, by sending out wireless messages that hinted at a forthcoming attack, and by driving trucks and light tanks backwards and forwards from the docks to the western sector of the perimeter in a cloud of dust, Morshead was able to convince the Germans that he was about to launch an attack in force against Hill 209. This ruse succeeded with the result that Rommel withdrew troops from the Sollum area to meet the threat to the Salient, while his sappers and pioneers hurriedly set about strengthening the positions around the Hill itself. But, although he did manage to shorten his front line by the end of June, Morshead was never able to drive the enemy from the high ground overlooking his fortress.

Life all along the perimeter was tuned to harrying the enemy. Except in the Salient where our positions were within easy range of the Afrika Korps' mortars and machine-guns, our troops in the forward area were free to move about in daylight in comparative safety and our trucks could drive up almost as far as the Red Line without risk of surprise attack. This freedom of movement was largely due to the patrols which kept Rommel's troops so far back that no-man's-land along the greater length of the perimeter was never less than a mile wide and at some points as much as four miles of open desert lay between the opposing forces.

After the May battles, this no-man's-land virtually belonged to the garrison, or, at least, our troops had the free run of it. For a while, the Austrailians and the Indians shared it between them. Amongst the Indians were a number of Rajputs, warrior-caste Hindus from Jodhpur, of whom the enemy went in terror. They could move through the darkness without a sound, and never returned from a raid without claiming a high score of Germans and Italians. Indeed, so successful were they that their senior officer became suspicious and lectured them sternly against over-estimating the number of enemy dead. A few nights later, when the patrol returned through the wire just before dawn, its leader, saluting smartly, laid two small sacks at the senior officer's feet. They contained irrefutable, if macabre, evidence of the night's operation, for in one were sixteen right ears, and in the other sixteen left ears, all still oozing with the blood of their former owners.

Apropos of the stealth with which these Indians moved by night, I remember the alarming experience of a South African sapper major while lifting German mines under cover of darkness near Sollum.

"It was one of those nights," he told me, "when the desert was as quiet as the grave. I was on my knees dealing with a detonator when suddenly a hand was clapped over my mouth and a thin arm wrapped itself round my neck. I was so numb with fear that I couldn't move. But my hair stood on end! I felt someone running their fingers over me; feeling the buttons on my tunic, my revolver, my pockets. When they reached the crowns on my shoulders, they seemed to hesitate. Then, just when I'd made up my mind that I was as good as dead, I was released. I heard a voice whispering, but I couldn't hear what was said because the blood singing in my ears deafened me. But I did catch the single word 'Sahib.' I don't know, but I may even have passed out in sheer terror. But when I pulled myself together, I was still kneeling on the ground staring up at two bearded Sikhs. They were out on patrol, and since I was in the Jerry minefield, I'd had a pretty close shave. I still get the trembles every time I think of it!" the Major told me with a shiver.

Every night our patrols went out from Tobruk across no-man's-land, and as the siege lengthened, the men became better and better equipped for their task. In the early days, the Diggers set out with socks over their boots and even in their stockinged feet, while the Indians made themselves special sandals from the rubber of old motor-tyres. Later, the patrols were provided with thick desert boots with soft rubber soles, and special one-piece patrol suits reinforced at the elbows and knees as protection against the thorn bushes and stony ground.

The patrols usually consisted of between ten and twenty men, each with a rifle with fixed bayonet, and carrying two or three hand grenades. In every patrol there was at least one man with a Bren, which he fired from the hip, and often as many as six armed with Tommy-guns. Usually, they were supported by a Bren- or mortar-carrier to give covering fire as they withdrew, and, when necessary, to pick up the wounded. Fortified with a hot meal and a tot of rum, they set out in the darkness, moving on a compass bearing across the featureless desert to the enemy's lines. To achieve surprise, it was their practice to attack a strong-point from the flank or rear; a manoeuvre which called for very accurate navigation by the patrol leader.

One of the main objects of these night raids was to capture a prisoner for interrogation.

One moonlight night when two officers and fourteen men of the 2/23rd Battalion were out on patrol on the Bardia road sector, they had a strange experience.

"As we went forward," their leader, Captain Rattray, told afterwards, "we saw the shadowy figure of a soldier moving out from the forward enemy position to the patrol. . . . Every few yards he would stop and give a low whistle. When he whistled the third time, McMaster whistled back. The figure turned towards us and as he got nearer we could hear him calling: *'Herr Leutnant! Herr Leutnant!'* McMaster called back *'Si, si, Comradio!'* and the Eytie walked right into our arms. We had been sent out to get a prisoner and so now we could go back. . . . Next day we all had badly lacerated knees and elbows, but we had the unusual distinction of having whistled a prisoner in."

Such patrols played havoc with the enemy's nerves, particularly the Italians, and to protect themselves against the night raiders the Germans sowed the ground round their strongpoints with mines and booby-traps linked together with trip-wires. They also covered their whole front with an ever-increasing number of mortars and machine-guns. But throughout the siege they were never able to prevent the nightly sorties made against them. They were constantly on the alert and for ever in fear that one of these night patrols might be an overture to a full-scale breakout from the fortress.

It was the spirit of the men in Tobruk which defeated Rommel. Yet that spirit which inspired the garrison is hard to define.

"Throughout all those months," an officer wrote of it afterwards, "it so permeated the whole atmosphere of the place as to be almost tangible. Everywhere one was as conscious of it as the very sand that filled the air we breathed, the food we ate, and the vile brackish

115

water we drank. It manifested itself in the manner of the men. Although most of them looked like scarecrows, and many of them, owing to the lack of fresh vegetables and in spite of the vitamin C tablets, were covered in suppurating 'desert sores,' they bore themselves with pride. Instinctively, one recognized them for what they were; dedicated men, resolutely, grimly determined to endure fear, discomfort, hardship, and, if needs be, death, rather than surrender. Rommel couldn't hope to defeat such a spirit any more than he could understand it. When he came up against it, he was confounded by it. Those ridiculous pamphlets he showered on us from the sky calling on us to surrender proved that."

Yet Tobruk cast something very like a spell over the men who lived there, so that years afterwards they remember it with nostalgia. It would be easy to say that time had lent enchantment to the scene, were it not for the fact that at the height of the siege there were men who wrote home with genuine affection for their beleaguered fortress.

Returning from a twenty-four-hour stint in his battery observation post, a young gunner wrote home of his "day off" by the sea.

"It's my turn down to the beach tomorrow, so I'll have a good scrub and do some washing," he told his mother. "I'm black, or at least grey. This sand gets everywhere, and my clothes stand up by themselves when I get undressed. Sweat and sand make good concrete. I won't have much washing to do, only pants and socks. I don't wear anything else. Furthermore, I'll have to walk around in my boots until my clothes dry. It's nothing here for the boys to walk around stark naked for half the day as most of them have nothing else to wear while their clothes are drying, so at meal-times they line up with nothing on but their boots and hats. . . .

"The sea was like a mill-pond when we got there, the day glorious, so things couldn't have been better.

At night, another chap and I lit a fire and cooked some tinned food, and then lay in bed and had a good feed. . . . You know, when lying there in bed I remarked to my mate that I wouldn't swop beds with anyone in the world, and he agreed. It was beautiful lying there on the sand about five yards from the Med., a lovely still night with every star visible. We were wonderfully warm and comfortable and hadn't a care in the world. . . .

"You women back home sit and worry about us. You don't realize the good times we have, days that we have at the beach or days when Jerry is quiet and we have a euchre party at threepence a game. . . .

"I awoke the next morning feeling great, just crawled out of bed, stripped off, and had a swim before breakfast. . . .

"I'm extremely happy here; I don't know why! There ain't no bird to sing, no flowers or lawns or trees or rivers to look at, but I'm just happy. . . .

"I suppose I enjoy company and I enjoy the wonderful feeling of comradeship in Tobruk. We are more or less cut off from the world, and we have one job and one job only, that is, to hold this place. This is an experience I shall always relish. It will be a privilege later to say 'I was there. . . .' "

Those simple words written home during the summer of 1941, sum up the spirit of the garrison of Tobruk.

But as the months dragged by there crept into those letters an insidious note of resignation—an undertone of philosophic contentment—towards their utterly unnatural existence. They wrote almost with affection about the fly-blown Libyan port in which they were virtually prisoners. In spite of the Stukas, the shelling, the eternal bully beef, the brackish water, and the absence of women, they said they were happy. They didn't know why, but there was something about Tobruk, the blue of the Mediterranean by day and the dark indigo of the desert sky by night, even its detachment from the rest of the world, that tugged at their heartstrings.

Then, one morning towards the end of July, three strange officers presented themselves at the 9th Divisional Headquarters. They wore grey shirts and shorts, comical little pith helmets, and glittering silver insignia. They were very smart, clean, and freshly laundered, and they smelt slightly scented. Clicking their polished heels, they saluted and shook hands with everyone in sight, and then saluted again. They were Poles! And one of them was a general called Kapanski.

Even when the advance party of the 1st Battalion of the Polish Carpathian Brigade arrived, the Diggers had their doubts whether they had come as reliefs or reinforcements. But by mid-August it was confirmed that the Poles were there to release the 18th Brigade. But still there were sceptics who were prepared to wager a month's pay that the old 9th was destined to stay in the fortress until the siege was raised. They were not pessimists, but wishful thinkers.

The Polish Carpathian Brigade had been formed in Syria by General Kapanski. It consisted of regular soldiers who had fiercely resisted the German invasion in 1939, and a large number of volunteers. The majority of the former had been officers who, having escaped from Hungarian, Rumanian, and German prison camps, had made their way to Syria to join the Brigade as N.C.O.s and private soldiers. The rest were patriots who, rather than live under the Nazis, had left their homes and families and suffered ghastly hardships tramping across Europe in order to fight for the Allied cause.

When France capitulated, Kapanski, ignoring orders from Vichy, marched his force into Palestine, taking with him all the arms, equipment, and vehicles supplied by the French. For more than a year the Brigade had remained in Palestine and Egypt, and it had been camped outside Alexandria for several months before the decision was made to send it to Tobruk to relieve the 18th Australian Infantry Brigade.

There were Staff Officers in Cairo who predicted that this move was doomed to failure from the start. Everyone knew, they said, that the Poles were raring to kill Germans. But they also had quite a reputation as lady-killers, and so were what was technically known as a "bad security risk." Even if their leave were stopped prior to departure, there were bound to be those truants who would sneak out of their camp at Agomi to take passionate leave of their "lights o' love" in Alexandria. There would be wild farewell parties in the Monseigneur Bar and Pastroudi's, these Staff Officers warned the Navy, and every Axis agent would know exactly what was afoot.

The Navy shrugged its shoulders and remarked that conveying the Poles to Tobruk looked like being a sticky business. So they gave the operation the code name "Treacle."

But no one, least of all Cunningham, really treated this undertaking lightly. The evacuations of Greece and Crete were still fresh in his memory, and although "Treacle" was not an evacuation, it nevertheless entailed the withdrawal of large numbers of soldiers from under the very nose of the enemy. The risks were enormous and the odds even more heavily weighed against his ships than they had been during those desperate days in the Aegean, for now the Luftwaffe were in possession of the Cretan airfields as well as those around Tobruk.

To succeed, "Treacle" would have to be a combined operation in the fullest sense of that term. Its success would depend upon split-second timing and perfect planning by the Staff Officers of the three Services in co-operation with Morshead, the Fortress Commander, Poland, the Senior Naval Officer Inshore Squadron, and Smith, the Naval Officer in Charge, Tobruk.

It was fortunate indeed to have these three able, level-headed officers in Tobruk at such a time; officers who not only inspired confidence in those under them, but who were masters of improvisation. And in Tobruk, where there were no facilities for the quick unloading of ships and handling large numbers of troops, a positive genius for improvisation would be needed.

Morshead had twice left the fortress to confer with the planning staffs in Cairo,* and was confident that his Transport and Movements Control Officers, together with Smith and his staff at Navy House, could cope with their end of the operation. He had given orders that extra mobile 3.7s were to be moved in from the perimeter to strengthen the harbour defences, and had arranged with the Poles that the 'A' lighters and other small craft arriving in Tobruk should be retained there to ferry troops between the ships and the shore. His pioneers, sappers, and the Docks Group had further improved the berthing facilities alongside those wrecks used as wharves by the destroyers. The men leaving would take with them only what they could carry on their backs; the rest of their equipment, including vehicles, would be left behind for the Poles.

No amount of planning, however thorough, could insure against all the hazards of an operation involving so many lives. It was for this reason, therefore, that Operation "Treacle" was an experiment. If it succeeded—and that was a very big "if"—Cunningham, Auchinleck, and Tedder were prepared to repeat it until the 15,000 Australians in Tobruk had been replaced by a like number of British and Polish troops. But in no event could this relief be allowed to delay the start of the new offensive in November, before which all the available destroyers, "A" lighters, and other ships of the Inshore Squadron would be engaged in carrying tanks, guns, ammunition, and supplies to the fortress. Auchinleck made this point clear in his telegrams to Whitehall, and Churchill, who loyally supported his decisions, forwarded them on to Canberra.

A great deal, therefore, depended upon "Treacle." Everyone concerned knew that if the operation was to work it must do so with clockwork precision. Yet, in their hearts, few believed that Rommel would allow it to work. He had vowed that he would either overwhelm the garrison or starve it out. Now that his reputation was at stake, it was

*In June 1941, General Wavell had been removed and General Auchinleck was given the command of the Western Desert Campaign.

inconceivable he would permit the Diggers to escape without making a supreme effort to destroy them.

"Treacle" began on the first day of the moonless period in August when three destroyers and the minelayer *Latona*, loaded with nearly a thousand troops and some two hundred tons of stores, sailed from Alexandria, escorted by other destroyers. All during the day relays of fighter squadrons flew over the ships. Then, as darkness fell and the Hurricanes turned for home, the first of the bombers and long-range fighters set out from their bases in Egypt, heading west for the Axis airfields. Their task was a dual one; to bomb the runways and then circle the airfields so that the Germans would not dare to light the flarepaths for their pilots to take off into the inky darkness.

As the convoy approached Tobruk other bombers roared out of the east to Bardia to drop bombs and flares over the German long-range guns. As they did so, a destroyer was detached from the convoy to fire salvoes into the gun positions. Then, as the three destroyers and the minelayer neared Tobruk bay and swung to port, the batteries of 60- and 25-pounders opened up on "Bardia Bill" and his mates. The timing was superb. Blinded by the smoke-shells and under a deluge of high explosive, the German gunners could see nothing, while the star-shells bursting in the sky guided the ships up the narrow swept channel into the harbour.

In Tobruk the Diggers waited. They stood shoulder to shoulder on the only jetty, on the rusting decks of two half-sunken hulks, packed like cattle in the cavernous holds of the "A" lighters, and on the decks of launches and tugs. On the quay below Navy House, and at the edge of beaches, the lorries waited. All round the harbour, the crews of the 3.7s and the Bofors and the "UPs" waited.

But now, at last, the sun was setting and it would soon be dark—pitch dark, for tonight there would be no moon. Tobruk was strangely quiet. Usually, at the end of these stifling summer days, the port came to life with a sigh of relief. The crews of the landing craft came ashore, the Aussies working on the quay ambled off to wash their sweating bodies in Anzac Cove, the Indian troops, who had been unloading stores, began to chatter like starlings, and a few of the staff of Navy House brought their "Plonk" into the evening air. But this evening Tobruk appeared like a ghost town. Then, as the sky grew dark and the stars came out, the still air was filled by the rumble of approaching trucks. Operation "Treacle" had begun.

Below me, although I could not see them, I knew the Aussies were clambering down from their lorries, rifles slung over their shoulders, and were humping their kit on to the jetty, into the launches and tugs, and over the ramps of the landing craft. I marvelled that so many men, keyed up with excitement, could make so little noise, and listened for the sound of their tramping feet against metal decks. Then I remembered that they were wearing their rubber soled desert boots.

Suddenly, I heard the distant drone of aircraft. All day long I had waited for that sound, and now that I heard it I felt sick. Getting up from the bench, I gazed into the starry sky, expecting at any second the rhythmical hum of the distant planes to be drowned by the ear-splitting crash of the ack-ack batteries. Instead, I heard the far-off thud of exploding bombs and saw their flashes like summer lightning in the southern sky beyond the escarpment, so that I knew the R.A.F. must be bombing El Adem airfield.

The reverberating drum beats of those bombs were the opening notes of an Olympian symphony that I felt was composed by Thor himself. They were joined by the pulsing beat of diesel engines and the throb of giant petrol motors, and, as the tempo quickened, this wild orchestra was swelled by the crash of heavy artillery, the shrill whistle of speeding salvoes, and the staccato crack of bursting shells. The very earth trembled as the symphony soared to a mighty crescendo.

Awed and dazed by this cataclysm of sound, I watched the great pall of smoke rising like a curtain over Bardia change from black to deep crimson, and saw silhouetted against it the shapes of the approaching ships. I saw, too, the jagged wrecks rearing out of the water like dinosaurs.

Slowly, *Latona* glided up the harbour and lost way, and the onyx water sparkled with phosphorus as her anchor cracked its surface. Through my night-glasses I watched two of the destroyers until they vanished into the shadows of the wrecks crowded with waiting troops. The third nosed her way towards the quay, to come to rest alongside yet another wreck. I could see the soldiers lining her deck four deep, and heard above the thunder of the bombardment the clatter of gangways.

Almost before the shore parties had secured her lines, the Indians were aboard off-loading boxes of ammunition, while down the narrow gangplanks the Poles came ashore. As the last of them landed, the Aussies swarmed aboard. There was no noise, no shouting, no flashing of torches, not even a lighted cigarette to be seen; and no confusion.

In less than ten minutes some 350 men had left her deck and another 350, including wounded on stretchers, had taken their places, and the destroyer was going astern on her engines.

Within thirty minutes the four ships were heading for the harbour entrance. High over their masts screamed the salvoes from the 60- and 25-pounders as one by one they merged with the darkness.

The story of "Crusader," which began at dawn on November 18 in a downpour of rain, has been told often enough. Its pattern followed those of all battles waged in that tactician's paradise, the Western Desert, where the protagonists are the armoured units rather than the infantry battalions, and victory is won by the flow of petrol and water rather than blood of soldiers. With their swift outflanking movements by light tanks and armoured cars, their clashes of heavy armour, when, mounting an escarpment, the opposing tanks meet face to face, breathing fire at each other like legendary dragons, and their moments of savage in-fighting between infantrymen with bayonets, rifles, and hand grenades, such conflicts should be an inspiration to any writer. Yet, because they range over the vast, featureless desert, their ebb and flow hidden in swirling dust-clouds, as the opposing armies fight for some un-charted hillock, these battles defy description and accounts of them are deadly dull.

For the first three days of "Crusader" everything went well for the 8th Army, although the reports coming in from the front, in the Commander-in-Chief's own words, "grossly exaggerated enemy tank losses." Nevertheless, Rommel was taken by surprise and forced to give ground.

Briefly, the plan was for the two divisions of the 8th Army, under General Alan Cunningham, to advance north and east towards Tobruk. The 30th Corps, under General Norrie, which comprised the 7th Armoured Division, the 4th Armoured Brigade Group, the 22nd Guards Brigade Group, and two brigades of the 1st South African Division, was to deliver the main attack. Its orders were to make a wide sweep on the desert flank, engage Rommel's main armour, and, having defeated it, to strike north to Tobruk. It was for Norrie to order the garrison to make its sortie from the fortress at the crucial moment. Meanwhile, the 13th Corps, commanded by General Godwin-Austin, and composed of the 4th Indian Division, the New Zealand Division, and the 1st Army Tank Brigade, was to attack and pin down the Axis frontier defences from Halfaya in the north to Sidi Omar in the south, outflank them, and press on to Tobruk. In this overall plan, the relief of Tobruk was merely incidental, for the purpose of the operation was to drive the Axis Army out of Cyrenaica and, finally, North Africa.

The 7th Armoured and the 1st South African Divisions, together with the 4th Armoured Brigade Group, had started off at a gallop in spite of the heavy going. By night-fall on November 18th, they had advanced across the El Abd track running from Sidi Omar to El Gubi, where they split into four columns, which would the next day search out the enemy's armour.

In the morning, the 22nd Armoured Brigade attacked the Trieste Division near El Gubi and knocked out forty-five of its tanks, but lost twenty-five of its own. As the Italians withdrew, the South Africans advanced into El Gubi. Meanwhile, the two center columns were heading north and west. The right-hand column, the 4th Armoured Brigade Group, advanced towards the Capuzzo track leading from Bardia to Gambut, while the 7th Armoured Brigade, finding the going ahead too soft, swung northwest towards Sidi Rezegh. This hundred-foot-high ridge overlooking the Capuzzo track about fifteen miles south-east from Tobruk became the hub of the battle for it virtually was the key to the fortress.

But, at first, Rommel chose to ignore the threat to this important position, and despatched a force of some sixty tanks to attack the 4th Armoured Brigade, whose main armour consisted of some 166 light American Stuart tanks. Although the attackers were outnumbered and forced to withdraw, they had tested the strength of these light tanks and discovered the weakness of their armour and firepower. Thus, the next morning when the 4th Armoured Brigade renewed the attack, it found itself up against a vastly superior German force. It was outgunned as well as outnumbered, but it put up a brave fight. Throughout the whole of November 20, the battle raged, and the reports reaching Cunningham's headquarters led him to believe that not only were Rommel's Panzer divisions committed in battle but had lost a considerable number of tanks.

In fairness to all concerned, these reports were not so inaccurate as they may have seemed. For the Germans did have a number of tanks knocked out. Our troops saw them hit and brought to a standstill. But they underestimated the brilliance of the enemy's recovery organization which enabled many of these tanks to return to action. Even as the battle was on, the Germans sent up their huge wheeled and tracked tank-transporters to recover their damaged tanks and drag them back out of range to the repair bases.

While this battle was being fought, the 7th Armoured Support Group had captured Sidi Rezegh, and the 7th Armoured Brigade had established itself on the aerodrome there. Thus, these two brigades had reached a position of great strategic importance only about fifteen miles from the Tobruk perimeter. Cunningham, therefore, allowed orders to be given for the 13th Corps to start operations and for the sorties from the fortress to begin.

For two days the garrison had been poised ready to spring. Its Commander was no longer Morshead, but General Scobie, G.O.C. British 70th Division, for "Ming the Merciless" had handed over the fortress on October 19 and sailed for Palestine to join the rest of the Australian Corps. Now the only Diggers in Tobruk were the 2/13th Battalion. The new garrison was composed of the British 70th Division, the Polish Carpathian Brigade, and the 32nd Army Tank Brigade.

Its task in Operation "Crusader" was to sally forth from the fortress on the morning of November 20 and drive its way through to El Duda, a point on the ridge about three miles northwest of Sidi Rezegh and approximately the same distance from Bel Hamed. Having done this, it was to hold open this corridor and cut the enemy's lines of communication along the Axis by-pass road.

All through the 19th the men of the garrison sat waiting and listening to the gunfire. But that evening when no signal came from Norrie, they resigned themselves to another bitterly cold night in their posts behind the perimeter wire. The next day, Scobie received the order to break out at dawn on November 21. But this order was tragically premature, for by the time it reached the fortress headquarters everything had started to go wrong for the 8th Army.

Suddenly, Rommel reacted violently to the capture of Sidi Rezegh and hurled the full weight of his armour against the 7th Armoured Brigade and the 4th Armoured Brigade Group. This savage assault changed the whole situation. Now it became a question whether our armour could hold out on the high ground at Sidi Rezegh until the Tobruk garrison could reach El Duda.

The Germans and Italians crouched in strongpoint "Tiger" facing the eastern perimeter, stiff and heavy-eyed after the long winter night's vigil, heard above the intermittent crash of gunfire, the eerie wail of pipes. Borne to them on the chilled dawn wind, the alien sound made their flesh creep, and with numbed fingers they gripped the triggers of their machine-guns and rifles.

Then, like phantom figures in the grey light, they saw

their attackers, fanning out to left and right of the tanks. Company upon company, with bayonets fixed, they came charging across the desert, yelling and screaming wild, high-pitched war-cries.

But these were not the mad Australians, whom the be-siegers had grown to dread, or the Indians, who attacked at night with the stealth of panthers. They were wild men from north of the Border—the Black Watch—led into battle to the skirl of their pipes. What would the Englishers think of next? The men in "Tiger" had seen Yeomanry officers who led their men with walking-sticks and hunting horns. And, now, these savage Scots with their bagpipes! No wonder Rommel called them amateurs in war.

Even when their piper fell mortally wounded and the music of his pipes died with him in a last fearful screech, the men following him never faltered. On they came, howl-ing like dervishes, their short bayonets glinting in the first light of the rising sun. As they met the first hail of fire from "Tiger," they leapt into the air to fall, kicking like shot rabbits, and then lie still. But there was no stopping them.

By the time they had overwhelmed "Tiger," half the 2nd Battalion of the Black Watch were casualties. But they went on to capture a second strongpoint, known to the garrison patrols as "Butch," and by the afternoon they had taken more than a thousand prisoners, of whom the majority were German. By nightfall, the garrison troops had shortened the distance between themselves and their ob-jective to seven miles. But the enemy's defences were deeper and stronger than had been expected. Furthermore, they were held by Rommel's crack troops brought up for his assault on the fortress. The minefields, too, were thick on the ground, and these, together with the heavy guns, in-flicted fearful damage on our tanks, so that it was soon apparent that there was no chance of reaching El Duda by the following day.

Although in Tobruk Scobie had only the haziest idea what was happening at Sidi Rezegh and to the east of Capuzzo, he was left in little doubt that things were not going ac-cording to plan with the relieving force. But, by the morning of November 22, the Garrison Commander was in a predicament. His small force of tanks had taken a terrible hammering in the sortie and were sadly in need of maintenance. Without their support, his infantry could make little impression on the enemy's strongpoints. Casualties had been high, the ground gained was thinly held, and there was no telling that if Rommel discovered this, he might not launch an attack against Tobruk at any moment.

But, although Scobie could not know it, Rommel had even more ambitious plans. Flushed with his success against the British armour at Sidi Rezegh, he sent for General von Ravenstein, in command of the 21st Panzer Division, telling him somewhat melodramatically that he was to be given the chance of ending the campaign that very night.

Ravenstein's orders were to take tanks, motorized infantry, and mobile artillery and anti-tank guns, and make a dash for the frontier. He was to look neither to right nor left, but push through and beyond the frontier wire and then swing northward to Sollum. While Ravenstein was doing this, Rommel explained, another force from the 15th Panzer Division commanded by General Neumann-Silkow would follow up and attack General Cunningham's headquarters at Fort Maddalena, while a third force would move east to capture the railhead at Bir Habata with its supply dumps.

Von Ravenstein's force dashed headlong eastwards, shooting up everything in sight. It outflanked the 7th Armoured Division, and threw the 30th Corps headquarters into a state of confusion, so that its administrative and supply trucks turned and fled for the frontier like a flock of panic-stricken sheep before a pack of wolves. By the afternoon of November 24 the rot had set in, and hundreds upon hundreds of British vehicles were streaming eastwards, and they did not stop until they reached the boundary fence. So rapid was both the advance and the retreat that there were times when the fleeing British troops and the pursuing Germans passed and repassed one another in their trucks without recognition, and von Ravenstein's tanks and armoured cars actually swept by our two huge supply dumps at Bir El Gubi and Gabr Saleh and never spotted them. When von Ravenstein was told about them, after he was taken prisoner, he was amazed and said that if he had known of their existence the Axis would have won the battle.

By this dramatic thrust to the frontier Rommel hoped to cut our lines of communication, and so force Cunningham to withdraw right back to his starting point. Once he had achieved this, Tobruk would be at his mercy. And, first and foremost, Rommel's heart was set on capturing Tobruk.

In fact, Cunningham proposed calling off the offensive. To continue it might mean the destruction of his entire tank force and the loss of Egypt. Thus, Rommel's gamble so nearly came off. But he had reckoned without Auchinleck.

Rommel's raid deep behind the 8th Army's lines had left havoc in its wake. The 5th South African Brigade had been cut to ribbons, its headquarters overrun, vehicles blown to pieces and left burning, and some 4000 of its men were either prisoners or missing. Scattered all over the desert were units, which a few hours before had been holding part of a continuous line, now completely cut off. Little groups of guns and tanks, by-passed by the enemy, were stranded in the desert. Hospitals and field-dressing stations found themselves surrounded, their staffs taken prisoners and as quickly abandoned and left to treat British and Axis wounded alike. Their signals trucks destroyed, brigade and battalion commanders, at a loss for orders, manned the machine-guns along with their men, shooting up enemy tanks and armoured cars as they dashed by in a fog of dust. At Army Headquarters, intelligence officers buried their aching heads in their hands and gave up trying to plot the course of the battle.

Into the midst of all this utter confusion Auchinleck arrived by plane, accompanied by his Deputy Chief of Staff, Ritchie, and Tedder.

Faced with such chaos, a lesser man might have conceded to his Army Commander's proposal to withdraw from the battle while the going was good and while there yet remained some armoured units to be regrouped and refitted. But Auchinleck gave his categorical refusal to such a plan and issued orders to "attack and pursue the enemy with all available forces, regain Sidi Rezegh, and join hands with the Tobruk garrison," which was to co-operate by attacking the enemy on its front.

This was undoubtedly the Commander-in-Chief's finest hour, for by his refusal to accept even the possibility of defeat, he saved the day. Then he returned to Cairo where he immediately decided to relieve Cunningham of his command, since in his own words he had "reluctantly come to the conclusion that he was unduly influenced by the threat of an enemy counterstroke against his communications."

So at this crucial moment Cunningham went and Ritchie took his place. But from then on it was Auchinleck who fought the battle.

On November 25, Scobie received a signal at the Fortress Headquarters telling him that the 2nd New Zealand Division would make a concerted effort to reach Sidi Rezegh the next day, and that by then the garrison was expected to have captured El Duda. With his tanks hurriedly serviced, Scobie launched an attack early on the morning of the 26th, and after fierce fighting his infantry captured the last enemy strongpoint, "Wolf," between them and their objective. But there was still neither sight nor sound of Freyberg's New Zealanders.

At one o'clock the garrison troops saw some tanks on the horizon, and from the turret of one of them three red flares rose into the clear blue sky. There was a pause and then three more red flares burst above the tanks. As they did so, the men from Tobruk broke into wild cheers, for those six red flares were the 8th Army's recognition signal, and for the first time for seven months the troops from the beleaguered fortress were within sight of the relieving force.

From that moment the men of the Northumberland Fusiliers and Essex Regiment, supported by the tanks of the 32nd Army Tank Brigade, raced for El Duda. By four o'clock that afternoon, after violent hand-to-hand fighting, they had driven the last of the Axis troops from the ridge and the corridor to Tobruk was open at last.

But all through that night the weary garrison troops clung grimly to their positions on the high ground. And it was not until the early hours of the morning of November 27 that the 19th New Zealand Battalion with a squadron of British "I" tanks battered their way through Sidi Rezegh and Bel Hamed to meet men from the fortress at El Duda crest. Then it was that General Godwin-Austin made his famous signal: "Corridor to Tobruk clear and secure. Tobruk is as relieved as I am."

But, once again, this jubilant signal was dangerously premature. For even while it was being despatched, Rommel was regrouping his tanks for another blow at the 8th Army.

On November 29, having gathered his strength together, he launched a major assault into the Sidi Rezegh-Bel Hamed-El Duda area with the 15th and 21st Panzer Divisions, supported by some Italian troops. His scheme was to cut right through the corridor from east and west simultaneously.

Fortunately, through an intercepted radio signal, the 8th Army was warned of Rommel's plan, and was able to muster some tanks to send into the attack. But it was touch and go whether the corridor could be held open. On the ridge at Bel Hamed and Sidi Rezegh, Freyberg's troops, probably the finest fighters in the Western Desert, resisted all the enemy attacks. But at El Duda, the 1st Battalion of the Essex Regiment, finding themselves up against a strong force of German heavy tanks, were forced to give ground.

When night fell it looked as if the western wall of the corridor might cave in altogether and the garrison be forced to retire within the perimeter again. For eight of Scobie's fourteen infantry battalions were already trying to hold the corridor, thinly supported by the remainder. He then received a signal from 8th Army Headquarters, saying: "At all cost corridor must be held."

Scobie had only one fresh battalion in reserve—the 2/13th Australian. But it had been mutually agreed between

Blamey and Auchinleck that only in an emergency were the Diggers to be committed to battle. Now, however, there was an emergency and a desperate one, and so Scobie sent for the Battalion Commander, Lt.-Colonel "Bull" Burrows.

On paper, he said, the 2/13th no longer existed on the garrison's strength, but, in fact, it was still there, and now, no matter what promises had been made in high places, he was calling upon the Diggers to fight once more for Tobruk.

By six o'clock that evening Colonel Burrows had given his orders for the battalion to move out to El Duda immediately. Two and a half hours later the troops were on their way to the gap in the perimeter to rendezvous with their Commanding Officer, who had gone ahead to contact the Commander of the 16th Infantry Brigade, under whose command they would be.

As they passed through the perimeter wire the oldest inhabitants of the fortress felt a strange thrill—a strange sense of unreality—at driving through the wire in their vehicles, instead of crawling through it on their bellies as they had done so often before.

At "Tiger" strongpoint the convoy halted to await the arrival of another convoy and their escort of armoured cars. Then, at midnight, in the bitter cold, they set off across the eight miles of desert to their positions on the eastern slopes of El Duda, where they were to spend the night.

Their orders were to attack at 11 o'clock the following morning, through the positions held by the Essex Regiment, over some 4000 yards of open country, and to drive the enemy from the lower slopes of Sidi Rezegh.

At first light, the Australians found they were bivouacked on a long low hill, and soon discovered that this position was within range of an enemy heavy battery. Moreover, this proved to be a German battery whose gunners plastered their positions with high and low angle salvoes, forcing the Diggers to scratch shallow holes in the rocky ground with their bare hands to escape the shrapnel raining down on them.

That day the Australians' orders were repeatedly countermanded as the battle for the corridor ebbed and flowed, and all the time they were under heavy shell-fire from the German artillery and tanks.

By dark, when they were due to attack again, Burrows spotted two dozen German tanks ahead of him. While his men took cover, he went back to call up the garrison's tanks. Six of the latter attacked, but the Germans could not be shifted, so Burrows called for artillery support. The heavy barrage knocked out two of the enemy tanks, setting them ablaze, and as the others retired the Australians prepared to attack. As they did so, they were joined by odd troops from the Essex Regiment determined for revenge.

As the moon waned, Burrows gave his men their last orders, telling them to yell "The Australians are coming!" as they charged. And yell they did, as they raced up the slope in the darkness, leaving the lumbering "I" tanks behind them. Ahead they could hear the enemy chattering excitedly and recognized the words: *"Englander kommen!"*

Then, by the livid green light from a Very pistol and to a shout of "Come on, Aussies!" they went in with hand grenades and fixed bayonets.

The odds were more than four-to-one against them, but the sheer weight of their charge overwhelmed the Germans before they had a chance to resist. Indeed, the attack was over so quickly that, except for those in the immediate vicinity, the Germans did not realize El Duda had been recaptured. Throughout the rest of the night the Australians and the Royal Horse gunners were shooting up Staff cars and trucks as they drove unsuspectingly up to their positions.

During the mopping-up after the attack, Private Clarrie Jones took a German captain prisoner. The latter demanded to know the name of Jones's regiment, and, when told, refused to believe it. All the Australians had left Tobruk, he declared knowingly. In the fading moonlight Jones thrust his metal shoulder-titles under his prisoner's nose, and told him to look for himself.

But the German laughed. *"Ach!* You are the English dressed as Australians to frighten us!" he insisted.

For two days the 2/13th held their position at El Duda

before they were withdrawn and their place taken by the 4th Battalion of the Border Regiment. Later, they left in convoy for Tobruk.

"Never did we dream, during those weary months of siege," Lt.-Colonel Colvin wrote afterwards, "that we would ever welcome a return to the perimeter, but it was with a feeling of relief that we finally passed through the perimeter wire to take over a position from the Durham Light Infantry, astride the El Adem Road."

Day after day the two armies fought for those ridges around Tobruk. When El Duda resisted, Rommel switched his armour against Bel Hamed and Sidi Rezegh, and under the weight of his attacks we were driven from both these positions. Now, although the garrison troops still clung resolutely to El Duda, Tobruk was once more surrounded.

Next, Rommel made a desperate bid to relieve his troops bottled up in Capuzzo and Bardia. But now Auchlinleck was at Desert Headquarters, and never for one moment did he allow his armour to rest. His orders were: "Attack everything you see, and keep on attacking." And the "Jock" columns, small roving tank formations that took their name from Brigadier "Jock" Campbell, V.C., one of the finest of all desert fighters, constantly harried Rommel's flank, racing into the attack and off again before the Germans realized what was happening. In this battle of thrust and counterthrust the initiative slowly but relentlessly passed to the 8th Army.

In daylight, Rommel's armour was ceaselessly set upon by the R.A.F., while night after night our bombers went forth to raid his supply bases.

In the first days of December the New Zealanders retook Bel Hamed, while the 4th Border Regiment repulsed no fewer than three heavy attacks on El Duda. On December 5, our fighters reported shooting up huge concentrations of enemy transports all heading west past Tobruk. Two days later, the 11th Hussars from Sidi Rezegh and the South Africans moving up from Bardia joined hands again with the garrison, and it was the turn of the Axis reconnaissance planes to report huge concentrations of enemy transports moving west towards Tobruk.

On the night of December 9–10, the Polish Brigade captured Ras El Meduuar in the Salient, and by the next morning stood triumphantly on Hill 209.

After 242 days of siege the fortress of Tobruk had been relieved.

Stand By to Ram

The German battleship, Tirpitz, anchored at Trondheim, Norway in early 1942, was a dangerous threat to all North Atlantic convoys. But once the Tirpitz broke out on a raid, the British were sure they could block her return to Norway. The only other Atlantic Coast harbor big enough to handle her was at Saint-Nazaire. "Destroy the Normandie Dock at Saint-Nazaire, and the Tirpitz would not dare to venture out into the Atlantic," so ran the argument in high British naval circles.

The task of blowing up the huge lock (a drydock capable of handling the largest ships in the world) and adjacent installations was entrusted to Lord Mountbatten's Combined Operations. The original objective of this group was to conduct quick hit-and-run raids all along the Atlantic coast—"one operation a fortnight" was Mountbatten's announced goal.

To reach the lock at Saint-Nazaire, it was necessary to sail up the Loire River about six miles. Unless surprise could be attained the mission could hardly succeed, because the river banks were studded with gun installations. Furthermore, the channel was narrow, and on both sides mud flats discouraged ships of more than light draft. Only during extraordinary spring tides could heavier ships get up the river out of channel. Ironically, this "flaw in the defense" appealed to Mountbatten's command as an excellent risk for a spring raid.

The plan of attack finally decided on was as follows:

"A gutted and 'expendable' destroyer of light draft, carrying a commando force, was to cut through the anti-torpedo net and ram the outer caisson (of the lock). A large weight of explosives would be packed at the point of impact and the ship blown up by delayed-action fuses. . . . The troops in the expendable destroyer would meanwhile have landed and would proceed to destroy with explosives all lock gates leading into the Submarine Basin, with the intent of making it tidal.* Bomber Command would be asked to engage the attention of

*German submarine pens had been constructed to service the U-boats in the South Atlantic.

the enemy's guns, searchlights and radar by a bombing operation to be begun before the expedition entered the estuary and to be maintained throughout the assault. Finally the commandos and the skeleton crew of the expended destroyer would withdraw in a second destroyer, which would have followed up and proceeded alongside." *

This plan, if fully supported by the other services, seems almost foolproof in light of what happened. Unfortunately, the inevitable conflict between services during wartime prevented its full acceptance. The Navy was unwilling to risk a second destroyer. CO had to settle for a fleet of lightly armed motor launches. The destroyer chosen to ram the lock was the *Campbeltown*, originally the *Buchanan* and one of the fifty old U.S. destroyers the British received as Lend-Lease in exchange for U.S. use of certain Caribbean ports.

A further blow to the CO battle plan was felt when the R.A.F. Bomber Command reduced the size of their requested contribution, both in numbers of planes and the time span devoted to the operation— Bomber Command hated to give away anything from their own operations.

Because so much depended upon surprise, the overall risks in the operation were now even higher. How high, Lord Mountbatten made clear to Colonel Newman, who would lead the Commando units ashore.

"I want you to be quite clear," he said, "that this is not just an ordinary raid; it is an important operation of war. . . . It is also a very hazardous operation. I am quite confident that you will get in and do the job all right; but, frankly, I don't expect any of you to get out again.

"If we lose you all, you will be about equivalent to the loss of one merchant ship, but your success will save many merchant ships. We have got to look at the thing in those terms.

"For that reason, I don't want you to take anyone on the operation who has any serious home ties or worries. No married men. Tell all your men that quite openly, and give very man the opportunity of standing down if he feels he should. Nobody will think any the worse of him and we must have that quite clear, too." **

The Greatest Raid of All, by Anthony Heckstall-Smith, published by Little, Brown & Co., pp. 22-23.

** *Ibid.*, p. 37.

At two o'clock on a sunny afternoon on March 26, the little fleet set sail. "They numbered, apart from the escorts (two destroyers) 611 souls —345 naval officers and ratings, 166 all ranks in the fighting parties from 2 Commando, 91 all ranks in the demolition teams of the combined Commando, together with the medical party, three liaison officers and two press representatives." *

As a feint, their course was set well out into the Atlantic to a point 160 miles west of Saint-Nazaire. There they turned toward France but headed toward a point a good bit south of the Loire River destination. At eight o'clock on the evening of March 27, they turned and sailed toward the open jaws of the Loire estuary.

Mile after mile went by, the little fleet still undiscovered. At 11:30 p.m. British bombers were heard going over but their fleet's position was still a few miles off the coast.**

At 12:30 a.m. the ships entered the river mouth. Their luck held until 1:22 a.m. when the column of ships was suddenly caught and held in the beam of an enemy searchlight. For a few minutes the raiders were able to confuse the Germans with false signals but not for long. Then the firing began from both sides and sounded as though all hell had broken loose.

"Campbeltown was going fast now, making a good twenty knots, her bow wave splaying wide. Every German gun that could bear was now converged upon her; not now those lower down the river but those at point-blank range in the dockyard area itself—from the Old Mole, from either side of the Normandie Dock, from the top of the submarine pens, from the roofs of buildings—and from the east bank of the river. Repeatedly hit, she was now suffering very heavy casualties, among her sailors and soldiers alike, her decks spattered with fallen bodies. But miraculously Campbeltown escaped damage to any vital part as she raced forward. The gunboat and the motor launches of Boyd and

* *The Greatest Raid of All,* p. 68.

** Editor's note: The air raid did little damage, but it did make the Germans suspicious and they went on the alert for that night. To make matters worse, because of an overcast, several bombers continued to cruise over Saint-Nazaire for unexplained minutes before leaving.

Irwin were backing her up at close quarters. Boyd's gunner, Able Seaman MacIver, observed a Bofors immediately to starboard of the caisson engaging the destroyer. With a steady hand, he caught it in the sights of his Hotchkiss and silenced it with a direct hit.

"Not till he was within 200 yards did Beattie see the great steel gate of the lock, discernible as an indistinct black line beyond the 'spill' of the searchlights, dead ahead. At the last moment an incendiary bomb, of the nature of thermite projected by no known agency, but conceivably dropped from one of our own aircraft, landed on the forecastle and burst into flames. *Campbeltown* held steadily on her course. In the wheelhouse there was complete silence. Beattie and Montgomery propped themselves against the front of the wheelhouse, ready for the shock of impact. Throughout the ship every man braced himself.

"Denser and denser grew the black line ahead. A momentary check told them that they had ripped through the anti-torpedo net. All hands could feel the wire dragging along the ship's bottom. The caisson was scarcely fifty yards away and only now could Beattie clearly see it. With extraordinary presence of mind, in order to hit the caisson in the center and in order to swing the ship's stern to starboard, so that the Old Entrance should not be blocked, he crisply ordered at this last moment:

" 'Port 20!'

"Instantly Tibbits obeyed and at 1:34 a.m. with all her Oerlikons blazing at the enemy guns only a few yards away, with her fo'c'sle in flames she crashed into the caisson.

"She struck with such accuracy and force that her bow, up to the level of the caisson, crumpled back for a distance of thirty-six feet, leaving her fo'c'sle deck, which was higher than the caisson actually projecting a foot beyond the inner face.

"Beattie turned to Montgomery with a smile and said, 'Well there we are.' Looking at his watch, he added, 'Four minutes late.' " *

*The Greatest Raid of All, pp. 98-99.

THE RAID ON SAINT-NAZAIRE*

by Anthony Heckstall-Smith

Beattie's achievement, executed with such cool precision, marks the attainment of the chief purpose of the expedition. There now began a medley of events difficult to describe in ordered sequence. The battle spread like a flame, to the whole scene by land and water. The motor launches, coming up astern of *Campbeltown*, pressed towards their designated landing places with the greatest daring, adding to the lurid scene the glow of their own conflagrations and the smoke and stench of burning petrol as, one by one, half their number burst into flames or blew up. The battle splintered into innumerable little actions. From the moment of committal command and control of the action was lost, partly through the very nature of the operation and partly through the failure of the gunboat's wireless, so that each boat and each group of soldiers pursued, or attempted to pursue, its predetermined part alone.

At the moment that *Campbeltown* crashes into the caisson, we may imagine Curtis's gunboat and the motor launches of Boyd and Irwin standing off to support her and the two columns of troop-carrying craft coming up close astern, with Platt leading the port column and Stephens the starboard. These beheld the bows of the destroyer erupting in flying timbers, smoke and flames. They saw the commandos leap to their feet on deck and, under a covering fire from the destroyer's Oerlikons overhead, begin to move

*A condensed version of several chapters from *The Greatest Raid of All*.

forward. The guns of both sides began to concentrate their fire on this small area.

Campbeltown herself began to prepare for her last moments. Beattie, excited enough beneath his icy exterior, forgot to give the order to ring off the engines, and for a few minutes there was a little confusion in the engine and boiler rooms, accentuated by the darkness which now enveloped the whole ship below deck. The engines might have been required to hold the ship on to the caisson, but Chief Engine Room Artificer Howard went up on deck, found Gough in the storm of fire that crackled and flashed up there and got sanction to shut off steam. The ship was still being repeatedly hit and down below, where the engine-room staff were bearing themselves with exemplary courage, shells and explosive bullets were still penetrating. Stoker Petty Officer Pyke was going about quietly, maintaining machinery by torchlight. Engine-Room Artificer Nelson was killed while evacuating hands from the forward boiler room.

The first, the most imperative duty, however, was to disembark the commandos as rapidly as possible. Not till this had been done did Beattie give the order to abandon ship. Winthorpe's medical party, their hands more than full to the last minute, were routed out. Howard and Engine-Room Artificer Reay proceeded to scuttle ship by torchlight, opening the valves that would let in the sea and removing the condenser doors. To make assurance doubly sure, scuttling charges were fired under the direction of Hargreaves, the torpedo gunner. Finally Beattie and Gough then went round the ship to make sure that no one was left behind. Then they themselves went onto the upper deck while the ship, held fast by the bows on the caisson, was beginning to settle at the stern.

From this moment we must imagine the seven parties of the commandos, steel-helmeted, with whitened webbing, scattering to their several targets, moving at the double under heavy weights of arms or explosives, past tall cranes, buildings, railway trucks and piles of timber; now brilliantly illuminated by the searchlights, now in a moonlight gloom; sometimes unopposed, sometimes having to fight bitterly for their objectives. In the midst we see the handfuls of the commandos moving to their stations—Roderick scattering his enemies, Roy holding his bridge, the teams of destroyers fixing their charges.

Thus the two assault parties carried out their tasks. The demolition teams were hard on their heels. Let us remind ourselves what the targets were they had been ordered to destroy.

These numbered five. At the southern end of the dry-dock area was a group of three tasks entrusted to teams under officers of 5 Commandos. Stuart Chant had the formidable task of destroying the big pump house; Christopher Smalley was to go for the winding-house where the machinery for moving the big southern caisson in and out of position was situated; Robert Burtenshaw was to destroy the caisson itself with magnetic "wreaths" and 18-pound charges if *Campbeltown* should fail to ram satisfactorily. The protection party for all these teams was provided by Hopwood, of the Essex Regiment.

At the northern end of the big dock, Etches, with Gerard Brett and young Corran Purdon, was charged with destroying the caisson at that end, and the winding-house associated with it. For these demolition teams the protection was provided by "Bung" Denison, of Roderick's Troop. All these five demolition tasks in the drydock area were under the control of Pritchard's friend, Bob Montgomery.

During *Campbeltown's* approach Chant's party were lying behind their steel screens, face up and feet forward against the shock of impact. A moment before the destroyer rammed, a small shell burst beside Chant and Chamberlain,

142

wounding them both. A sticky feeling running down his leg told Chant that he had been hit in the knee; splinters wounded his arm and fingers also. The bittersweet fumes of high explosive blew over him. He lay momentarily dazed, but an inner compulsion told him to rise and slip into his rucksack with its load of explosives. Three of the sergeants rose with him, but Chamberlain said, "Very sorry, sir, but I can't move."

Between them, however, they lifted up his hundred and eighty-nine pounds and half-carried him as they moved forward to disembark, together with Smalley's and Hopwood's teams. Then, heavily laden with their explosives, sledge hammers, axes and incendiaries, they scrambled, slid or fell down the scaling ladders on the port side. Somehow Chamberlain was got down and the team made for the pump house by the route printed on their minds through a scene vividly lit, but checkered by the dense angular shadows of the buildings, swaying from time to time as the searchlights swung their beams.

Chant was limping but could move fairly freely. They were right on Roy's heels, seeing the kilts flying just ahead. Without waiting for him to attack the German gunners on the roof of the pump house, they went straight for the entrance, but met an unexpected obstacle when they found it barred by a heavy steel door. Chant was momentarily at a loss, but at that moment Montgomery appeared and from the spare explosives that he carried he took out a small magnetic charge, clamped it on the door and stood back. Chant made to light the short length of safety fuse, but found it difficult to strike the fuse with his bleeding fingers. He was disconcerted to find his hands trembling and he said to Montgomery, "Bob, for God's sake help me light this bloody thing; the chaps will think I'm scared."

Montgomery complied, the door was blown in and Chant and his sergeants entered the pump house.

Chant's team had rehearsed over and over again, including provision for casualties. The task required two demolitions—the first, that of the great impeller pumps forty feet below ground, and the second, the electrical gear on the ground floor where they now stood, particularly the electric motors that drove the impeller pumps below, and the transformers. They flashed their torches around and, with the help of the glow coming in from the searchlights and the fires outside, they noted that everything was exactly as they had seen it in the King George V Dock at Southampton—the straight line of the motors, the transformers, the switch gear, the indicators, all laid out in orderly precision.

Chamberlain was by now weak and moving slowly. Chant was reluctant to take so heavy a man down the steep, zigzag staircase that led to the pumping chamber far below, but to ease the sergeant's chagrin, he said,

"Stay up here and do guard for us. Don't let anyone in."

The big sergeant lay down at the top of the stairs and Chant started on the long descent below ground, Butler and Dockerill helping him down, with King following, and carrying between them Chamberlain's sixty pounds of explosive besides their own.

Utter darkness lay beneath them, a darkness that the torches at their belts penetrated only as a cold, unfocused beam. Below ground level a cold dampness at once struck their faces. Their blindfold exercises at Southampton came back vividly to them as they counted the steps, but these were not quite the same. The impulse to make haste was upon them, held in check by the risk of losing balance and by thought of the results of taking a false step or of straying off the stairs on to the galleries that ran round the walls of the pit. Chant, limping down by jerks, fought the threat of giddiness.

At the foot of the long stairs, in the pumping chamber at last, their torches showed them that the impeller pumps were exactly as they knew they would be—four main pumps of the turbine impeller type and two subsidiary drainage pumps. They looked rather like giant lifebelts, or huge inverted mushrooms. Inside these big steel ring castings were the fast-revolving vanes which impelled the water in or out of the dock. Standing up in the middle of each ring was the long, shining, steel shaft connecting with the motor that drove it far above at ground level. Each of the four sergeants was to blow up one of the main pumps and Chant himself the two subsidiaries, but Chant now took over Chamberlain's target, leaving the subsidiary pumps to be attacked collectively.

Not much need for torches now. They knew every step and every movement by heart. They wriggled out of their harnesses, laying them on the concrete floor, and took out the specially prepared plastic charges in their waterproof covers. These, reaching up and over the big circular tubes, they slapped and molded firmly onto the casting joints of the impeller pumps, which they knew from the Southampton dock engineers could not be replaced in less than a year. Disturbed by two deep muffled thuds overhead which shook them deep below, they were told by Chamberlain far above that it was "only Captain Donald blowing up the guns." They worked quickly and confidently. Dockerill was quietly singing "Blue Birds over the White Cliffs of Dover" and the other two sergeants chatted casually in broad Norfolk. Their homely, easy voices gave Chant a glow of affection, overcoming the pain of his wound and the handicap of his lacerated fingers. He heard one of them say:

"Nearly finished, sir. Can I help you?"

"No, thanks, I'm all right."

The charges laid, out came the ring main. Together they unrolled and laid it out, hands feeling forward to other hands dimly seen in the checkered light. Out next came the cord-tex leads to connect each charge to the ring main by a clove hitch. Chant, on No. 3 pump, heard successively reports of his companions:

"No. 2 done, sir."

"No. 4 done, sir."

And finally, with a note of triumphant finality:

"No. 1 done, SIR!"

The subsidiary pumps were quickly connected likewise. Finally, out came the two lengths of safety fuse, with igniters and detonators already connected, to be crimped on to the ring main.

A hundred fifty pounds of high explosive were now ready to be detonated at the touch of the duplicated percussion igniters. Three feet of safety fuse gave a delay of ninety seconds, which would give a fit man ample time to run up the stairs and out of the building. It was Chant's duty to fire the charges himself, sending his sergeants up first and being himself last man out. But he was wondering how on earth he was going to get up those forty feet of steep stairs. His knee was now slowing down all his movements. He decided to keep Dockerill with him, sending King and Butler upstairs with instructions to remove Chamberlain to safety and to shout down when the way was clear.

He took one of the igniters and gave the other to Dockerill. Two long minutes passed in the underground darkness. Dockerill continued humming his song. No other sounds were audible and the battle above seemed far away. At last came the expected shout from above and Chant, by prearrangement, gave a simple "one-two-three" to Dockerill. Simultaneously they pulled their igniter pins and the slow fuse began to burn along its three feet passage to the detonator and the cordtex. Subaltern and sergeant turned and made for the stairs. With Dockerill leading and Chant clinging tight to his arm, they went up in the dark as fast as possible, Chant hopping two or three steps at a time.

They arrived out into the bright light and the din and Chant ordered his team to take cover behind the concrete anti-blast wall opposite the door of the pump house, but Montgomery was at hand and ordered them at once to cover further off. They had no sooner reached it than the charges went up, bursting in the confined space below with great violence—"a great roar of sound that cracked our eardrums," as recorded by Copland, who was passing through not far away—shaking the ground and throwing down a great concrete block upon the very spot where they had lain just before. Clouds of debris billowed out and bright showers of broken glass burst outwards from the windows. The "great roar" impressed itself on the whole battlefield, heard with satisfaction by both Ryder and Newman, both now ashore, and heard even by the motor launches in the agony of their river battle.

It was not quite two o'clock.

Christopher Smalley, fresh at the nearby winding-house, came up at a trot to make his report to Montgomery before withdrawing to his last rendezvous. They exchanged quick congratulations and Stuart Chant led his team back to the pump house. They had now to go in again to destroy the motors and electrical gear on the ground floor. Quickly in, they found the building filled with clouds of smoke and dust, the concrete floor caved in, two of the electric motors fallen through it to the pumping chamber far below and the other two lying at crazy angles. It was obvious to them all that the place had already been sufficiently wrecked and that another destructive explosion was unnecessary. Chant contented himself, therefore, with ordering King to smash the transformer pipes and the gauges with his sledge hammer, which that broad-shouldered sergeant did with relish and precision, and as the oil poured out of the transformer pipes it was set on fire with tar babies.

Thus, leaving the pump house completely destroyed and burning fiercely, Chant and his sergeants set out to withdraw according to plan, supporting between them their wounded companion.

When all was done, Montgomery, having observed a large shed at the side of the pump house, opened the door and threw in an incendiary. There shot up, in the words of Copland, "a colossal burst of continuous yellow fire," adding yet another to the series of fires that were now raging in the white beams of the searchlights.

Meanwhile Christopher Smalley and his small demolition team had had equal success in their attack upon the southern winding-house close by. Smalley, of the Manchester Regiment, was somewhat aloof, squarely built, had good looks and a heavy mustache. His little team consisted of Sergeant Bright, the miner, Corporal Howard, Bombardier W. Johnson and Corporal E. Johnson.

His was the nearest of the objectives to *Campbeltown*. Within the building he saw the two big wheels by which the caisson was moved and the motors that drove them. On these motors and on the spokes of the wheels he placed his charges, connected all up with cordtex, and, having had permission from Montgomery, pulled his igniters. There was no result. He reported to Montgomery and fresh igniters and safety fuse were fitted. These fired successfully and the

147

whole building and all its machinery went up with a shattering concussion, the bricks and debris showering down upon the motor craft now in the Old Entrance and narrowly missing Ryder as he stood by the caisson watching *Campbeltown* sink.

Leaving it in ruins and blazing fiercely, Smalley went quickly to report to Montgomery, as we have seen, saying to him, "Bob, I have finished and I'm going to withdraw now." Returning to his team, he saw at that moment Burt's motor launch in the Old Entrance, disembarking his troops, and he decided to take this opportunity of effecting his withdrawal, instead of going to the Old Mole. He and his team ran to the quayside and embarked, but the boat was heavily engaged by the minesweepers and harbor defense boats in the Submarine Basin. The forward Oerlikon was jammed and Smalley took charge of it in an attempt to free it, but was almost immediately shot dead.

All the commandos' demolition objectives on the machinery of the great Normandie Dock had now been fulfilled with almost complete success in less than half an hour from the moment *Campbeltown* had rammed. Even if the destroyer herself should fail to blow up, it was now impossible to operate either of the caissons and impossible to pump out or refill the dock. The great Forme Ecluse was useless for certainly a year at least, useless to the *Tirpitz*, useless to every kind of ship. It was, indeed, to remain useless until long after the war was over. This feat is unique in military and naval annals. No other example exists of damage so vital and so far-reaching in its results being carried out so swiftly and with such economy of force. No guesswork, no "hundred per cent zone," no "permissible error," no "near misses" obscured the exactitude of the commandos' attack, for they placed their charges on those small, vital pinpoints which might never have been hit at all by projectiles launched from bomb rack or gun.

The achievement was not only the visible record of the daring of the men who performed it; it was also a triumph for the man, now at this moment about to die on the doorstep of fulfillment, who had planned it. It was Pritchard whose imagination, invention and fanatical persistence had built the way to this technical achievement, it was his midnight assiduity that had calculated every charge and written out every item of each man's task and load to the last fusee, and it was his patient and meticulous training that had taught each man precisely what to do. In the honors and memorials of the Charioteers his name, denied by death the award of any decoration, stands among the highest.*

Having thus completed all their tasks, the commandos of Group Three began their withdrawal according to plan. Their work was finished and they were now to re-embark for home again.

Except in one instance which will shortly be related, the commandos had not the least difficulty in dealing with any of the troops that they met; what was much more serious to them than the superiority of numbers was the superior weight of fire from the fixed gun positions and from the minesweepers and harbor defense craft, some of them firing from extremely close quarters, to which were quickly added several machine guns. These weapons, particularly those of the ships in harbor and the hastily mounted machine guns, very soon began to turn their attention from the motor launches to the little parties of men that they now saw darting about in the searchlight beams or among the shadows of buildings and dumps and railway tracks. Later the quadruple 20 mm. beyond the Submarine Basin began to sweep this area with their more venomous fire and occasionally, from some unidentified battery, there came the sharp crump of an airburst shell overhead.

With Moss and his important-party missing, Newman was therefore very relieved when his tiny headquarters was augmented by the "special task party" of Troop Sergeant-Major Haines, which joined him soon after he had taken up his impromptu headquarters. The rugged little sergeant-major, in fact, had arrived before Newman and then moved off for his special task of silencing the guns reported to be on the sea wall between the mole and the Old Entrance. Finding none there, he reported to Newman in accordance

---

*The award of the DSC to Tibbits was made before it was known that he had been killed.

with his orders. Standing to attention as on the parade ground, he listened as Newman told him:

"Stay near me in case I want you; because you are the only reserve I have now got."

He very soon did need him, for fire from one of the 20-mm. guns beyond the Submarine Basin and from machine guns mounted on the roof of the pens began to harass them. Newman called up Haines and said:

"We have simply got to stop those guns. What have you got you can take them on with?"

"I've got a 2-inch mortar, sir. No sights, but it's the only thing we've got."

With extraordinary unconcern, Haines took forward in his great hands a little 2-inch mortar, siting it slap in the open near the quayside of the Submarine Basin just beyond the end of one of the warehouses. Here he knelt down and, taking the small bombs that were passed to him by a chain of hands, including Newman's, from behind the cover of the building, dropped them down the barrel of the mortar, to go soaring high into the air and onto the enemy positions only two hundred yards away. With the enemy fire plunging down on the very spot where he knelt, he successfully silenced one position after another, if only temporarily.

There then came against him one of the armed vessels in the basin, the flash of his mortar and the crump of its bombs being only too apparent. Coming close in, the ship made his position "a veritable death trap." Quite unperturbed, however, Haines leaped over to a Bren gun that some fallen comrade had left, and although the fire from the ship's machine guns was "cascading" in the very place where he was now lying, he sent a series of bursts so well directed that the ship ceased fire and sheered away.

All this time Newman was quite in ignorance of the progress of the battle elsewhere, for he never succeeded in establishing wireless communication with Ryder, though the 38 set on the gunboat had its own independent rod aerial. Sergeant Steele opened up his own set immediately in the shelter of Newman's headquarter building, and almost at once heard Lance-Corporal Fyfe, Copland's signaler in the Normandie Dock area. But Newman was not interested in Copland. He kept anxiously asking, "Have you got the boat yet?" But Steele, swinging his dial from time to time, chanted "Newman calling Ryder—Newman calling Ryder" for over an hour without any effect, till at length there was disclosed a situation in which wireless could only too clearly have no value.

The silence of the radio, however, was not matched by the din and clamor all around, and very soon sounds of fresh Tommy-gun fire on his left told Newman that something was afoot there also.

This was the party successfully landed at the Old Mole by Collier's ML 11, containing Philip Walton's team for destroying Bridge D, Watson's protection squad and Pritchard's demolition control team. Pritchard's tasks were to control the timings of the demolitions, to help where necessary and to attack targets of opportunity.

With Watson's squad leading, followed by Walton's, followed by Pritchard, this little band ran quickly up the steps to the landward end of the mole. Watson had orders that if his was the only squad to gain the mole he was to attack and hold it himself. He could probably have done so, had he not been led to believe that Birney had already arrived. As it was, he stopped to examine and empty his Tommy gun into what appeared to be a new gun position at the top of the steps, until the cry came up from Pritchard in the rear:

"What are you up to, Tiger? Get on!"

Without more ado, the three parties made straight for Bridge D, but very soon came under fire. In commando fashion they did not wait for each other's support, but made straight for their objectives independently. Pritchard, passing two bodies dead or wounded on the ground, reached Bridge D the first, having probably taken a different route from Watson and Walton and perhaps having seen the trouble into which they both ran.

Pritchard's party consisted of four corporals—I. L. Maclagan, a Royal Engineer Territorial, J. Deans and H. Shipton, all of 9 Commando, and S. Chetwynd, of 12 Commando. Approaching the lock of the Southern Entrance, they beheld before them the steel latticework swing bridge which was Walton's objective, looming in the half-darkness ahead of them like the ribs of some giant skeleton. There was no cover at all on the bare and open quay, except for a small concrete hut, about ten feet square, a few yards from the bridge. To this Pritchard and his corporals sprinted, dumping their rucksacks on its sheltered side—four men alone in the half-light with the enemy just across the bridge and all behind them also. Pritchard, looking round at once for prey, saw two ships berthed alongside each other against the quay of the Submarine Basin, forty yards to his right, and he whispered to Maclagan:

"Mac, I'm going to sink those two ships. Get out two five-lb. charges."

Under full observation from an enemy scarcely sixty yards away, the two men ran to the quayside, jumped onto the nearer ship, crossed to the second and lowered the charges between the two ships, three feet below water. They tied them to the rail of the ship, pulled the igniter pins and hurried back to the shelter of the hut.

There Pritchard gave instructions to the other three corporals, in the absence of Walton's party, to "do what you can" to the swing bridge, while he and Maclagan went round to visit, as he hoped, the other demolition parties in that area. He lingered a moment, however, listening for what he hoped for, and before they separated, smiled happily as the charges between the two ships blew up with a muffled roar, followed by a violent and prolonged hissing which told convincingly that the charges had been accurately laid against the ships' boiler rooms. When Newman passed there nearly two hours later he found the two ships sunk. They were the tugs *Champion* and *Pornic*.

Having accomplished this impromptu act, Pritchard and Maclagan, the tall Welshman and the smaller Scot, set out at a trot towards the South Entrance, going boldly and silently along the open lock side, in the half-light from the "spill" of the searchlight beams and from the moon that shone through the high cloud. But they passed in turn one lock gate after another, and the farther bridge likewise, disappointed to find no demolition parties yet arrived. At the most southerly gate they turned left to visit the power station that operated all these southern lock gates, close by on the edge of the Old Town. They could hear the tread of leather-soled boots but they saw no one.

At the power station Pritchard therefore decided that he must go back to find out what was happening. Together with his corporal, he turned about lefthanded and began trotting across the Old Town, making for Bridge D again, Maclagan on Pritchard's left. They passed through a labyrinth of small buildings, making their way through back yards and narrow streets.

They were nearly halfway across the Old Town when, at a sudden corner in the half-light, Pritchard ran straight into a German. The end came swiftly. At one second they met and in the next Pritchard had fallen backwards, possibly bayoneted, for no shot was fired by either. Maclagan took a quick pace forward and riddled the German with his Tommy gun.

He then dropped down on his knee beside his leader. Pritchard was breathing "terribly heavily" and for a few moments could not speak. Then he said:

"That you, Mac? Don't stop for me. Go straight back and report to HQ. That's an order." So far as we know, he never spoke again.

This order the corporal was desperately unwilling to obey, but the tall, strapping Welshman was far too great a weight for his smaller frame. He resolved therefore to return to the concrete hut, send one of his comrades to headquarters, and bring the others to Pritchard's assistance.

He made his way back alone through the eerie, hostile streets and reached the concrete hut safely, but all that there was to be seen was a dead body. It was that of Philip Walton.

Still quite alone, therefore, in the heart of enemy territory, Maclagan continued on his way, across the dangerous and exposed Old Town Place, through the rows of warehouses and so to Newman's battle headquarters. There he asked for help to bring Pritchard in, but was told it was out of the question. At some time or other Corporal Deans and Corporal Chetwynd were also killed, Maclagan and Shipton being the only survivors of Pritchard's party.

Watson's tiny squad comprised young Sergeant Wickson, Lance-Corporal Grief, an irrepressible, ribald Cockney, Private Davidson and Private Lawson.

Coming up immediately behind them was Philip Walton the schoolmaster, with his demolition team for the critical Bridge D, consisting of Sergeant Dick Bradley, Sergeant Alf Searson, Corporal George Wheeler and Lance-Corporal Homer. Watson set off at a smart pace, too smart indeed for Walton's heavily laden demolition team, from whom they soon became separated. At the first group of buildings after passing the landward end of the mole, Watson saw in the half-light what appeared to be a group of French civilians. He shouted to them, as he had been instructed, *"Dedans vite"* (Inside quickly), and fired a burst from his Tommy gun over their heads as he ran. They disappeared, and he saw also a group of German soldiers running away into the Old Town—the second group that he had already seen to run away.

Full of confidence, therefore, he doubled along the broad open space of Old Town Place, but had gone only about one hundred and fifty yards before he met some Germans who did not run away. He called to them, *"Hände hoch!"* (Hands up!) But they answered him with a grenade and a similar summons. Himself a little way in front of his squad, he therefore dropped to the ground to engage them, his orders having been to keep the enemy occupied while the demolition team went on, then to disengage and join up again.

Disengagement became difficult, however, when a machine gun opened up on him from a rooftop to his left. He was almost stunned by a grenade that fell and burst beside him. With a metallic clang a litter tin attached to a lamp-post just above his head was riddled with bullets. Another bullet or other projectile burst open his haversack of grenades and the movement of scrabbling about to pick them up drew fresh fire. From an emplacement beyond

Bridge D another machine gun began spraying the area at random. Watson therefore lay low for a minute till the shooting stopped, then rose quickly and darted back several yards to rejoin his squad, who had taken cover behind a railway truck and who would have shot him but for his blue pinpoint torch.

Watson was upset to find the demolition party here also, but without Walton; they had seen him fall while running across Old Town Place, but in fact, unknown to all, Walton was making his way to the bridge alone, there to die in an attempt to lay his charges singlehanded at point-blank range. The subsequent study of the battle by the German naval staff reveals that German troops found charges actually laid on his bridge, though whether by Walton or by one of Pritchard's corporals who was killed we know not.

To Watson's urgent inquiries, Corporal Wheeler replied that they had been unable to cross the road and that he thought Walton must have been killed. Watson shouted for his friend, without result and turned to question Sergeant Bradley, when the sergeant was shot through the lung by the rooftop machine gun. While bending down to administer morphia, Watson himself was wounded in the buttock. Bradley was dragged under better cover, but before long he was shot again.

Some reinforcement was clearly necessary for Watson's tiny squad, but when he raised his Very-light pistol to fire the required signal it was shot out of his hand. He therefore sent Wheeler to run to Newman's HQ with the request for help. He then attempted a new approach, moving half-right through the sheds and warehouses north of him towards the Submarine Basin, closely accompanied by Private Lawson. He had nearly reached the quayside when he heard German voices at the end of an alley between the warehouses, and, instead of ignoring them, he hurled a grenade.

He was answered by a violent burst of machine-gun fire, which enveloped him in clouds of dust from shattered bricks at head level from the wall alongside him and from cement stored in the warehouse. This brusque stoppage came from one of the ships of 16 Minesweeper Flotilla still berthed at the quayside only a few yards from him; he saw her outline clearly, heard her engine-room telegraph and heard the orders from her bridge. He saw also some cement bags lying in the road and thought in the half-light that they were his comrades. His calls to them brought no answer and the way ahead was blocked by wire. Frustrated a second time, he made his way back through the shadows to Newman's HQ, accompanied by the bewildered but obedient Lawson and pursued by the ship's machine gun.

Among all the clamor and the darting tracer Watson found Newman—who was not yet aware of the failure of the Old Mole landings—jovial, kind and reassuring.

"Hard luck, Tiger," he said. "You've done jolly well. I can let you have a couple more Tommy-gunners. Go back and have another shot."

Not much relishing this order, but determined to do his damnedest, the little officer, still accompanied by the faithful Lawson, retraced his steps. "I was convinced," he said, "that it meant certain death, but orders were orders." He made contact again with Sergeant Wickson and the remainder of the party and they turned about. His blood was up. Observing one man straggling, he shouted at him angrily:

"Do you want to live forever?"

The effect of this startling challenge was magical, and by the time that they had all reassembled on the dangerous edge of Old Town Place, they had all become charged with the same ardor. They were at a point close to where they had left Sergeant Bradley, of whom they could see no sign. What they did see on that spot was a party of Germans standing easy, and these they wiped out at a few yards' range.

While they were bracing themselves for the new effort, a runner arrived from headquarters canceling the order and instructing them to assemble with the other parties, for it must have been about now that Newman had seen Maclagan, had learned from him that none of the demolition teams for the Southern Entrance had yet arrived and had begun to realize accordingly that these targets might be beyond accomplishment. Watson complied with mixed feelings, for from now till the end he was in an angry mood, burning to have it out with the enemy in atonement for the failure of his mission; but he had done better than he knew, for his little fight had created a valuable diversion, distracting enemy attention from what was now a more vital area and keeping at bay superior forces that would otherwise have been a danger to the remainder of Newman's troops, who were now beginning stealthily to muster together.

The sounds of Watson's fight had told Newman that some at least of his troops had landed at the Old Mole and were about their business. He had no reason yet to suppose that the mole was not in our hands or that anything on the left wing of the battle had gone seriously wrong. On the contrary, one by one the explosions on his right flank and rear began to tell their tale. He heard Purdon's and Smalley's winding-houses go up, Chant's deep underground explosion in the pump house, and the dull thud and boom of the northern caisson's underwater burst. He felt tremendously exhilarated and began to crack jokes with his staff. On the left, however, no such detonations interrupted the unceasing crash and clatter of guns and machine guns.

Apart from those who were already in his designated headquarters, parties of the enemy in this confused situation were extremely close to Newman's small team. One party was no more than twenty yards away, occasionally lobbing grenades, and small-arms fire seemed to be coming from every direction, besides the vicious air crumps from some unidentified battery from time to time. Mindful of the need of being personally out in the open with his men, Newman abandoned the idea of occupying his proposed headquarter house, and after some grenades had been thrown into it, took up a fresh position behind a shed near the quay (where Haines had fired his mortar), from which he could check the demolition parties as they came in and direct them, as he hoped, to the point of re-embarkation on the Old Mole.

One by one these parties began to come in, the young officers in charge of each—all of them wounded, though

Montgomery only slightly—reporting personally. All those who could do so stood up and saluted as though on parade. Tremendously pleased with them all, Newman said, "Well done, old boy. Better move along now towards the mole and wait for Major Bill."

Copland came in very soon after, giving Newman the good news from the Normandie Dock area, and the less promising news of Burn's lone arrival far away at Bridge M. The time had therefore come to fire the rain rockets that were the signal for the withdrawal, but there were no rockets, for they had all been lost when Regimental Sergeant-Major Moss had gone down in the river. Newman therefore called upon Lance-Corporal Harrington to go out and take verbal withdrawal orders to Roderick, a quarter of a mile away, and to Roy. Harrington set out alone at the double. He crossed Roy's fireswept bridge after due challenge and reply, and swung to the right to traverse the dangerous no man's land beyond which lay the *Campbeltown*. On the way he was fortunate enough to meet Roderick, who, as we have seen, had already begun his withdrawal. The lance-corporal returned, passed the order to Roy also and reported back to his CO.

"When the situation is uncertain or confused, collect your forces." By the time that Roderick and Roy had completed their withdrawals, this maxim was being complied with. Newman and his commandos, now reduced by fatal casualties and by the re-embarkation of Smalley's party to something just under a hundred, of whom many were wounded, had collected loosely together in the warehouse area. Newman now knew that the main purpose of the expedition, as Haydon had set it out, had been achieved. The situation on the left was dubious, but, so far, no more than that. The general impression on his buoyant mind, therefore, was that the operation was developing favorably. Of the fate of the motor launches he had little or no knowledge, for where he stood the warehouses and railway trucks acted as a baffle to any view of the river.

Thus when Copland said that he would "push along" to organize the re-embarkation, for which the parties from the north were now ready, Newman said, "I'll come with you, Bill."

Together they made their way southeastward through the ranked warehouses, keeping to the selvage of black shadow that bordered the buildings under the harsh, white beams. Emerging from the buildings and coming to a line of railway cars, they had their first glimpse of the river north of the mole and were all brought up standing.

Struck with consternation, Newman exclaimed:

"Good heavens, Bill! Surely those aren't ours!"

Nothing, in the recorded words of Copland, more exactly resembled a scene from the *Inferno*. The river itself was on fire. Close in to the mole the hulks of burned-out motor launches still glowed red on the water, while in the night beyond, seemingly suspended in the air, there blazed a sea of burning petrol which had spread outwards from each burning ship or had been splayed far and wide like so many fountains of fire as other craft blew up. From this floating furnace a pall of black smoke, frustrating the glare of the searchlights, rolled indolently towards the northwest in the almost still air, mingled with the white withdrawal smoke of the escaping launches. From out this curtain of smoke shot the burning trails of cannon fire from the batteries at Mindin Point beyond. In all this forbidding scene there was no sign of life, or of movement, except the leaping flames and the slowly drifting smoke. And on the Old Mole itself the still-glaring searchlight at its tip and the emplaced gun halfway along its length, firing far downstream on some target that they could not see, betrayed to the watching officers in whose hands the pier still remained.

For a moment they both gazed in silence, the import of the scene only too apparent. Then, with a little, wry laugh, Newman said:

"Well, Bill, there goes our transport!"

The first requirement was to rally, consolidate and organize for the new situation. Copland set briskly to work to re-form the little force, choosing as the rallying ground the loop in the railway 150 yards north of the Old Mole, where there was some field of fire and where a few railway cars gave a little protection. Using the well-armed assault troops to form protective screens, he put out Roy on the southern flank, whence increasing fire was being directed from the Old Town, and Haines to the west, where stood the ranks of warehouses.

Here at this rallying point an extraordinary situation existed. Until the commandos were re-formed, both sides were in considerable confusion. Often only a few yards from each other, friend was not instinctively distinguishable from foe. The winking blue torches, the white webbing and the occasional kilt proved their value but were not infallible. The tread of boots and the shouted orders likewise gave clear indication of German presence, but no one knew who was on the other side of a building nor who had thrown a grenade. In Newman's words, the enemy "were shooting at us round corners." The gaunt dockyard reverberated to the bursts of Tommy and Bren gun, the explosions of hand grenades, the crack of rifle and pistol and the answering fire of the enemy, echoing among the warehouses and accented by the cries of the wounded of both sides.

Steadily augmented in numbers, the Germans were now on all sides of them, except to the north, probing forward with caution, but were kept at bay by fire from troops far more highly trained in the use of infantry close-quarters weapons at night.

Virtually surrounded and their means of withdrawal gone, the commandos nonetheless intended to retain the initiative as long as possible. Newman himself, with the responsibility for men's lives on his shoulders, alone had a moment's doubt. They had, he reflected, accomplished the major part of their mission. To satisfy his mind, he sought a second opinion, calling Bill Copland into a short conference. Did Copland think, he asked, that they ought "to call it a day"?

"Certainly not, Colonel. We'll fight our way out."

Nothing pleased Newman more. He made a quick plan to divide his force up into groups of about twenty, fight their way out of the dockyard, through the town, into the open country beyond and try to make their way in pairs to Spain and thence to Gibraltar.

He told Copland and Day his plan, a grenade exploding at their feet as they talked. Copland then moved off to divide the force into detachments of twenty and brought the group leaders to Newman for their orders. Newman's own words vividly illustrate this moment. "The scene at the Old Mole," he said, "is hard to describe. There were flames and smoke everywhere. Some wounded Germans were screaming down an alley and small-arms fire was coming from all the buildings around us. Our own chaps were forming a perimeter round the Old Mole; some railway trucks gave them cover and from behind these they were coolly returning the fire with ever-decreasing ammunition. When the group leaders came up to me for my orders, they saluted and grinned. I told them that, as usual, there was no transport to take us home, and that we should fight our way into the town and from there to open country. No one seemed at all surprised."

Their shortest route into the town was by Old Town Place and Bridge D, 200 yards away, but this broad, open approach was so covered by enemy fire that it would be rash to attempt it. The route decided upon, therefore, was through the area of sheds and warehouses to the north of them, and thence back along the quayside of the Submarine Basin, which Watson had already attempted, this route being chosen because by any other they would have to pass between warehouses with the enemy on both sides of them, for the whole of the warehouse area was now alive with Germans. It was a run of some 650 yards, which would have to be undertaken by the wounded also.

Copland marshaled the force into their groups. Making a final round of the positions, accompanied by Private Fahy, he found a party of Germans trying to break through a weak point, and saw them scatter with casualties as Fahy opened up on them with his Tommy gun.

Then, when all was ready, Copland reported to his colonel.

Some time after 3 A.M. this extraordinary column, encumbered with wounded, short of ammunition, began its dash straight through the serried rows of buildings thronged with enemies. They were fewer than a hundred now, a third of them armed with pistols only and nearly one man in three wounded.

They moved by bounds, keeping to the shadowed ways at the edges of the long warehouses and halting from time to time to squat in some dark patch and collect together—sometimes to rush some open stretch by parties under covering fire, or to overcome some point of enemy resistance or to give time for the straggling wounded to catch up. These, obedient to the precept that the lame must not impede operations, fell out to await the inevitable when they could no longer keep up. Gerard Brett, with manifold wounds, could move no further than the first twenty or thirty yards and, giving his Colt to a man who had lost his own, he sank down in a warehouse.

Throughout the whole route, from concealed positions a few yards away in the dark, a ragged fire, now feeble, now bursting into an angry challenge, was sprayed upon the silent-footed column.

Stumbling through a bomb crater made that night by the RAF, they ran the gauntlet through the warehouse roads, turning left, right and left again, and reaching the approach to the old headquarters building. Contact with Burn had somehow been lost at the first or second turn and Donald Roy was now in the van, a splendid figure in his kilt, a grenade in either hand, now striding along in the middle of the road. As he led, Day and Haines served as whips to the field under Copland's mastership, running up and down the column to bid Roy slow down or quicken up, to urge forward any stragglers and to keep the column closed up. Somewhere always in the van was to be seen the figure of Newman, still cracking jokes, never taking cover, always on his feet and directing fire or calling out, "Keep going, lads!"

Reaching the Submarine Basin, the commandos swung boldly left along the quay. An hour earlier this route would have been impossible, but the minesweepers had now moved from their berths at the quayside and, appreciating that the attack might be directed against the submarines, had taken up positions in front of the pens. In their place, however, the commandos met the fire of the guns across the water on their right, while on their left small-arms fire assaulted them at a few yards range from the sheds. Halted by one troublesome party, Copland took a squad right into the shed to silence them.

Watson trying to rush a rifleman who was firing at close range from round a corner, was hit in the left arm, the bullet shattering the humerus. He sank to the ground and prepared to shoot it out with his Colt, but Roderick appeared, killed the German, administered morphia to Watson and began to carry him, but Tiger called in pain to put him down. Hopwood was there, too, and together they put him down at the side of the road. Very quietly, ignoring the boy's cry of "Hoppy, what the hell are you doing with my gun?" Hopwood slipped his Colt off its lanyard.

Roy, meanwhile, was sweeping along to the southern extremity of the Submarine Basin. At the end of the quay came the most dangerous place of all—the wide, open stretch of Old Town Place, which, turning right, they must cross before reaching Bridge D. At Newman's order they halted accordingly in the pale moon shadows aslant the buildings on their left hand, while Newman himself, accompanied by Roy and Haines, darted across the open space for a quick reconnaissance from the buildings opposite. Immediately they came under fire from a machine gun in a pillbox beyond the Southern Entrance, commanding the open way by which they must all go.

There lay the girdered Bridge D, gaunt and ghostly in the curious light. It was barely seventy yards away. Beyond it the German machine guns looked down from roof and window. Astride it on the far side, and stretching along the quayside, lay a line of enemy riflemen, last remaining elements of the German naval troops.

No means of indirect approach to the bridge was at hand, no cover, no opportunity for finesse. Haines, at his own suggestion, sited a Bren gun to give a little covering fire. Then Newman called to his waiting soldiers:

"Away you go, lads!"

The commandos went for it, moving at a steady double as a hurricane of fire burst upon them from beyond the bridge. The astonished Germans, quite in the dark about the purposes of all these confounding occurrences, shot high and wide, as they had done all that night. A violent storm of bullets swept over the commandos' heads.

Donald Roy made on right in the middle of the road, Newman now beside him. Close behind him were Sergeant Rennie, Denison, Montgomery and Haines. They saw the German riflemen athwart the bridge scramble to their feet and retire. They passed the ships that Pritchard had sunk, passed Philip Walton's dead body and swept over the Bridge of Memories, their rubber boots thudding on the hollow road while the bullets rang and sparked on the steelwork or whistled overhead into the night. To all those who took part it was the most inspiring moment of the night. In the pages of British history there have been many glorious charges, but, on its smaller scale and in its more modest intent, the break-out of the commandos at Saint-Nazaire ranks high among them as a manifestation of soldierly purpose and of the will and determination to defy odds.

As they reached the end of the bridge Sergeant Rennie fell, shot in the knee. A German grenade hit Corran Purdon in leg and shoulder, bowling him over on top of Day. At that moment Copland went straight for the pillbox, emptying his magazine into the slit and others followed his example. Roy, seeing a German run out from behind it, attacked him with a grenade. He ran to a roadside pit with Denison, Haines and a sergeant to attack with fire another machine gun in action from a window a little way up the street. A motorcycle combination, carrying machine-gunners, came suddenly from round a corner at a crossroads. Every commando in sight opened fire and the Germans, riddled with bullets, crashed into a café wall. Further up the road what appeared to be an armored car drove up very fast, spitting out fire at random in every direction and taking station at a crossroads 150 yards ahead, thus barring further progress by that route.

So, about a hundred yards beyond the bridge, ended the commandos' dockyard battle. For the motorcycle combination and the armored vehicle gave notice of the arrival of the first troops of the German Army. They were units of 679 Infantry Brigade, a partially motorized formation, consisting of one or more infantry companies, half a company of machine-gunners, two companies of 559 Construction Battalion and probably a unit of the 333 Division's artillery regiment. The brigade commander himself arrived in the town about this time and took over command of the operations at 4:30 A.M. These troops had arrived too late to mar the splendor of the commandos' break-out from the dockyard, but just in the nick of time to stop them from getting any further. Had they been fifteen minutes later, all the commandos who were fit enough would have made their way through the town and into the marsh country beyond, for once over the bridge, there were no more naval troops to oppose them.

Immediately after having crossed the bridge, the little force, deflected by the armored car, turned left and soon broke up into separate parties. Copland, finding a lorry parked at the roadside, seized the opportunity for escape but inside the cab the only switch he found to work was the one for the headlights, which illuminated Denison, who gave vent to the familiar wartime cry: "Put out those bloody lights!"

From this point all becomes confused as the small parties of commandos, with no maps and not knowing which direction to take, made their way through the streets, sticking close to the shadows of walls. All over the town the Germans were now rushing in reinforcements, uncertain what was afoot, believing that the raid was the spearhead of an invasion. Armored cars or machine guns were being posted at every road intersection. Newman squeezed into a doorway to avoid an armored car that shot past. Everywhere the Germans were shooting at any object that moved, frequently firing at each other, as the watching commandos observed.

To avoid all these patrols and pickets, now being augmented each minute, the British began to forsake the streets, and to engage in what they were afterwards to term the "Saint-Nazaire Obstacle Race," clambering over walls, passing through one back yard after another, even going through houses from front to back. Private Hannon dropped over a wall into a chicken-run, awakening the startled fowls to a premature reveille. Newman also dropped into a chicken-run and, going head-first through a window, entered a parlor with the breakfast things already laid out on a blue-checked cloth, and so passed through the house to the front door.

By now, however, time was running out. It was somewhere about 4 A.M. and only two hours of darkness remained in which to find lying-up places for the day. Ammunition was very short and, with every street corner now picketed by the enemy and every street swept by fire, effective progress became difficult. Worst of all was the condition of the wounded. By now about three men out of every four had been hit. All but a few had kept up but were now weak from loss of blood and fatigue. Here and there small parties, becoming broken off from their main groups, began to seek shelter in cellars and outhouses.

Michael Burn and Rifleman Bushe were surprisingly caught in the boiler room of a ship in the docks. Very few of them had any luck.

Donald Roy, at the head of a party, seeking water for the wounded who were with him, called at a building which unfortunately turned out to be a police station, and the police, after stalling him, had a squad of German bayonets round in a few minutes, for the French police, under orders to collaborate with the invaders, were nearly as dangerous to escapers as the Germans themselves.

Newman himself, with about fifteen others, found refuge in a large cellar equipped as an air-raid shelter, with eighteen palliasses. Of them all, only himself, Copland, Day and Steele were unwounded. Steele was posted as lookout near the head of the stairs and wounds were dressed as far as possible. Here Newman intended to stay until night, when they would set out in pairs for the open country. "But I also decided," he said, "that if we were found in the cellar I should surrender, as the wounded were in a pretty bad way and a single grenade flung down the stairs would see the lot off."

They were indeed discovered, the commander of 679 Brigade having ordered a systematic search. Newman himself at once dashed upstairs and offered surrender. Roughly handled, the party was frog-marched across the road and taken into the house immediately across the road, which turned out, to the amusement of Newman, to be the German headquarters. Under heavy guard, they were stripped of their weapons and interrogated by a German officer without much success.

While this was going on one of the commandos had some occasion to take out his fighting knife, which they all wore strapped to their legs inside their trousers and which, as we have noted earlier, they scarcely thought of as weapons, the British instinct (and, one thinks, the German too) being averse to the use of the knife as a soldier's weapon. The interrogating officer, who was what Newman called an "office type," observed this action and flew into a rage. Why had they not surrendered all their weapons? They were then all stripped naked under the muzzles of Tommy guns and lined up against a wall. "I really thought," said Newman, "that that was going to be the end of things." At that moment, however, another German officer appeared who was not an "office type," and he quietly gave orders for the prisoners to resume their clothes.

Back in the dockyard Chant lay by the quay, unable to rise. Wounded a second time in the legs, he had been bowled over in the dockyard battle. Sergeant Butler and Private Brown, of the Argylls, had come to his aid and carried him onward as far as the Submarine Basin, but there he had bidden them leave him. He lay in "the weird half-light" looking straight across to the submarine pens and watching the Germans moving about and manning their weapons on the housetops. A dazed young soldier whom he did not know came and sat down beside him.

There they were found in the morning by a German patrol, who came up to them, Tommy guns leveled, and, shouted, *"Herauf! Herauf!"* (Get up! Get up!). The young soldier, prompted by Chant, obeyed and was immediately shot dead. They turned to Chant and again ordered *"Herauf! Herauf!"* Chant, mad with anger but helpless, pointed to his injured leg. One of the Germans then noticed the stars on his shoulder, and said *"Offizier."* They searched him, taking all his personal possessions, and carried him to a café at a corner of Old Town Place, where Gerard Brett and several other wounded or dying prisoners already lay.

Not far from here Roderick, Hopwood, Sergeant Searson and one or two others, all wounded before or during the break-out (Roderick had been hit a second time), were lying up in a warehouse stored with bags of cement. They all managed to climb to the top of a pile of bags high off the ground and for some hours they avoided capture, watching the German search parties at work.

It was not until 10:30 in the morning that a German, on a higher level than they, looking out from a shed across the dock road, saw, through a bomb-splinter hole in the wall of their warehouse, the bandaged and bloody head of one of the commandos. In next to no time the place was alive with Germans. The wounded men were roughly manhandled to the ground, searched, lined up against a wall, and, like Newman's party, thought that "they had had it." Again, however, some responsible German intervened and instead of being shot they were hustled off to a ship in the Submarine Basin before rejoining their comrades in captivity.

Thus, little by little, what was left of the commandos began to come together again. "It was just like a reunion," Newman recorded. "In spite of personal misfortunes our spirits were high. We never gave in to the Jerries. We all felt that a good job of work had been done, and as each newcomer arrived we pieced the story together. What we were all waiting for, and straining our ears to hear, was the big bang of *Campbeltown* going up in the air."

Not all, however, could maintain this high note. Many were wounded very badly. Wherever the wounded lay, the camera-mad Germans gathered round, clicking from all angles and stepping over bodies to take close-ups. Private McCormack, grievously wounded in the head, lay in an open space in Saint-Nazaire town, with his head between his kilted legs, dying. The Germans gathered round him in crowds, jeering and laughing, while their cameras clicked. One of these pictures was published throughout Europe in the German armed forces magazine as a whole-page picture with the derisory title "Picture of a British Commando."

While the commandos were fighting their dockyard battle and trying to effect their "withdrawal by land," the little motor craft of Ryder's force, or what was left of them, had begun their withdrawal by sea. For some of them the fighting had by no means been ended.

Seven of the seventeen craft we have already seen lost in flames in the immediate neighborhood of the docks—those of Stephens, Platt, Burt, Beart, Tillie, Collier, and Nock. The remaining ten which include Curtis's gunboat and "Wynn's Weapons," have begun their homeward journeys, setting course at full speed for the open sea. There they are to make rendezvous at Point Y, twenty-five sea miles from Saint-Nazaire, with their escorting destroyers *Tynedale* and *Atherstone,* with whom they parted company at 8 P.M. It was intended that, having assembled at Point Y, the force should be well on its way home before first light, which was at 5:48 A.M.

Tweedie and Jenks, commanding *Tynedale* and *Atherstone* respectively, had passed an anxious night, having had no news at all of what was happening in the river. All that they had heard on the air, picked up between 2:18 A.M. and 3:25 A.M. were the "leaving" signals wirelessed by only five of the MLs. Their anxiety had been added to by the knowledge that the five small German destroyers of the 5th Torpedo Boat Flotilla, which had left Saint-Nazaire early that night as a result of the signal from U593, were somewhere in the vicinity and might be encountered at any minute.

While the destroyers waited, the ten remaining motor craft, passing beyond range of the small, rapid-firing flak guns in the harbor area, came under fire from the heavier and more dangerous guns of the coastwise batteries. With the exception of the 75-mm. battery at Pointe de l'Eve, which was not manned, all these batteries engaged them hotly, even the big 9.5-inch guns on railway mountings at La Baule. The 6.6-inch battery at Pointe de l'Eve fired no fewer than 400 rounds that night, mostly in this withdrawal phase, their shells of about a hundred and ten pounds splashing up great fountains of water as they detonated on the surface. Yet all but two of the withdrawing craft successfully ran the gauntlet.

As one may suppose, the Germans lost no time in boarding *Campbeltown*. A group of very senior officers and many technical specialists, to the number of about thirty, climbed on board by the ladders that the commandos had left and carried out an examination. It is said that the Admiral-Superintendent of the dockyard himself arrived and, immediately suspecting the existence of an explosive charge, ordered a search to be made; but none was found, so shrewdly had it been concealed in its steel and concrete jacket. On being so informed, he said, we are told, "Well, the British must be very stupid if they think we can't deal with this." For the problem of disengaging the destroyer from the caisson was not one of serious engineering difficulty. It was apparent that she would sink in the lock entrance if simply towed out, and the methods to be adopted for getting her clear without immobilizing the dock for longer than necessary were being discussed. The acting Harbor Commander also visited the ship, but neither he nor the Admiral-Superintendent stayed very long. Mecke also came, driving up from his headquarters at St. Marc, and he took some photographs.

But these were by no means the only visitors. Orders had been given for a cordon to be placed round the dock, but either the order was never carried out or the cordon was ignored. For the word very quickly flew that here were plenty of cigarettes and chocolates to be had for the taking and a throng of curious sightseers of all sorts began to arrive by car and on foot—the submarine commanders, the gun position officers, officers of the naval shore staff and so on.

And their lady friends. Looking for souvenirs, they roamed the littered upper deck from the shattered bows, where the displaced twelve-pounder stood precariously by the big hole in the fo'c'sle, on past the tangles of twisted metal, underneath the bandstands where the Oerlikons had been so bravely served, and so down the steep incline towards the sunken stern, where the falling tide lapped quietly on the quarter-deck. They penetrated to the darker chaos below, where the officers' sherry lay spilled and wasted in the wardroom, where the butter was plastered on the mirrors, where broken glass, cigarettes, clothing and little personal things littered the cabins and the mess decks and where the inert corpses indifferently lay.

While this tour of his ship was being made Beattie, blanketed and barefoot, was brought ashore in Saint-Nazaire with the other survivors of Rodier's boat. It was probably some time after ten o'clock and he was disappointed to see *Campbeltown* still intact on the caisson. The latest possible computed time for Tibbits's fuses to act was 9:30. What had gone wrong? He supposed that the Germans had discovered the arrangements and found some way of disarming the fuses, though he thought that Tibbits had provided against that contingency also. He had no opportunity, however, to stand and stare and was hurried on, very cold, to some German office, where he was taken for interrogation by a pleasant-mannered German Intelligence officer, who spoke English well. The Intelligence officer got nothing out of Beattie, but he was persuasively talkative, and he remarked:

"Your people obviously did not know what a hefty thing that lock gate is. It was really useless trying to smash it with a flimsy destroyer."

At that precise moment the glass from the window crashed to the floor, as the room, and indeed, the whole town, was shaken by a thunderous explosion sustained for several seconds.

"That, I hope, is the proof," observed Beattie dryly as the vibrations began to abate, "that we did not underestimate the strength of the gate."

The interrogation was brought to an abrupt close.

This heartening evidence of their success was heard, or even seen, by nearly all the Charioteers who had now been swept up. The time, as nearly as can be judged, was 10:35 A.M., not earlier. Between them, Beattie and Tibbits had done better than either could know. *Campbeltown* erupted with an enormous flash and a column of black smoke. Under the impact of this blast, reinforced by the hammer-blow of the inrushing sea, the great 160-ton caisson burst open inwards. The sea poured like a tidal wave into the empty dock. The northern caisson, the inner face of which had not been destroyed by Brett and Burtenshaw, held, but the two tankers that lay inside the dock—*Schledstadt* and *Passat*—were flung against the dock walls and damaged and the sunken stern-half of HMS *Campbeltown,* cut off as by a giant saw, was swept inside by the force of the flood. Of the rest of her nothing remained but the fragments that were flung far and wide. All the Germans on board the destroyer—men and women—went with her. So, too, did large numbers of those who clustered about her on hand, dismembered by the violence of that blast.

How shall one explain the fact that this explosion took place so long after the extreme limit of time expected of its fuses? Not one fuse, but at least three. Under normal functioning, they should have burned through at 7 A.M. Even under the extreme expected tolerance, they should have acted by 9 A.M. When they did act, they were nearly four hours overdue.

There persists a belief in Saint-Nazaire that a British officer, either voluntarily or involuntarily, went back on board and, in a deed of self-immolation, refired the quiescent charge. Workmen are said to have seen one or more go on board. The finger of surmise points at once to Pritchard. He understood the charging and the fusing of the explosive ship. He had the professional competence.

Did Pritchard die in the Old Town where Maclagan saw him fall? No shot was fired and the corporal did not know by what weapon he had been struck. Had he only been very badly winded? Or had the wound been not a fatal one?

If there is any truth in the legend, it would, of course, explain the delayed explosion; but it is a legend not easy to

172

sustain. For Bill Pritchard lies buried in the cemetery at Escoublac. Had anyone else gone back on board the destroyer, it is difficult to explain how, without the requisite gear, which he is unlikely to have carried, and in the presence of the Germans, he could have fired the great charge. It was recognized that these fuses were of an experimental and uncertain nature in regard to their timing and we can do no more than suppose that some unknown factor of temperature, moisture or material led to an excessive delay in the action of the acid on the copper. Yet it remains very odd that all the fuses should have been so long delayed without failing altogether, and even a man so little given to fanciful speculation as Hughes-Hallett thinks that "some hero" may have gone back on board and immolated himself.

An alternative interpretation of this persistent French legend is that some one or two British officers, on being ordered or invited by the Germans to go on board, did so in order to encourage the belief that the destroyer was not armed with a deadly charge. That is entirely possible, but there is no positive evidence.

Whatever may be the truth in this matter, nothing detracts from the brilliance of the demolition plans conceived and carried out by Nigel Tibbits, which so conclusively prevented the enemy, for all the remaining years of the war, from using against our most vital convoy route the most dangerous ship that they possessed. And to the memory of Pritchard we owe a like acknowledgment for those acts of demolition against the operating machinery which would have put the big dock out of action for at least a year even if *Campbeltown* had never blown up.

Dieppe at Dawn

The Dieppe Raid was launched at dawn on August 19, 1942. Churchill has called the raid a "successful reconnaissance," a rehearsal for the main landings at Normandy two years later—for it was deemed vital by the Allied commanders to gain experience disembarking major forces of men and tanks from landing craft in face of heavy fire. But in terms of numbers of troops lost, the landings were a disastrous failure. Out of approximately 5000 troops, the casualties numbered 3614, plus 215 officers. And by the end of D-Day, the German commander, Field Marshall von Runstedt, could announce to the world, "no armed Englishman remains on the continent."

The decision for the assault was taken by the Planning Committee of Combined Operations Headquarters presided over by Vice-Admiral Lord Mountbatten. The attack force was made up of 252 ships, of which eight were destroyers assigned to escort duty; air cover was provided by the R.A.F. which had agreed to commit sixty squadrons of fighters and seven squadrons of bombers.

The first landings were made on the outer flanks of the Dieppe sector, British Commando units being landed on Orange and Yellow beaches. They were to destroy big gun emplacements that overlooked the Channel and which threatened the ships in the attack force. The landings on Orange and Yellow were successful.

On the inner flanks of Dieppe, landings were made at Blue and Green beaches. The Royal Regiment of Canada landed at Blue, on the left flank. Here the troops were immediately stalled by anti-troop barriers and then devastated by overpowering fire from the cliffs. Out of 27 officers and 516 men only three officers and 57 men got off the beaches. It is not surprising when one reads the description of Blue Beach.

"The beach of Puits enclosed within the gentle-looking cliffs is a little more than 200 yards from end to end. A sea wall of very solid masonry fills most of this expanse above high-water mark, and at normal tides there is about fifty yards of shingle bank between the wall and the water's edge. This shingle is of large rounded flints of from four to six inches in diameter. It is not an easy or a pleasant beach to walk on.

"At low tide the beach extends to a depth of up to about 300 yards. The shingle soon gives way to sand and flat rocks, and these rocks build up into rocky ledges which narrow the sea entrance to this small haven to less than 120 yards. Even under good conditions the approach is not an easy exercise in navigation, and it is not difficult to miss Puits altogether in the ramifications of that coast.

"The sea wall at Puits is a solid piece of masonry rising vertically about ten or twelve feet above the shingle. The whole crest of the wall was crowned with wire, and the two flights of steps which break the front were filled with tangles of heavy barbed dannert wire . . . From concrete pill-boxes embedded in the sea wall heavy machine-guns were firing point blank, themselves impregnable to small-arms fire, to mortar bombs, and even to the sustained covering fire from the guns of the motor gunboat standing in as near as she dared." *

The South Saskatchewan Regiment landed on Green Beach and moved off the beaches inland with comparative immunity. Its men were up the cliffs by ladder and blowing up gun positions along the tops with a momentum that carried them inland several miles. The Regiment of Queen's Own Cameron Highlanders of Canada followed on their heels and they, too, fared better than the troops on Blue. By nine a.m. the Camerons were more than two miles beyond the beaches.

So far, there was limited success at Green beach, but only a shambles at Blue. Greater success might have been achieved at Green and Blue if the men landing on the main beaches in front of Dieppe had been able to sustain a solid coordinated attack on the objectives handed them, thus mounting pressure on the German defenders at Green and Blue. Failure at the center meant trouble for all.

Let us now turn to the story of the main assault at Red and White beaches in front of Dieppe.

*At Whatever Cost, by R. W. Thompson, pp. 70, 72-73.

THE MAIN ASSAULT

by R. W. Thompson

1

The growing thunder of war closing in upon them from the flanks before the dawn had aroused the people of Dieppe from sleep with a sense of excitement, compounded of hope as well as of fear. They were accustomed, in these years of the Nazi occupation of their land, to the alarms and dangers of air raids. They had listened often, and without comfort, to the harsh roar of anti-aircraft fire and the crump of bombs, but this rousing din of war was of a different texture and pattern.

On all that broad sea front of Dieppe the Germans, too, had awakened to a new alertness. In the grey light of dawn they could see little beyond the fringe of the sea, but the sense of some crisis impending was unescapable, as battles raged on the flanking beaches.

Along the whole length of the foreshore from the end of the west jetty breakwater to the steep white cliffs of the western headland, the heavy barbed coils of triple dannert wire grew out of the half light, seeming a fragile barrier, little more than a snare for the unwary in its almost delicate filigree of outline. Fifteen feet behind the rolls of dannert, a seven-foot wire apron fence built on the knife-rest principle gave a more solid impression to the watchers at their posts behind the sea wall, on the house tops, in the pill-boxes and casemates, behind the anti-tank blocks and barricades, and in the caves of the headlands. Even then, as they stared outwards to the quiet sea, they also looked over their shoulders, for the threat—if threat there was—might come equally well round the flanks of the headlands from Pourville and Puits.

The beach of Dieppe is a steep shingle bank rising from about 1 in 40 gradient to 1 in 10 under the solid masonry and concrete of the sea wall. In places, the high tides had piled up the shingle almost to the top of the wall, which normally rose vertically ten feet above the beach. But this might prove more of a hindrance than a help to an enemy seeking a foothold. The sea wall, protecting the wide promenade, filled all the front for 1500 yards from the harbour to the West headland. It was well fortified. At regular intervals along its whole length men peered out from under cowlings such as shield "prompters" on a stage. These men were Forward Observation Officers. Their stage was the wide beach, and those they must prompt were far behind them, manning the batteries of mortars and field-guns that could bring down concentrations of fire anywhere upon all that steep and stony foreshore at a word. This was in addition to the predicted fire of mortars that would fall upon the angles of the wooden groynes which run up out of the sea to space the beach into tracts 150 yards wide. There were, in fact, a wealth of weapons in great variety concentrated upon this shore.

The Germans, when their own invasion hopes had dwindled, had worked with an energy and skill born of a growing fear throughout all the summer in their preparations to meet an invader. There had been much talk and clamour for an invasion, and the Germans had constructed skilfully an "iron coast" to meet it when it should come. They had burrowed tunnels and dug crawl trenches to their "prompters" boxes and grenade pits from the hotels and boarding houses that stood in gaunt and sombre outline in the half dark beyond the wide boulevards Marechal Foch and Verdun. These boulevards were wide enough to take three lines of traffic, and between them lay lawns and gardens, a seemingly peaceful expanse, 1200 yards long by more than 150 feet wide, and lending a spaciousness to the front of the huddled seaport town. The line of those tall buildings seemed like a wedge, imprisoning the rambling town and holding open the mouth of the narrow valley of the D'Arques that encloses Dieppe within the limits of its white chalk hills.

To the casual eye there were few signs of life at five o'clock on the morning of the 19th August. In all that sober row of hotels and boarding houses looking bleakly out over the grey sea, no guest lay waking or sleeping, and no light burned. The white mass of the casino building with its forecourt and steps breaking the line of the sea wall at the western end of the promenade had a blank deserted look, as though long abandoned. It had long since ceased to be a place of gambling and amusement, and had become instead a minor fortress. In the white cliffs of the headlands there was no sign of weapons or of movement in the blank sockets of the caves. In the docks of the inner harbour armed trawlers and invasion barges lay dark and silent at their berths, while the incessant bursts of gunfire flickered staccato patterns in the sky above the headlands, and beyond to the east and west.

At that hour of five o'clock in the morning the sea in front of Dieppe appeared as deserted as Dieppe itself, revealing nothing to the eyes of the watchers. Even from the snipers high up on the roofs of many buildings the last of the dawn twilight hid its secret.

Three miles offshore at that hour a great concourse of little ships, deployed in a wide arc and carrying the men of the main assault, bore steadily in at 10 knots to close the beaches at the appointed hour. They hoped simply to come in tight on the heels of a brief bombardment from the air and sea. Greater surprise than this they could not hope to gain.

The motor gun boat of Lt. Commander Mullen was in the lead. Gun boats and motor launches, flak and support landing craft guarded the heart and flanks and rear of the convoy, ready to give close support with their machine guns and Oerlikons.

On the left sailed the assault landing craft with the Essex Scottish Regiment under Lt.-Colonel F. K. Jasperson, bound east for the Red Beach. On the right were the assault landing craft of the Royal Hamilton Light Infantry under Lt.-Colonel R. R. Labatt, bound west for the White Beach.

And in their midst with the flak and support craft, and

in the van of those who must be first to land, were the Beach Assault Group of nearly 400 sappers of the Royal Canadian Engineers with their special roles of blasting the sea wall, and all else that might stand in the way of men and tanks.

Keeping station close in along the line in the second rank loomed the larger shapes of the tank landing craft of the first wave. Behind them again came the landing craft with the mortar detachments of the Black Watch of Canada and the Calgary Highlanders, and the machine-gunners of the Toronto Scottish.

Bravely, they came on with all the expanse of Dieppe and its beaches in their minds' eyes, knowing well the slope of the shingle, widening in an arc from left to right from a depth of 180 yards in the east, the Red Beach of the Essex Scottish, to 360 yards in the west, the White Beach where the Royal Hamilton Light Infantry must land. Much they knew; much more they imagined. Above all, they knew that they must seize the beaches at one bound, and press on to their tasks. So they waited like runners poised for the starter's pistol, ready to dash for the sea wall.

In the rear and on the eastern flank of the convoy six assault craft altered course eastward as they made the landfall of the Dieppe Gap. These were the assault craft of the Infantry Landing Ship *Duke of Wellington,* carrying the mortar detachment of the Black Watch for their appointment with death on the Blue Beach of Puits. The main body of ships held on its course, dead ahead. The moment of revelation was at hand.

Out of the northern sky the low hum of aircraft grew to a roar as Bostons and Blenheims swooped in upon the East headland pouring out a dense curtain of smoke, while Hurricane cannon fighters, fighter-bombers and Spitfires dived in a fierce blaze of guns and hurtling bombs to bring all that grey and quiet-seeming front to an instant uproar of smoke and flame, spurting red veins into the sky from the arcs of the answering tracer.

The time was exactly ten minutes past five o'clock.

The leading craft were then less than 1000 yards offshore, and as the aircraft swerved up and away from their brief

179

assault, the guns of the destroyers opened fire to set the whole promenade ablaze and fill the sky above the landing craft with the curious quiet shuffle of shells.

For five minutes that harsh and sibilant music filled the ears of 2000 men crouched ready and waiting for the ramps to go down, and for the rasp of stones that would send them rushing over that shingle bank to storm the wall.

The last half mile narrowed swiftly to 200 yards. Three red Very lights from the leading craft signalled the destroyers, and the barrage switched at once to the flanks, leaving more than a score of tall buildings burning behind the Boulevard de Verdun.

With 200 yards to go, the support landing craft began to lob their smoke bombs to veil all the fringe of the sea. The dawn was shattered now. The silence was ended. Through the smoke and into the guns, the assault craft reached that 1700 yard long curving arc of beach, and deployed upon it from end to end, from the wooden breakwater of the West Jetty in the East to the West headland.

Then the enemy guns roared out, suddenly, to drench all the sea approaches and the foreshore with a deluge of fire that tore the water to frayed shreds of wild spray.

Behind them and in front of them as they landed, the wild uproar of the guns enclosed the Canadians in a terrible cage of din and death from which somehow they had to break out.

The time was twenty-three minutes past five o'clock. They were three minutes late.

2

A terrific battle raged at once on the sea fringe as the Royal Hamiltons charged out of their landing craft to struggle for a foothold on that bleak desolation of stones fenced with its deep barriers of wire. In those first moments the flak and support landing craft joined with the gun boats, motor launches and destroyers, to pour fire into the enemy positions in an attempt to cover the infantry while the smoke held over the East headland. In that opening outburst of fire, the crews of the little ships threw caution to the winds to rise to heights of courage and audacity that were to sustain throughout the long-drawn-out hours of the morning. They were hopelessly outgunned, sitting ducks in the drifting veils of the smoke-screens from which they emerged like Davids to confront the monstrous Goliath of the defence with their puny weapons. From one point alone, near to the Casino, four 3.7 cm. and one 4.7 cm. anti-tank gun with a range of 9,000 yards fired point blank over open sights. A 10.5 cm. gun-howitzer added the weight of its fire from the same area, while from the West headland, Hindenburg, and from a hundred unidentifiable points a deluge of heavy, medium and light machine-gun fire weaving in with the light A/A batteries,* wrought dreadful havoc and confusion.

The tank landing craft, attempting to close the beaches with their ramps down and their doors open, and meeting the full force of the heavier weapons, were stricken, like wounded animals, to wallow in the shallow water, their ramp chains cut, their hulls riddled with the penetrating fire of armour-piercing and high-explosive shells. Yet with a terrible persistence they crawled in while men remained alive upon them.

Worse was yet to come as the smoke cleared, meanwhile the mortars and the machine-guns combined with the brilliant deadly sniping to make a death-trap of the beach as the Royal Hamiltons were caught in the open. Yet in face of that bombardment, spurred on by the courage they knew at their backs, the Royal Hamiltons began to cut and blast their ways through the heavy wire barriers. Many men in that assault were bewildered and confused by the sheer force of the reception, but swiftly those who lived began to fight, to answer with rifles and Brens the deluge that poured upon them.

Within ten minutes of the touchdown, the Beach Assault Groups, many of them trying to land from the crippled tank landing craft, died in scores. Of seventy-one men of one

* Many light A/A guns had dual-purpose roles.

group of sappers only nine survived, and of those, four were wounded. Out of a total strength of eleven officers and three hundred and fourteen other ranks of the Royal Canadian Engineers, nine officers and 180 men were killed or wounded at the moment of landing. Thus at the outset the power of the assault force to demolish their targets was gravely curtailed.

Very few coherent voices speak out of that landing. Private Prince of C Company of the Royal Hamiltons is one of them:

"When we landed, we were confused for some time but finally got down and began to return some of the fire. We encountered barbed wire and began cutting it. We found it could be crossed without cutting. I tried to go under the last two strands but got hung up. Corporal J. Hartnett was also hung up and was wounded. I think the German sniper is a real specialist. They are wonderful shots and go for the officers and N.C.O.s. We found that they are mostly planted on roofs or in very high buildings.

"The Germans seemed to be able to lay down mortar bombs where they damned well pleased. The beach was well covered by L.M.G.s from the buildings and by Heavy and Medium M.G.s from our flanks.

"After we got over the wire we got down behind the beach wall and were forced to stay there. Going up that wall four of our N.C.O.s were put out of action. Our Platoon Officer was also wounded then. Major C. G. Pirie crawled up and told us to stay put. He got the Colonel on the '18 set' and gave our position and the Colonel told him to stay there. Colonel Labatt was asking the Air Force to bomb the hotels further on. A tank appeared at this moment and after changing direction finally got on the beach. It got a couple of men who were too slow in moving. The tank was hit at this point, three times in the tracks and twice just below the turret, by some sort of A/Tk gun. The tank, after a few attempts, turned round and returned the fire. We stayed in this position until time for withdrawal when we organized parties to help wounded. I would like to mention an act of bravery I saw—the man concerned being Private G. McRichie. He is now missing. McRichie was himself quite safe from fire behind the wall we got to. He looked back and saw Corporal Hartnett who was hung on the wire. George (Private McRichie) got a pair of wire cutters and walked out into that heavy M.G. fire and cut the Corporal loose. He then began to roll him through the remainder of the wire and brought him back into the shelter of the wall."

Even in the first half hour before the smoke cleared from the formidable bulk of the eastern headland, Bismarck, it was plain that the attempt to seize the beaches in one bold stroke must fail. Without the Sappers, the sea wall could not be breached. Without the covering fire of the tanks in close support, the infantry were almost as helpless as men with bows and arrows. Yet after the first moments of confusion they rallied to fight back. With Bangalores and wire cutters they breached the wire while many men struggled over and under the barriers, firing into the yawning cavity of Dieppe as they crawled over the stones. There were very few gaps in that carefully laid pattern of direct and enfilade fire, but in the face of it the Royal Hamiltons reached the wall, and behind them came six tanks that had got ashore in the first wave, climbing, skidding and swerving over the steep shingle. Of these six, five clawed their ways over the wall, and the six climbed the broad steps of the Casino to reach the esplanade. Flying the yellow pennant of C Squadron, three moved off at full speed along the Boulevard Marechal Foch. Two more got into positions on the esplanade east of the Casino, and began at once to shell machine-gun posts and anti-tank guns on the West headland. The sixth tank was caught in a tank trap on the esplanade and its crew died fighting. Seven more tanks were stuck on the edge of the sea, four of them disabled, and three of them with cold engines trying to warm up while fighting their guns with great determination, but unable to withstand the battering that engulfed them.

Nevertheless the partial success of the six tanks in reaching the esplanade had given some cover to the right flank of the Royal Hamiltons, and small groups of determined men were quick to take advantage of the chance to move.

All this time the fighters and fighter-bombers of the R.A.F. dived incessantly upon the enemy. It was in vain. At six o'clock, as the smoke cleared from the East headland, the enemy played his trump card. At that same moment, the gunboat *Locust* was trying to probe the outer defences of the harbour to lead in the Chasseurs, and the second wave of tank landing craft were struggling to close the beach. These met the full force of the terrific armament hidden in the East headland caves. All available destroyers, and *Locust,* turned their guns upon the headland in an endeavour to quell this new fury. It was hopeless. Guns of heavy calibre, probably 88s and 75s, came forward to fire, and immediately withdrew out of sight, invulnerable to guns or the bombs of the R.A.F.*

The official record reads as follows:

> "This appalling enfilade fire made the capture of the beach impossible and all the rest of the plan fell to the ground."

By six o'clock two companies of the R.H.L.I. should have been joining with the South Saskatchewan Regiment in attacks against the light A/A batteries, the Goering battery, and in the assault against Quatre Vents Farm; while a third company should have joined with one company of the Essex Scottish to hold the Dieppe perimeter. But the R.H.L.I. were no longer a battalion measured in companies, platoons, and sections. Units were shattered out of recognition; most of the leaders were killed or wounded, cohesion was lost. The battalion had become

*Constant air reconnaissance and daring low-level photographic sorties had failed to reveal the secrets of the caves in the East headland. And they had not been imagined.

simply small groups of men ready to take and to accept leadership wherever they could find it. Some of these groups were prepared to do more than sell their lives dearly. A few there were hemmed in under the cover of the wall who could do little, but many more were resolved to harry the enemy wherever they could find him. If the battle could not be won, at least there were many ways in which it might be lost.

The Casino was the first objective. Two groups of men following Capt. Hill and Sgt. Hickson, D.C.M., went in to the attack. Lt. Bell led a third group into the town, while yet a fourth group under an unknown officer attempted to storm the West headland. This officer was seen to fall when halfway up the cliff, and there on the cliff all that group perished.

3

The mile-long beach of Dieppe sweeps away from the East headland and the harbour in a south-westerly direction, broadening like the blade of a scimitar. The Essex Scottish Regiment landed up near the "hilt" where the beach has a depth of approximately 180 yards at high tide. This did not confer any benefit upon them. Instead, they met a weight of fire no whit less than that which greeted the Royal Hamilton Light Infantry on the broad expanse of White Beach, and it was concentrated in a narrower and more devastating field. High velocity artillery fired from concealed positions in the fortified hotels and houses behind the Boulevard de Verdun. Mortars used as howitzers responded instantly to the directions of the Forward Observation Officers using field telephones from their covered positions behind the sea wall. The cross-fire of machine-guns firing from innumerable fortified positions was fully co-ordinated with the mortars, the A/A guns with dual-purpose roles, and the 4.7 cm. anti-tank guns in pill-boxes three to four feet thick, and embedded deeply in the ground.

Yet in the brief interval while the smoke-screen still

blinded the gunners in the East headland to their targets, the Essex Scottish landed and, supported most bravely from the sea, many reached the wall.

In attempting to give a true picture of this succession of events, I find myself imprisoned by their terrible similarity in a narrow framework of words. Men land from landing craft; the beaches are of stones varying from three to six inches in diameter; sea walls, cliffs and headlands enclose them. And within these confines, almost devoid of cover, men are enfiladed by merciless fire and slaughtered in droves. These things beat upon my mind like the strokes of a hammer, day after day. But there is no way out. I must pursue this repetition, seeking constantly to curb the use of words such as "heroism," "courage," "devastating," and "fury" that spring constantly to the end of my pen. Yet even the official record of these events is at times unable to avoid the purple phrase. These things happened. In their emphasis the tragedy may emerge the more starkly.

When they landed on Red Beach the Essex Scottish rushed the first of the wire barriers, flinging themselves down upon it, making bridges of their bodies that their fellows might cross. In that first deluge of fire, men knew instinctively that there was no time for wire cutting, and that only by sheer speed might the battalion hope to reach the wall. There was no shelter, save only the shallow folds of the shingle. While many charged the wire, others burrowed in the loose stones and began to return the enemy fire with rifles and Brens, thus to give some cover to those advancing. In their wake the mortar detachments and some of the machine-gunners of the Toronto Scottish with their guns on A/A mountings, strove to land and set up their weapons. One mortar detachment lived long enough to direct a score or more of bombs against enemy positions before the Forward Observation Officers under their cowlings directed shells upon them. The "average life" of static elements upon that beach was measured in a handful of seconds.

Meanwhile officers and N.C.O.s, the individual prey of snipers, led on towards the wall, many of them maintaining their impetus while suffering mortal wounds, ready only to die when the first objective might be gained. Among these, Lt. D. Green, with one foot blown off by mortar fire within a few seconds of landing, led his men a further hundred yards hobbling on the bleeding stump until a second mortar bomb killed him.

The courage with which Lt.-Colonel F. K. Jasperson led his men is amply testified, but he could not lead them beyond the wall. The role of his battalion had dwindled to this. And there, under that shallow and dangerous barrier, the Essex Scottish fought like animals snarling in a trap. Some of them did more. C.S.M. Stapleton, with twelve men hurling grenades into the grenade pits of the enemy, crossed the wall, the esplanade and gardens, to gain the houses. These few, moving fast in the rear of the hotels lining the Boulevard de Verdun, entered two houses in the town. Firing from the windows for more than an hour, they engaged enemy patrols, killing many, before, by a miracle of retreat, they rejoined their harassed comrades.

The East headland had long since emerged from the veils of smoke to withstand easily the repeated attacks of cannon Hurricanes and fighters and the bombardment of the destroyers. There was no help and little hope for the Essex Scottish. Under the wall, suffering constant casualties, they settled down to fight to the end.

From first to last a wireless operator of C Company maintained contact with Brigadier Southam, at first on White Beach, and later on in the Casino. The incessant crackle of fire in the headphones told as clearly as words of the conditions under which the Essex Scottish were holding out.

4

It had been planned to land four troops of tanks in the first wave; two troops to assist in subduing the armed trawlers in the harbour; two troops to help clear White Beach and silence light anti-aircraft guns, and then to help in the capture of the Goering battery and Quatre Vents

Farm. Three scout cars were to go with Tank Battalion Headquarters, and remain with 6th Infantry Brigade Headquarters. These headquarters with signallers and the beach signalling party were to be established at St. Remy Church in Dieppe and share with the 4th Infantry Brigade landing at Red Beach. With the tank landing craft were also the sappers to demolish the sea wall and let the tanks through.

The first flight of six tank landing craft of Group 8 were less than five minutes behind time when they began to close the beach. The East headland was still masked in smoke, while Dieppe itself was barely visible beyond the swirling chaos of smoke, a cauldron brewing with the appalling din of war, and festooned with the red ribbons of tracer in monstrous profusion.

Two hundred yards out, the tank landing craft met the full force of the anti-tank and light anti-aircraft guns sited and ranged especially to meet them as they emerged to close the beach. Even as the infantry on the beaches met the full force of mortars and machine-guns in the first moment of assault, so also these tank landing craft met the full force of the heavier weapons.

In the face of this great weight of fire, the lightly armed supporting vessels, disdaining the protection of smoke, closed in to point-blank range in their attempts to cover the tanks. On the tank landing craft the machine-gunners of the Toronto Scottish, in exposed positions, offered themselves as sacrifices, manning and fighting their guns until they died.

Shuddering to the frightful impact of fire, the landing craft crept on over that brief stretch of sea. It seemed that not one of them could hope to reach the shore, still less to loose their burdens upon the enemy. The ramp chains of two were cut, the ramps swinging and folding back under the hulls.

The Tank Landing Craft 145, hit in a dozen places, yet with her ramp intact, touched down successfully and landed three tanks. It was her last desperate effort. Hit again as she tried to draw away, she drifted broadside on to the beach and sank fifty yards out.

Next to her, the Tank Landing Craft 127 forced her way in with her ramp smashed, and with her engine-room, her ammunition and magazine all on fire, her crew almost all dead or wounded. But a rating still lived at her helm, and two gunners of the Toronto Scottish manned their guns as the tanks crawled out of the burning oven the vessel had become.

The third craft, with her ramp chains cut and her doors jammed, stuck helpless on the beach. A fourth got in on fire, unloaded her tanks, and sank in shallow water. A fifth landed her tanks and struggled out from the beach for sixty or seventy yards before she lost way, and wallowed helpless and sinking.

At the last came Tank Landing Craft 163 fighting a dogged battle with disaster. Early on she had been hit in the engine room and had caught fire. A moment afterwards the vessel veered sharply to port as the helmsman collapsed, overcome by fumes. At once a naval rating took the helm, and brought the vessel round, head on, before a direct hit killed him. A third rating took his place, and the distance narrowed in a kind of slow motion to seventy yards before this helmsman also died. A fourth rating then brought Tank Landing Craft 163 to the beach to land her tanks, and with the same rating at the helm of the burning vessel she pulled away from the beach, making a bold attempt to take the sinking craft in tow. In this she failed, but it seemed that the enemy had done his worst to her, and, miraculously, Tank Landing Craft 163 made her own way out to sea.

There were seventeen tanks on shore as a result of this brave endeavour, and six of them reached the esplanade. Of these, the three that had gone off at speed in a westerly direction along the Boulevard Marechal Foch flying the yellow pennant of C Squadron, little is known. A tank commanded by Lt. W. C. Patterson knocked down a house. Another was seen in the Rue Grande. At least two tanks finally made their way back to the beach with all their ammunition gone. No man lived to tell of their exploits.

There were many unlooked-for tank obstacles, especially on the Boulevard de Verdun, that had not been revealed by air photography. By day the enemy had removed all trace, and had hidden his anti-tank guns. These reappeared each night at dusk, and were removed at dawn. Road blocks protected all the entrances to the town and promenade. These were eight feet high and four feet thick, with sloping backs on which fire-steps had been built.

Of the tanks on the beach, two lost their tracks, one lost its turret, and a fourth had the turret badly damaged. An officer climbed out of this tank with one of his eyes shot out, and ran at once to a second tank following up behind. He climbed in, and a moment later this tank knocked out the gun that had wounded him.

But none of these, lurching and floundering, burrowing grooves in the loose shingle, and in the face of deadly fire, reached the wall. Nevertheless, they fought to the last, and gave some cover to the Royal Hamiltons in their fight for the Casino.

Meanwhile, throughout the landing, the large flak landing craft, commanded by Lt. E. L. Graham, R.N.V.R., was conspicuous, closing the beach to attack the enemy at point-blank range. One by one the guns were fought until they were put out of action and the gunners killed. When the Captain was killed, Surgeon-Lt. M. P. Martin, M.R.C.S., the only surviving officer, took command and fought the ship until she sank under him. By so doing, he afforded some protection to the four tank landing craft of the second flight. This medical officer was finally rescued, wounded, from the sea and put aboard *Calpe*. There, throughout the day, despite his own condition, he tended the wounded.

5

The smoke had cleared from the East headland as the four tank landing craft of the second flight came in, exactly on time, at five minutes past six o'clock. They carried with them not only tanks, but also Brigadier Lett and Staff Officers of the 4th Infantry Brigade, together with

Lt.-Colonel Parks-Smith, R.M., of Combined Operations Headquarters, in command of the Beach Provost Party, and Lt.-Colonel J. G. Andrews, commanding the 14th Canadian Army Tank Battalion of the Calgary Highlanders.

These officers were on board Tank Landing Craft 125, to which Lt.-Colonel Andrews had transferred offshore, coming in slightly astern and to starboard of Tank Landing Craft 214. These two craft met the full weight of the barrage unleashed at that moment out of the caves of the East headland. Nevertheless, No. 214, brought almost to a standstill by direct hits, closed the beach in a sinking condition to land her tanks under a tremendous concentration of fire.

This was the target the enemy had longed for and waited for, and a great number of guns were designed and ranged for this purpose. As soon as her cargo was landed, No. 214 crawled away almost along the sea bed, holed like a sieve, and to sink as soon as she was out of her depth.

The Tank Landing Craft 125 with her cargo of commanders and tanks had gained some slight cover in the lee of the stricken vessel. She managed to close the beach and get one tank away before she met the full force of the enemy fire, and then in one burst, with her crew killed or wounded, it seemed that she must be overwhelmed. The vessel was no longer head on to the beach, and those among the wounded who could still move got some way on her astern, trying then to square her up for a second attempt.

The stricken craft had become a vortex of fire, her crew out of action as she drifted again towards the beach. Brigadier Lett had suffered severe wounds, and Lt.-Colonel Parks-Smith lay mortally wounded and dying by his side. At this stage, Lt.-Colonel Andrews, seeing his hopes of getting ashore to take command of the tanks rapidly fading, decided to get away. The vessel was only a few yards offshore, her ramp down and damaged by shell fire that threatened to cut it loose at any moment. It must have seemed to Andrews that he was unlikely to gain another yard. His tank was already out on the damaged ramp, and with a sudden lurch, it left the ship and was drowned in eight feet of water. The tanks had been water-proofed to a depth of six feet.

Like men escaping from the hatch of a submarine just above water, the crew climbed out and swam for the beach. At the last, Lt.-Colonel Andrews climbed from the hatch, paused for a moment to look round, and was heard to shout: "I'm bailing out," before jumping into the sea.

A motor launch, swooping in with her guns blazing in an attempt to cover and rescue the survivors, picked up the Colonel and was immediately engulfed in flames from a seeming deluge of direct hits. It is probable that all on board were killed in that instant before the motor launch sank in the shallows.

Meanwhile, Tank Landing Craft 125 was still afloat, and those alive on board were fighting to save her and the wounded. A Sergeant of Royal Marines had at once cut the ramp cables after the loss of the second tank and the last of the crew. The Sergeant then took the helm. In the engine-room Major M. E. P. Garneaux, a Staff Officer of 4th Infantry Brigade, had reversed the engines, and immediately afterwards manned a pompom.

Slowly, crawling astern, the Royal Marine Sergeant at the helm spotted the engineer struggling to regain the vessel from the water. He had been blown overboard by blast, but was unhurt. Major Garneaux got him back on board, and he at once took charge of the engines. In such fashion the vessel gained the cover of the outer smoke-screens protecting the heart of the convoy, and was taken in tow by a motor launch to safety.

The remaining two landing craft had fought their way in to land their tanks, but with little success. The third vessel, covered to some extent from the full weight of fire from the East headland by the two vessels almost abeam on her port side, landed her tanks without a hitch. Within two minutes all three gained the wall, only to founder there, unable to grip the shingle and to climb to the esplanade.

On that desolation of shifting stones, swept by a fiendish pattern of gunfire no armoured vehicle could withstand, the tanks had the aspect of unwieldy wounded beasts, seeming to flounder almost blindly as they strove to bring their guns to bear upon the targets on the headlands.

Tank Landing Craft 165, the fourth in line, also reached the beach, but the fortune of her tanks was worse. The first tank stalled on the beach, and was an easy prey for enemy guns. The second tank fouled an airduct, and caught fire from a direct hit within a minute of landing. The third tank fouled the port side of the door, and was hit while still on the ramp.

This was a position of the utmost danger for the tank and the vessel, and then with a roar the engine started, and the tank lurched off violently into the sea, pushing the landing craft astern, and dragging a scout car after her through four feet of water. The driver of the scout car hung on, swaying wildly in his small vehicle in the wake of the tank as it roared over the shingle, and on up over the sea wall to the esplanade in one great bound. There, the scout car got free and moved off at full speed along the Boulevard Marechal Foch, while the tank fought like a beast at bay, pouring fire into the hotels and boarding houses that were now wreathed in smoke and flames.

This was the last tank to cross the wall. Of the twenty-four tank landing craft which had sailed, ten landed a total of twenty-eight tanks. Seven of these crossed the wall. One was drowned. Twenty were swiftly casualties. All were lost.

The remaining fourteen tank landing craft of the third and fourth waves, due to go in to land at intervals up to a final landing at ten o'clock, awaited offshore the order to land. It was never given.

All these craft were equipped with barrage balloons to defend them from air attack, in the event no balloons were flown. The R.A.F. controlled the air above all that battle-ground on land and sea, as yet unchallenged by enemy bombers. Had it been otherwise, the shambles of the beaches might well have been matched by the shambles of the sea.

Through all that day the pennant of Lt.-Colonel Andrews flew from the turret of his drowned tank, a forlorn symbol in an aching void of desolation as the tide receded to leave the tank high and dry on the smooth sands beyond the stones.

Soon after six o'clock the Military Force Commander had decided to commit his Floating Reserve to the support of Red Beach. The messages received at that hour from Brigadier Lett and Lt.-Colonel Andrews, stating that they were about to land, had seemed reassuring. The Military Force Commander could not know that these messages had preceded, by a few minutes the severe wounds of Brigadier Lett and the death of Lt.-Colonel Andrews.

Accordingly, the Fusiliers Mont-Royal, embarked in twenty-six large personnel landing craft, led by Lt.-Commander J. H. Dathan, R.N., set course for Red Beach under cover of smoke. Two of the landing craft were lost by gunfire on the way in, but the smoke-screens in the main masked the approach effectively up to the last moments. Unfortunately, they had also inevitably masked Dieppe itself from view.

At any time up to six o'clock that would not have mattered, but, meanwhile, the tide had taken a strong westerly set, and this was an unexpected and unobserved factor unknown to Lt.-Commander Dathan at the head of the column. Forced to navigate blind through the smoke, and without a chance of a landfall until it was too late, the landing craft missed Red Beach by more than one thousand yards with the left flank, and was off the beach entirely on the extreme right.

Out of the chaos and confusion of the landing, three men had towered above their fellows, and had rallied many to follow them. These three men were Capt. Vandeloe, Sergeant-Major Dumais and Sergeant Dubuc. They were men of rare quality, seeming larger than life even in the bald official record of their deeds. There were no orders now. No battalion. These three, assuming leadership of all who would follow, went in to fight in their various ways, determined to come to grips with the enemy, and to tear him out from behind his guns.

Capt. Vandeloe leading a score of men, and covered by Lt. Loranger's party from the folds of the shingle, stormed up and over the sea wall. Some little way to his right Sergeant-Major Dumais led a smaller group into the attack against the Casino to join with the Royal Hamiltons and Sappers resolved on the same purpose.

Meanwhile, Sergeant Dubuc had landed with his men at a point opposite the western end of the Casino. He had taken in something of the plight of half the battalion under the West headland, yet with no means of knowing that they were trapped. Dubuc's first aim was to liquidate as many enemy guns as possible covering what might be the exit from under the headland. It was the kind of situation for which such men seem to have been born, and which others recognize instinctively in a crisis. With an utter disregard of danger, careless even of whether or not others were with him, Dubuc rushed upon two pill-boxes threatening his immediate front, and overwhelmed them almost, it seemed, with his bare hands.

Sergeant Dubuc now looked for new fields to conquer. At that moment the pennant of Lt.-Colonel Andrews, flying from the drowned tank, caught his attention.

The tank had been left high and dry on the sand by the fast ebbing tide, and Dubuc realized from its position that it must have fallen off the ramp of its landing craft, and that its guns and ammunition might be intact. Without hesitation, beckoning one man to his side, Dubuc bounded off over the stones and the widening fringe of hard sand beyond, running like a stag with his mate at his heels. Together they gained the tank, and from that small isolated fortress on the edge of the sea, Dubuc turned his guns upon the West headland, fighting under the pennant of the Calgary Highlanders until his ammunition was exhausted, and at least six machine-gun posts and anti-tank guns had ceased to fire.

Meanwhile, in the shallows a tragedy was played out to avert a tragedy. In that dreadful moment of revelation, as the assault craft came out of the cover of smoke, it had been as if a curtain had lifted suddenly upon inferno. Upon the instant Lt.-Colonel J. P. Phillipps, the Commanding Officer, recognized the utter hopelessness of the situation. For himself, and all those with him in the first few vessels, there could be but the merest chance of survival. But for those behind, there might be hope. Without a moment's hesitation, and before any man realized his purpose, the Colonel pulled on his white gloves and leapt to the small forward deck to stand upright in face of the enemy. Easily recognizable by his white gloves, he was too prominent to be missed either by the enemy or by his men. He had resolved to halt the landing, if it were possible, and save all those who followed. He had but a few seconds to live, and in those seconds with his white-gloved hands above his head, a proud and most noble figure, he signalled, and clearly made his purpose known, to the landing craft to put about and head back into the shelter of the smoke.

For perhaps ten seconds his body remained upright before he fell mortally wounded to the deck, yet knowing with his last breath, as his men lifted his body, that he had probably saved two hundred men from the murderous fire that must have added their numbers to the final count.

Six landing craft managed at once to turn about on the fringe of the smoke at the Colonel's signal, but the seventh, under Capt. R. R. Devereaux, R.M., remained behind in an attempt to save a few who still lived from one of the sinking vessels. Only then did he turn about to gain the smoke cover with his own assault craft in a sinking condition. The effort would have been in vain had not the Chausseur 43, standing by in close support, gone at once to the rescue to take all on board.

The task of rescue was, indeed, all that now remained to be done. On the Red and White Beaches, in Dieppe itself, in Pourville, and in the woods behind Green Beach, perhaps three thousand men still lived and fought. Even behind Blue Beach some might still survive.

Everywhere, the enemy reinforcements were closing in, and large forces were on the move. The battle could not be won, but all was not yet lost. In the air the R.A.F. remained supreme, still challenging the enemy to fight, and the Navy still ruled the narrow sea.

It was nine o'clock; six hours since the infantry landing ships had put the assault craft into the water.

It is known that at least six small groups of men made

effective raids through the town. There may have been more. At least two tanks fought on in the heart of Dieppe until their ammunition was exhausted, and of their fate nothing is known. But outstanding in the roll of these few are the exploits of Sergeant Dubuc of the Fusiliers Mont-Royal.

For an hour Dubuc and his one companion had fought the stranded tank of Lt.-Colonel Andrews from its exposed position on the sand. As soon as the last shell had been fired, Dubuc decided to make a dash for the sea wall. Two men might easily live where fifty would almost surely die. With his companion, he reached a point under the sea wall close to the invisible boundary between Red and White Beaches. In that area the wounded Lt.-Colonel Ménard strove to hold together a nucleus of his regiment and to organize as much aggressive defensive fire as possible. He was still unaware of the fate of nearly half of his men. They had seemed to disappear, and no contact had been made. In Dubuc's mind was a very strong awareness of his Colonel's plight, and a burning desire to do something to redeem, in however small a fashion, the débâcle of the landing. He was fully aware, too, that his regiment had been sent to the relief of Red Beach.

It is impossible to measure such men as Dubuc by normal standards. It does not seem to have entered his head to sit down under the wall in a defensive role, and at once eleven men of the Fusiliers Mont-Royal rallied to his side. Well armed with tommy-guns, Brens and grenades, they followed their leader in swift bounds to cross the esplanade.

By this time, a murky acrid pall of battle overlay the whole scene, the incessant gunfire, the smoke and flames of burning buildings, the smoke-screens laid continuously at sea and wafted inshore by the freshening wind from the West, all combined to make a twilit world of the broad boulevards and the gardens of the sea front.

The crossing of these wide open spaces presented no problem to Dubuc. Gaining the backyards of the hotels and boarding houses, he pressed on with his men into the town, clearing the streets with bursts of Bren-gun fire, and reaching the Rue de Sygogne almost without incident. There, Dubuc's party came up with Captain Vandeloe of their own regiment, marauding with a body of twenty men in high fettle, having found themselves more than a match for all the enemy they had encountered.

Captain Vandeloe had attacked in the rear the hotels and boarding houses with their fronts on the Boulevard de Verdun. Most of these buildings had been fortified as strong-points, and had added greatly to the direct fire-power of the enemy in the early stages. This much, at least, the withdrawal would be spared, for Vandeloe's party had winkled out the enemy with great effect. They had also brought down most of the snipers from these roof-tops, and those few who remained were no longer able to concentrate with any sense of detachment upon their deadly work.

These successes had inspired Vandeloe, and he proposed to carry on clearing enemy out of houses and key points until it was time to go.

The meeting of these two, the Captain and the Sergeant, seems to have been brief and buoyant, and mutually inspiring.

Dubuc turned East. There lay the tasks he would find for himself, for it was not only in his mind to inflict as much damage upon the enemy as possible, but also to do this in the area to which his regiment had been committed. As for his men, they were eager to follow wherever he might lead. His personal magnetism was astounding, in keeping with the kind of character beloved of a Dumas or a Sabatini, and but seldom encountered outside the pages of romantic fiction. Dubuc led on swiftly towards the docks.

Approaching the dock area, the small party were at once held up by machine-gun posts covering intersections and entrances, but not for long. Moving with great speed and determination round the flanks, and skilfully using covering fire, Dubuc succeeded in destroying the machine-gun posts with grenades used with great daring, and forced a way through to the edge of the *Bassin Duquesne*. Here they were still under intermittent machine-gun fire and sniping, and confronted by a seeming emptiness, bleak and desolate.

It was as though they had burst through an outer wall from a world of din and known danger, to an unnatural silence, and a sense of being watched. There were few shots, but those few held a note of peculiar personal menace in the thin whine of their coming.

It would have been simple to have turned back, as men do confronted with a cul-de-sac, and for a moment Dubuc halted on this eerie edge of the dockland, waving his men to crouch in the shelter and shadow while he got his bearings. The *Bassin Duquesne* was empty. Skirting the *Bassin,* moving swiftly in sharp bounds, setting the tempo to those who followed, Dubuc pressed on. There was something indomitable about him, and even at this time an aura of seeming safety.

So they came quickly through to reach the *Bassin du Canada,* and to find there two of the invasion barges that had been earmarked as the prey of the Navy. These were the prizes Dubuc sought. His party was still under intermittent fire, and it was vital to act swiftly before this fire gave warning to the barge crews. A sense of exhilaration seems to have uplifted these few men at this moment: it may have been that their French blood gave them a sense of "belonging," of being native against the alien Nazi. They followed Dubuc as stealthily as cats, to swoop silently and suddenly upon the barges, and to overwhelm the crews in brief and fierce hand to hand fighting. In five minutes Dubuc had won the barges, and it would not have been beyond his imagination to have attempted to sail them out to sea. That task would have been impossible.

Leaving the barges with their dead, Dubuc then turned South on the railway tracks with the idea that his party might in some way hold up enemy reinforcements. This was unwise. Well armed, keeping the initiative, it was credible and even probable that Dubuc and his men might have overwhelmed three times their numbers, but they were now out of grenades, and their ammunition was almost used up.

For about 1000 yards, divided into two groups, one on either side of the tracks, taking what cover they could find, Dubuc and his men moved forward apparently unseen. It was, by that time, nearing half past ten o'clock.

Little time remained, and strong enemy patrols were already moving in Dieppe in the vanguard of reinforcements.

It was in Dubuc's mind to give up this barren course, and move off into the town, when he came suddenly under heavy fire from an enemy patrol. It was impossible to get away. The small party with one mind stood their ground, and fought to the last round. In five minutes it was all over, and Dubuc surrendered. That in itself was a delicate operation, for it is sometimes easier to be killed than to be captured in such circumstances.

At that moment Dubuc appeared to be overcome with exhaustion, and utterly disconsolate. The stuffing seemed to have been knocked right out of him, but the Germans were not disposed to take any chances. Not content with disarming their captives they took the unusual precaution of forcing them to strip down to their underclothes, but they left them their boots. In that sorry state the prisoners were lined up with their faces to a wall near a siding, and left under guard. At a command from the guard they kept their arms above their heads. They were helpless, and to most men, however brave, it must have seemed that the game was up. But Dubuc was acutely alert, his ears tuned to the diminishing beat of boots as the patrol moved on, and sensitive to new sounds.

There could be but a few minutes in which to act— if it were possible to act at all. Dubuc's head had slumped down to his shoulder. He stood in an attitude of dejection, and from that position he was able to watch the guard. The man stood with his rifle at the ready, alert, half turned to keep his prisoners in view while also watching the lines of approach. In postures of weariness and despair, his prisoners appeared to need the support of the wall. Dubuc himself was breathing heavily.

Two or three minutes went by in a silence broken only by the harsh small sounds of men in distress, and the pattern of gunfire that seemed almost to come from another world.

Dubuc had carefully revolved in his mind the chances of a break. He braced himself for action, determined somehow to lure the sentry within reach of his hands. Dubuc, of course, was completely unarmed, standing there, rather ridiculous at first glance, in his Summer singlet and shorts, and with his heavy ammunition boots. He made a sound like a dry groan to gain the attention of the sentry. His hands above his head lay against the wall, as though but for that he must have fallen.

"Water!" he croaked. "Water!"

The guard took two steps towards him, and for an instant was off guard. In that instant Dubuc turned with the speed of a panther and smashed the man down with his bare hands, and killed him.

"Go!" he ordered. His voice was very quiet and gentle. "Back to the beach. Each man for himself."

Within a minute the twelve men had gone without trace, each man taking his way, alone, through the back streets of Dieppe, heading for the beach. If they were seen by the enemy, it may be that the strange sight of men running at full speed through the streets in singlets and shorts was strange enough to make reaction slow. In their various ways they reached the beach.

It was almost exactly eleven o'clock when Dubuc found his wounded Colonel, and reported, excusing himself for his unmilitary appearance. It was a moment of decision. The squadrons of the R.A.F. were swooping down exactly on time over the East headland laying the curtain of smoke that must be a shield to all these men in their hopes of escape. And out of that massive pall, the enemy guns had begun to blaze fiercely at the invisible targets, too numerous and too confined to be missed. In an instant the whole foreshore became an inferno of smoke and sound and fury, and of men moving down over the stones.

Out of the sea smoke Dubuc could see the assault craft coming in through the shallows. It was no short passage now over a steep shingle bank, but a long and perilous journey. Without a word Sergeant Dubuc stooped to lift his wounded Colonel in his arms, and strode out towards the sea.

Casting the Net

Two huge Arctic convoys with supplies for the Russians were scheduled to be sent on the Murmansk run in November and December, 1943; they would be escorted by strong units of the British Navy. Since the previous May, when it was necessary to draw off Allied naval strength for the operations in the Mediterranean, none had been sent by the Northern route. Now the pressure was building up from the Russians to renew the convoys to Murmansk.

The Germans, who had suffered defeats on the Russian front, were determined to prevent the convoys from making their delivery; they knew from past experience that the arms and supplies delivered by the Allies to the Russians immediately stiffened their resistance to German attacks.

The terrible toll of convoys by the German U-boats had been effectively reduced in 1943 but any British convoy traveling north still must be on constant guard against enemy submarines, as well as the danger of a hit-and-run raid from the German 1st Battle Group which lay at anchor in the Alta Fjord of northern Norway. This group was comprised of the battle cruiser *Scharnhorst* and five destroyers. The real killer in the Group was the *Scharnhorst*; if she could once get into a merchant ship convoy, with her nine 11-inch guns, her secondary complement of twelve 5.9 inch guns and fourteen 4.1's, she could do great damage. She was also able to outrun any heavy British naval ship because of her speed.

The first convoy in November got through safely. But the December convoy was spotted by German air reconnaissance. Quickly, the German Naval High Command issued orders for 1st Battle Group to sail on Christmas Day and make contact as soon as possible. The weather conditions could hardly have been worse—for all ships at sea in northern waters. "A southwesterly gale was blowing in the operational area. A heavy sea had come up while dense snow squalls seriously reduced visibility. The term 'heavy sea' as used by seamen meant waves up to thirty feet high. They rolled up in long roaring swells, dark, foam-flecked, white crested. The gale tore sheets of spray from the crests and shot them flat across the water. The eddying snow was thicker and heavier than the men had ever known it before, either in the North Sea or the North Atlantic, and it was cold as the icy breath of the Pole itself.

"The Arctic convoys sailed round the most northerly end of Norway to Murmansk. The farther north they kept, the safer they were from attack, but their voyage took proportionately longer and this was at a time when hours could be decisive. Furthermore, the sea to the north became increasingly rougher. The wind which blew in directly from the Pole churned up mountainous seas, while visibility was obliterated in furious flurries of snow. The dark sky precluded light and it was, literally, impossible to see one's own hand. Only occasionally would the green-yellow or red-violet Northern Lights cast an unsteady, erratic gleam. At noon the day would turn a pale grey for about two hours, although the sun never rose above the horizon. The cold was almost unbearable. Watchkeepers on warships and freighters shivered in spite of sheepskin clothing and many layers of woollens. Depth charges froze fast to the decks, gun-sights and breeches became encrusted with ice, and the lubricants on the munition-hoists froze hard. A warship which failed to take special precautions to safeguard the lives of her crew and keep her armament free of ice, could not hope to survive an action in these waters." *

The British convoy escort was made up of fourteen destroyers and three cruisers. To the southwest of the convoy was the battleship *Duke of York*, the cruiser *Jamaica* and four destroyers; this unit was attached almost solely for the purpose of doing battle with the *Scharnhorst* should she sally out after the convoy.

*From *Holocaust at Sea,* pp. 48-49 and 72-73.

SINKING OF THE SCHARNHORST*

by Fritz-Otto Busch

During the night of December 25–26 the *Scharnhorst* proceeded on her sortie with the five escorting destroyers. Set on a northerly course, blacked-out, with war-watches closed up at action stations, the battleship rolled on before the south-westerly gale. Slowly the Radar beams scanned the darkness, while look-outs on the bridges, control positions, searchlights, and guns scrutinized their allotted sectors.

Sailing before the wind with the gently swaying motion and rhythmical pitching characteristic of the long ship, the *Scharnhorst* was spared the worst effects of the gale blowing from astern. But snow squalls impeded visibility, the sky was as dark as the sea, and the escorting destroyers were hardly discernible. From time to time a breaker reared up before the battleship, stood for seconds in a column of pale foam, then collapsed over the bows, and ebbed away before the breakwater in gurgling eddies. Smaller breakers, churned up to left and right by the great curving bows, disintegrated in white pennants. The night was icy cold. Cold, too, were the lashes of salty spray which flung themselves across the armour of the forward triple turrets and whipped up to the bridge.

Little was to be heard above the roar of the sea and the intermittent howling of the gale. Here, a water-tight door would bang; there, the clatter of heavy boots on wooden gratings could be heard as one of the watches on the bridge stamped to keep his feet warm. The soft regular hum of the electrical generating plant spread its soothing sound

*Condensed from several chapters of *Holocaust at Sea*.

through the stillness of the control positions and turrets. Otherwise there was silence. Every man was tense with expectancy. Any moment the alarm might sound and the ship that was gliding so smoothly ahead would be suddenly transformed, as if ignited, into a volcano belching fire.

During the whole of December 26, Acting Chief Petty Officer Willi Gödde stood at his port forward searchlight-control column on look-out duty. These installations, known to the ratings, not quite correctly, as "director columns," were fitted on either side of the bridge, some-what abaft the armoured fire-control position, and were used for look-out duty because of their outstanding optical performance. P.O. Gödde, a quiet, serious type of man with religious leanings, could not be relieved all day because the Petty Officer who usually took over from him, a trainer in "B" turret, was away on leave.

Gödde was wearing his telephone apparatus slung round his neck and so was in constant communication with the ship's command. He was able to listen to everything that was discussed at the control position and follow the entire sequence of events.

Suddenly, at 0920 hours, huge columns of water, nine feet in diameter, spurted up out of the darkness about 500 yards abeam of the control column. Phantom-like in their pale unreality, they were clearly visible through the drifting snow.

"Shell splashes," darted through the P.O.'s mind "Eight-inch shells at least." He turned the speaking-switch of his telephone . . .

And then everything happened at once.

The forward Radar reported the enemy. Alarm bells rang. Gödde heard a confusion of voices; directors on all stations picking up the target; orders, commands. Then the barrels of the after "C" turret began to thunder.

An action had started, but not against the convoy and its cargo ships; warships had opened fire on the *Scharnhorst*.

A far-off angry rumbling snarled across the sea and the night was lit with flashes of fire. On the port quarter, on a bearing of 245°, orange-red flames burst out of the darkness. Gödde could see quite clearly the snowflakes dancing in the fiery light, and shortly after the German guns had fired their second salvo, he heard the answering roar of the enemy's guns. Then he was momentarily dazzled by the long sheets of flame which burst from the *Scharnhorst's* own armament, while the ship was wrapped in a cloud of warm acrid fumes. Gödde pressed his eyes hard against the rubber-cushioned lenses of his apparatus, but in vain; he could see no more than the enemy's gunflashes; of the ship that was firing he could see nothing. Perhaps there were two ships, perhaps three—he could not tell. But one thing was certain: the ship that was hidden there, sending over salvo after salvo, must be a heavy cruiser with 8-inch armament.

Starshell was also being fired, obviously from another ship, to allow the heavy cruiser to observe the fall of shot around her target, the *Scharnhorst*.

The action lasted fifteen minutes, that is until 0940 hours. It was impossible to say whether any hits had been scored on the enemy. Shortly after opening fire, the *Scharnhorst* altered course to 150°, almost a complete turn round, and increased her speed to 30 knots. Her task was to annihilate the convoy. To engage in battle with enemy cruisers that were certainly armed with torpedoes, in the pitch darkness—dawn would not begin to break until 11 a.m.—was certainly no part of her duty. The German Commander-in-Chief could now assume that the cruisers were standing to the southward of the convoy, and that he would certainly have come upon the convoy itself had not the cruisers fallen upon the *Scharnhorst* like angry watch-dogs. The convoy could not be far off now; it must be steaming somewhere to the north of the cruiser line, and as the speed of the *Scharnhorst* was thought to be superior to that of her opponents, she could easily disengage, try to work round the cruisers and attack the convoy from a different direction.

The *Scharnhorst* did not, however, emerge from this

encounter unscathed. A report reached the forward fire-control position from the port III 5.9 gun:

"Hit between port III gun and torpedo-tubes. Shell has not exploded."

Ordinary Seaman First Class Sträter serving in the IV 5.9 turret heard later that this shell had penetrated the upper deck, and come to rest in compartment IX, the office of the technical P.O.s in the forward crew space of the 4th Division. The gun crew had only just been apprised of this when the Signals-Transmitter turned the talking-switch of his telephone and raised his hand:

"Attention! The foretop Radar is out of action. A direct hit in the foretop. Casualties among the A.A. crew."

As a result of the same hit, splinters were falling, fortunately, without causing further damage, on to the small open platform where P.O. Gödde stood at his control column. Through his earphones he, too, heard the reports of the two hits. He learned also that fire had broken out on the lower deck when the unexploded shell had come through, but that it was quickly got under control.

While the *Scharnhorst* was disengaging, the Captain ordered a smoke screen, and as the ship sped away at 30 knots great clouds of dense white smoke formed a solid wall behind her. Then the loudspeaker was heard again:

"Lull in action. We are trying, once more, to get at the convoy, the destroyers from the south, we in the *Scharnhorst* from the north."

The sequence of events during the first encounter between the *Scharnhorst* and the cruisers of Force 1 were, from the British point of view, as follows:

At 0840 hours the Radar in the *Belfast*, Admiral Burnett's flagship, picked up the *Scharnhorst* at a range of 35,000 yards. At this time Force 1 (10th Cruiser Squadron) was heading for the convoy which was still 48 miles distant to the north. The *Scharnhorst* was at this time 36 miles away from the convoy. From 0900 to 0930 hours the British Radar recorded a second echo. It was assumed that this was either one of the merchant ships in the convoy or possibly an enemy destroyer seeking to approach the convoy. As the cruisers intended to attack the *Scharnhorst*, the echo was ignored as being of only secondary importance. Vice-Admiral Burnett, therefore, kept course in the direction of the German battleship. At 0924 hours the *Belfast* opened fire with starshell, and five minutes later Force 1 was ordered to engage with main armament. The *Norfolk,* the only cruiser with 8-inch guns, opened fire with her four twin-turrets at a range of 9800 yards. She continued firing until 0940 hours. Upon firing the second and third salvoes, the British observed that the *Scharnhorst* had been hit. The *Belfast* and *Scheffield* did not participate in the direct firing.

When the *Scharnhorst* retreated and the range opened, the *Norfolk* ceased firing and the squadron pursued the German battleship to the southward. When, at 0955, the *Scharnhorst* turned on to a northeasterly course, the Admiral appreciated at once that she was trying to work round to the northward of the convoy and attack again. As the *Scharnhorst's* speed was estimated at 30 knots and Force 1 could steam at a maximum speed of only 24 knots in the prevailing gale and sea, Admiral Burnett decided to take a short cut and interpose his force between the convoy and the *Scharnhorst.* He knew that the cruisers' Radar could sight and report the enemy in good time. He had the cruisers alter course accordingly so that at 1020 hours contact with the *Scharnhorst* was lost. The last Radar echo was obtained from the *Scharnhorst* at 36,000 yards when she was steering to the north-east.

The *Scharnhorst,* concealed by her smoke-screen, had disappeared on a southerly course. As contact with the British cruisers appeared to have been broken, Rear-Admiral Bey gradually altered course to the northward. His plan of action had been well considered. The battleship's superior speed should allow her to turn the enemy's flank and take him completely by surprise. The one thing which the Commander-in-Chief and his Staff had not reckoned with was the great range and—as was later explicitly acknowledged by the British Commander-in-Chief in his despatch—the outstanding performance of the British "Rotterdam apparatus."*

The black Arctic night at last yielded to a faint grey dawn. Gale, sea and snow squalls increased. The *Scharnhorst* men remained closed up to action stations, the Commander-in-Chief was on the bridge. With the collar of his heavy sheepskin coat turned up and the big Zeiss nightglasses hanging on their leather slings round his neck, Rear-Admiral Bey gazed into the dancing snow flurries. Next to him stood the Captain, hands encased in fur-lined gloves and thrust deep into his pockets. Korvettenkapitän Bredenbreuker, the Gunnery Commander, in company with his Chief Signals-Transmitter, stepped from his control position on to the bridge. In such thick weather more could be seen from outside than through the lenses of the directors and gunsights. The Gunnery Signals-Transmitter, an able seaman of long service, leaned nonchalantly against the armoured walls of the control position. He had put on his head-phones and the telephone cable coiled like a thin black snake at his feet. With the sea on her quarter, the ship rolled with a smooth and gentle rhythm. Shortly after 1100 hours, the Navigating Officer appeared on the bridge with a wireless message. It was now sufficiently light for him, immediately, to recognize the Captain's broad-shouldered figure and he made his way straight to him:

"Report from a reconnaissance aircraft, Sir."

Captain Hintze freed his right hand from his pocket and took the wireless message.

"Splendid. It's remarkable how these chaps manage to keep it up in this foul weather!"

He read the text, frowned and turned to the Commander-in-Chief:

"Not too pleasant, Herr Admiral. But it need not worry us for the time being."

The Admiral took the message form. The report was disquieting. Five units had been sighted far to the north-westward of North Cape, approximately 150 miles to the

*Radar.

westward of the *Scharnhorst*. The Commander-in-Chief looked at the Captain with half-closed eyes:

"We'd better make sure exactly where it is. Come along."

They went down to the chart-house together. The Navigating Officer, Korvettenkapitän Lanz, had already plotted the position on the chart. He indicated it with his pencil:

"Here, Herr Admiral."

Rear-Admiral Bey considered for a while:

"In my opinion," he said, "it can only be an enemy Battle Group. One or more heavy units with the usual screen. Or just one heavy unit."

The Admiral took a packet of cigarettes from his coat pocket and offered it to the Captain, while Chief-Quartermaster Jürgens—who had been keeping respectfully in the background—stepped forward to offer them a light. Inhaling deeply, the Admiral thanked him and offered the tall, fair Friesian a cigarette. Then, in company with the Captain, he left the chart-house and returned aloft. Back on the bridge, he said:

"The look-out, Hintze, must be first-class. Everything depends on it. Do impress that again on the Gunnery Commander."

In the *Scharnhorst,* between 1100 and 1130 hours, P.O. Gödde, at the port forward searchlight control column, heard the voice of his Captain. Captain Hintze did not, on this occasion, use the loudspeaker system, but spoke, instead, on the artillery telephone:

"From the Captain to all stations: Situation Report. This morning as expected, we ran into the forces covering the convoy—three cruisers of the 'town class' type. We have altered course and are now trying to get at the convoy from the other side, that is from the north. We have shaken off the cruisers. An important reconnaissance report has just come in from the Luftwaffe. A British heavy battle group has been sighted 150 miles to the westward; I repeat 150 miles to the westward. That is to say, well out of our way. We are forging on towards the convoy. End of announcement!"

Gödde nodded. He was satisfied. It was very satisfactory,

he thought, how the Captain always took the men into his confidence, and kept them informed of the situation. He knew from comrades serving in other ships that this was not always the case.

About two hours after the first engagement of that day, Gödde heard contact with the enemy again reported by the after Radar. Soon the alarm bells were sounding their shrill warning through all decks.

Gödde applied himself to his apparatus with redoubled concentration; carefully he scanned the way ahead.

At 1221 hours Gödde thought he saw a patch of darkness against the midday twilight on the port and starboard bows. Soon afterwards, this became definite shadows. Turning the wheel of his director apparatus with his right hand, he felt for the talking-switch with his left and pushed it over:

"Port and starboard ahead three shadows!"

At the same time Gödde was able to hear how similar reports were coming in at the control position from other stations. As the initial orders went out to the heavy guns, and the directors in the control tower picked up the target, flashes of fire came from the distant shadowy forms, the silhouettes of which were gradually sharpening against the twilight. Once, twice, three times gun flashes broke from the dark shadows that were the enemy ships. Dull explosions above his own ship, and the sudden appearance of a yellow glare around him, caused Gödde to take his eyes off the targets and look upwards. Three or four dazzling yellow-white suns hovered phantom-like above the *Scharnhorst*, their falling rays starkly illuminating her superstructure and decks. The outlines of the triple turrets and barrels, the bridges and tower roofs rose sharply delineated out of the whirling snow.

"Starshell!" The thought was mechanical, objective. Gödde again glued his eyes to the sights of his apparatus. Great splashes raised steep plumes from the sea close to the ship, and at the same moment, the two forward 11-inch triple turrets of the *Scharnhorst* opened fire against the enemy ship lying to starboard. The second encounter of December 26 had begun.

Standing in the open on the bridge, Rear Admiral Bey observed the enemy's fire, while the Captain and Gunnery Commander rushed to their stations in the control position immediately the sighting of British forces was reported. The Admiral then stepped to the port armoured bulkhead of the control position which was still open and shouted his order to the Captain:

"Turn to port; we must get out of this!"

"*Jawohl*, Herr Admiral! Hard a-port! All engines full speed ahead! New course: 135°. To Gunnery Commander: Ship is turning hard a-port."

Quickly increasing her speed, the *Scharnhorst* hauled round on to her easterly course, heeling over heavily to starboard while the fire-control directors of the main and secondary armament held steadily on to their target. In the turrets, the gunners followed the pointers to offset the ship's turning. Now, the after "C" turret on the quarter-deck could also pick up the target and add the golden-red flames of its triple barrels to the second and third salvoes. Kapitänleutnant Wieting, the Second Gunnery Officer, added the fire of the two forward 5.9-inch twin turrets for as long as they could still reach the target.

P.O. Gödde observed that after the first three or four salvoes from the *Scharnhorst* fire broke out in one of the three British cruisers—the outlines of which were now clearly visible—roughly abreast of her after funnel. Another cruiser was evidently also well ablaze at bows and stern and was giving off a great deal of smoke. Between two salvoes Korvettenkapitän Bredenbreuker announced:

"To all stations: Heavy explosions with the enemy."

Then the heavy guns fired their next salvo. Ahead and astern of the British cruisers the splashes of the 11-inch shells rose mast-high from the sea, stood erect for several seconds, like giant fountains, and then broke. Broad circles of foam formed in their place and swung up and down with the rhythm of the waves. Gödde noted to his satisfaction that the salvoes which the Gunnery Commander was ordering in quick succession were straddling the enemy almost in every instance. The *Scharnhorst* kept turning round on to her easterly course and the British cruisers were dropping more and more astern and to port. Once more Gödde, who was keeping his sights trained on the enemy, observed what he thought was a hit in the bows of one of the cruisers. A giant sheet of flame shot from her fore-deck but soon subsided in a cloud of black smoke. It appeared that the enemy's fire, which at first had been well placed, began to falter under the quick-firing salvoes of the *Scharnhorst's* main armament, though the range was much closer than during the first encounter in the morning. After about twenty minutes the enemy was, in the driving snow and rain, completely out of sight.

At 1241 hours the British checked their fire. A quarter of an hour later, at 1300 hours, the Captain transmitted an order to the Gunnery Commander which was thereupon repeated by all Signals Transmitters:

"Lull in action!"

In this action, the second encounter with Force 1 (10th Cruiser Squadron, Admiral Burnett), the *Scharnhorst* was not hit.

Everywhere, the gun crews set to work. The brass cartridges of the used ammunition were salvaged or thrown overboard where they had not already been washed away by the heavy seas. The heavy turrets, from which the cordite gases could not always be drawn off quickly enough, were briefly turned into the wind for ventilation. Munition hoists rattled; munition racks were replenished, and the ordnance personnel checked consumption in turrets and batteries. Minor damage was quickly repaired by the artificers. Soon the all-clear reports were reaching the Gunnery Commander.

Meanwhile, the Commander-in-Chief was discussing the situation with his staff, the Captain, and the Navigating Officer, in the charthouse.

"Damn it," grunted the Admiral, "we're not getting at the convoy at all. The cruisers are always just where we want to strike. They were the same ones as this morning, weren't they, Hintze?"

The Captain pulled the leather cover over the lenses of his big double glasses and remained thoughtful for a moment before replying:

"I'm inclined to agree, Herr Admiral. The AO (Artillery Officer, i.e. Gunnery Commander) thinks so, too. It was impossible to see the cruisers this morning, but the shell splashes, which I observed myself, were of the same calibre. The AO thinks they were 8-inch and 5.9-inch shells."

"Apparently we're still being shadowed," continued the Rear-Admiral, "according to the after Radar reports at any rate. There's nothing actually to be seen. Let's hope we shake her off in due course. I can see no point in making a third attempt to get at the convoy."

He paused and everyone was silent.

The Admiral went up to the chart table, checked once more the distance to the north Norwegian coast, glanced at the course and speed indicators and looked at the Captain:

"Return to Norway, Hintze. Alta Fjord."

A few minutes later, the *Scharnhorst* slewed round on to her new course. She now had the gale and the sea ahead and to starboard as, her bows washed by the heavy breakers, she pitched southward. The short twilight was already over. Darkness had settled around the ship. She was no longer closed up at action stations, but intensified look-out had been ordered.

It seems probable that Rear-Admiral Bey—possibly concerned by the report that five enemy units had been sighted—chose to make for the Norwegian coast after his second attempt to strike at the convoy had failed, so as not to be cut off by the British Force. From the measures taken by the Commander-in-Chief and from the Captain's words to the crew—as recalled by survivors—one may conclude with reasonable certainty that in the *Scharnhorst* they thought that one of the five units reported was a heavy unit, and the Grand Admiral's explicit instructions were that the *Scharnhorst* was on no account to enter into an engagement with a heavy unit.

At 1345 hours, that is to say, after the conclusion of the second encounter with Force 1, the 4th Destroyer Flotilla received an unsigned wireless signal:

"Fourth Destroyer Flotilla break off!"

Upon inquiry from the destroyer leader in Z 30 it was

stated that the signature *Scharnhorst* had been transmitted in a garbled form. To Captain Johannesson, leader of the flotilla, the order—quite naturally—seemed incomprehensible. As it was not clear to him whether it referred to the attack against the convoy as located by U-boat Lübsen, or meant that the entire operation was being called off, he asked the Commander-in-Chief, by wireless signal, for further instructions. The *Scharnhorst's* reply, received at 1420 hours, was:

"Return to base!"

The British dispatch concerning the second engagement of Force 1 with the *Scharnhorst* contains, among other things, the following details:

At 1024 hours the 10th Cruiser Squadron closed the convoy and met up with the 36th Destroyer Division. Then the cruisers—because of the danger of U-boats—zigzagged 10 miles ahead of the convoy, with the 36th Destroyer Division disposed ahead of the cruiser force as a screen.

Towards noon it became clear to Admiral Fraser in the *Duke of York* that, owing to the fuel situation in the destroyers, he would be obliged either to turn back or go on to Kola Inlet for refuelling. If the *Scharnhorst* had already been on her way back to base at this time, there would have been no chance of catching her.

At 1155 hours Admiral Fraser ordered the convoy to alter course to 125°, that is, more to the south, his idea being to keep the cruisers between the convoy and the *Scharnhorst*. At 1137 hours the *Norfolk* made contact with the German battleship by Radar at 27,000 yards, but lost it a few minutes later. Then, at 1205 the *Belfast* picked up the *Scharnhorst*, this time at 30,500 yards. Vice-Admiral Burnett now concentrated the 36th Destroyer Division on his starboard bow and altered course to 100°. At 1221 hours the *Sheffield* reported, "Enemy in sight," and Force 1 was ordered to open fire at a range of 11,000 yards.

At the same time the 36th Destroyer Division was ordered to attack with torpedoes. The destroyers, however, owing to the extraordinarily bad weather conditions which greatly reduced their speed, and to the fact that the *Scharn-*

215

horst was all the time retreating, did not come within torpedo range at this stage of the battle. The *Musketeer* opened fire at a range of 7000 yards at 1222 hours and continued firing for 14 minutes.

During this second action, at 1233 hours, the *Norfolk* received a serious hit through the barbette of her after turret "X," which put it out of action, and the turret's magazine had to be flooded as a precaution. A second shell hit the *Norfolk* amidships. All the cruiser's Radar apparatus became unserviceable except for one set of the Type 284. One officer and six ratings were killed and five ratings were seriously wounded. At the same time an 11-inch salvo straddled the *Sheffield* and pieces of shell— some the size of footballs—according to the British report —crashed inboard; smaller fragments also penetrated the ship at various places.

With the *Scharnhorst* retreating at 28 knots, the range, which during the action had narrowed to 4½–8 miles, opened more and more. Vice-Admiral Burnett decided to check fire and shadow with the whole of Force 1 until the *Scharnhorst* could be engaged by Admiral Fraser with Force 2. The 10th Cruiser Squadron, therefore, increased speed to 28 knots so that from 1250 hours onwards the enemy range remained steady at 13,400 yards. The 36th Destroyer Division, too, continued the chase. Later the range between the *Scharnhorst* and the pursuing cruisers opened to 20,000 yards and then remained steady.

.

Admiral Sir Bruce Fraser, sailing in the *Duke of York,* and acting on enemy reports received from Vice-Admiral Burnett, had on this December 26 been proceeding eastward with Force 2. His sole aim was to approach the *Scharnhorst,* cut off her retreat to Norway, and sink her, thus disposing of the most serious threat to the Arctic convoys.

A quarter of an hour after the *Scharnhorst* had been

216

engaged by the cruisers of the 10th Squadron, one of the young officers from the Radar plot of the *Duke of York* reported in the chart-house of the Admiral's bridge:

"Enemy reconnaissance aircraft, Sir."

The Admiral, who with his Chief-of-Staff, had been checking Vice-Admiral Burnett's reports on the first action just concluded, looked up quickly:

"German reconnaissance aircraft? Where?"

"Eight and a half miles on the starboard quarter, Sir. We picked them up by Radar as well as by D/F. Three aircraft. One of the planes must have Radar; it's started sending radio location signals and is transmitting reports."

Sir Bruce exchanged glances with his Chief-of-Staff and placed the report sheet on the chart before him:

"Nothing else? No further signals?"

The Sub-Lieutenant shook his head:

"No, Sir. We're keeping contact with the aircraft."

"Good. Thank you."

For about four hours the *Duke of York's* Radar observed the German reconnaissance aircraft shadowing the Force and sending out signals. Then it was seen no more; either it had lost contact or had returned to base.

At 1400 hours Sir Bruce sought out his Chief-of-Staff in the plotting-room. "I'm beginning to wonder," he said, "if our respective positions have been incorrectly reported. They seem too good to be true."

The Chief-of-Staff pointed with conviction to the large-scale chart on which all data were precisely recorded as they came in:

"Impossible, Sir. The D/F bearings here fully confirm the positions. Our approach is being made on a steady bearing."

Sir Bruce was relieved. "If the *Scharnhorst* maintains roughly her present course, she will run directly across our bows. I shall attack with the *Jamaica* on the same course, open fire at 13,000 yards and at the same time give the escort destroyers the order for torpedo attack. Burnett is keeping excellent contact."

The Chief-of-Staff traced with his pencil the course of the 10th Cruiser Squadron, Vice-Admiral Burnett's Force 1.

"Up to now, Sir, there's no indication that the reports of the German reconnaissance aircraft have influenced the movements of the *Scharnhorst* in the slightest. If she continues as she's going now," he cast a quick glance at his watch, "we shall be in action with her at about 1715 hours."

About two hours later, at 1617 hours, the Admiral was seated on a metal stool by the rapidly rotating disc which permitted a clear view through the large window of the bridge, in spite of the driving snow, when suddenly one of the officers from the plotting-room appeared before him like a spirit conjured from the darkness.

"We've got her, Sir! The first report has just come in: 45,000 yards, bearing 020°. The Chief-of-Staff wishes to report that the bearing agrees with the plotted course. The *Scharnhorst* has turned on to a rather more southerly course. Force 1 has made the same report."

The Admiral jumped to his feet:

"Splendid; well done, Radar. Flag-Lieutenant: Pass on this Radar report with our own position to all ships!"

"Yes, Sir," came the voice of the Flag-Lieutenant out of the darkness.

Exactly twenty minutes later, at 1637 hours, the escorting destroyers received the order to take up the most advantageous positions for torpedo attack in subdivisions. (Sub-divisions stationed on either bow of the *Duke of York* had previously been formed.) At the same time, it was reported that the Radar had also picked up the *Belfast* which was coming up behind the *Scharnhorst* in pursuit.

Five minutes earlier, the *Duke of York's* fire-control Radar had found the *Scharnhorst* at 29,700 yards.

Sir Bruce gave a further order to the Flag-Lieutenant and requested the Captain of the flagship to come to the voice-pipe connecting the Admiral's bridge with the ship's bridge below. When Captain Russell reported, the Admiral himself was already standing at the voice-pipe:

"In two minutes Force 2 will turn to 80°, Russell. You can then bring all heavy guns to bear at once."

At 1647 hours the *Belfast* opened fire with starshell. One minute later, at 1648 hours, the *Duke of York* joined in also with starshell, and at 1650 hours the first heavy salvo thundered from the ten 14-inch barrels of the British flagship. The *Jamaica* followed with her twelve 6-inch guns, while the *Norfolk* and the *Belfast* opened fire somewhat later. The initial range was 12,000 yards.

Stationed at his control column, P.O. Gödde, who was searching slowly and systematically from dead ahead to the port beam, became suddenly aware that the Radar reports were taking a new shape. He took his eyes from the lenses, all attention now on the headphones. What was that? The after Radar, which had been putting through in routine fashion reports on the British ship shadowing astern, had suddenly discovered another target to starboard. And now, at the Captain's request, it was reporting the range and bearing of the new target. The P.O. suddenly recalled what the Captain had announced to all stations at 1130 hours: that an enemy Force was 150 miles away. Gödde pondered on this. Three hours previously the *Scharnhorst* had turned on to her present southeasterly course; before that she had been in the second action with the cruiser squadron. What would be the speed of this new Force? Twenty-eight to 30 knots, Gödde thought. That would mean 90 miles in the last three hours at the most. But this Force would obviously have been receiving continuous reports on the speed, course and position of the *Scharnhorst*—from the shadowing cruiser; hence, Gödde reasoned, if the enemy are out to intercept us on our return journey, they will have been able to take a short cut. This battle group must now be just about ready to strike.

Suddenly the piercing sound of the alarm bells shrieked through the ship.

It was 1600 hours.

Heeling over heavily, the *Scharnhorst* slewed round and increased speed at the same time. The unbearable pitching changed into rolling, then into a soft rhythmical swaying now that the battleship was almost running before the sea again.

The Signals-Transmitter passed on a further announcement from the Gunnery Commander:

"Enemy opening fire to starboard. A.A. crews below deck. Skeleton crew only to remain on deck."

Then it came. Blow upon blow. In a matter of seconds ship and crew were swept along in the confused headlong rush of events. Gödde observed gigantic splashes 100 to 150 yards on his port side from what must have been shells of the heaviest calibre. Then, while the battleship was still turning round, her own heavy turrets opened fire. Gödde heard the Second Gunnery Officer, Kapitänleutnant Wieting, order single guns of the starboard secondary armament to fire starshell in between salvoes, evidently with the idea of enabling the visual range-finders to pick up the enemy. The enemy's own starshell firing seemed to slacken during the few starshell salvoes of the German 5.9-inch guns. The P.O. now heard an interchange between the Gunnery Commander and the Second Gunnery Officer on the artillery telephone. The Gunnery Commander thought it inadvisable to take guns from the batteries and thus weaken the defensive fire. The Second Gunnery Officer, accordingly, stopped the firing of starshell, and the guns which were ready for the next salvo were at once unloaded.

The enemy's shells which had been falling to port and starboard of the *Scharnhorst*, now began to fall wide and well behind the ship.

Anxiously Gödde searched for an enemy on the port side. Nothing could be seen but the glistening white columns of water which rose steeple-high as the 14-inch shells hit the sea. They rose from the water like pale phantoms trailing white shrouds, stood poised for a while, and then fell in mighty cascades of water. The German heavy armament kept up continuous fire from all triple turrets.

At 1655 hours a 14-inch shell hit the starboard bows abreast of "A" turret and the blast threw P.O. Gödde to the deck. Overcome with shock and the greenish-black lyddite fumes he gasped for air and lay for several seconds on the wooden grating of his small platform, incapable of moving. Just at this moment the Captain appeared. The lenses of the optical apparatus had become temporarily unusable—from the effects of the hit and the fumes—and had to be cleaned from the outside by ratings sent up from below. Captain Hintze saw the prostrate man and helped him to his feet:

"Are you wounded, Gödde?"

The P.O. pulled himself together:

"No, Herr Kapitän, only stunned."

The Captain pointed to the apparatus:

"Stay at your post. We can't afford to be taken by surprise from this side."

"A" turret was now jammed in its bearings with its barrels elevated and could no longer be trained. Shortly after the first hit, a second was scored amidships.

Later, when Gödde's artillery-telephone had been put out of action, and he had switched over to the ship-control telephone system, he heard a report from one of the stations to the Gunnery Commander:

"A" turret is no longer reporting. Fire and smoke around the turret prevent entry."

This meant that "A" turret was completely out of action and that the *Scharnhorst's* defences were deprived of three 11-inch guns. Her remaining heavy guns, six 11-inch barrels, meanwhile stepped up their fire to a quick succession of salvoes and the range opened to 17,000–20,000 yards. It was observed that the enemy was frequently straddled by salvoes and that many near misses fell close to the British ship. This gunnery duel lasted some twenty minutes and was conducted by both sides with the utmost ferocity. Throughout this period a continuous stream of starshell were exploding over the *Scharnhorst*. The flares hung over the ship for minutes on end like so many huge floodlights exposing everything with stark, pitiless clarity, the cruel brilliance sharpened by the fiery flashes of the German's own salvoes. The whole battleship from bridges to foretop, masts and funnels was bathed in a ghastly pink to blood-red light. Smoke and cordite fumes clung to the ship, driven now by an almost following wind, and at times completely obscured visibility in the direction of the enemy. Through the thunder of the German salvoes, the British shells could be heard screaming over and thudding into the sea, while those that met their target caused the ship, already rocked by the recoil of her own guns, to tremble from stem to stern.

P.O. Gödde concluded from the gunnery orders that the range was opening while German and British fire slackened appreciably. The *Scharnhorst* was steady on her easterly course and seemed to increase speed still more. The intervals between salvoes lengthened and visibility gradually improved.

As the action was being fought to starboard, the crews in the port IV 5.9-inch twin turret could open the turret trap-hatch occasionally and observe the continuous explosion of starshell over the ship stabbing the darkness with their glare. At 1650 hours the turret Signals-Transmitter repeated an announcement from the Captain:

"From the Captain to all stations. The heavy enemy units are turning away, they can't match our speed." Then after a short pause: "The *Scharnhorst* has again proved herself."

The lull following the Captain's last announcement, during which the *Scharnhorst's* heavy artillery temporarily checked fire, lasted only five to ten minutes. Then once more the ship was exposed to the dazzling light of starshell and the heavy shock of an underwater explosion, amidships on the starboard side, shuddered through her hull. Soon after this, her speed slackened.

In the port IV 5.9-inch turret the Signals-Transmitter passed on the report:

"Torpedo hit in boiler-room 1. Speed 8 knots."

By 1840 hours the first sub-division (*Savage* and *Saumarez*) were astern of the *Scharnhorst;* at the same time the second sub-division (*Scorpion* and *Stord*) closed in from the south-east to about 10,000 yards, and were on the *Scharnhorst's* starboard beam ready to fire their torpedoes. The *Scharnhorst* opened heavy fire against the *Savage* and *Saumarez* with her secondary armament and

222

A.A. guns which the two destroyers returned. At the same time they fired starshell. The second sub-division *Scorpion* and *Stord* turned for the torpedo attack, *Scorpion* firing eight torpedoes at 2100 yards and *Stord* another eight at 1800 yards. *Scorpion* observed one hit. The *Scharnhorst*, turning to southward ostensibly to get out of the line of fire, put herself just where the first sub-division wanted her. Thus, while the second sub-division on its retreat came under heavy secondary armament and A.A. fire from the *Scharnhorst*, the first sub-division hastily trained its torpedo tubes from port to starboard and turned in to attack. *Savage* fired her eight torpedoes at a range of 3,500 yards. *Saumarez*, which owing to casualties and damage had only one set of tubes clear for action, and lying as she was under heavy fire, could launch only four torpedoes at 1800 yards.

Savage remained miraculously intact, but *Saumarez* was damaged above the waterline and sustained casualties. Shells hit her director and penetrated below her range-finder director without, however, exploding. Splinters from other shells caused further damage which reduced her speed to ten knots on one engine only. One officer and ten ratings were killed and eleven ratings wounded. *Savage* claimed to have observed three hits on the *Scharnhorst*, *Saumarez* one.

The attack of the two sub-divisions was carried out without support from the *Duke of York* or the *Jamaica*. The *Duke of York* observed three heavy underwater explosions on the *Scharnhorst*, the *Belfast* six—an indication of how uncertain and unreliable observations made during a night action are, though they may be made and reported in good faith.

After delivering their attacks the destroyers withdrew to the northward.

While the *Scharnhorst's* heavy guns were still firing at the retreating destroyers, P.O. Gödde heard the after Radar reporting new targets; the Captain asked for their respective bearings and ranges, and these were given.

Shortly afterwards, the 11-inch guns opened fire on these as yet shadowy opponents, one of which was soon identified as a battleship; heavy shells fell into the sea around the *Scharnhorst*. The Second Gunnery Officer, Kapitänleutnant Wieting, ordered the secondary armament to open fire on the battleship and on a second opponent which, judging by its shell calibre, was obviously a cruiser.

Hit upon hit crashed on to the *Scharnhorst*. Heavy explosions followed one upon the other, and as each bout of violent rocking subsided it was replaced by a slow vibration as if the very hull were trembling. Steel crashed upon steel; fire broke out and the smoke which billowed from the quickly spreading flames mingled with the acrid cordite fumes of the German salvoes and the strangely stinging odour from the British explosives. The two remaining triple turrets kept up their relentless fire in company with the 5.9-inch battery and the 4.1-inch A.A. guns. Between the German salvoes one could hear the dull rumbling noise of starshell exploding over the battleship, the detonations of torpedoes and the impact of shells. The rending steel groaned and hissing splinters hammered like hail on superstructures and decks. The enemy's wide shots came screaming over the *Scharnhorst* and fell with heavy thuds into the sea beyond, flooding decks and guns with the swell and marking their trail with a rain of deadly splinters.

This hurricane of fire, this ghastly concentration of assault from heavy guns and torpedoes, took place—according to the British dispatch—between 1901 and 1937 hours.

In the fearful din of battle in which the *Scharnhorst* was now enveloped, none but the well-trained ear, tried in exercise and action, could distinguish voices and interpret the reports and orders which the ship's telephone system was picking up from every side. P.O. Gödde possessed such a practised ear. He had his eyes pressed closely to the lenses of his control column, raising them only occasionally to look round him, when a particularly heavy explosion shook the ship. Through the noise came word from the Captain:

"Scharnhorst immer voran!"

It was the ship's motto. Gödde gritted his teeth and looked up. He realized that the long bows of the *Scharnhorst* had nosed straight into the path of a shell. The noise of the explosion mingled with the sight of wood, iron and steel torn asunder as by giant, flaming ploughshares. Then the blast flung the P.O. from his apparatus, lifted him bodily into the air and threw him violently on to the deck. Gödde lost consciousness and lay inert. When he wearily opened his eyes again he saw the Captain.

Captain Hintze had left the control position through the port door opposite Gödde's control column to take a quick look round. The lenses of the optical instruments in the control position had for the most part been destroyed by flying shrapnel; the rest had been made temporarily unserviceable by clinging snow, water and slime. Just as the Captain was squeezing through the narrow aperture of the slightly open armoured door, the 14-inch shell—the one which tore Gödde from the control column—hit the bows. Splinters grazed the Captain's face but he seemed hardly to notice them. He had only the sensation of something warm trickling down his forehead and on to his cheeks and he dabbed it with his handkerchief. Then he saw Gödde crumpled up on the wooden slats of the control column platform. He bent over him:

"Are you wounded, Gödde?"

The same question as he had asked the P.O. two hours previously. The Captain helped the prostrate man to his feet. Gödde rubbed his eyes and looked at his apparatus.

"No, Sir. It was only a few splinters. The gear's all right."

The Captain nodded:

"Good. See what's wrong with the starboard control column. It's not answering."

With this the Captain withdrew once more to the control position and Gödde hurried round to the other control column. In the harsh light of starshell one glance sufficed. The men on the platform were all dead. The apparatus was totally destroyed. All that remained was an unrecognizable mass of twisted steel, shattered instruments and torn, half-melted cables. As quickly as he could Gödde rushed back to his own control column, slipped on his telephone and reported:

"Starboard forward control column destroyed. Crew dead."

This hit must have occurred a few minutes after 1900 hours. About twenty minutes later, roughly at 1925 hours, Gödde felt the impact of a torpedo which brought the battleship practically to a standstill. Then a shell of medium calibre, fired no doubt by one of the cruisers now stationed to the north and south of the *Scharnhorst,* crashed into her bows. A fragment of this smashed the upper mobile portion of the control column at which Gödde was stationed and flung it from its bearings, while other splinters severed the cables of the head-phone. He himself remained unscathed. While Gödde was still occupied in investigating the damage, a Quartermaster sent out by the Captain appeared:

"The Captain wants to know what's happened here? Why don't you answer?"

"The control column's gone. And the telephone too."

The Quartermaster disappeared into the control position again and then returned once more.

"Order from the Captain: Come into the control position. The old man says there's no point in staying outside any longer."

Casting a last look at the shambles around him, Gödde followed the Quartermaster and squeezed himself through the armoured door into the control position.

It was the British torpedoes which finally brought about the end of the German battleship.

One, two torpedo detonations thundered above the indescribable pandemonium of the battle and the *Scharnhorst* slowly took a list to starboard. Whatever there was that could still fire—"C" turret and the remaining 5.9-inch guns—went on firing. And again two, three torpedo detonations crashed forth. They hit on the starboard side and the list increased. Simultaneously came the order:

"From the Captain to all stations. Destroy all secret papers and installations. To damage control party: prepare for scuttling! All men detailed for scuttling to their stations!"

More violent explosions. Torpedoes again. The port 20-mm. A.A. gun was still firing from the fore-top, the only one which had remained in action after the fore-top had been hit during the morning. It fired down from the main A.A. gun tower and with it the port IV 5.9-inch twin turret. Then, because of the heavy list, the hoist in the twin turret jammed in its shaft. At the same time, the order was passed down from the bridge:

"Abandon ship."

Staff Chief Gunner Wibbelhoff rose from his seat:

"Leave the turret!" he ordered.

The men hesitated. During the whole operation the turret had suffered neither damage nor casualties.

"Leave the turret, boys," Wibbelhoff repeated, raising his voice. "I'm staying where I belong."

Chief Petty Officer Moritz went at once to Wibbelhoff's side:

"I'm staying too."

Not another word was spoken. Slowly, the men turned away and prepared to leave, returning the Battery Commander's last salute.

They clambered out slowly, one after the other, still a little uncertain, turning round for a last glance. Sträter, one of the last to leave, saw Wibbelhoff put his hand in his pocket and quietly produce a packet of cigarettes. He saw him light up and in the calm deliberate manner so familiar to his men, swing back into his seat. Moritz, likewise, lowered himself onto his laying-seat. Sträter felt a lump in his throat as he gazed on the scene for the last time, a scene which was to be indelibly printed on his mind and swim before his eyes whenever he thought of his ship.

Both men were still at their stations when the *Scharnhorst* capsized and sank.

Shortly before the first torpedoes of this last phase of the battle hit the *Scharnhorst,* Gödde, now in the control position, heard that enemy destroyers were closing from astern.

The Captain, who received the report, looked at the Commander-in-Chief:

"They want to finish us off like the *Bismarck,* Herr Admiral. Torpedoes into rudder and screws!"

He stepped to the side of the Signals-Transmitter at the emergency line which the Torpedo Officer, now standing by at the torpedo tubes, had had hurriedly laid. Then Captain Hintze gave the order to fire torpedoes. By a supreme effort, the Torpedo Officer, Oberleutnant Bosse, and those of his men who were left, had carried out emergency repairs on the damaged tubes; now with the help of a few ratings, he succeeded in training them and firing torpedoes first to port, then to starboard at the targets indicated by the Captain. After the appropriate interval the stern look-out reported to the control position that he had observed a brilliant blaze astern.

According to British sources, this was yet another of the mistaken claims made in good faith by both sides during the night battle.

The *Scharnhorst* was hit by the first enemy torpedo salvo at about 1927 hours, and six minutes later, at 1933 hours, by the second. Four minutes after that, at about 1937 hours, the last torpedoes detonated with a thunderous roar against the ship's starboard side.

The fate of the *Scharnhorst* was sealed.

Gödde, deeply moved, heard reports coming in from all parts of the dying ship; in accordance with the Captain's orders to prepare for scuttling, the damage control parties had fitted the explosive charges, and, one-by-one, the various installations were being destroyed or rendered useless.

The *Scharnhorst* was listing more and more to starboard as Captain Hintze beckoned the Navigating Officer to him.

"Pass to the Action Information Centre," he ordered, "a last report of our position in clear text. Quickly Lanz. Time is running out!"

Then he gripped the Chief Signals-Transmitter by the arm:

"To all stations. From the Captain: Abandon ship. Every man to the upper deck. Life-jackets on. Prepare to jump overboard!"

Summoned by the Captain, the First Officer, Fregatten-kapitän Dominik, had come up from the Commander's office through the armoured shaft. Rear-Admiral Bey, Captain and First Officer now discussed the measures still to be taken. Then Gödde saw the slim figure of the First Officer leaving the control position to go across the bay of the bridge and down the port companion-way to the upper deck. The list was becoming increasingly marked and Captain Hintze urged the twenty-five men in the control position to leave.

"Off with you, men. Put on your jackets. Just think of yourselves now. And don't forget to inflate them. Don't go overboard to starboard, my friends. Go over from the port side, and slide from the rail into the water."

As Gödde prepared to leave the bridge, the *Scharnhorst* was rolling heavily in the rough sea and was enveloped in dense smoke and fumes, but she was still moving slowly. Her starboard side lay in the water practically to the folded wing of the bridge, while the highest waves washed the main mast. Snow squalls, mingled with hail, had again set in and starshell still hovered over the sinking ship.

In the target area there were present at this time: one battleship, three cruisers and eight destroyers. The *Duke of York* withdrew to the northward to avoid the mêlée of ships. All that could be seen of the *Scharnhorst* was a dark glowing mass within an enormous cloud of smoke lit up by starshell and the searchlights of the surrounding ships. From the British side neither the glare of the starshell nor the beams of the searchlights could penetrate behind that smoke-cloud. Thus no ship actually saw the *Scharnhorst* sink. It seems certain however that she sank after a heavy underwater explosion which was heard and felt by various ships at 1945 hours.

Jamaica, Matchless and *Virago* were the last ships to sight the *Scharnhorst* (at 1938 hours). When the *Belfast* turned in for her second torpedo attack at 1948 hours the German battleship had finally sunk. She went down in approximately 72° 16′ N., 28° 41′ E. The *Jamaica* joined the *Duke of York* on her northerly course while *Belfast, Norfolk* and most of the destroyers continued until 2040 hours to search for survivors. During this time *Scorpion* picked up thirty survivors and *Matchless,* six. *Scorpion* reported that the German Admiral and the *Scharnhorst's* Captain had been seen in the water seriously wounded. The Captain was dead before he could be reached. The Admiral grasped a life-line but died before he could be hauled on board.

The deck was already tilted at a steep angle, so Gödde and the Bos'un's Mate, Deierling joined hands and moved carefully across the icy surface. As the port companion-way was crowded with men, they decided to use, instead, the starboard companion-way leading to the upper deck. The starboard bridge was already on a level with the water and heavy breakers lashed the main mast. Suddenly the two Petty Officers lost their footing and a receding wave swept them from the ship, separating them.

Gödde was drawn down by the suction around the hull. He felt an unbearable pressure in his ear drums, then he was tossed to the surface. He tried desperately to get clear of the whirling waters which eddied round the ship.

It was a gruesome scene that met his eyes as Gödde, lifted on to the long crest of a wave, looked about him, a scene illuminated by starshell and the chalk-white beams of searchlights. Where their light met the blue-black ice-cold water it shone in flashes of dazzling silver. Gödde swam on slowly and steadily, his head turned towards the capsizing *Scharnhorst.* Through the whirling veil of great snowflakes he saw, garishly illuminated, the outline of the battleship now lying practically on her side. The sight seemed unreal, improbable. It flashed through his mind that a fighter plane, banking, would have seen the *Scharnhorst* like that. Everything was oblique, foreshortened, contradicting the laws of gravity. Only a few men were swimming on her starboard side, most of them having followed the advice of the Captain and left the *Scharnhorst* over the rail on the port side.

He saw the light of an emergency raft flickering close to him. Uncannily, like a ship's distress signal, its flame quivered restlessly in the gale. Gödde could see a young officer and several men on the raft. He swam towards it and saw the officer suddenly stand up. Through the raging storm he heard him shout: "Three cheers for the *Scharnhorst!*"

Gödde was two to three hundred yards from the ship which was now lying so much on her starboard side that he could look right down her funnel as into a dark tunnel. He was amazed that she was still afloat. He and many of his shipmates could still plainly hear the turbines revolving inside her. Fuel oil had spread across the sea, covering the surface with a tough, pungent, rainbow-colored film. It was nauseating if it was washed into the mouth or even came into contact with the face. But, as Gödde quickly observed, it cushioned the violence of the breaking seas.

At the same time Sträter saw the *Scharnhorst* capsize and settle deeper into the water, bow first. All three propellers were still revolving at fair speed.

Gödde now tried to reach a raft which was drifting near him. Some twenty men were already sitting on it or clinging to it, so that, pressed below the surface by the combined weight of the men, nothing could be seen of the raft itself. Seeing this, Gödde abandoned his attempt and swam towards some wooden props such as were used by the damage control parties for propping up hatches, etc. They were drifting close together and when at last he reached them, they offered him some support. Of the ship's rafts only a few were in the water. Most of the rafts and life-boats had, on the Captain's orders, been cut free from their lashings in good time, but splinters and fragments of shell had riddled them with holes and rendered them useless. Clinging to the wooden props Gödde let himself drift about in the swell. Now he could relax sufficiently to look back to his ship; the *Scharnhorst* had turned turtle after capsizing and her superstructure, which Gödde had been able to see for so long, had disappeared. The wreck was drifting on the sea, bottom up, and men were moving about on the ship's keel, among them Artificer 1st Class Johnnie Merkel, one of the survivors. He remained perched on the keel until he saw a raft drifting by, then he jumped into the water. Sitting on the raft Merkel then helped several men over from the ship's bottom.

Meanwhile the cold began to take hold of Gödde; paralysis crept from his lower extremities and threatened to numb his whole body. Lumps of ice were drifting by, the snowstorm was still raging, and gusts of hail drove almost horizontally across the dark waters. Gödde was weakening. He had just reached the point when he felt he could keep his grip on the props no longer when he caught sight of the raft bearing Merkel and three other men. Summoning his last reserves Gödde managed to reach the raft. He let go of the props and Merkel helped the half-paralysed man to push the upper part of his body over on to the raft. Utterly exhausted Gödde cast a last glance back to the *Scharnhorst*. Only part of the stern was showing above the water. Then the long rolling swell of the Arctic sea closed over her.

Gradually, the sound of starshell firing ceased and darkness reclaimed the sea. The little groups huddling on the few rafts could hardly see each other, still less the isolated swimmers. A young rating who had left his own raft because of overcrowding joined Gödde's company. He too was helped on by Merkel so that he could keep his hold by lying, like Gödde, with his body across the raft. They were all completely exhausted, incapable of feeling, half-numbed, stricken by a leaden weariness. For one to one and a half hours they drifted, the raft swinging up and down with the sea, floundering in monotonous rhythm between wave-crest and trough. Pressed tightly together, one supporting the other, they would, whenever the raft was lifted to the crest of an unusually high wave, look around them with eyes red-rimmed and swollen, encrusted with hoar-frost and caked with salt and oil.

Then, suddenly, they started: there was a flash quite near them, the thunder of guns broke loose again and the screaming of shells passed over their heads. Were they under fire? There came the sound of dull detonations, then the sky lit up around them. Flares shed their harsh light and a few seconds later the long white arms of searchlights pierced the darkness. For a moment the men thought that their raft was being fired on, then they realized their mistake. A great ship had concentrated her searchlights and was now spot-lighting the raft. In the light of starshell they saw two destroyers approach and stretch the thinner fingers of their searchlights too on to the raft, their raft. Then one of them turned away. The other continued towards them and, maneuvering cautiously, approached the raft. It struck Gödde, now fully conscious again, how skilfully the destroyer was managed in the heavy sea-way; she left the raft on her starboard side and then let herself drift with the wind towards it. Great climbing nets were laid out on the side of the destroyer and as soon as the vessel was close enough the British seamen threw bowlines over the heads and shoulders of the men on the raft. They were pulled on board one after another in this fashion. When Gödde had the sling thrown to him he had not the strength to slip it over his elbows, and as the British seaman went to pull him up he slipped out of the sling and back into the water. Four times they threw him the line: at the fifth attempt the end of the line hit him directly across the mouth. In desperation he sank his teeth firmly into the hemp rope and in this manner was hauled up. As he reached deck level he felt a pair of giant fists grasp the collar of his uniform and pull him over the rail.

The Invasion of Sicily

The decision to invade Sicily was made by the Allied Combined Chiefs of Staff at the Casablanca Conference in January 1943. S. L. Morison, the U.S. naval historian, says there was a "serious divergence of views" between the U.S. and Britain as to the next strategic objective after the successful Allied landings in North Africa. There was, however, agreement on the following points:

1. "The basic strategic principle of March 1941 that the European Axis, as the most dangerous enemy in military might and potentiality, must be defeated first.

2. "Anti-submarine warfare was the most pressing and urgent problem.

3. "Some sort of 'second front' must be opened against Germany in 1943.

"The divergences, however, were very wide. The British wished almost complete concentration on the European war and merely to "hold" or "contain" Japan until Germany was defeated. The Americans, especially General Marshall and Admiral King, felt that it was absolutely essential to maintain momentum in the war against Japan, lest she consolidate her conquests and become impregnable. Regarding China as having the same geopolitical relation to Japan as Russia had to Germany, they believed that something must be done in 1943 to relieve Chiang Kai-shek. Admiral Leahy at JCS. meetings kept saying to General Marshall: "Remember this: who controls China at the end of the war, controls Asia. Don't overlook China." The British, on the contrary, regarded China as of slight account as an ally, Chiang as undependable, and the obstacles to rendering him aid through the Japanese blockade as insuperable.

"The English-speaking allies also disagreed as to their next move after TORCH. The Americans wished to leave only token forces in North Africa, to concentrate on the United Kingdom build-up and the bomber offensive, and prepare to launch a cross-channel invasion during the summer of 1943. The British, on the contrary, believed that no cross-channel operation had any chance of success before 1944. They proposed to exploit the capture of North Africa by using the ships and troops already there to take Sardinia or Sicily around mid-summer 1943, in the hope of knocking Italy out of the war, and perhaps bringing Turkey in on the Allied side." *

The CCS decided to postpone the cross-channel invasion until 1944, and the U.S. would continue all-out war against Japan in the Pacific. But the Chiefs agreed that "something" must be done in the European Theater in 1943.

"The British Chiefs proposed occupying Sardinia; the Americans, Sicily. Sardinia as the less strongly held of the two could probably be taken about two months earlier and with fewer forces. It would be a good base for bomber raids on the industrial cities of northern Italy, and for commando raids on the coast. But, although Nelson once called Maddalena Bay 'the finest harbor in the world,' it was not ample enough to mount a large modern amphibious operation. Admiral King scoffed at the Sardinia proposition as 'merely doing something just for the sake of doing something.' He predicted that Sicily would have to be taken eventually, and that it could best be taken immediately. Admiral Pound and General Somervell pointed out that the Straits of Sicily were still too risky for troop and tanker convoys, that Allied possession of Sicily would render unnecessary the roundabout Cape route to India, affording a saving in time equivalent to the employment of 225 freighters. On 19 January 1943, the CCS decided on the occupation of Sicily, with four objects in view: (1) securing the Mediterranean line of communications, (2) diverting German forces from the Russian front, (3) increasing the pressure on Italy, and (4) creating 'a situation in which Turkey can be enlisted as an active ally.' " **

Sicily was heavily fortified; 405,000 Axis troops were stationed there to defend against an invasion. The terrain was most difficult for tanks and trucks, because of narrow roads and mountainous country.

The plan of assault called for a week's bombardment in advance of the landing to knock out the enemy's air and naval defenses. Then

*S. L. Morison, *Sicily-Salerno-Anzio*, published by Little Brown & Co., p. 5.

** *Sicily-Salerno-Anzio*, pp. 9-10.

on July 10, the invasion forces, consisting of 160,000 men, 14,000 vehicles, 600 tanks, 1800 guns and 3000 ships and landing craft, would land on the Sicilian beaches.

The U.S. Seventh Army was to land between Cape Scaramia and Licata on the southwest coast. Its six divisions, including the 82nd Airborne, were under the command of General Patton. The British Eighth Army, commanded by General Montgomery, would land seven divisions, including the British 1st Airborne, on the southeast coast.

On July 9, bad weather made the prospect of coordinated landings extremely hazardous. But by the morning of D-Day, July 10, the seas had calmed and only moderate surf was on the beaches.

Earlier, airborne troops had been dropped to knock out installations, set up roadblocks, and delay reinforcements. They had only limited success with their tactical objectives. However, the assaults on the beaches by the landing forces were successful and the troops were soon organized into attack groups to move inland.

The Hastings and Prince Edward Regiment of the Canadian 1st Division took part in the Eighth Army assault. Facing only Italian defenders, they had a comparatively easy time of it in the landing operation. But soon the orders came through to form up for the march inland to make contact with German troops who had withdrawn to defense positions in the hills.

Farley Mowat, the Regiment's historian, describes the march.

"The Regiment moved off from its olive grove at noon, turning its back on the sea. The heat was brutal and the dust rose so thickly that it became an almost palpable barrier through which men thrust their whitened bodies with an actual physical effort. It gathered thickly on their sweating faces and hardened into a heavy crust. Their feet sank ankle deep in dust as if in a tenuous slime. There was no water; the occasional foul well along the route dried up when the first few platoons fell upon it. The sun was an implacable enemy, and there was no escape from its brutality. Steel helmets became brain furnaces. The weight of the battle equipment, weapons and extra ammunition was one more agony. The marching troops straggled along the verges where there was no grass, but only dust, eternal dust. Occasional tanks rumbled past, obliterating whole companies in the hanging shroud. They marched.

"Not least of the qualities of good fighting men is their ability to endure. Bravery, military knowledge and expert marksmanship— these things have their place in the making of a soldier, but they are

236

as nothing if the man cannot endure the unendurable. The men of the Regiment were soldiers. They endured.

"The attenuated column, strung out in single file over many miles, worked its way steadily inland, and upward into the hills. There were brief halts each hour, and in those intervals a few men looked back at the broad blue bay with its minute ship models. Most of them looked down at their feet. They dragged at the incomparably bad issue cigarettes that came with the 'compo ration' packs on which the fighting units subsisted; and the smoke was bitter and acrid in their parched mouths. They got to their feet and their boots slithered, clumped, and the dust clouds rose into the shimmering air.

"Before dusk fell the column had passed the limit set for the third day of the invasion. There was no halt. Darkness brought some surcease from the heat, but none from the dust and thirst. The roads became steeper and exhaustion began to take its toll. Men slept on the move; an old habit learned in the English schemes, and they were guided by their companions. Here and there an N.C.O. shouldered extra rifles for those who had reached the apparent limit of their endurance. The troops marched on. Perhaps a dozen men could not go farther and were loaded on the backs of donkeys, to sit swaying with eyes shut.

"At midnight the unit passed through its first Italian town, Rosolini, but the place left little impression on men's minds, and few have any memories of it except that in the central square there was a well.

"A few miles beyond the town, and nearly thirty miles from the start point of the march, the Regiment was halted. Sections and platoons staggered into the open field and fell where they stopped. They were beyond caring even about food. They died on the hard ground, and three hours later they were dragged from their graves, and set upon the road once more." *

"In launching the Sicilian invasion, the Allied Commanders had as their prime objective the capture of the crossings to the mainland of Italy at the Straits of Messina. Accordingly, Eighth Army had been instructed to go directly for this objective up the eastern coastal route while on the far left the American Seventh Army was intended to contain and destroy the major German forces which were then concentrated in the western and central interior.

"But as so often happened, the inital plan had to be drastically

*The Regiment, published by McClelland and Stewart, Limited, pp. 63-64.

modified as a result of the enemy's failure to conform to it. Quickly disengaging the bulk of their forces from the battles with the Americans in the west, the Germans abandoned most of Sicily and concentrated their armour and their best divisions in the path of Eighth Army's coastal thrust. Thirteen Corps on the Catania plains at once became involved in a series of savage and exhausting battles of attrition that gained little ground, and that took much precious time. Its role became that of a holding force engaging the bulk of the German armour. And it was left to someone else to force the path northward towards Messina.

"Thirtieth Corps of Eighth Army, including First Canadian Division and Fifty-first Highland Division, had during the first few days been operating in a secondary role through the interior mountains on an axis parallel to that of Thirteenth Corps. Now Montgomery gave it the formidable task of making the major thrust northward and of opening up the front." *

MONTGOMERY'S MOUNTAIN GOATS

by Farley Mowat

First Canadian Division's thrust through the mountainous heart of Sicily, in its attempt to force the withdrawal of the strong German forces in the Catania plains, was approaching its climax. Catania itself already lay south of the line of the advanced Canadian units and it was nearly time for the Division to swing eastward and drive towards the coast. But before the turn could be made there was a most formidable gate to be opened.

The enemy had established himself on the Leonforte-Assoro base where the mountains swelled abruptly out of the bed of the Dittaino River and lifted steeply towards the peak of Etna to the east. Of the many almost impregnable

*The Regiment, p. 68.

positions available to the Germans, this was by far the strongest. Astride the two roads leading out of the valley the Assoro feature rose nearly 3000 feet from the dead river and thrust itself forward from the main mountain massifs like a titanic bastion. On the slope of the highest peak the village of Assoro clung precariously while a few miles westward the town of Leonforte guarded the back door to the citadel. As long as this position was held by the enemy there could be no further advance of Thirtieth Corps towards Messina; and the Germans had chosen the formidable Fifteenth Panzer-Grenadier Division to garrison this natural fortress.

By July 20 the forward Canadian unit (the Edmontons) had reached the Dittaino and had established a bridgehead across it. From the valley floor men could now look up to the sheer cliffs of Assoro and to the narrow, tortuous road that climbed the crags.

The German defenders were unperturbed by the appearance of the Canadians. They had no reason to be worried, for it was obvious that any frontal attack must be suicidal. And they believed Assoro to be one bastion that could not be outflanked for its only open side, upon the east, was a cliff face rising 900 feet to terminate in the ruins of an ancient Norman castle on the very peak of the mountain.

Brig. Howard Graham, entrusted with the assault of the fortress, believed differently. He knew as well as did the Germans that a frontal assault would be disastrous. But remembering Valguarnera, he found some faint hope in the prospects of an attack from the right flank and rear. The hope was very faint; nevertheless, he called Lt.-Col. Sutcliffe and asked him if the Regiment could do the job. Sutcliffe agreed to try.

With his Regiment committed, the C.O. immediately went forward across the Dittaino to the most advanced positions in order to estimate the chances of success. With him was the Intelligence Officer, "Battle" Cockin. The two men crawled through an olive grove and far down the exposed northern slope, in their anxiety to get a clear view of the enemy position. Crouched beside a single tiny foxhole, too small to hold them both, they were soon engrossed in their study of the great mountain thrusting high out of the dun-coloured earth.

On the Assoro scarp the crew of an 88-mm. gun laid their weapon over open sights. And when the cloud of yellow dust rose clear of the foxhole, Sutcliffe was dead, and the I.O. lay dying.

Prior to this moment all of the soldiers of the Regiment who had been killed had died in the confusion and tumult of action. Their loss had not been deeply perceived as yet, and hatred had not grown from their graves. This new stroke of death was something else again.

The tragedy had a remarkable effect. It irrevocably and utterly destroyed the pale remainder of the illusion that war was only an exciting extension of the battle games of 1941 and 1942. The killing of the C.O. *before* the battle seemed to be an almost obscene act, and when the news came to the men it roused in them an ugly resentment. The emotions stirred by the first skirmishes with war were only awaiting crystallization, and now they hardened and took form. Hatred of the enemy was born.

One more element had been added to the moods of battle and with its acquisition the Regiment reached a new level of efficiency as an instrument of war.

With Sutcliffe's death the command passed to the Regiment's adopted Canadian, Major Lord John Tweedsmuir. Tweedsmuir took over at a moment when the Regiment was faced with the toughest battle problem that it had so far encountered. He reacted to the challenge by accepting and putting into effect a plan so daring that failure would have meant not only the end of his career, but probably the end of the Regiment as well.

It was his appreciation that only by a wide right-flanking sweep through the mountains, culminating in the scaling of the Assoro cliff, could the enemy's position be reduced. Therefore the Regiment would scale the cliff.

It was already late afternoon and preparations had to be hurried. Alex Campbell was ordered to form a special assault force, a volunteer unit, consisting of one platoon from each of the regular rifle companies. The men in this special group were stripped of all their gear except for essential arms and ammunition, for it was to be their task to lead the Regiment; to scale the cliffs, and before dawn broke clearly, to occupy the mountain crest.

The approach march began at dusk and it was the most difficult forced march the Regiment ever attempted, in training or in war. The going was foul; through a maze of sheer-sided gullies, knife-edged ridges and boulder-strewn water courses. There was the constant expectation of discovery, for it seemed certain that the enemy would at least have listening posts on his open flank. Absolute silence was each man's hope of survival—but silence on that nightmare march was almost impossible to maintain.

There were terrifying moments; once, when the scouts saw the loom of a parapet that could only be a masked machine-gun post. Incredibly it was deserted, but so recently that fragments of German bread upon the ground were still quite fresh. Hours later there was a faint sound of stones, disturbed by many feet, ahead of the assault company. Men sank into the shadows tensed for the explosion that never came. Instead a young Sicilian boy came sleepily out of the darkness driving his herd of goats. The youth stared unbelievingly at the motionless shapes of armed men that surrounded him on every side and then passed on, as in a dream.

There was a desperate urgency in that march for there were long miles to go, and at the end, the cliff to scale before the dawn light could reveal the Regiment to the enemy above. A donkey, laden with a wireless set, was literally dragged forward by its escort until it collapsed and died. The men went on.

By 0400 hours the assault company had scaled the last preliminary ridge and was appalled to find that the base of the mountain, looming through the pre-dawn greyness, was still separated from it by a gully a hundred feet deep, and nearly as sheer as an ancient moat. It was too late to turn back. Men scrambled down into the great natural ditch, crossed the bottom, and paused to draw breath. First light was just an hour away. Under the soldiers' hands were the cliff rocks towering a thousand feet into the dark skies.

Each man who made that climb performed his own private miracle. From ledge to ledge the dark figures made their way, hauling each other up, passing along their weapons and ammunition from hand to hand. A signaller made that climb with a heavy wireless set strapped to his back—a thing that in daylight was seen to be impossible. Yet no man slipped, no man dropped so much as a clip of ammunition. It was just as well, for any sound by one would have been fatal to all.

Dawn was breaking and the whole cliff face was encrusted with a moving growth that like some vast slime-mould oozed upward almost imperceptibly. This was the moment. If the alarm was given, nothing could save the unit from annihilation.

The alarm was never given. The two men at the head of the leading assault platoon reached the crest, dragged themselves up over a stone wall and for one stark moment stared into the eyes of three sleepy Germans manning an observation post. Pte. A. K. Long cut down one of the Germans who tried to flee. The remaining enemy soldiers stood motionless, staring as children might at an inexplicable apparition.

Ten minutes later, as the sun cleared the eastern hills, the Regiment had overrun the crest and the companies were in position on the western slopes overlooking the whole German front. Close below them the village of Assoro showed a few thin spirals of grey smoke as peasant women prepared the morning meal. Half a mile below, in the steep valley leading to the front, a peaceful convoy of a dozen German trucks carried the day's rations forward to the waiting grenadiers.

Twenty Bren gunners on Assoro's crest vied with one another to press the trigger first.

The appearance of the Canadians must have come as a shattering surprise to the enemy and had his troops been of a lesser calibre, a debacle must have resulted. But the Germans here were of a fighting breed. Although they were now at a serious disadvantage, they had no thought of giving up.

From the ditches beside the burning trucks German

drivers returned the Regiment's machine-gun fire with rifle shots. The crews of four light anti-aircraft pieces, sited beside the road, cranked down their guns to fire point-blank at the Canadians upon the crest. Machine-gun detachments, hurriedly withdrawn from the front, scrambled up the road, flung themselves down behind stone fences and engaged the Brens in a staccato duel. With commendable, but frightening efficiency, the enemy's batteries, which had been concentrating their fire on Second Brigade in front of Leonforte, slewed their guns around to bear upon Assoro. Within an hour after dawn the crest of the hill was almost hidden in the dust of volleying explosions.

The Regiment dug in. Able company and the assault company on the south and southwestern slopes; the balance of the unit on the north and northwestern side. A series of narrow terraces gave scant shelter but the men scraped shallow slit trenches in the stony soil, using their steel helmets as shovels. The enemy's fire grew steadily heavier, while that of the Regiment died away as realization dawned that this would be a long battle, and there would probably be no new supplies of ammunition until it ended.

But the surprises of that morning were not all one-sided. Before the infantry companies moved off it had been agreed that two green Verey flares, fired by the assault group, would indicate that the enemy position had been overrun and that it was safe for the unit's transport to move forward. Sometime after midnight, while the infantry was still struggling through the maze of hills and valleys far from the objective, a German in the positions overlooking the Dittaino sent a routine signal to his own artillery. The signal that he fired was two green flares.

Although there had been no sounds of battle as yet, the transport group accepted the evidence of its eyes and began moving north. Before dawn it had crossed the valley and the leading carriers had been halted by a crater blown in the road by German engineers some time earlier. Things were still quiet and some of the men of "F" echelon got out of their vehicles and lay down on the gentle slopes to catch a little sleep.

The Panzer-grenadiers defending the road must have

found it hard to credit their eyes as the grey light revealed thirty Canadian trucks and carriers drawn up in a neat line almost under the muzzles of the German guns.

The men of "F" echelon were rudely awakened. Some of them, leaping up out of a pleasant sleep, yelled horrid threats at their comrades who, they believed, had gone mad and were firing upon them. Others, more alert, realized that they were in a most unhappy situation and did what they could to remedy things. While one of the three-inch mortars was hastily put into action, the drivers tried to turn their vehicles on the narrow road. Someone, thinking with great rapidity, began throwing smoke grenades around the leading vehicles and under this thin protection the carriers managed to turn and clatter wildly down the slopes. One of them was driven by a motor-cyclist who had lost his own mount. He missed a turn and his carrier skidded off the road and somersaulted all the way down to the valley floor. The driver was miraculously uninjured and when he had dragged himself to his feet he stood for several minutes, in full view of the enemy, cursing his steed as if it had been a horse that had thrown him, and angrily banging its steel flanks with his boot.

It was fortunate for the transport and carrier men that at this juncture the balance of the Regiment on Assoro's crest carried the battle to the enemy's rear. In the ensuing confusion, and not without casualties—four trucks destroyed and four men badly wounded—"F" echelon managed to make good its retreat to the Dittaino and beyond. But it was in a chastened mood, and for some weeks afterwards it was notably suspicious of all orders to move forward to a "captured" area.

Meanwhile the position of the men on Assoro was becoming critical. The 500 infantrymen were almost completely surrounded on the three-acre crest of the mountain, and they could neither withdraw nor advance. Patrols were sent scuttling through the curtain of small-arms and shell-fire into the village. The place was cleared, but its capture brought little relief. The Regiment's threat against the enemy supply route could not be fully implemented, for already the scanty ammunition supplies carried on men's backs up the cliff, were growing perilously low. Confined to the congested area on the crest, the Regiment was exposed to an increasing fury of artillery shelling which was suddenly, and terrifyingly, supplemented by the fire of a number of German rocket batteries. This was the unit's first experience with the weapon nicknamed "The Moaning Minnie" and there was not a man who was not shaken by the initiation. The shells were nine inches in diameter and they were fired in salvos of five or six. The screaming of their rocket motors was an intolerable sound, as if the heavy shells were being forced through interminable rusty cylinders, slightly too small for their diameter. In addition there were single twelve-inch rockets, each containing 150 pounds of high explosive, that screeched their way slowly overhead and burst with a tremendous blast. More than 400 rocket and artillery shells crashed into the crest of Assoro in the first two hours of that bombardment.

But if the Regiment could not attack, it was not content to remain simply passive under this punishment. The Germans had decided that the crest of Assoro must be held by a very small number of Canadians and that, under cover of the shelling, it would be safe to withdraw the many vehicles which had been at the front. It was not safe. As the armoured half-trucks and open trucks came scuttling up the road the Regiment caught them in a withering small-arms fire and destroyed or forced the abandonment of almost a score of them. The Germans promptly reassessed the danger and prepared to counterattack the hill in force.

The Regiment's situation now became desperate. Unless it could somehow silence the enemy artillery it could not hope to hold on. Desperation sharpens men's wits, and in this extremity someone remembered the captured German observation post. It had been equipped with a fine pair of 20-power scissor telescopes and these were now hurriedly moved to the north end of the hill where Tweedsmuir and his second-in-command, Major Kennedy (who had originally trained as an artilleryman), could sweep almost the entire area from which the enemy guns were firing. There was only one radio—the short-range No. 56 set that had been miraculously carried up the cliff on a man's back. It sufficed to save the unit.

In the next hour the Regiment gave the distant Canadian artillery a series of dream targets. As each German gun fired up at Assoro, its position was radioed to the rear and within minutes salvos of Canadian shells fell upon it. There was no escape, for every movement of the German gunners could be seen. Methodically, carefully, the officers at the telescope directed the counter-battery fire until by noon well over half the enemy's artillery was out of action, and the rest was hurriedly withdrawing to safer sites.

But the vicious bombardment of the hill had added a new emotion to the battle mood. Men had discovered fear.

It was met by the beginning growth of a special type of fatalism, relieved by wit. The sort of thing that led one man to say: "When you dig a good slit-trench nothing can get you except a direct hit, and if it *is* a direct hit, it's because you teased your grandmother—or pulled the wings off flies." And another. "There's no use trying to hide out from a shell. If it's got your name on it, it'll chase you into the house, follow you upstairs, push the pot aside and get you under the bed." The humour was not uproarious— but it was adequate.

On the forward crest of the hill, pinned down behind a rock by a salvo of mortar bombs, Paddy Gahagen replied to the shout of his platoon commander who demanded to know what in the name of all the furies he was doing. "Looking for goddam four-leaf clovers with my nose" was the muffled reply.

Never had there been a greater need for the solace of humour than on Assoro. As the first day drew on, the heat grew worse and though the continuous heavy shelling had ceased, there were spasmodic outbursts from hour to hour. Water was a problem for there was only one well on the crest and those attempting to reach it were exposed to sniping fire. There was little food, for the emergency rations had long-since been consumed. In Charlie company, Pte. Greatrix became the hero of the moment when he produced a can of sardines that had been secreted in his haversack, and gravely offered each man in his platoon one fish.

A small cave near the well had been converted into a medical station and here the wounded lay in silent rows. The padre, Capt. Reg. Lane, a man of more than forty-five years of age, who was not equipped either by nature or by training for the hardships he had undergone, performed his own private miracle of endurance as he helped the stretcher bearers care for the living, or helped the living bury the dead.

In the late afternoon the C.O. gave up hope of a relief column breaking through to the Regiment that day, and called for two volunteers to return to the Canadian lines and attempt to guide a carrying party forward with rations and ammunition during the night. The R.S.M. and an officer accepted the task and set out down the great cliff, and across four miles of enemy dominated country, finally reaching safety in a state of complete exhaustion. But when darkness fell they were still able to guide a hundred men of the Royal Canadian Regiment laden with food and ammunition, back through the gorges to the foot of the mountain. The next morning the garrison received its first rations in thirty-six hours.

While the supply party was toiling over the hills and gullies, the battle situation had reached its climax. The Germans were being fiercely attacked at Leonforte by Second Brigade and they could not stand firm there while the threat of Assoro lay on their supply routes. They understood that Assoro would have to be retaken or the whole position would have to be abandoned; so at 2200 hours the enemy counterattacked. They came through the north end of the town, two companies of grenadiers, under cover of an intense mortar and artillery barrage, and they met Dog company on the lower slopes. Dog had very little ammunition left, but when the attack broke and fell away, Dog company had not given any ground and had taken a heavy toll of the attackers. It was the Germans' last effort. As darkness fell, they began to withdraw both from Assoro and from Leonforte to the west. The gates were opening.

The ordeal of the men on the mountain was not yet at an end for the road up to Assoro had been so badly cratered that it was not until late on July 23rd that the Regiment could be relieved.

At the precious well a group of a dozen soldiers relaxed contentedly, drinking to their hearts' content, and splashing cold water over their faces and arms. Below the town, supply trucks at last rumbled forward. Now the Regiment could rest.

And then, somewhere far to the north, the crew of a German rocket-launcher prepared to abandon their position. One 21-cm. rocket was set up for firing with its electric igniters wired and ready. And someone, in a last defiant gesture, paused for a moment to close the circuit and send the rocket screaming into the quiet sky.

The indecent shriek of the projectile drifted over the brown hills. The men by the well heard, but they had only time to stiffen warily before the rocket struck. It hit the curbing of the well, and when the black and acrid smoke had cleared, four dead men lay in the new crater, while five others moaned in mortal agony.

It was a brutal way to learn the grim lesson that in battle there can be no escape—until the war is done.

The Treetops Raid

About one-third of the oil—especially the high octane fuel necessary for aircraft—used by the German war machine came from refineries in Ploesti, Rumania. In the early years of the war, an oil refinery did not receive top priority in the bombing lists of the Allied air forces; rather, electrical plants, transportation centers, and industrial centers manufacturing tanks, planes, etc., took precedence. But in May 1943, during a meeting in Algiers, the Allied leaders decided a strike should be made against the Ploesti refineries.

In June, the 44th and 93rd groups of the VIII Bomber Command, 2nd Bombardment Wing, then undergoing combat over Europe, were withdrawn and given special new flying assignments. At the end of the month they were sent to Benghazi where they joined two other groups of the Ninth Air Force, the 98th and 376th. Altogether a force of approximately 200 B-24 Liberators was now assembled for the 2700 mile strike.*

In July, during the invasion of Sicily, these bomber crews were sent on daily missions against carefully selected targets. It was not until several planes were shot down that air force brass realized that some of the crew officers had already been briefed on the Ploesti strike. As a precaution against information leaks from any captured officers, all future combat missions were canceled until August 1.

According to Leon Wolff, the Ploesti "complex as a whole was fairly

*This would not be the first Allied raid on Ploesti. On June 11, 1942 a small force of 13 B-24s took off from the Egyptian air base at Fazid and dropped two tons of bombs. Little damage was done but the Germans and Rumanians immediately took pains to improve antiaircraft installations and warning systems against further raids.

concentrated around the major refineries and their most vital installations—mainly the six cracking plants. Distilling units, too, were particularly fragile, as well as the boilerhouses, power plants, and a few gas-liquefying plants. A vast scattering of over 2000 storage tanks dotted the area. Snake-like rail lines threaded everywhere, requiring in turn several key marshaling yards. A network of pipe lines connected the distant oil wells with the refineries. It all added up to a dream of an aerial target . . ." *

A most important condition for the success of the raid was surprise; a new and daring tactic was to be tried—planes were to hit Ploesti in successive waves but at "zero altitude." ** The planners believed such a maneuver would cause the greatest possible damage to the refineries.

The B-24s were fitted out with additional armor plate to protect against small-arms ground fire; an extra .50 caliber machine gun was placed in the nose, and the top turret guns in lead planes were made operable to fire forward to increase the overall strafing power of the leaders.

There were many doubts about the tactics of the low-level raid. For instance,

"The enlisted gunners were not told of the detailed bombing plan until the night before the mission. But unofficially the word had seeped down, or the men had made a remarkably good guess, and they too expressed many doubts. Some top officers began to wonder whether an unusual number of personnel might not find a reason—such as illness—to evade the mission. It cannot be doubted that fear had begun to permeate the five groups as the date for the ominous venture neared. Daily it seemed more and more suicidal. The consensus was that surprise was improbable, low-level or high. Flak would slaughter the low-flying, cumbersome monsters. Fighters would knock down dozens, at least on the way back, if not sooner. The balloon cables would be murderous. And 2700 total miles of unescorted flying, in itself, was no joke over enemy territory or water. It all seemed to add up to a desperate and needless gamble.

"In the desert, in July, everything was that much more exasperating. It was hot. Countless little sand flies made the fliers fretful. Scorpions

*Low Level Mission, by Leon Wolff, published by Doubleday & Co., Inc., p. 84.
** Minimum possible altitude.

prowled through the tents and took up lodging in the men's clothes and bedding; their sting was nasty, flashlights were prized, and walking barefoot was unheard of.

"But first, last, and foremost was the sand. Reddish and talclike, it seeped into everything and became an invariable part of life. Every afternoon the wind came up and the desert began to swirl. To evade the dry, gritty, blinding sandstorms, men even welcomed combat flying. The wind tore out tent stakes, it ballooned out the canvas tents in an afternoon, it covered everything inside with sand piled inches deep. The battle was without end." *

Then on July 31, the day before the mission, official briefings were held and the success of the assignment could be seen to depend on unusually delicate timing. "Plans called for the five groups to proceed northward in column after the original forming up over Benghazi. Then, regardless of what happened in the interim, there would be a time check over the Danube. Each group had its own assigned time of arrival at that point. From there the five groups would proceed in column to their first Initial Point. And finally, still in line, one after the other according to their time of arrival at the I.P., they would bomb their targets in the order that had been designated in the field order and by the briefing officers day in and day out for weeks on end. While the less experienced 389 had been assigned the easier separate target of Campina, the other four groups would be bunched together from Pitesti onward. This was the first I.P.; the second was Floresti, from which the run would be made to the target in bunched waves as swiftly as possible." **

*Low Level Mission, pp. 100-101.
** Low Level Mission, pp. 121, 122.

"TARGET: PLOESTI"*

by Leon Wolff

SEVEN-TEN A.M.

It began badly. One of the planes from the 98th never got off the ground, ran to the end of the runway, crashed, and exploded, killing all crew members aboard instantly.

Take-offs continued amid billows of orange-red dust, with the 44th and 98th using the adjacent Benina field and the other groups taking off from the strips near Benghazi proper. The weather was good except for a slight haze which reduced visibility to about ten miles. Each plane was flown to 2000 feet. There it wheeled overhead awaiting the remainder of its group. The men plugged their radios into the jack marked "interphone," and the pilots interrogated each man in turn ("pilot to navigator . . . pilot to radioman . . . pilot to tail gunner . . ." and so on). Each crew member stated that his guns and station were in order, that he had checked his oxygen (it would probably not be needed on this trip), that his Mae West was on (they would be over water half the way), that his parachute was in proper condition (it would be useless during the low-level phase). Everybody checked his machine gun by firing short bursts into the Mediterranean.

7:40 A.M.

Now all five groups were aloft and formed up. One aircraft had been scratched before dawn, one had already

*A somewhat condensed version of several chapters from *Low Level Mission*.

252

crashed, and the remaining 176 assembled in follow-the-leader order behind Compton's 376th. Next came Baker's 93rd, then Kane's 98th, then Johnson's 44th, with Wood's 389th bringing up the rear. The first group flew low over the water. Each successive group was a little higher than the one in front of it, and the last group, Jack Wood's 389th, held an altitude of 4000 feet. In this alignment the great task force swung north and headed across the Mediterranean Sea, cobalt-blue, brilliant, and glistening in the slanting morning sun that glanced off the whitecaps.

7:50 A.M.

One of the planes (the Kickapoo) flown by a squadron leader of the 376th began a long curving sweep out of formation to the right. Major Ramsey Potts had stood up to stretch, turning his controls over to his co-pilot, when he noticed this. "He seemed to slide off on his right wing and burst into flames. The radio operator on my airplane, who was standing beside me looking out across the sea—toward the lead formation which was off to our right and below us —said, 'Gee whiz, look at the flame!' And that was quite an incongruous sort of reaction, I thought, so I half-pushed him back into his seat and told him to shut up . . . We were all keyed up, and to have this happen to a lead plane in the lead formation was kind of shocking."

The Liberator on fire was still partially under control, and the pilot thought he could make it back to the Benina strip. This he did, but as the ship neared the ground it was flying fast and not quite level. The field was still a swirling fog of red dust stirred up by the prop-wash of the last planes to take off several minutes previously. With a sickening jolt the Kickapoo hit the runway, bounced twenty feet into the air, hit again, skidded down the extreme edge of the field, smashed into a concrete telephone pole, and exploded. Eight of the ten men were killed. Sergeant Eugene Garner came out almost unharmed, but the navigator, Lieutenant Russell Polivka, survived with fearful burns from head to waist.

Radio silence had been put to the test during this incident, but not a word was spoken by the horrified on-lookers aloft. The plane behind the ill-fated one moved into the vacant slot, and the group flew wordlessly on.

All across the Mediterranean the planes flew on in a flat V, wing tip to wing tip, none more than twenty-five feet away from another. It was a pleasure, at least, to be flying so low that annoying, efficiency-robbing oxygen masks were not needed. As time passed planes began to turn back because of mechanical failures. Captain William Banks of Kane's 98th observed: "Every once in a while I would look off to my left and see one or two Liberators feather a prop, wheel out of formation, and start for home. A little later one of the crew would call over the interphone, 'Another plane's turned back!' Most of them went under us. We could see them about halfway down between us and the sea, trying to make it to safe, Allied land before they piled into the Mediterranean. Others would turn back close enough for us to see the men in the plane. We waved goodbye . . ."

Eleven planes in all aborted. Major Shingler thought that the number was "a little high," but pointed out that "it was up to the pilots to use their own discretion," and that a mission as long and hazardous as this called for aircraft in top condition "especially as we were anticipating the interception of fighters from the time we entered the coast off the Adriatic Sea, all the way in and all the way back." (It is true that seven of the eleven aborts came from Kane's group. This percentage seems out of line and may have been caused by the fact that Kane often strongly advised his people to fly beyond their operational limit. It is known that in this mission, especially, he had exerted great pressure, even to the point of delaying certain men stateside leave until their return from Ploesti.) As each plane turned back the hole in the formation was plugged up. Each group remained intact, but the haze had caused the five groups to become partially separated from each other. The 98th, for one, had become completely isolated after three hours. No enemy shipping or planes were sighted; thus far the element of surprise was still on the side of the invaders.

11:30 A.M.

While the 376th Group was proceeding over the coast line of the island of Corfu, Brian Flavell's lead plane spun into the sea with the loss of all crewmen, including the lead navigator, Captain Anderson. When this crucial plane and officer went down, a chill of foreboding passed through all members of the group. Momentarily the 376th began to scatter in confusion, trying to select a new leader. Then the plane carrying Compton and Ent moved out of their section and up into the lead position of the group. In theory lead navigating was now in the hands of a young, inexperienced second lieutenant. In actuality Compton and Ent took over, since they doubted the ability of the youngster to handle the assignment of penetration to the target accurately.

The attacking formation, which had originally been conceived by General Brereton to include 178 aircraft, was now reduced to 163 effective sorties, and the five groups were considerably scattered as they began crossing the coast line in the vicinity of the Greek-Albanian border. Now they turned gently northeastward. Over the land, swelling white cumulus clouds were beginning to form well under 10,000 feet. As the planes crossed Albania and approached Yugoslavia they began to climb, for ahead of them lay the North Albanian Alps.

12:20 P.M.

Here the cloud build-ups had become fairly dense and towering, rising to about 15,000 feet, a mile and a half above the average height of the mountains. Four of the leaders elected to fly above the clouds, while Kane led his group under them at about 12,000 feet. The winds at the higher altitude favored those groups. Imperceptibly their ground-speed increased.

1:30 P.M.

As the four high groups crossed the final mountains above the clouds and neared the Bulgarian border, a certain amount of confusion had taken place. Even some individual squadrons were now quite separated. In going through clouds twice (up and down) most aircraft had temporarily lost sight of each other. Obviously many adjustments would have to be made if each group individually were to pull itself together before reaching the target.

Killer Kane and his outfit were, for the moment, nowhere. Unfavorable winds had left them far behind, struggling somewhere over the Alps. Keith Compton's aircraft were first to break through into the open country. In fair order they headed for the Danube without pause. By now Jack Wood had overrun both Addison Baker and Leon Johnson (unavoidably so, because of his higher altitude and speed). Since he was supposed to be last in line, this would require a correction. Under ordinary circumstances the use of inter-plane radio communication would have straightened the jumble out, but this was not possible today. So the four groups proceeded toward the little town of Lom on the Danube, losing altitude and trying to sort themselves out in the process. By the time they reached the great river most squadrons were down to about 2500 feet. The clouds had thinned out. A beautiful, nearly clear, sunny day welcomed them in Rumania.

1:50 P.M.

At this point the laggard 98th broke through the Alps and the cumulus and headed for the Danube in the vicinity of Lom, Bulgaria. There much skillful but nerve-racking maneuvering was already taking place. Compton and Baker had reorganized in good fashion and were precisely on time as briefed. Congratulating themselves on their accuracy, they set out for their first I.P.—the town of Pitesti.

This was an understandable but regrettable move, for it brought the 376th and 93rd toward the target far ahead of the other formations. For during this interval the succeeding groups continued to circle over the Danube, arranging themselves into their proper elements; and while so engaged they were surprised to see Killer Kane's straggly collection of aircraft approach from the south. Since these

256

belonged in front, the others were forced to wait for them.

The feelings of the men during this seemingly interminable delay can well be imagined. At 2500 feet they were in plain view of anybody on the ground. The entire mission had been planned on the basis of at least partial surprise, and this had been one reason for the decision to execute it at low level. Now the concept was being apparently nullified by faulty timing, which in turn had been caused by a mere cloud obstacle.

More than likely the defenders had already been alerted, especially since Compton and Baker had already gone on to the I.P. Yet minutes passed without a sign of enemy fighters or anti-aircraft fire. The Rumanian Cabinet, including Marshal Antonescu, weekending at the little town of Snagov, heard the sound of airplanes above but thought nothing of it.

2:10 P.M.

After these agonies of readjustment and realignment the three late groups set off toward Pitesti, losing altitude and picking up speed in a shallow dive. They knew they were twenty minutes behind schedule.

It was about now that the crew of Hadley's Harem, piloted by Lieutenant Gilbert Hadley, claims they were spotted and shadowed by two enemy fighters who made no attempt to close. (If true, this meant that the attacking bombers had lost the element of surprise long before reaching even the first I.P., a likelihood more or less verified by subsequent information and events.)

2:30 P.M.

The two early groups, under Compton and Baker, reached the first I.P.—Pitesti—at an altitude of 200 feet. Here they came down even farther, perhaps to twenty or thirty feet above the ground.

The reaction of the people below to this fantastic sight and sound was one of wild excitement. Details could be seen vividly from aloft. An elderly man and woman fell to their knees and prayed. People in the villages stood still and gaped upward. Most of them had their Sunday finery on. "You could see people going to church . . . man, wife, and child walking along the country roads." Bombardier Herbert Light, through his binoculars, saw an open-air festival in progress, with the women dressed in colorful skirts and blouses. One of them threw her apron over her head in panic.

As they roared over the wheat fields, the first unfriendly acts occurred: farmers threw stones and pitchforks at them. One farmer leading two horses was startled by the advancing planes and leaped into a nearby stream. A girl swimming in another river was reported by ten separate crews.

And still there was not a plane, not a gun to challenge the Americans. At about 200 mph and rock-bottom height (one plane had to pull up to avoid hitting a man on a horse) everything went by swiftly and dreamlike. In fascination the men watched the kaleidoscopic sights hurtle below them, and looked above for the enemy interceptors that they had been awaiting for two hours. They cleared their guns in short bursts, stared, and waited, but nothing happened and nobody came.

2:50 P.M.

The remaining three groups arrived at Pitesti and began to drop to treetop level, the 98th and 44th for the run to Floresti, the 389th for its private target: Campina. The 98th had been specifically "directed to get down to fifty feet, and we knew fifty feet would put us below some of the stacks in the refinery. But we figured we could pull up over those and get back down . . ."

Meanwhile the new lead plane of the lead group, piloted by Colonel Compton, in which General Ent was a passenger, was on its way to Floresti, the second and final I.P., from which the turn to the target would be made. A railroad line led from Floresti straight into Ploesti. The same was true of Targoviste; and here a blunder of major magnitude was made. As their aircraft approached the latter, Compton and Ent decided to turn with that railroad, having mistaken the town for Floresti—an error not too difficult to make in a plane moving so fast and so low. Their young navigator protested, but General Ent hastily overrode him. Scarcely before anyone could realize what was happening, they had turned sharply down the railroad and were roaring downhill to the southeast at nearly 300 mph, followed by the rest of their group and Baker's 93rd. But this route led to Bucharest, not Ploesti. What ensued is described by Major Potts of the following 93rd:

"We had gone through this maneuver of turning from the run-up to the Initial Point and make the run-down on the target many times. And as we drew near that point I had a map of my own in the cockpit, and my navigator was checking with me constantly. I was trying to jockey myself into position so I would be trailing a little bit, so when the turn to the right took place I could wheel into line and we could present a frontal string of airplanes to the target as we came into it.

"However, just about nine minutes before we were due, according to my calculations and those of my navigator . . . the lead formation started to turn to the right. And the second formation, taken by surprise, turned in a kind of following position. We were boxed in, and I had no choice but to turn. At that point I broke radio silence and started calling the leader . . ."

It will be noted that radio silence had been enforced thus far. However, all surprise was lost now—the formation led by Compton, followed by Baker's puzzled group, was already on the outskirts of Bucharest. The spires of the buildings in the center of the city, white and delicate in the distance, could be seen clearly. German and Rumanian staffs were already in an uproar, and no doubt wondering why the Americans would want to attack Rumania's innocent capital city. Dozens of air-raid sirens began to yowl. All flak batteries had been called into action. Radio and telephone had alerted every fighter field in the Balkans.

"At that point the leader of the formation called back and said he realized he had made the wrong turn and was turning back to the left. We made a left turn but this maneuver had taken us south of the target, and we were now coming in on an axis of attack for which we had not been briefed, and with which our navigators and bombardiers were unfamiliar.

"I thought that I might turn left again and go back to the Initial Point. But by the time I had run the thought through my mind I found that we were practically on top of some of the refineries, and we were getting shot at in all directions. It just would have been useless to try to turn around and come back on the right axis."

3:00 P.M.

Unaware of all this, Jack Wood and his aircraft had reached Campina; Killer Kane and Leon Johnson had made their turn at Floresti and were running toward Ploesti. It did not strike them as unusual that the defenders seemed unusually alert, although this was largely caused by the premature turn made by the 376th some twenty minutes earlier. One of Lieutenant Robert Sternfels' gunners called him on the phone to ask, "When can I start firing, boss?" He replied, "Any damn time you see something worth shooting at." A few miles from the main target the raid paid its first dividend. Gunners of Kane's own plane blew up several dozen oil cars sided at a rail junction along the Floresti-Ploesti spur.

At this point Kane was shocked to see several pink B-24s pass under him heading southwest. Since pink identified Compton's outfit, Kane realized for the first time that the 376th had already entered and left the target area.

As yet not a single one of the five groups had reached their assigned target, but already they had run into a small-caliber hornet's nest. Most of this was ordinary machine-gun fire. One or two planes had already been brought down by it, and others had been seriously damaged by the puncturing of hydraulic lines and injury to electrical systems. Dozens of these smaller flak batteries and machine-gun nests sprouted from nowhere. Roofs of cottages unfolded and guns swung out; haystacks parted to reveal gun emplacements. Lightninglike duels were fought between many air crews and these gunners, in which some of the latter were killed. But as yet there was little or no interference from heavy flak batteries, partially because the planes were too low to be hit by them. This factor and the approach to the target are described by Colonel Johnson:

"We got down on the deck . . . most of us had studied those maps so much that we needed no maps from the time we left the Danube. I remember them saying, 'North of this town on a hill there will be a monastery four miles out of town.' I remember seeing it distinctly. 'You will cross a big sandy river and there will be two bridges across it.' So from the time we crossed the Danube to the time we turned in to the target I personally never needed a map. We had moving pictures of the target area, and we had sand table models made up—it was so similar to what we'd seen that we had no difficulty . . .

"We turned—98th, 44th, in that order—until we came to a point where we all turned in abreast . . . And the 389th had pulled out to go to their target, which was in a little valley up ahead.

"As we approached Ploesti we could see heavy smoke and fires over the town, and at the same time we could see guns firing at us in the vicinity of the target and to the north of the target, as we were running from north to south. As these guns fired we would dive to get as low as we could. I remember distinctly being lower than some high-tension wires and pulling up over them in formation.

"We had over a hundred airplanes there down below treetop level . . . because our salvation seemed to be there. They couldn't get their artillery trained on us if we were that low . . ."

All the ingredients necessary to bring about a calamity of the first water were now present:

The cloud structure which had caused a mix-up of the formations also brought about a long delay over the Danube which, doubtlessly, had led to their tentative detection.

The premature attack of the two leading groups would

bring in its wake two penalties for the following two groups attacking Ploesti itself: First, the immediate defenses would be even more alert to subsequent aircraft. Second, these would have to fly into the fires left by their predecessors.

The false turn toward Bucharest finally and definitely alerted all defenders elsewhere, as well as in the immediate vicinity, twenty minutes too soon. This particularly meant fighter aircraft and insured that the bombers would receive their maximum attention on the way back.

The 376th and 93rd would now be forced to approach the target from its most heavily defended sector and, as pointed out by Major Potts, from an angle with which they were not acquainted. Therefore there was likely to be a good deal of waste motion in their bombing of the assigned objectives, assuming that they would be able to recognize them at all.

The element of surprise having been dissipated, lack of friendly fighter escort would tell even more heavily than had been expected.

Thus, long before the various elements had begun their final run into the targets assigned them, nearly 400 German, Rumanian, and Italian fighter pilots were already racing toward their waiting ME-109s, HE-111s, and Macchis, which were being hurriedly warmed up on a dozen flight lines by startled mechanics in Italy and Hungary as well as Rumania itself. As for flak and machine-gun emplacements, every one had been at least partially manned a half hour ago, and by now the full complement of each crew was ready and waiting. And, to complicate matters, the defenders had been given enough time to set off several dozen smoke pots at the southeast section of Ploesti which were beginning to obscure, to some degree, the various aiming points assigned to the bombardiers.

So the worst of all possible nightmares was now a definite reality: surprise was lost, the defenders were 100 per cent alert, the bombers were stranded twenty feet above the ground, 1350 miles from home without escort, and were about to be hit by fighters . . . "flak, small arms, everything but slingshots." Already some of the younger, more panicky American gunners had begun to fire at anything that moved, including cows that grazed quietly in the fields below.

After the run-up through the valley (referred to as "difficult" by General Brereton in his memoirs) and the wrong turn toward Bucharest instead of Ploesti, Compton found his formation in an uncomfortable predicament. To go back toward the I.P. and start all over again seemed impossible. Pandemonium had already broken loose. On the other hand, to run through the strongest sector of anti-aircraft guns in a dubious effort to locate the target from an unfamiliar direction would, in effect, base the entire 376th operation on pure guesswork. After discovering the mistake he had, at most, one minute in which to make up his mind. All thirty planes were now flying over the suburbs of Bucharest itself.

Following a hurried conversation with General Ent, Compton decided to head straight for Ploesti from the southwest. Thereupon, the 376th, still followed by Addison Baker's group, executed the tightest possible turn toward the target twenty-five miles away. The closer Compton's men approached Ploesti, the more intense became the flak, fired by German gunners at remarkably oblique angles directly into the path of the oncoming planes; 88-mm. cannon fired point-blank over open sights, like so many shotguns. Machine-gun bullets came up in sheets. Three bombers apparently crashed during this phase.

In desperation Compton then led his remaining aircraft in a great twenty-mile semicircle around Ploesti, hoping to get at it from a northerly direction. While this would be a roundabout route, at least the final approach would be more or less as planned, and the planes would be coming in from the direction where Intelligence had forecast the least number of defending guns.

So the 376th drove in from the new angle, northeast of

Ploesti. Though obscured by smoke, their target, Romana Americana, could be dimly seen in the distance. However, the volume of AA fire seemed as great as it had been previously to the south. At this point General Ent himself got on the inter-plane radio and directed the 376th Group to attack "targets of opportunity." This was, in effect, an admission that the individual attack of this group had misfired. The five squadron commanders, each leading six planes, were now on their own.

Most of these planes ranged over the general Ploesti target area and unloaded on anything that looked good. It was in this action that the volunteer, Major Jerstad, and most of his crew were killed. When a burst of flak caught his plane it began to burn. He continued to fly toward the refinery that he had selected, and stayed on course for three miles while the flames sheathed both wings and began to envelop the body of the plane as far back as the top turret. After bombing the plant, his plane plummeted into the target area.

Major Norman C. Appold, a tall, thin youth with a large Adam's apple, decided to make a try for the Concordia Vega installation. He led his squadron straight in, and all aircraft unloaded practically at once. An inferno of fire and smoke burst skyward. The six planes plunged through it and emerged on the other side, miraculously unharmed but covered with soot. While the target was in this fashion well plastered, it had been intended for Addison Baker's target force.

And, finally, a few planes from the now thoroughly dispersed lead group set out for Campina, where they bombed the Steaua Romana refinery, which had already been smashed by Jack Wood's outfit.

Bitter and frustrated over the turn of events, Colonel Baker and his 93rd had been dragged willy-nilly into this imbroglio from the south, behind Compton's formation. Compton, as noted, had turned right (east) at the outskirts of Ploesti. It was the second time his group had turned unaccountably right, and perhaps Baker was becoming annoyed, for he ignored the leading group and the

AA fire and plunged directly into the target from the south, followed by his intact group of thirty-five aircraft. Prior to the mission Baker had emphasized the stringent necessity of keeping a tight formation so as to hit their small targets with the greatest number of bombs. He had warned: "If anything happens to the lead ship pay no attention. Don't swerve. No matter what happens, keep straight . . ."

Baker's Target Force No. 2 Liberators had been assigned Concordia Vega, but they could not locate it from their reverse approach. However, as noted, Major Appold's squadron had been kind enough to bomb it by mistake, and with excellent results.

Meanwhile, Target Force No. 3, also under Colonel Baker and commanded by Major Potts, was doing its best to find something resembling its assigned targets. As related by the Major, "Several of the planes in my formation had dropped by this time . . . we went ahead and bombed what we thought was the right target, but probably not more than five planes in my formation bombed the right target. The others were dropping their bombs on what they thought was the target, but they were confused. As we went over . . . coming in, as I say, from the south, the wrong direction, the planes on my right and left went down . . ."

Meanwhile a shell had struck the right side of the cockpit of Colonel Baker's Liberator, killing the co-pilot and injuring the colonel. The forward section of the ship began to burn. Almost immediately it was hit again, by a heavier-caliber shell. A wavering mass of flames, the bomber stayed on course long enough for Baker's bombardier to dump his entire bomb load into a single refinery a few dozen yards below. Baker tried to pull up so that his crew could bail out, but the plane would not respond. It began to somersault end over end lightning-fast, like a boy's toy, and then crashed heavily on the edge of the refinery it had just bombed, with all men still aboard.

Enemy fighters, portents of things to come, had already begun to appear in small units. In spite of them and the flak the 93rd accurately bombed its improvised targets from heights as low as 100 feet. These later turned out to be Astra Romana, Phoenix Orion, and Columbia Aquila, refineries which had been intended for the attentions of Kane and Johnson and their respective men. Eleven B-24s from the 93rd Group were lost over these targets alone. One plane crashed into a women's prison, allegedly killing about a hundred inmates.

The easiest objective had been given to Jack Wood and his somewhat less experienced collection of thirty crews, the 389th Bombardment Group. They were to fly to the suburb of Campina and bomb only the Steaua Romana refinery, giving Ploesti and the other squadrons a wide berth coming and going. But here again things did not work out quite as planned.

"We had been warned," said Colonel Wood, "to avoid drifting left after we crossed the Danube because of a G.C.I. station in that direction, and to stay strictly on our northeast course. But what do the two groups in front of us do but veer left at exactly that point.

"I was checking my navigator to the fraction of an inch —I wasn't at the controls—I had a pilot and co-pilot flying the plane and I was squeezed in almost between them with a map on my knees. As soon as I saw Kane and Johnson swing left I turned to my pilot and said, 'I don't know where the hell those fellows are going, but from now on we're on our own.' We kept straight on for Pitesti."

Wood could afford to be more independent than the other commanders, for his group was the only one with a single, separate target not in Ploesti proper. After reaching their I.P. they banked slightly northward and at 4000 feet headed laterally across the mountain ranges which temporarily prevented them from coming down to zero altitude. Their task was to pick out a particular valley about three miles wide, and then to follow it straight into Campina. They then proceeded to descend into the wrong valley. When this mistake was discovered, Wood calmly led his outfit up to 4000 feet again, and over into the next valley, which turned out to be the right one. The bombers coasted down to minimum altitude once more, and raced toward their target. At this stage machine-gun nests on the sides of the hills were firing down on them—a novelty, certainly, in anti-aircraft annals. Some of the planes ripped their wings through the treetop branches. As they approached the target many gun duels ("like a wild-west movie") took place between the bombers and the flak and machine-gun batteries concealed below in haystacks, in railway flatcars, and in farmhouses. Over four hundred .50-caliber American machine guns, including the new nose armament, which was used to good advantage, poured a flood of millions of bullets from all directions at anything that moved. This sweeping mass of fire killed, wounded, and scattered great numbers of the defenders during the earsplitting sweep toward the town.

Youthful Second Lieutenant Lloyd Hughes was among those killed at Steaua Romana. His plane was hit by machine-gun bullets during the run-in through the valley, and sheets of gasoline poured out of the left wing and bomb bay. But since the plane was not yet afire, Hughes decided to make his run to the target. In doing so he passed through a tongue of flame which touched off the left wing. After releasing his load of explosives and incendiaries he tried to land in a dry creek bed, found a bridge in the way, pulled up and tried again; but it was too late, and his B-24 spun into the ground. (From another plane moving pictures were taken of the entire sequence of this tragedy, from the moment when gasoline started pouring out of the tanks until the flaming machine crashed—a remarkable film still on secret Air Force file.)

Lieutenant John Fino, bombardier of the 389th lead plane, dropped a thousand-pound bomb directly through the large double doors of one power plant which apparently had not had time to reduce its steam pressure. As a result this single bomb created innumerable explosions within the plant by tearing out high-pressure steam conduits.

Another plane from a later wave was destroyed like a moth in a flame when a boilerhouse hit by a previous bomber blew up just in time to catch it in the explosion. But the 389th hit Campina accurately and as briefed. In ten narrow waves of three planes each the group passed over the target exactly as planned and practiced over the mock-up in Libya. At this point one stray squadron from Compton's 376th began to show up, for, it will be recalled, some of them had decided to go to Campina after General Ent's order to attack "targets of opportunity."

"We could see these aircraft about three or four miles to our right coming in at right-angles to our line of approach, and we couldn't figure out what they were doing around here, especially since they were bound to arrive after we were all finished." And several minutes after the 389th made its turn back to home base the bombers from Compton's group reached the holocaust that had once been the Campina refineries, and inflicted further damage on the roaring, blackened remnants of this installation.

"We had expected to take losses," Colonel John Kane said, "but I never will forget those big Libs going down like flies." His radio operator, Ray Hubbard, added, "I looked through the open bomb-bay doors and could see flames from exploding gas tanks shooting right up into us. The fire wrapped us up. I looked out of the side windows and saw the others flying through smoke and flames. It was flying through hell . . . I guess we'll go straight to heaven when we die. We've had our purgatory." Official AAF historians admit that the 98th and 44th Bombardment Groups would have been morally justified in turning back from the target under the circumstances.

Kane's 98th was after Phoenix Orion and Astra Romana, but Baker's squadrons had been there first. So for Killer's aircraft to bomb them, which they proceeded to do, they were forced to fly directly into the fires and explosions left behind by their own people. In addition, the delayed-action bombs were now beginning to detonate. This, in fact, was the most insidious hazard of all, not only for Kane's group but later for Johnson's as well. A sheet of flame and a billow of smoke could often be avoided by an oncoming plane, but nothing could be done about sudden explosions from delayed-action fuses dropped previously by planes which had attacked refineries not assigned to them. Possibly a total of six aircraft were cremated in mid-air by these gigantic and unexpected blasts.

Kane's plane itself was hit in one engine just as it came over one of the targets. He feathered the propeller and added power to the other three engines. "From below, ack-ack batteries were firing at us point-blank . . . like a skeet shoot."

Wringing wet with perspiration from the roaring fires on the ground and from the emotional tension of the mission, Kane's men severely damaged Phoenix Orion, left it behind, and drove on doggedly for the great Astra Romana plant. It was unbearably hot in the planes from the wall of flames and explosions rising over 300 feet, the August heat of the day, and the machine guns, which had been firing steadily until the gun barrels were blistering to the touch. The colonel reported, "We could see reservoir tanks exploding, with fire shooting up like ruddy tongues in the middle of the smoke. It was so hot the hair on my arms was singed. I thought I could smell it burn . . ." The smoke was a constant worry, for it obscured chimneys and balloon cables lurking within it.

An unexpected factor over the target area was the violent turbulence caused by flames and explosions. At best a B-24 is not easy (like a B-17) to fly steadily; even in routine formation it tends to wander and slide when not on automatic pilot. Over Ploesti this defect was dangerously magnified. Only with difficulty could the planes be kept under control near the heart of the inferno. They rolled and pitched like sheets of paper in a breeze. Many a bomber could be seen hanging crazily on a wing tip; others sagged and then were wafted upward by a hot billow of uprushing air. Crew members had to strap themselves down. Pilots and co-pilots flew their ships simultaneously; the job was too much for one man. There is little doubt that several planes went into the ground purely through accidental dives and sideslips. Sometimes pilots were forced to change course right in the middle of a bomb run; off they veered to attack another refinery instead, in split-second switches caused by the simple necessity of avoiding collisions with other bombers off course or out of formation.

The ships swept on, weaving in and out of the smoke-stacks, through several miles of storage areas and small farms. "We [had] many airplanes come back with corn stalks hung in their bomb-bays," remarked Major Shingler. "In a B-24 the bomb-bays open up like a clam-shell, and of course we were right down on the deck. When they shut the bomb-bay doors . . . they just gathered up a little corn with it." The remnants of the 98th hit Target White 4 in four waves at a speed over the objective of about 185 mph. The smudge pots, fortunately, turned out to be no great nuisance.

Enemy fighters began to hover over the wild scene, wait-ing for the bombers to leave the area and come up from the floor. A few of them tried to attack the heavy planes hugging the ground, but the majority of the ME-109s and other interceptors grimly bided their time. The bombers stuck to their assignment, manifold and prop settings as low as possible, and mixtures lean, to save gasoline.

"Our pinpoint was a smokestack," said Captain William Banks. ". . . all we needed was a split-second to sight it. And we had to get it with the first try; there would be no time to turn around for another run this trip. Somebody ahead of us had bombed our target by mistake. We all felt sick when we saw the oil tanks exploding and great swirls of smoke pouring up from the ground. There was nothing to do but try to hit it again . . .

"Oil tanks were still going off right under us, and on both sides German ack-ack batteries were firing in unison. We were so low that they were actually trained down on us.

"We kept straining our eyes for that stack. We couldn't see it yet, and I began to worry. It looked as if we weren't going to get the damned thing after all . . . We just plowed on, sweating blood and not saying a word. The *Sad Sack* was bristling with guns for this mission and we were firing every one of them as we roared in. The whole plane shuddered with the fire.

". . . Finally I decided to pull away. We had finished our run and hadn't even seen our pinpoint. At that moment

Joe Souza yelled. He had spotted our smokestack and power plant through an opening in the smoke. I held her steady for a split second while Joe sighted and let his bombs go, and then I almost jumped out of my seat. Carl shouted, 'Jesus!' and I pulled back with all the strength I had. Right in front of us, square in the middle of the windshield and looming up almost out of sight was the tallest . . . smokestack I have ever seen.

". . . Shaking all over with the racing of her motors, the *Sad Sack* leaped up and climbed for the top of it. I prayed as she lost speed and the stack rushed at us. We cleared it as if we were pole-vaulting . . ."

Some contact bombs failed to explode, but few of the crewmen noticed this in the confusion around them. Banks continued: "There were B-24s going down all around us now. We saw two fall right in front of us that had apparently climbed up out of formation and had been hit by pursuit planes. The ground was spotted with them, including some that had managed to land safely. The crews of these last were beside them, watching the planes burn and waving to us as we went by . . . We ducked even closer to the ground and scooted for home."

The squadron in which Captain John Palm was flying had been ordered to climb to 100 feet when they arrived thirty seconds from their assigned target. This he did, but when he reached it his plane was the only one of the six left. And as he was nearing the refinery, his own forlorn Liberator was finally hit. An anti-aircraft shell knocked out three engines. The plane went into a shallow dive. Two men in the nose were killed outright. Captain Palm's right leg was blown off. He glanced down and noted, almost absently, that it was hanging by a few strands. At the moment he had other problems. The plane was going in fast, just above the refinery that was to have been bombed. He yanked the emergency release.

As the action increased in intensity, a pall of dense black smoke added to the difficulties and caused several near-collisions. B-24s were crisscrossing the area. Much of the confusion was caused by Compton's earlier aircraft, which were roaming haphazardly over the entire target area seeking targets of opportunity, as instructed by General Ent. This meandering, plus the maneuvers of Baker's aircraft in bombing installations not under their briefed jurisdiction, and from a reverse direction, created a particular hazard that no one had dreamed would take place during this meticulously planned operation. Yet all but eight of Kane's element got over the target, one having cracked up in the take-off, and seven others having turned back with mechanical troubles. This group suffered the worst losses of all; twenty-one of Kane's thirty-eight American heavies that arrived at Ploesti were knocked down.

The last was the most unfortunate group of all, for it perforce arrived at a scene of unparalleled confusion left by the previous three groups assigned to Ploesti proper. This was the 44th, originally from England, led by Colonel Leon Johnson.

"It was more like an artist's conception of an air-battle than anything I had ever experienced," Johnson said. "We flew through sheets of flame, and airplanes were everywhere, some of them on fire and others exploding. It's indescribable to anyone who wasn't there." Engineer James E. Cailliar added, "As we passed over [Brazi] our ship filled up with smoke and it was quite awhile before it all cleared out."

Two of the planes from this group (and possibly others from other groups) ran into balloon cables and crashed. However the British briefing officers were partially vindicated, for other planes had in fact snapped the cables, as predicted, though their wings were slashed back to the main spar in the process.

The 44th experienced the same keen disappointment as Kane's formation before them: their Ploesti target (though not the one in Brazi) was burning before they arrived. So they would have to bomb it all over again, or go home emptyhanded, or find something else to bomb. The decision is described by Colonel Johnson: ". . . we had all agreed ahead of time that we weren't going that far without trying to get our targets, so even though they had been fired on . . . we made our runs . . . and we'll point out for the interest of the people that weren't there that the fires were so close together that some of the planes had the paint on their wings burned and scorched . . . I remember the cracking plant loomed up and we let our bombs go.

". . . we found that we could weave around the fires like we weaved over the trees and over the high-tension wires, because the fires were not a continuous line across. There would be a tank burning on your right, and maybe one staggered back—well, it seemed like only the width of an airplane, but it must have been more than that. You could weave through with a formation, although it looked . . . too narrow to get three airplanes through."

Thus Columbia Aquila was tagged again for good measure, and the first blows were delivered to Creditul Minier at nearby Brazi. Each time one of the incendiaries struck home there would follow a hoarse roar, a sheet of flame, and a billow of black smoke. In the course of these actions eleven of the big planes were shot down by machine guns and heavier AA fire, or burned to a crisp in gigantic explosions beneath them.

Johnson later remarked: "We saw the 93rd and 376th groups swinging below us . . . or even with us, and some of us had to pull up to let the others go by. It was a sight that was hard to forget, because you see planes going in on fire, and I remember seeing one pull straight up, and two chutes come out of the window of this big bomber, and I saw it pull straight up and then fall to the ground.

". . . Then the anti-aircraft opened up on us. We were headed almost parallel to it . . . We decided that the only thing to do was to head over it—we didn't think they would traverse 180 degrees overhead . . . If we went parallel we knew they'd knock us all down. As a result we flew immediately over them. And we shot and fired at all the gunners as we went by . . . I distinctly remember seeing a number of them leaving their guns and running for cover . . ."

If the two early groups (Compton and Baker) had been even earlier, or if the two later groups (Kane and Johnson) had been later, affairs would not have been so bad. As it was, the time spent by the formations that had gone to Bucharest and then belatedly swung around toward Ploesti and Campina brought them there, by an unfortunate coincidence, at almost the same moment that the other formations arrived, and from an opposite axis of attack. Thus, according to Johnson, "We had airplanes going in at just all the directions you could think of . . . We'd have to pull up and find airplanes below us and other airplanes above and around us. I mean, it was just a general confusion around the target area—of squadrons and groups, not individual flyers." But part of Compton's lead outfit had arrived several minutes earlier—for example, Appold's squadron. When later aircraft came in, they saw what had happened. The timing was all wrong. The delayed-action bombs of the first wave were going off ahead of them and under them. They barreled through nonetheless and unloaded. Twelve of one outfit went into the smoke and only nine broke through on the other side.

There is a saying among bomber crews that while en route and over the target they were employed by Uncle Sam, but after "Bombs away!" they were out of work. The Ploesti raid of August 1, 1943, was over to the extent that the explosives had been laid on the target to the best of the ability of the participants. Their problem now was to save their skins. From this standpoint the raid was less than half finished.

All the ground fire that had been traversed on the way in would now have to be met on the way back. Also, there had been no fighters worth mentioning on the way to the target and over the target, but now they were wheeling overhead in swarms, and they would hang on all the way out into the sea "like snails on a log." Many bombers had already been lost. Therefore the concentrated fire power of the rest was reduced. And all planes were damaged now to some degree. Some were limping on three and even two engines. These could not possibly keep up and had to be more or less discounted from defensive calculations. Many crewmen were dead or wounded, reducing the gun strength of their aircraft that much more. The odyssey of the Ploesti warriors was many hundreds of miles, many hours, many deaths from done.

By a stroke of unpremeditated luck, the scurrying bombers were for the moment relatively safe from the enemy fighters above them: They were actually too low. To dive on them at roughly 300 mph would not allow enough time to pull out. Some enemy planes tried it, and either pulled up before coming within effective range or dove in too close, sprayed their opponents briefly, and then piled into the ground an inevitable split second later. After several Germans had killed themselves in this manner, the others gave it up and turned to different methods of disposing of the disorganized Liberator formations clinging to the protection of the ground and streaking for home. They could not stay down there indefinitely; in fact they would have to start climbing very soon in order to clear the Alps.

A renewed hail of flak met the bombers as they emerged into open country, knocking down a few more and damaging almost all the rest in varying degrees. There the interceptors got to work in earnest. The experience of Captain Young of the 98th is typical of many return trips:

"After the bombs were away, we dropped back to twenty feet and about fifty ME-109s and 110s jumped us from the right. We were flying so low they couldn't dive on us, but they did lazy-8s all over our formation and caused us plenty of trouble.

"The housing around the propeller and three cylinders of our No. 4 engine were shot out. Two feet of the prop on the No. 1 engine was smashed, tearing a foot-and-a-half hole in the left aileron. The motor was vibrating like a bucking bronco. And we had a wing-cell leak in No. 3 . . . The fighters kept coming in, and we acounted for three. They attacked for about twenty minutes, and we just put the ship on the ground and ran like hell.

"We muddled through the fighter attack, and staggered away from the target on two-and-a-half engines. About 200 miles south of the refineries, we realized that we couldn't return over the Mediterranean with our battered ship. We decided to hug a land route going back. The chief topic of conversation was picking a good place to set her down. Everybody was pestering our navigator, Lt. Norman Whalen . . . He finally had to tell the Colonel, 'Look, if you guys will just leave me alone for a while, maybe I'll find a field.' We left him alone. Whalen was navigating for two other damaged planes which were following, and the three of us were being covered by Lt. Royden LeBrecht. Nothing had happened to his ship.

"We crossed an enemy airfield at 1500 feet, and the flak batteries opened up. I don't know who was more surprised. But we got away without trouble.

"In order to gain altitude to cross a mountain range, we threw out everything that was movable. We released the extra gasoline tank and tossed out oxygen bottles, gas masks, ammunition, radio equipment, and anything that a screw driver could dismantle. LeBrecht called and inquired: 'What the hell are you doing, redecorating?'

"We finally got up to 6600 feet, but we needed 7000 to cross the mountains. By picking our way through canyons and ravines, and with some lucky updrafts, we managed to get over.

"The plane was hobbling along now at 130 mph, and we knew that it might stall around 125. We kept plugging along. We had a choice of putting her down on land or flying across open water to the nearest Allied landing field. The Colonel and I realized that there was a good chance the ship would flop into the water, but we had come too far to worry about that. As we crossed the coast, Whalen gave us an ETA (Estimated Time of Arrival) of 2110 for the selected airfield.

"Whalen was on the nose to within a minute. Exactly fourteen hours and forty minutes after we left Africa, we let her down.

"We had to crash-land the plane, but nobody was hurt, and the first thing I did after we got away from the ship was to kiss the navigator. Yes, I really kissed him."

The Axis threw every available fighter at the Americans, scraped the bottom of the barrel, and even came up with a few obsolescent biplanes—Gloster Gladiators built by Britain in 1935 (top speed 250 mph), a few of which had been sold to other countries later in the decade. They, said Major Shingler, "had a chance of making just about one pass at us. And then of course they had their other fighters . . . and they would hover over you and drop fragmentation bombs . . . I saw a few B-24s lose their tails that way. Nobody dove into us, but I did see B-24s with their tails knocked off, and the minute you knock off one of the verticle fins it goes into a chandelle, stalls in, and then comes right straight in on its nose.

". . . They were right down on the deck . . . strafing the whole bomber formation at fifty or a hundred feet. And they seemed to have an intercept system, whereby they would relay us from one control point to another . . . and then when we'd go fifty or sixty miles another control point would pick us up, and we'd have fresh fighters coming in."

Theoretically the plan was for all surviving aircraft to assemble at a rendezvous point some fifty miles from Ploesti, whereupon those in good condition would group together and head for Benghazi, while the cripples were supposed to make a formation of their own and try to get to Cyprus or some other escape area. The 376th and 93rd Bombardment Groups had come and gone about twenty minutes earlier than the others and headed south at once in fairly good order. But the three later groups got together more or less as briefed, after hitting their targets.

The situation, however, was too confused and dangerous to permit any leisurely maneuvering and regrouping. Lurking in the background, also, was a gasoline problem, especially in the case of those planes flying on three (or two and a half, or even two) engines. The cripples knew that their chances were better in formation; for even a battered, limping B-24 carries a good deal of fire power, and in combination with other such casualties is hard to knock down. So most planes, in good condition or otherwise, hurriedly contrived something resembling a combat box and turned south.

Shingler continued: "We climbed up to about 12,000 feet, as I remember, and we were still being intercepted by fighters. About 45 minutes before we got to the coast the fighters stopped. We came out over the Adriatic in good weather, and my personal opinion is that everyone relaxed. I think they said, 'Well, the show is just about over' . . . The formation got sloppy . . . we started letting down to around 8000 feet. All of a sudden we looked up and here were Italian fighters coming across from Foggia, which was across the sea. They came in under us and they did shoot down five aircraft—*zip, zip, zip,* just like that . . . I still think they wouldn't have shot down any of the boys if we had been in formation and the gunners had been manning their guns. They were taking care of some of the boys who had been shot up on the aircraft and trying to make them comfortable . . . I would say there were in the neighborhood of twenty-five or thirty fighters that hit us just as we came out over the Adriatic, heading back to Benghazi. We lost about eighteen aircraft."

Shingler blames his own people for this crowning misfortune, but Colonel Johnson of the 44th is more lenient: "[The enemy fighters] ran out of fuel and couldn't keep up with us. They took quite a beating, too. We knocked down quite a few of those fighters that came up against us. There were no more fighters until we got over the Adriatic . . . A number of us started chattering back and forth on the radio . . . and fighters did come up from the heel of Italy and knocked down a few of our bombers. Actually, if I remember correctly, they took five out of the 98th Group. Fortunately, although we were talking just as much, they didn't hit my particular group—it was just happenstance more than anything else."

As the laborious exodus continued, Liberators continued to fall, new fighters rose and pressed their shallow attacks, occasional ack-ack continued to annoy the bomber crews hanging on grimly with their precious gallons of fuel, forcing them to make small, wasteful detours to avoid them. The planes that "had lost an engine had to start lightening their load for the climb [across the Alps]. It startled us at first to see equipment fly out . . . and float back under us. We thought the planes were disintegrating in mid-air. The crews threw out everything that was loose or could be yanked loose, and we left behind us a long, wobbling trail of seats, tanks, belts, shoes, boxes, and first-aid kits with gauze bandages unrolling in great circles, figure-eights, and curious, sometimes beautiful designs."

It began to rain. The atmosphere aboard the plane carrying Ent, Compton, and their navigator was particularly depressing.

Flying at 100 feet, Major Potts started down a valley he hoped would afford a little extra protection from AA fire surrounding the main target. "The tension relaxed just a bit. A young gunner that was flying the left waist gun position—named Sherman, not more than nineteen—let go at what looked like a distillation plant—not one of the [assigned] targets . . . it suddenly exploded and burst into flames. Everybody on the plane started cheering . . . it was kind of an anti-climax and a good feeling to see something burst into flames that you figured was sort of a dividend.

"Well, as we started back other planes in my formation, numbering nine, gathered around and we started to climb back over the mountains . . . One of my very close friends, Captain Roper, was . . . leading two other planes . . . He pulled off a little bit so he wouldn't be flying in too close to me. He seemed to go into a cloud. And we suddenly saw dropping out of this cloud various pieces of airplane. Well, that was a shock . . . much more than losing somebody in the target area . . .

"After we landed back on base I realized that only seven planes out of thirty-seven had come back from the mission. That created an additional damper on everybody's feelings. Matter of fact, I was feeling so depressed that I had a hard time sitting through the interrogation by the Intelligence officers . . . It was kind of an ordeal . . ."

The 44th, under Leon Johnson, was so mauled and dispersed in the course of the strike that he was able to gather only three other planes around him for the return trip. Following a skirmish with enemy fighters, one of these feathered a propeller and headed for Turkey. The remaining three plugged on, cleared the mountains, and reached the Adriatic, where one plane was forced to ditch into the sea. Two got back to Benghazi.

The aircraft flown by Captain Banks, of the 98th, was one of eleven which made it to Cyprus. "The next morning we spent hours refueling the plane. The airfield didn't have any fueling apparatus, and we had to fill her up with piddling little five-gallon cans of gasoline. It was one hell of a job. We finally got her refueled and checked over, and took off at noon. It was an easy run down to Tel Aviv." There the captain distributed a wad of "escape money" to his crew and said, "I don't want to see a sober man within the hour."

Killer Kane wound up in typical style, crash-landing spectacularly in Cyprus, where he dined on pork chops and a bottle of wine in a night club. But he got little sleep that night. "I kept thinking about those guys going down, some of them in flames—big Libs like broken flies."

One of the favorite stories of Keith Compton's outfit had to do with the plane known as the Lucky, flown by "Hap" Kendall. It had two insignia—one a Teddy bear holding a bomb, and another (for no special reason) of a girl. Damaged and running out of fuel, this plane had no chance of reaching Africa, and Kendall decided to try a landing at a small British field in southern Sicily. The first complication arose when it was discovered that a break in the hydraulic system required the landing gear to be cranked down by hand. The brakes were also gone. When the great bomber landed on the tiny 800-foot strip it raced to the end of it in a flash, ran over a ridge, smashed through two fighter planes under repair, crashed through five tents, and finally stopped with the camp kitchen directly under the starboard wing. A gunner named Miller jumped out, yelling, "At least we can eat!" and the rest followed.

Hadley's Harem had been hit hard before reaching its target. One large hunk of flak blew off part of the nose of the ship. Another slammed into the chest of the bombardier, Bud Storms, killing him instantly, and at the same time Harold Tabicoff of Brooklyn, the navigator, was also wounded. Engineer Russell Page decided to go aft to see what could be done and, since Storms had not had the chance to get his bombs away, Page salvoed them simultaneously by using the emergency release. He administered first aid to Tabicoff and then noticed Storms, whose chest had been torn to shreds. Page hurried forward, muttering, "I never want to see a mess like that again."

Lieutenant Hadley had turned south, warily watching the No. 2 engine upon which burning oil was flickering. He feathered the propeller. At this point the Harem staggered and went into a steep dive, but Hadley and his co-pilot pulled back on their wheels to the limit and the plane came out of it. Wind was now pouring like a torrent through the gaping nose. The forgotten bomb-bay doors were still wide open.

When the next burst of flak hit, the floor of the ship buckled like a smashed tin-can, throwing the men about and knocking two of them unconscious. Three birds were flying overhead. In a daze the waist gunner cut loose at them, thinking they were enemy interceptors.

In their doomed bomber the men watched two others settle on the ground of Rumania with their tanks aflame. Then a third was seen flaming from wing tip to wing tip. She climbed agonizingly to nearly 3500 feet; then, in a single, blinding explosion, the Liberator totally disappeared. "I guess they were trying to get up and bail out," said Blacky Holweger, the armorer-gunner. The vision preyed on him for a long time. "For a split-second I saw that. It was the most horrible thing I had ever seen. It is stamped on my mind."

The Harem, too, was climbing tortuously for altitude with which to clear the Alps. When they passed over a Sunday excursion train, the passengers leaned out and waved. Farmers saluted them from the fields below. Chickens scurried for safety in tiny eddies of dust. One girl in a brilliant peasant blouse ran out of her house to look up. The No. 3 engine cut out just as they reached the Aegean Sea when they were at 5000 feet. All hands were told to be ready to bail out and warned not to smoke, for gas fumes were leaking throughout the fuselage.

The day was turning hazy and dim at eight-fifteen, when the No. 1 engine began to lose oil; in a flash the gauge dropped to zero. Hadley turned to the co-pilot: "What do you think we'd better do?" Lindsay suggested that they should try to make land first, but pointed out that engines Nos. 1 and 4 would soon be definitely out. Hadley then queried the crew over the intercom; all the men said they preferred to stay with the ship. The discussion, at any rate, was now academic, for the plane had lost so much altitude so quickly that parachuting was impossible. Everybody took off his shoes and adjusted his Mae West. When they were less than a mile from Turkey, Hadley asked Page to read the air-speed gauge. He replied, "No, the co-pilot will read it," for, to do so, Page would have had to lean over while standing between the two pilots and would have been killed instantly in that posture if the plane hit. He opened the top escape hatch and braced himself against the armor plate behind the pilot.

Just as the last two engines sputtered out the plane went in. There was a paralyzing shock as the right wing tip snagged a wave and twisted the plane into the water at an awkward angle. The Mediterranean rushed through the flak holes and especially the torn-open nose, filling the Harem instantly with water. Outside a slap of water slammed the escape hatch shut. The crew was now trapped.

The nine live men groped and swam in their underwater tomb. As Page held his breath a hundred confused thoughts passed through hs mind. He saw his wife's face and said to himself in wonderment, "My God, am I going to die this way?" He, Hadley and Lindsay, half blind from the salt water, tried without success to burst open the jammed escape hatch. With his lungs near bursting Page worked back to the top of the gun blister and tried to break through the Plexiglass. In despair he turned and saw the pilot and co-pilot splashing frantically in the nose. A half minute had passed since the plane had gone under.

Lindsay and Hadley never did get out. Trapped in a welter of debris, they drowned while the Harem settled slowly to the bottom of the sea. The remaining seven men forced their way through various natural and artificial openings and reached shore. As they staggered up the long beach they found fifteen ragged peasants awaiting them with long rifles, relics of wars long since ended—"Just like those revolutionary movies." They dozed on the beach under guard beside a big fire all night long, and the following morning were spotted by an English Wellington bomber. Later an air-sea rescue boat from Cyprus landed, three British Navy men furnished first aid, and arrangements were made to smuggle the Americans back into Allied hands.

The experiences of the hundreds who crash-landed or parachuted in or around the target area were perhaps the most grueling of all, in addition to which they faced the bleak prospect of untold years in concentration camps awaiting the end of hostilities. A few were shot by Germans in the process of being captured. Most of the others were treated reasonably well, one of whom was Captain Palm. Holding the remnants of his right leg, he had dived through the window of his crashed plane and hopped into a cornfield while hanging to a crew member, Bill Love. There the rest of the crew congregated abjectly, waiting for Rumanians to surrender to, and hiding from the Germans. Finally a group of peasants appeared, and the fliers shouted, "Doctor!" at them—a word they believed was similar to the Rumanian word. For a few moments nothing happened. The Rumanians looked at the Americans. The latter began to wonder how popular they were. At this stage several German soldiers arrived. A discussion followed as to who was entitled to the American prisoners. Eventually the Germans left, but not before one of them had reached over and snatched Palm's wrist watch, while he was clasping the remnants of his leg with both hands.

When the Rumanians tried to carry the captain, he nearly fainted from the pain, and because his dangling leg kept slapping him in the face. A litter was hurriedly whipped together out of saplings and he was lifted into a truck. Next he was driven to a hospital for women and children, where he was turned away, and then moved again to another hospital where a Dr. Petrescu—"a hell of a good old Joe"—snipped off the leg.

Now Rumanians began to come in to see Palm. He understood their curiosity. It was as though Chicago had been bombed by Rumanians, or it was like a visit by a man from Mars. In Palm's ward lay five other Rumanian victims of the American bombing. "I wouldn't have blamed them for being sore," Palm relates; but, in fact, they tried to shake hands with him. Delayed-action bombs continued to explode throughout Ploesti during the entire evening. The six men in the hospital ward tossed and muttered, and tried to sleep.

The sun had set, leaving in its wake a cloud-streaked twilight, when word came at seven-thirty that the first planes were calling in from a hundred miles out at sea. Officers and men jumped into jeeps and staff cars and dashed over to the Benghazi strip. Some ground crews were already there, looking for their own planes, and as the ships arrived they called out their names—Old Baldy, Vulgar Virgin, and so on. On one the bomb doors were still grotesquely swinging open. A few arrived with dead engines. All were riddled by machine-gun bullets or the scars of 40-millimeter shells. Brereton personally greeted Ent and Compton as they crawled unhappily out of their plane. Many bombers had a curiously blackened appearance, as though they had been toasted over an open fire. Some fired flares during their approaches, to indicate wounded on board. The main spar had buckled on the right wing of one bomber. Holes in the tail surfaces could be clearly seen from the ground. Some of the landings were poor, for the planes were now so light that they bounced like rubber balls down the strip, too battered to respond efficiently to the controls. It was a sorry, bedraggled formation that made the initial landings at Bomber Command.

One of the bombers in Jack Wood's section had the manual controls shot away, but by putting the ship on automatic pilot and manipulating the engines the pilot got it back to Benghazi. Remarkably enough, he even managed to make a fairly decent landing despite the absence of tail or aileron controls.

Still another bomber from the 389th had been the cause

of much anxiety on the way home. Over the Mediterranean the pilot began to complain by radio that his gas was running low. Every few miles he reported that the end was near, and finally he drifted away. There was nothing to do but hope that he had been able to ditch safely so that the men could be picked up later by rescue boats. But when Wood landed at Benghazi the first people he saw were these supposedly doomed fliers, who had not only reached base but had even beaten him there.

The night dragged on, black as Pharaoh's tomb. There was no moon. At infrequent intervals other forlorn single planes found their way home, guided by the thin, bluish glare of a searchlight that swung slowly back and forth over the field. The service and officers' clubs stayed open all night; there was much drinking and strained, nervous celebrating. Every man had a whole Southern fried chicken for dinner. Voices and incongruous laughter drifted across to the Operations tent, where a little group of men still watched the pitch-black sky, against which the stars shimmered with a hard, gemlike intensity. The Ploesti raid was over.

Avalanche

The decision to invade Italy at the Salerno beaches, with the main Allied objective the port of Naples, was finally made by the CCS on July 26, 1943. This would be the task of the newly formed 5th Army, composed of the U.S. VI Corps, with the 36th and 45th Divisions for the assault, the 3rd and 34th Divisions in Reserve; and the British X Corps made up of the 46th and 56th Divisions. September 9 was D-Day.

On September 3, the British 8th Army under Montgomery moved across the Strait of Messina on to the toe of Italy, almost unopposed; their progress was slow up the boot. There was little opposition but roads were mined and bridges blown and the 8th Army, used to traveling on wheels, took its time. This was unfortunate because the Allied command had hoped that the 8th Army would reach the Salerno beachhead quickly in order to put pressure on the left flank of the German defenders. However, it would take the 8th until September 16 to make contact with the 5th Army, and then only advance patrols of each Army had met.*

Operation Avalanche commenced with some degree of optimism on the part of the Allied Commanders. In retrospect, it does not seem justifiable. Hugh Pond, author of the recently published *Salerno* says:

"The beaches along the thirty-six-mile curve of Salerno Bay were ideal for an assault landing. There were no shoals or river-mouth ridges to impede the boats and the sand shelved gently and evenly. But the coastal plain behind the beaches—largely reclaimed land—was narrow, and in some places almost non-existent, dominated by the mountains from which a beachhead could be observed and pounded by artillery. The only exit from this plain was through two narrow passes, which could easily be held by light, strongly entrenched forces.

*Twenty-four hours earlier, several war correspondents had driven the length of the gap between the Allied Armies and had met no enemy resistance.

"The nearest air bases for our fighters, apart from carrier-based planes, were in Sicily, which meant that Spitfires fitted with ninety-gallon wing tanks would be able to remain over the area for a maximum of twenty minutes, an operation which called for tremendous coordination to be effective. For the first three days the ground troops would have the support of a hundred and twenty Seafires of the Fleet Air Arm, operating from five Royal Navy carriers under the command of Rear-Admiral Sir Philip Vian.*

Again, optimism plus plain bad strategy seems to have overcome the 5th Army Commander, General Mark Clark. Admiral S. L. Morison says:

"Of all decisions about AVALANCHE, the most unfortunate was the Army command's insistence on no preliminary gunfire support, in order to obtain tactical surprise. Admiral Hewitt argued against this in vain, as he had before HUSKY. He pointed out that the Germans knew something was on, as evidenced by their August air raids on Bizerte; that any officer with a pair of dividers could figure out that the Gulf of Salerno was the northernmost practicable landing place for the Allies; that reconnaissance planes would snoop the convoys; in short, that it was fantastic to assume we could obtain tactical surprise. He was right in every particular. Implicit in the denial was the fear that preliminary bombardment would attract German forces to Salerno. But on 6 September the Germans had already sent the 16th Panzer Division into the Salerno plain. The enemy had several days in which to set up 88-mm and other guns, cut down trees, build strong points, site the Italians' Breda machine guns and fieldpieces on the beaches and their exits, bring up tanks, and cram nearby airfields with their planes. As it turned out, a good selective shoot on strong points on the edge of the Salerno plain, for a day or two before D-Day, would have rendered the landings much less arduous." **

In the meantime negotiations between the Italians and General Eisenhower were carried on, which led to the unconditional surrender of Italy. The announcement of the surrender was made by Eisenhower on September 8 while the assault troops were approaching the Salerno beaches. "In justice to the Italians the armistice had to be announced before we landed on their soil, but it was singularly ill-timed

---

Salerno, by Hugh Pond, published by Little, Brown & Co., pp. 40-41.

** *Sicily-Salerno-Anzio,* pp. 249-250.

with reference to embarked troops. These, naturally assuming that they were to have a walk-over at Salerno, proceeded to relax, mentally and otherwise. Senior officers tried to undo the mischief by warning the men by loud-speaker that they would still have to fight Germans; but Admiral Cunningham states 'that many took no heed of these warnings and viewed the proceedings with a sense of complacency.' Complacency is hardly the word for it; the general impression seemed to be that the war was over. We were landing in Italy, and the Italians had quit, hadn't they?

"So the tenseness that one usually feels just before an amphibious landing dissipated; the approach continued under a sort of spell. It was a beautiful, calm, bright night. To many of the ships Capri was visible, swimming in a silver sea; the jagged outline of the Sorrento peninsula made a dark cut-out against a floor of heaven . . . thickly inlaid with patines of bright gold and beyond lay the Bay of Naples redolent with history, beauty and romance. . . .

"This illusion lasted even after the beacon submarine—HMS *Shakespeare*—flashed her guiding light seaward, and until the transports began easing into their release points at one minute past midnight. Then orders rang out, boatswains' whistles shrilled, and the clang and clatter of lowering landing craft broke the spell." *

SALERNO*

by Samuel E. Morison

Paestum, the American Sector

Daylight revealed to lookouts in the crow's nests a superb panorama, unsurpassed even on the west coast of Italy. The Gulf of Salerno, Longfellow's "blue Salernian bay with its sickle of white sand," loosely embraced by a jagged mountain wall, stretches 30 miles from the Sorrento peninsula to Cape Licosa. Between mountains and sea lies a plain shaped like a second-quarter moon, with the bright little city of Salerno at the upper and the small town of Agrópoli at the nether tip. The Naples–Reggio coastal highway and railway pass through Salerno, skirt the plain, and at the town of Battipaglia are met by another road and railway from southern Italy.

The planners for AVALANCHE decided to put the British X Corps ashore near the northern end of the gulf, for prompt capture of Salerno, Montecorvino airport and Battipaglia; while the American VI Corps landed opposite the temples of Paestum in order to protect the Allies' right flank and make contact with Montgomery's Eighth Army marching up from Calabria. It may seem odd that the two sets of beaches should have been eight miles apart, instead of contiguous; but the beaches near the mouth of the Sele are more obstructed by sand bars than those farther away, and the exits are not good.

At 0001 September 9 the leading transports, three British LSIs, were in position. *Marnix van St. Aldegonde* had her

* A somewhat condensed version of the Salerno chapters in *Sicily-Salerno-Anzio*.

landing craft in the water in 20 minutes. She and four United States transports carried the 142nd RCT, which was to land on the two northernmost beaches (Red and Green) at H-hour, 0330. Simultaneously, five U.S. transports were to land the 141st RCT on the two southern beaches, Yellow and Blue. Five other U.S. transports and one LSI carried the 143rd RCT, which was destined to follow up on Beaches Red and Green at 0630.

The same Scouts and Raiders who had functioned in HUSKY were embarked in four scout boats (LCS), one for each beach. Using a radar fix on Monte Soprano obtained by *PC-624*, reference vessel for the Southern Attack Force, each of the four scout boats took a position a few hundred yards off its assigned beach, and started blinking seaward, to guide the boat waves. The boat commanded by Ensign G. Anderson USNR arrived at a point 400 yards off Beach Red at 0230 and began blinking red. That of Lieutenant (jg) Grady R. Galloway USCG located Beach Green by sighting, against the starlit sky, the Torre di Paestum—a medieval stone watchtower that adjoins the road exit between the two pairs of beaches. Galloway started blinking green at 0310 from 100 yards off shore. Ensign J. G. Donnell's boat found the center of Beach Yellow from a bearing on the tower, and took station 600 yards off shore. (During the hour of waiting, the men in this scout boat heard clanking and clattering ashore and saw the lights of vehicles; German troops were moving down to the water's edge.) Ensign Ross E. Schumann USNR, commanding the guide boat for Beach Blue, found that beach by a bearing on Monte Sottane.

Next after the scout boats came Commander Richards's minesweepers to clear a channel through the mine field reported to lie between the line of departure (6000 yards off shore) and the transports. This was done by the same group of fleet minesweepers (*Seer* flag) that had been used in Sicily, and ten small motor minesweepers (YMSs). According to Admiral Hewitt, the sweep plan was too ambitous, requiring not only the boat channels but fire support areas to be swept by 0330. That was more than the available craft could possibly accomplish. Several boat waves were held up by reports of floating mines, and one LCVP was blown up.

The American beaches were well selected for an orderly night landing. There would have been no trouble if tactical surprise had been obtained, or if the enemy had been luke-warm fighters, as had happened on the coast of Sicily. Un-fortunately for us, the Germans were almost as well pre-pared to contest landings at Salerno as the Japanese would be at Tarawa two months later.

General von Vietinghoff, commanding the German Tenth Army, had been expecting a landing in the Salerno Gulf for several days. On 7 September when he heard that large convoys were heading thither, the 16th Panzer Division and the Italian 222nd Coastal Division were al-ready busy installing mine fields along the beaches, building strong points at the most likely landing places, digging tank traps and preparing bridges for demolition. By D-day there was a series of strong points along the shore between Salerno and Agrópoli, armed with light and heavy machine guns, quads of antiaircraft 20-mm, and either 75-mm or 88-mm cannon. In the hills and along the Salerno-Bat-tipaglia road were several batteries of 88-mm mobile artil-lery, and the Germans were in process of taking over all Italian coastal and fieldpieces. The commanding general of the coastal division, who objected to taking German orders, was quietly taken out and shot. By D-day all beaches between Salerno and Agrópoli had been mined, and pioneers were preparing the port of Salerno for demolition.

When Vietinghoff got the word of the Italian surrender, during the evening of 8 September, he ordered the 26th Panzer Division, then delaying Montgomery's advance in Calabria, to break contact and hasten north. Still uncertain of the main Allied target, Vietinghoff made no further troop dispositions until daylight revealed that the Allies had made a *Grosslandung,* not a Commando raid.

The higher levels of German command also were well prepared. Hitler's headquarters, as early as 1 August, had drawn up a plan for Operation ACHSE, to start when and if

Italy surrendered. This involved the swift occupation of Genoa, Leghorn, Venice and Trieste by Marshal Rommel, now commander in northern Italy; of central and southern Italian ports by Marshal Kesselring, commander in those parts of Italy; the evacuation of Sardinia and Sicily by German troops, and a brisk transfer of German divisions to Italy. At 1950 September 8, Kesselring ordered Operation ACHSE to be executed. When news of the Salerno landings reached him, the Marshal was apprehensive of an American air drop on Rome; but when nightfall came, with no paratroops, he felt confident enough to issue a grandiloquent proclamation:—

> The invading enemy in the area Naples-Salerno and southwards, must be completely annihilated and in addition thrown into the sea. Only by so doing can we obtain a decisive change of the situation in the Italian area. I require ruthless employment of all the might of the three army units. Every commanding officer must be aware of his historical responsibility. British and Americans must realize that they are hopelessly lost against the concentrated German might.*

As first light broke on D-day, at 0330, the initial waves for the four American beaches were nearing the ends of their eight- to ten-mile runs over a calm sea. All hit their respective beaches within seven minutes of one another (0335 to 0342) and the second and third waves followed at the proper intervals. Both waves were guided to the line of departure by patrol craft; but, unlike the British, they had no close fire support from that point to the beaches. Admiral Hewitt offered to furnish rocket craft or small gunboats, but the U. S. Army would have none of them; the soldiers imagined that they could obtain complete surprise if they landed silently. This decision was unfortunate; for want of close support, many men in landing craft were killed by German gunners ready and waiting behind the beaches. And, what made matters worse, the Luftwaffe at

*War Diary German Naval Command Italy 10 Sept. 1943.

the same time began to bomb and strafe the beaches, on a scale never before or since equaled in a Mediterranean landing. Fortunately this did not long continue.

Colonel John D. Forsythe's 142nd Infantry went ashore on Beaches Green and Red. Heavy fire from mortars, 88-mm cannon, and machine guns, descended on and around his landing craft, and the troops, even when wading ashore, came under machine-gun fire from the Torre di Paestum. Relentlessly they worked around to their prearranged assembly area, and made it by sunrise, 0436. Plenty of Germans were left near the beach for later arrivals to mop up. Dukws carrying fieldpieces arrived from three Killer-class British LSTs at 0530. An hour later, the 143rd Regiment began to land on Beach Red. By 0800 that beach had become very congested, owing to the usual failure of Army shore parties to do their job of stevedoring.

Lieutenant Galloway's scout boat for Beach Green was, by exception, provided with a few rocket launchers which were used to silence gunfire directed at the first wave. The second wave of landing craft for this beach was delayed by mines and became mixed up with subsequent waves, beaching only at 0630. Thirty dukws hit Beach Green as early as 0525, one in every twelve bringing much-wanted 105-mm howitzers, and the others, ammunition. They unloaded in good order behind the dune line and most of them returned to the transports. No fewer than 123 dukw landings were made on the Amercan beaches between 0530 and 0730—a remarkable achievement. The 2nd Battalion of the 142nd Regiment here had a hard time getting through barbed wire and lost men from exploding land mines; but it managed to reach the same assembly area as the battalion from Beach Red. The southern half of Beach Green was interdicted by enemy gunfire throughout D-day.

Much of the trouble here and on the next beach (Yellow) came from machine guns mounted on the 50-foot stone tower and from one or two tanks that lurked behind the farm buildings attached to it. This tower was too near the beach for naval gunfire to take on. It was finally captured, the tanks put out of business, and all German defenders killed or made prisoner by the 531st Shore Engineers, who had already lost a number of officers and men in the early air attacks.*

The two southernmost American beaches, Yellow and Blue, were the most difficult for the invaders to negotiate. Behind them, the Germans had constructed a strong point, and both beaches were within range of coastal batteries near Agrópoli. As the landing craft approached, a loudspeaker blared in English "Come on in and give up. We have you covered!" The first three assault waves of the 3rd Battalion 141st Regiment were indeed covered. Tank fire from behind the stone tower stopped them, but there was no giving up; and a reserve battalion came in at 0500 to help them get off the beach. From 0830 to 1330 Beach Yellow was completely interdicted, and on Beach Blue the 1st Battalion was pinned down for 20 hours. Heavy gunfire prevented six tank-laden LCTs from landing there at about 0640. Four of the six were hit by 88-mm shell; in *LCT-244*, Ensign S. J. Cavallaro USNR, guiding the formation, was killed, and the tank nearest the bow started to burn; the crew promptly lowered the ramp and shoved the tank overboard. The LCTs retired out of range, awaited orders, started in again about noon with gunfire support from a destroyer, and at 1330 discharged their tanks on Beach Red. Tank-laden *LST-389*, which also carried pontoon units, beached at Blue at 1241. Her crew bravely rigged this pontoon under enemy fire and at 1354 her tanks began to roll off. Within twenty minutes enemy gunfire forced another closing of Beach Blue, but it was reopened at 1600 and became the principal beach for discharging tanks.

Thus, the 36th Division had very little armor ashore on D-day, but German Mark IV tanks had been active from 0700, maneuvering both in the open and behind the old Greek city walls, on which machine guns were mounted.

*Company D of this engineer regiment, commanded by 1st Lt. G. L. Shumaker USA, did fine work preparing the beaches with bulldozers and steel mat, under heavy fire from the tower. Disparaging remarks directed at Army shore parties do not apply to the 531st Shore Engineers.

The GIs, with the aid of a dismounted cavalry reconnaissance troop, bazookas, 105-mm howitzers and naval gunfire, prevented these tanks from reaching the beaches, and by noon forced them to retire; but some of their fire still reached Red and Green. At 1020 thirteen more Mark IVs rumbled down the highway from the north, threatening the 142nd Regiment's command post which had just been set up in the Capaccio railway station, a few miles north of Paestum. A dukw hauling a 105-mm howitzer arrived just in time to shatter two of the tanks; a third was destroyed by an Invader (A–36) divebomber; gunfire from a naval vessel, probably H.M.S. *Abercrombie*, accounted for two more, and the rest retreated.

The landings at Paestum and the British sector were among the most fiercely contested in World War II. Few soldiers suffered so severe a baptism of fire on landing as did those of this yet untried division, or came through it so well. Like the Sons of Tola, the 36th "were valiant men of might." Yet even they could not have carried on without naval gunfire.

Rear Admiral Lyal A. Davidson in *Philadelphia*, tempered by his experience in North Africa and Sicily, commanded naval gunfire support in the American sector. He also had *Savannah* at his disposal, and four destroyers, while H.M.S. *Abercrombie*, screened by Dutch gunboat *Flores*, stood by to serve when 15-inch shell was wanted. The monitor was the first to get into action. Between 0825 and 0915 she fired 11 rounds at an enemy battery, with aircraft spotting. At 1025, as we have seen, she fired on a tank concentration, and again at 1112. Next, she bombarded the town of Capaccio. All at ranges of over 25,000 yards. This hard-hitting monitor, whose help had already been appreciated in HUSKY, struck a mine that afternoon, took a 10-degree list, reached an even keel by counterflooding, but was so badly damaged that she had to steam to Palermo.

Delays in passing through mine fields and in establishing communications with harassed shore fire-control parties prevented the other fire support vessels from functioning as early as they wished. In Admiral Hall's opinion, they did not do so well this day as on D-day in Sicily; but there was no complaint from the troops. At 0914 *Savannah* established communication with her shore fire-control party, which wanted a railway battery silenced. That was accomplished with an expenditure of 57 rounds. For more than an hour, beginning at 1132, *Savannah* fired on a concentration of tanks at the good range of 17,450 yards, yet (so it was reported from shore) forced them to retire. Other targets were German infantry, artillery batteries, observation posts, and the town of Capaccio. The cruiser answered eleven calls for fire support on D-day and expended 645 rounds of 6-inch ammunition. For spotting she used her own SOC observation planes, as well as Army Mustangs; for the 111th Fighter Reconnaissance Squadron had been trained to spot naval gunfire. These P–51s, flying in pairs, turned in an excellent performance at Salerno; one would spot while the other covered against enemy air attack.

Flagship *Philadelphia's* work on D-day, the first of ten spent off the Salerno beaches, began at 0943 when, on call from shore fire-control party, she opened on an enemy battery. At 1033 she launched an SOC spotting plane, and two minutes later took a bridge under fire to hold up approaching panzer units. At 1057 she launched a second spotting plane and then followed a minesweeper through a swept channel to close the beach. From 1220 to 1309, with destroyer *Ludlow,* she fired at a German battery which was shelling beached LSTs on Beach Blue, then recovered her planes. Shortly before 1400 she launched another plane which, simultaneously with one of *Savannah's,* discovered a covey of German tanks concealed in a thicket adjacent to Beach Red. *Philadelphia's* 6-inch salvos flushed 35 of these birds and kept them under fire as they scurried to the rear; about seven were destroyed. Continuing almost to midnight, this cruiser expended 305 rounds of 6-inch shell on D-day.

Outstanding performance in gunfire support was given also by the destroyers.

Owing to the interdiction of Beaches Yellow and Blue by enemy gunfire, Beach Red became horribly congested after noon. A veritable mountain ridge of boxed ammunition and baled supplies lined the water's edge and extended several feet into the sea. Landing craft could not even find room to let down ramps. Troops detailed to unload drifted away, as usual, leaving boat crews to do the stevedoring. Admiral Hall at 1036 appealed to General Clark to assign 200 men to each beach to clear up the mess, and the General gave him about that many from his headquarters troops in *Duchess of Bedford;* but they were untrained for such work and were unable to cope with the sea-wall of supplies.

Landing craft crews functioned even better here than in HUSKY; discipline and seamanship alike were excellent. And although the sea was much calmer than it had been off Sicily, enemy fire on the boats was far heavier. The crews stuck by their craft, and worked around the clock to unload transports. When the operation was over, the incredibly small number of eleven boats had to be abandoned, and all but one of these had been knocked out by enemy action.

Despite this fine boat performance, the unloading of transports and assault cargo ships was unduly delayed. Distance of the transport area from shore (10 miles for some ships), beach congestion, lack of LCTs,* and defective combat loading at Oran were responsible. Disregarding the lessons of TORCH and HUSKY, the Army had again taken charge at that port, stowing equipment urgently needed for the assault where it could not be got at, and piling in stuff that would not be needed for days—as if the expedition were bound for some far-off Pacific island. At the end of D-day, the transports of the Southern Attack Force were only partially unloaded, the percentage ranging from 17 to 65. They would not have done even this well but for an extensive use of cargo nets which enabled bulk cargo to be hoisted out of landing craft by portable cranes onto trucks and dukws.

Surmounting all difficulties, the 36th Division reached important objectives by the end of the day. It had taken the

*Only 16 out of 54 LCTs promised from the Northern Attack Force area actually turned up on D-day.

459-foot hill called Templo San Paolo, two miles inland from Capaccio railway station; another hill south of it; and the town of Capaccio, from which the Germans had already retired. One company had fought its way almost to to summit of Monte Sottane. On the right flank, the 141st Regiment was still pinned down on Beach Blue. These fell short of D-day objectives, but General Clark was on the whole satisfied; he "felt that we had achieved as much as could be expected."

If anyone then imagined that the Germans had shot their bolt, he was destined for a great disappointment. They were still able to challenge from the air; they now had full control over the roads and railways of southern Italy, and of communications with the north. Reinforcements were rolling in from the mountains, and the Hermann Goering Panzer Division was coming south from Naples; leading elements of the 29th Panzer Grenadiers had reached the Salerno beachhead at 1900, less than 24 hours after they had been ordered north. During the three following days, the issue was continually in doubt.

That the Army achieved so much was, in some measure at least, due to the quality of naval gunfire support; the boldness of the destroyers driving in through mine fields to deliver accurate shoots was especially praised. It inspired a generous message from the divisional artillery commander of the 36th Division, Brigadier General John W. Lange, which was relayed to every fire support ship and joyfully entered in their logs:

Thank God for the fire of the blue-belly Navy ships. Probably could not [otherwise] have stuck out Blue and Yellow beaches. Brave fellows these; tell them so.

The British Sector

"What's the weather like at Salerno?" wrote Horace to a friend, about the year 20 B.C.; "and what sort of people shall I encounter there?" That's just what the Northern Attack Force wanted to know in A.D. 1943. The weather could not have been better for an amphibious landing; but the people, instead of the friendly Italians whom the troops expected to find on the beach, turned out to be very tough and uncooperative Germans of the 16th Panzer Division.

The general plan for this northern sector was for Commodore Oliver to land Lieutenant General McCreery's X Corps on beaches between three and six miles south of the city of Salerno. On the northernmost pair, designated "Uncle," the 46th (North Midland) Division, Major General Hawkesworth, was to swing left after landing and secure control of the high ground behind Salerno. One column was to capture Salerno and then move through the Cava gap toward Naples; the other to move up the valley of the Picentino and through a pass to Mercato, north of Salerno. The 56th (London) Division, Major General Graham, would land on the "Sugar" and "Roger" pairs of beaches south of Uncle, capture Montecorvino airfield and then drive toward Ponte Sele, apex of the desired beachhead line, ten miles inland. None of these objectives, unfortunately, were attained for many days.

On the Sorrento peninsula, whose astonishing beauty— a unique combination of rugged mountains and sophisticated building and planting—must be seen to be believed, two subsidiary landings took place. At Maiori, two miles east of Amalfi, there is a shingle beach with a gradient so steep that small cruising yachts anchor within a stone's throw of the shore. Maiori is the terminus of a road from Naples through the Chiunzi pass, and it was to seize this pass that three United States Ranger battalions were landed under Lieutenant Colonel Darby, the hero of Gela. A few miles farther east, and very near Salerno, the Marina de Vietri, with a short sand beach, lies at the foot of the Cava gap, through which the main road and railway run to Naples. British Army and Royal Marine Commandos under Brigadier R. F. Laycock RM, augmented by an American mortar battery, landed here to destroy nearby coast defenses and seize the gap.

Darby's Rangers, embarked in two LSIs and five American LCIs, began landing at Maiori at 0320. Unexpectedly, for Rangers, they met no opposition; succeeding waves and supply runs were sent in smoothly; by 0615 all supplies and equipment were ashore and the landing was completed. By this time the troops had reached the height of the Chiunzi pass, and the ridges which overlook the main road and railway running from Salerno to Naples. And their positions also dominated the defile of Nocera, a bottleneck where a network of roads converged.

At Vietri the British Commandos (embarked in *Prince Albert* and three British LCIs) were less fortunate. The first wave landed unopposed at 0330 after H.M.S. *Blackmore* and a gunboat had silenced a shore battery. For the next two and a half hours the landings continued "according to plan." But Vietri was too near Salerno for the Germans to ignore the threat. They infiltrated the town, mounted mortars and machine guns on several houses which overlooked the beach, and drove off landing craft attempting to come in after 0630. After almost two hours' fighting the enemy was driven out. As early as 0600 the Royal Marine section of the Commandos had reached the defile of La Molina about a mile inland, where they were counterattacked by a German force supported by tanks, and were pinned down for some time.

All these landings were subsidiary to the main operation. The main body of the Northern Attack Force sighted the outer ship of a string of reference vessels at 2317 September 8. Six fleet minesweepers of the Royal Navy and seven American YMSs preceded Admiral Conolly in *Biscayne*, commanding "Uncle" group, on its final run-in. By 0150 September 9 they had swept a channel through the mine field. Next after the minesweepers came three Hunt-class destroyers, which took fire support positions only one mile off the beaches—a bold plan, the wisdom of which was soon proved. Conolly received word from Admiral Hewitt at 2341 that shore installations were not to be engaged unless they opened fire—hoping that all would be abandoned, owing to the armistice.

The enemy soon canceled this restriction. At 0121, as the 15 six-davit American LSTs bearing assault troops were deploying in their allotted area, gunfire was observed on the beach ahead. Shortly after 0200, *Biscayne* and the LSTs were subjected to severe shelling by 88-mm guns. One LST had several members of her crew and 25 soldiers put out of action by the first three salvos. Admiral Conolly immediately ordered the supporting destroyers to return fire, while *Biscayne* stood across the inshore boundary of the transport area to lay a smoke screen. At 0225, when shore fire slackened, Conolly ordered the landing to proceed. As the first boat wave for the two Uncle beaches, Red and Green, made its run for the beach, gunboats picked up the ball from fire support destroyers and, just before the boats touched down, an LCR discharged 790 rockets onto Beach Red. The first wave landed precisely at H-hour, 0330, met stiff resistance and quickly overcame it. Artillery and ammunition followed, and at 0645 the Brigadier Commanding was on the beach with his staff.

Unfortunately the rocket barrage intended for Beach Green was almost half a mile off in deflection, and fell on Beach Amber of the Sugar pair. Guide boats were stationed off Beach Green and the commander of the first wave could easily have landed there; but, as rockets were considered necessary to explode beach mines, General Hawkesworth and Admiral Conolly had agreed that, if they went wild in the darkness, the boats must follow the rockets and not the plan. So the first wave destined for Beach Green landed at Amber instead, and three more waves followed at 15-minute intervals.

Landing behind the rockets may have saved some soldiers from being blown up by beach mines, but it crowded the 56th Division off Beach Amber, left intact an enemy strong point near Beach Green, and forced two assault battalions of the 46th Division to the wrong side of the Aso River. These battalions, working north to link up with the rest of their brigade, encountered German troops and, without vehicles or supporting weapons, suffered many casualties. And when their vehicles and artillery finally landed on the correct Beach Green, heavy 88-mm fire pinned them down.

German artillery and the Luftwaffe concentrated on the Uncle beaches and roadstead, and made things very hot afloat as well as ashore.

Throughout D-day, fire support ships were blazing away

in reply to aerial bombing and enemy artillery fire. Rangers and Commandos each had a destroyer and an LCG (converted beaching craft armed with 4.7-inch guns) to cover their landings on the Sorrento peninsula. Three British destroyers and three LCGs were assigned to support the 46th Division in Uncle, and the same number, with one more LCG, were assigned to the 56th Division in Sugar and Roger. Cruiser Squadron 15, commanded by Rear Admiral C.H.J. Harcourt RN in H.M.S. *Mauritius,* with *Uganda, Orion,* monitor *Roberts* and two destroyers, operated directly under Commodore Oliver in support of the entire X Corps, but the cruisers had such difficulty communicating with their F.O.O.s and ascertaining the relative positions of friend and foe that they were unable to do much on D-day.

The destroyers more than made up for the cruisers' silence. Off Uncle beaches, H.M.S. *Mendip* and *Brecon* and three small gunboats were busily engaged from 0215 on. They found it easy to silence enemy batteries temporarily, but the German 88s for the most part were mobile and constantly shifted position. When daylight made direct observation possible, enemy fire increased. The German artillery was so well camouflaged that gun flashes and smoke could seldom be detected by ships lying off shore. Admiral Conolly, from the bridge of flagship *Biscayne,* spotted a battery firing into the transport area from a hill southeast of Salerno. Unable at that moment to raise the destroyers by radio, he ordered his flagship to take care of the battery; she moved in and silenced it with 12 rounds from her two 5-inch guns. Soldiers and sailors had begun to call this flag officer "Close-in-Conolly" after his performance off Licata; this incident confirmed his nickname.

The same destroyers, together with H.M.S. *Blankney,* throughout the morning carefully pounded every German battery that they could detect. Liberal use was made of smoke to cover both transports and ships approaching the beach. Smoke provided good protection, since enemy artillery did not fire on floating targets unless they were clearly visible. When Beach Uncle Green was (falsely to be sure) reported overrun by the enemy, during the mixup over Green and Amber, these destroyers steamed so close to shore that they even came under rifle fire. *Loyal* had a boiler knocked out by an 88-mm shell. After *Laforey* had blown up the ammunition dump of a troublesome battery, a second battery nearby straddled her, but she silenced it at 0600, after receiving five hits. Her crew made temporary repairs in the roadstead, and she returned to action within an hour. The 56th Division reported that her fire had reduced several German guns to scrap and inflicted many casualties on their crews. *Lookout* closed Green Beach and put out of action a battery which had sunk an LCT. She remained off the Roger beaches all day, firing at every target seen, although she had but one contact with her F.O.O.

When a strong enemy tank column attacked the 167th Brigade on the right flank of the 56th Division, gunfire from *Nubian* was decisive in breaking up and driving off the assault.

Air defense of the beachhead, controlled by Brigadier General E. J. House USA from his fighter-director center in Admiral Hewitt's flagship *Ancon,* was adequate on D-day because the Luftwaffe put in but few and feeble appearances after the early morning attacks. The British escort carriers, operating well out to sea, placed Seafires over the transports and beaches from dawn to 0745, when fighter planes from the Sicilian fields took over. They started "home" at 1800, when the Seafires resumed combat air patrol and continued until after dark. There were only four "Red" alerts on D-day; and during the first three days, 10–12 September, only 156 enemy air raids were plotted by fighter-director control. Most of them were intercepted by Allied fighters and broken up before entering the assault area. Allied pilots had begun to feel that their activities were wasted, and top air force officers were beginning to suggest using them for "offensive missions," when the Luftwaffe disclosed a new secret weapon that made necessary an increase rather than a decrease of fighter support.

With the exception of the Uncle area, landings in the British sector were less strongly opposed than at Paestum.

But the X Corps became just as heavily engaged ashore as did the United States VI Corps at the same time. By evening the left flank of the 46th Division was about three miles from Salerno, whence its front ran east to a line about two miles inland, where the 56th Division took over. Its right flank joined the coast four miles northwest of the Sele River mouth, leaving a gap of about seven miles between the British X and the United States VI Corps. The Salerno harbor, Montecorvino airfield and Battipaglia—three important D-day objectives—had not been attained.

The pattern of assault in the British sector was very similar to that in the American. Amphibious technique was almost identical, troops were equally aggressive, landing craft crews as skilled and industrious and gunfire support ships equally bold. Commodore Oliver reported that "there was not enough space to bring into action all the artillery landed; naval gunfire filled the gap." Admiral Hewitt concluded that "without the support of naval gunfire, the assault of the beaches could not have carried and the Army could not have remained ashore without the support of naval guns and bombing aircraft."

Although the German command in Italy found D-day both confusing and critical, it quickly recovered balance. On 10 September the Hermann Goering Division and part of the 15th Panzer Grenadier Division began to move toward Salerno. With Rome secured, the 3rd Panzer Grenadier Division was able to start south from near Orvieto; and in Calabria the whole LXXVI Corps was hastening north, after disengaging Montgomery. At 1000 September 10 Kesselring received a cheerful report from the 16th Panzer Division at Salerno that the beachhead front was stabilized; half an hour later General Herr, commanding LXXVI Corps, arrived from the far south and took over. He promptly ordered the 16th Panzers to counterattack VI Corps from Eboli down the Sele Valley toward Paestum, and, as a diversion, to launch a tank attack from Battipaglia against the British X Corps. Both movements started at 1610, but neither succeeded.

Action ashore during the first four days, 9–12 September, is difficult to follow because almost nothing was "according to plan." Heavy fighting started even before the first landing waves beached, and continued with little let-up. We shall attempt to describe the ground action in a general way in order to lay the foundation for our account of the vital part that naval gunfire support played. The intensity and volume of naval gunfire delivered in direct support of troop operations here set a new high in that aspect of naval warfare; one that would not be exceeded in the Pacific until Iwo Jima and Okinawa. Unfortunately no accurate or complete log was kept of these shoots, or even of the calls. On the basis of incomplete reports it has been estimated that during the Salerno operation the ships delivered more than 11,000 tons of shell in direct support of troops ashore. This was the equivalent of 72,000 field artillery 105-mm high-explosive projectiles, and in total weight greatly exceeded that of the bombs dropped by the Northwest African Air Force on the Salerno beachhead, which amounted to only 3020 tons.

In the American sector of the beachhead, VI Corps met slight opposition, enabling it to reorganize, to get the floating reserve (two regiments of the 45th Division) ashore, and to consolidate positions. The gunfire support ships had a rest—few calls came. On the 11th the beachhead was expanded by nightfall against mounting opposition and VI Corps had reached a line starting at Agrópoli on the coast, running thence inland through hilly country and high ground for about ten miles, through Albanella and Altavilla, and to a point near Persano on the Sele River. The 179th Infantry of the 45th Division very nearly reached Ponte Sele, apex of the desired beachhead line, but was stopped short of it by German tanks and artillery. For the 29th Panzer Grenadier Division arrived that day in the foothills behind the Salerno plain, tipping the balance of forces in favor of the Germans; it attacked down the Sele

River, on the 45th Division front, while the 16th Panzer Division thrust outward from Battipaglia toward Salerno, in order to clear the way for the Hermann Goerings to reach the plain through the passes north of Salerno and Maiori. The 157th Regiment, just committed from Fifth Army reserve, moved up the right bank of the Sele River to help the rest of the 45th Division, but was held up by German troops who had occupied a large stone tobacco factory on the other bank of the river. The best the 45th could do by nightfall was to dig in along a line seaward of Persano.

Heaviest fighting on 10 and 11 September occurred in the British sector. Facing a long, 2000-foot ridge which dominated the beach and accommodated a strong concentration of enemy artillery, X Corps made little progress. From Salerno southeastward, Highway No. 18 skirts the base of this ridge and leads past the Montecorvino airfield to the rail and road center of Battipaglia, nearly five miles inland from the beach. On the right flank of X Corps, patrols of the 56th Division were in Battipaglia early on the 10th. Intense fighting continued there throughout the day. At dusk a counterattack by German tanks drove the British out. During the 11th, the 46th Division beat off several enemy counterattacks, and by nightfall it had captured Montecorvino airfield. But this important airdrome, the only one on the plain, remained under German artillery fire for several days. And X Corps had only a weak contact on its right flank with the American VI Corps to the south.

Toward Salerno itself the 46th Division had to fight on a narrowing strip of plain dominated by German artillery on the long ridge. The city was captured on the 10th. A British naval port party entered soon after to open the harbor, but their efforts were countered by the German gunners, who continued to range so accurately on the harbor that Salerno remained useless to the Allies for another two weeks.

At least 37 calls for naval gunfire were answered on 10 September in the British sector. Destroyers *Tartar*, *Lookout* and *Loyal*, which had been in the thick of the action on D-day, continued their active support on the 10th. *Loyal* departed for Palermo at 1030 to replenish ammunition, but was back on the job by dawn 10 September. Typical of the support rendered was that of H.M. destroyer *Nubian,* which fired 341 rounds of 4.7-inch shell on that day. In the early morning she broke up a German tank concentration, between 1000 and 1145 she bombarded and destroyed an enemy battery, besides demolishing a building which her F.O.O. thought to be a German strong point; for half an hour from 1250 she engaged an enemy battery that was firing on British troops, and destroyed it. Next targets were an ammunition dump and a concentration of enemy vehicles; at 1648 she shifted again to tanks, and closed a busy day at 1951. Cruiser *Mauritius,* flagship of Rear Admiral Harcourt, answered 17 calls for fire and expended nearly 500 rounds on a variety of targets ranging through enemy troops, artillery and tanks to road intersections. Cruisers *Uganda* and *Orion* and monitor *Roberts* joined in some of these shoots, which were very accurate — "Target destroyed" or "Battery silenced" being the usual closeout comment on a specific target. The cumulative effect of naval gunfire in checking German attacks and helping the hard-pressed British troops to hold their positions cannot be precisely assessed, but there can be no doubt that it was very important.

Commandos and elements of the 46th Division moved north through the pass from Vietri against mounting resistance, and held a good position against a heavy infantry and tank attack in which the Royal Marines suffered 198 casualties out of a total strength of 350. On the heights of Mount Chiunzi the Rangers held firm against determined German attacks. Dug in as they were in positions as high as 4000 feet, supply was their major problem; they fought on with skeleton rations and little water. Even mules collapsed when bringing water and ammunition up from the beach by the steep path. From observation posts high in the hills, the Rangers directed artillery and naval gunfire onto the roads below.

On 11 September, the 4th Battalion seized Monte Pendolo, far to the left of the 3rd Battalion, with a gap of several miles between. In order to strengthen their lines on these important positions overlooking the passes between Salerno and Naples, General Clark on 11 September lifted a battalion of the 143rd Infantry, reinforced with artillery, tanks, tank destroyers and engineers, in beaching craft, from the VI Corps sector to Maiori.

By nightfall 11 September, Fifth Army beachhead at deepest penetration reached about ten miles inland, but on the northern flank it tapered to about a mile. There was a lightly held gap between VI and X Corps north of the Sele River that was in the course of being plugged with the 157th Regiment.

Enemy air attacks on troops ashore on 10 and 11 September were little more than nuisance raids. But the Luftwaffe made serious raids on the roadstead, using the new radio-controlled glide-bomb. Two types of radio-controlled bombs, fitted with fins and with rocket-boosters, had been developed, one with a range of about 8 miles and maximum speed of 570 m.p.h.; the other with a range of 3½ miles and maximum speed of 660 m.p.h. Both were guided visually by radio from a high-flying plane which released them at a safe distance from the target; each carried a warhead explosive charge of 660 pounds. The existence of these bombs was already known to Allied naval commanders, since they had been used to a limited extent earlier in the war. Their employment in this theater was anticipated, but as yet no good defense against them had been devised.

Savannah was put out of action by one of these bombs. She was lying-to in her support area, awaiting calls for gunfire support, at 0930 September 11, when 12 Focke-Wulf 190s were reported approaching from the north. The cruiser rang up 10 knots' speed, which she increased to 15 knots after a heavy bomb had exploded close aboard *Philadelphia,* nearby. Ten minutes later, *Savannah* received a direct hit on No. 3 turret. The bomb, which had been dropped by a Dornier–217 from 18,000 feet, detonated in the lower handling room. The blast wiped out both the crew of the stricken turret and the No. 1 damage-control crew in central station, blew a large hole in the ship's bottom and opened a seam in her side. Fires were extinguished in several boilers, and for a short time the ship had no power. She settled by the bow until the forecastle was nearly awash. Surviving damage-control parties worked smartly to seal off the flooded and burned compartments; salvage tugs *Hopi* and *Moreno* moored alongside to assist. *Savannah* was kept on an even keel by shifting her fuel oil. At 1800 she retired under her own power, screened by four destroyers, and arrived safely at Malta.

Although enemy resistance had been so strong that several D-day objectives had not yet been reached, the beachhead seemed secure by the evening of 11 September. After a visit to X Corps, General Clark reported to General Alexander that he would soon be ready to launch an attack northward through Vietri toward Naples. The Germans, despite their rapid reinforcement and partial success in counterattacks, were none too happy. The commanding general of the 16th Panzer Division reported to General Herr that the situation was critical. His troops were under heavy pressure at Battipaglia and his lines had been breached by American tanks near Persano. But the tables were soon turned.

Ominous reports began to flow in to General Clark's headquarters ashore, shortly after 0930 September 12. Elements of the Hermann Goering Division moving south from Naples had been identified opposite X Corps, and the presence of the 15th Panzer Grenadier Division in the same area was ascertained. Elements of the 26th Panzer and 29th Panzer Grenadier Divisions arrived at the beachhead from Calabria and went right into action against VI Corps. The Eighth Army was supposed to be hot on their trail; Alexander on the 10th ordered Montgomery to hurry, and on the 12th sent his chief of staff "to explain the full urgency of the situation." But Montgomery's advance patrols did not make contact with VI Corps until 1400 September 16, after the crisis had passed.

On the right center of VI Corps, a battalion of the 142nd Infantry occupied Hill 424 behind Altavilla early on 12 September. Before it could organize this position, an important one to deny the enemy since it commanded a complete view of plain and beaches, the Germans counterattacked and forced them to adandon Altavilla. On the left of VI Corps, elements of the 45th Division drove the enemy out of the tobacco factory, with the help of gunfire from *Philadelphia,* captured Persano and advanced inland. General Dawley regrouped his troops during the night of 12–13 September to strengthen and tighten his lines; but there was still a wide gap between VI Corps and the British. General Dawley planned to drive against Hill 424 on the 13th.

On the extreme left flank of Fifth Army, the Rangers captured several more heights overlooking Castellammare on the 12th and sent a night patrol into that town, where they ran into stiff resistance. This thrust was little to the Germans' taste, as it threatened to break a way for the Allied forces to enter Naples. But the élan of the Rangers gave the enemy an exaggerated idea of their strength and he decided to reinforce before launching a major counterattack. The Rangers were strong enough to dominate the Sorrento peninsula and control the road-railway gap at Nocera, but too weak to exploit their positions.

No significant gains were made by X Corps on 12 September, although it was well supported by the gunfire of monitor *Roberts* and several destroyers. The 167th Brigade 56th Division was driven out of Battipaglia, sustaining such heavy losses that it had to be relieved. Despite comparative quiet in the British sector, X Corps had suffered some 3000 casualties—from 5 to 7 per cent of its strength—by the evening of 12 September, and the troops were exhausted.

Thus Fifth Army lost Battipaglia and Altavilla on 12 September, a day of more intense fighting than any that had preceded. It became obvious that the Germans were rapidly and dangerously building up their strength in front of Salerno beachhead. By the 12th, Kesselring had at his disposal 600 tanks and mobile guns, on which he relied to throw Clark into the sea before Montgomery could come up to relieve him. The day closed for the Allies on a very different note from that on which it had opened. General Clark began to think that he would have to evacuate the southern beaches and concentrate his entire army north of the Sele River.

Although the Montecorvino airport had been in British hands since 10 September, it was still dominated by German artillery fire on the 13th, and unusable. Army Engineers met the emergency by constructing a strip on the plain two miles north of the Greek temples at Paestum, and had it ready 12 September. On that day the British escort carriers had to retire to fuel at Palermo, but 26 of their Seafires were flown in to the Paestum airstrip from which they operated until replaced by planes of the Northwest African Air Forces. By 13 September a second strip was ready near the first, work had been begun on a third, and the British sappers had two emergency strips ready in X Corps area.

To strengthen the VI Corps left flank and also to close the dangerous gap between it and the British, General Dawley ordered many front-line units shifted during the night of 12–13 September. When news reached him that night of the German recapture of Battipaglia, he withdrew two more infantry battalions from the right flank of the 36th Division and sent them to the threatened left.

A tactical group, called the Martin Force from the Colonel commanding, composed of three battalions from the 142nd and 143rd Infantry, counterattacked Altavilla and Hill 424 at 0600 September 13. It did very well during the morning, but later in the day a German column isolated the Martin Force and stopped its offensive. It had to withdraw during the night of 14–15 September.

The crux of the German counterattack on 13 September came on the VI Corps left flank, especially in the angle formed between the Sele and the Calore River that empties into it.

At 1542, one column of six German tanks attacked the left flank of the 1st Battalion 157th Infantry, which was dug in on the north slopes of the tobacco factory hill, and at the same time 15 more tanks rolled down the road from Eboli, followed by a battalion of the 79th Panzer Grenadier Regiment and towed fieldpieces. They captured the tobacco factory and drove the 1st Battalion back to the railroad. Another force of infantry-supported tanks hit the 2nd Battalion 143rd posted on the road to Ponte Sele and forced it to retire across the Calore, with a loss of 508 officers and men.

Then, fortunately for us, the German commander made a bad tactical error. At 1715 he sent his main body of tanks right down into the fork between the Sele and the Calore. His intention, obviously, was to cross the Calore where the maps showed a bridge, and drive through the VI Corps to Paestum and the beach. But the bridge had been burned, the dirt road chosen by the tanks was lined with deep drainage ditches, so they could not deploy, and, on the rolling open grassland south of the burned bridge, two battalions of United States field artillery, the 189th and 158th, were posted. Lieutenant Colonels Hal L. Muldrow and Russell D. Funk USA stripped their batteries of all but minimum gun crews, commandeered every stray GI and truck driver they could pick up on the road, put headquarters company and band into line, and posted these improvised infantrymen, armed with rifles and machine guns, on the slope between the batteries and the river. The fire of these men, added to that of the artillery, crossed the tanks' "T" as neatly as Admiral Togo did that of the Russian fleet, and forced all surviving tanks to retreat.

Although *Philadelphia* and several destroyers were available, they were not called upon for gunfire during this critical battle. Probably there was no shore fire-control party among the impromptu defenders at the river fork. *Boise,* arriving off the beachhead that afternoon to replace stricken *Savannah,* divided 36 rounds of 6-inch between a German tank concentration and a battery at the rear, checking fire when her shore fire-control party reported the battery demolished. *Philadelphia* was busy brushing off enemy air attacks. Two of the new radio-controlled bombs were aimed at her, but nimble "Philly" eluded both and they exploded harmlessly in the water, one 100 yards, the other 100 feet from the ship.

Even after the tank attack in the river fork had been defeated the situation ashore was still critical. Several American units had been decimated, and there were few reserves to throw in next day. When the ground commanders assembled at VI Corps headquarters at Paestum that evening, things looked bad. Only the two artillery battalions had prevented a complete break-through, and X Corps was still heavily embroiled. General Clark, as a precaution in case the Germans had worse things in store for the morrow, sent Admiral Hewitt an urgent request to prepare plans to evacuate the VI Corps from the beachhead and re-land it north of the Sele to aid the X Corps, or vice versa. The Admiral did not like the idea—but, as the Navy was there to support the Army by any and every means, he went ahead with the plans.

Although the main strength of the German attack on 13 September was directed at the weak left flank of VI Corps, there was heavy fighting on the British X Corps front as well, especially near Battipaglia. To support the troops, H.M.S. *Roberts,* three cruisers and six destroyers delivered shoots on troops, batteries, tanks and road intersections, as called for by their F.O.O.s. Cruiser *Uganda* was struck by a guided bomb at 1440 when no alert was on; the attacking plane was not seen. The bomb penetrated seven decks and exploded below the ship. Although flooded with some 1300 tons of water, she was saved by prompt shoring of threatened bulkheads, and left the combat area early next morning under tow of U.S.S. *Narragansett,* escorted by three destroyers. Within an hour of *Uganda's* hit, destroyers *Nubian* and *Loyal* were narrowly missed by guided bombs. Now that two light cruisers were out of action, and other ships running low on ammunition, Admiral of the Fleet Cunningham ordered H.M.S. *Aurora* and *Penelope* up from Malta. They arrived off Salerno by sunrise 14 September.

Important reinforcements arrived on the 13th—the 82nd Airborne Division which would have performed the drop on Rome had it not been canceled. Some of the paratroops were landed at Maiori to reinforce Darby's Rangers; the rest, standing by on Sicilian fields, were requested by General Clark, at 1330, to fly in that very night. General Ridgway, equal to every emergency, organized the drops at an hour's notice. Mindful of what had happened in Sicily, he asked that all antiaircraft guns on the beachhead or in the roadstead be forbidden to fire that night; General

Clark and Admiral Hewitt so directed. The first planes took off at 1930. Led by three Pathfinders with paratroops and ground signaling equipment, 82 C–47s and C–53s, starting from Cómiso and Trápani–Milo fields in Sicily, dropped over 600 paratroops exactly where they were wanted behind the VI Corps lines south of the Sele; only one man was injured. The following night 1000 more paratroops were dropped successfully in the same zone.*

Throughout the night of 13–14 September weary Army officers worked to arrange a new defensive line, starting at the crossroads west of the tobacco factory, along the rise whence the artillery had stopped the tanks, and around the east edge of a line of foothills, almost to the hill town of Roccadáspide. At dawn 14 September the Germans renewed their attack with probing tank and infantry thrusts; but, thanks to the night time regrouping, VI Corps held its ground. In the X Corps sector the 46th Division was well dug in on hills near Salerno, but the 56th was still in the open plain southwest of Battipaglia, under enemy observation from the nearby hills. The Coldstream Guards and the 9th Royal Fusiliers repulsed a strong enemy tank attack during the night of 13–14 September, and on the 14th moved over to close the dangerous gap between the X and VI Corps. Although the rest of the 26th Panzer Division from the south, and a regimental combat team of the 3rd Panzer Grenadier Division from the north, arrived in the battle area that day, these were the last reinforcements available to the German command, and when darkness descended over the Salerno plain on 14 September the situation of the Fifth Army had greatly improved.

Naval gunfire support was a material contribution to this result. Of the 14th Vietinghoff wrote: "The attack this

---

*A third drop during the night of 14–15 September at Avellino was less successful, because the mountains forced it to be made from altitudes between 3000 and 5000 feet. Only 15 of the 40 planes carrying 600 paratroops hit the right place; the rest dropped their men from 8 to 25 miles away in small groups. Most were captured; some worked their way south and made contact with the Fifth Army.

morning pushed on into stiffened resistance; but above all the advancing troops had to endure the most severe heavy fire that had hitherto been experienced; the naval gunfire from at least 16 to 18 battleships, cruisers and large destroyers lying in the roadstead. With astonishing precision and freedom of maneuver, these ships shot at every recognized target with very overwhelming effect."

Philadelphia, as usual, was to the fore. She continued to shoot at targets designated by her shore fire-control party throughout the night of 13–14 September, firing 921 rounds of 6-inch on tanks, batteries, road intersections and massed troops, and receiving such messages as: "Very good—we are under attack—stand by," and "Thank you—stand by." Between 0844 and 1345 September 14, *Boise* relieved her, firing almost continuously at tanks and troops—18 different targets—and expending nearly 600 rounds. Shore fire-control party reported "Very well!" after a tank concentration had received 83 rounds. At 1503 *Philadelphia* returned for a two-hour session. There followed another lull in naval gunfire support; then, at 2130, *Boise* was called on for rapid fire on troops. With shore fire-control party reporting "No change" and "Straddle, straddle!" she unloaded 72 rounds in short order. An hour later she was called on again, and after firing 121 rounds got the word, "Cease firing; thank you, stand by." At 2310 she delivered interdiction fire on German troops marching down from Eboli; "You are doing well," said the shore party. All night 14–15 September she continued firing on call. In the British sector the pattern of gunfire support was much the same. Four light cruisers and four destroyers got into the shooting, with good results.

Although Fifth Army and supporting fleets were successfully beating off German attacks on 14 September, the situation still seemed grave to the higher Allied commanders. Admiral Hewitt, it will be remembered, had been making plans for a possible shifting of VI Corps to X Corps sectors, or vice versa, at General Clark's insistence. That afternoon he sent an urgent message to Admiral of the Fleet Cunningham: "The Germans have created a salient dangerously near the beach. Military situation continuing unsatisfactory. Am planning to use all available vessels to transfer troops from southern to northern beaches, or the reverse if necessary. Unloading of merchant vessels in the southern section has been stopped. We need heavy aerial and naval bombardment behind enemy positions, using battleships or other heavy naval vessels. Are any such ships available?"

Admiral Cunningham reacted promptly to the request for naval reinforcements. At 1732 September 14 he ordered Admiral Vian to expedite the loading of troops at Philippeville and to sail immediately with H.M.S. *Euryalus, Scylla* and *Charybdis* to Salerno. An hour later he ordered battleships *Valiant* and *Warspite* to depart Malta with six destroyers and report to Admiral Hewitt as soon as possible after daylight next morning. Unfortunately Hewitt's dispatch reached an important addressee, General Eisenhower, in a garbled form which suggested that he and General Clark were contemplating a complete evacuation of the Salerno beachhead. There was consternation at headquarters over what appeared to be going on, and consternation at the beachhead over what Hewitt thought he might have to do, if General Clark insisted. Both Commodore Oliver and General McCreery, in no uncertain terms, opposed the idea of transferring troops from one part of the beachhead to another, insisting that they should fight it out where they were, with all the gunfire support the Navy could provide.

General Alexander, after reviewing the situation on the spot, killed the plan for shifting troops. It was fortunate that the shift never had to be made, since a reverse amphibious operation under hostile fire is exceedingly difficult to carry out. But neither General Clark nor Admiral Hewitt at any time contemplated a complete withdrawal from the beachhead.

Northwest African Air Forces were not idle through all this. On 13 September General Eisenhower ordered Air Chief Marshal Tedder to send every plane that could fly against sensitive spots in the German formations. This great air attack was delivered on the 14th. Although in part ill-directed, owing to the lack of ground air-control units with the troops, it badly disrupted German mobility and communications, and materially helped the Allies to regain the initiative.

In retrospect, it appears that the German drive to the beaches was defeated not only by the stout resistance of all three Allied arms, but by the German dual command in Italy—Rommel in the north, Kesselring in the south. A single commander could, on 9 September have sent south to Salerno several divisions of the Army group stationed around Mantua, and they could have arrived by the 13th. But Rommel, who never believed in the southern Italy campaign, would not let them go. Even two divisions more would have enabled Kesselring to make good his threat, and wipe out the beachhead.

In The Hedgerows

Once the D-Day landings were secured, the town of Saint-Lô, approximately 20 miles inland from Omaha Beach, was a prime objective of the U.S. First Army. In the volume COMBAT: European Theater, the overall strategy of the operations of the First Army is discussed and the breakout from Saint-Lô to the Falaise Gap is described by Alan Moorehead.

The hedgerow country before Saint-Lô was especially rugged for infantry. Hedgerows were dirt banks lining the roads of Normandy approximately five to eight feet high and four feet wide. As tanks moved up the roads between the hedgerows, they were sitting ducks for German 88s emplaced just around curves. Machine guns and mortars were cleverly situated by the Germans to exploit the hedgerows as natural defenses. Instead of traveling up the alley-like roads, the infantry were forced to take to the fields. But soon they were sure to come to a hedgerow at right angles to the road. In consequence, it is not hard to see why progress before Saint-Lô was measured by one hedgerow after another, and there always seemed to be another one beyond the last.

Taking part in the war through this country was the 1st Battalion, 115 Infantry of the 29th Division, under the command of Major Glover S. Johns. These people landed at D-Day on Omaha Beach and were in combat steadily for the next two months. The Major's portrait of this action is remarkably frank for an officer; he unashamedly records his own feeling, his own inexperience in combat, and his times of indecision—all the while accepting the need to press on ahead.

Early on in his story he says, speaking of himself in the third person:

"They walked rapidly for a hundred yards. The firing began to die away. Then it stopped all along the whole front. The Major slowed a bit. These sudden changes in the tempo of the action puzzled him. He wondered if C Company had repulsed the attack, if A Company had driven in from the flank and forced the enemy to retreat, or if Ryan had been stopped and had pulled back into the woods to re-form and try it again.

While these questions passed through his mind a nasty feeling of failure grew inside him. Night was closing in. He had not succeeded in taking his first objective as a battalion commander. His stomach was knotting slowly but tightly with that overpowering fear, not fear of death or injury, but of failure. He kept moving forward." *

And, again:

"He looked at what he had written, but didn't like it. He was damned if he would squall for help so soon in the first fight.

"He was drawing a line through the last sentence when the world suddenly exploded all around him. Sharp ballistic cracks pounded his eardrums so rapidly they seemed like one impossibly prolonged rifle shot. He was instantly paralyzed with overwhelming fright.

"The radio operator, Jimmie, slumped forward at his feet, another man stumbled past to fall into the ditch ahead, and Newcomb cleared the eight-foot hedgerow apparently with one jump. But the Major was too shocked to move. His stomach knotted itself into a tight ball. It jammed against his pounding heart while his breathing stopped completely for an instant, then came in jerky gasps. The hair on his head felt as if it were rising like the hair on a cat's back. His skin prickled all over. But the most awful thing was the cold, empty feeling in his guts." **

Later as his men are hung up outside Saint-Lô he tells the story of attack and counterattack, the ebb and flow of infantry fighting which was the meat and potatoes of combat, and is still today.

BEFORE SAINT-LŎ

by Glover S. Johns

As the sun climbed higher the temperature rose with it. The day was going to be hot. And it was hot in

---

*The Clay Pigeons of St. Lô, by G. S. Johns, p. 11.
** Ibid., p. 13.

more ways than one. The Germans began warming things up all along the line by throwing over more and more artillery and mortar fire. By mid-morning there had been several casualties in each company and the command post had been shaken up twice. The battalion commander issued orders that no man would leave his position unless absolutely necessary. Obeying his own order, he stayed in the hole.

The battalion's mortars and supporting artillery were returning more than they received, but there was no quieting the Germans that day. Martin was watching the situation with interest. One of his jobs was to receive and forward "shell-reps." A shell report, or "shell rep," was supposed to be sent in by any man who witnessed the fall of enemy artillery fire. The report included the exact location in which each shell hit, its caliber, and, as nearly as possible, the direction from which it had come. At the Fire Direction Center, the artillery S2 placed the location of each hit on the map and projected the estimated direction of flight back into enemy territory. The lines thus plotted always crossed somewhere. If enough of these rays intersected near the same point, it was a good bet a hostile battery was located somewhere in that vicinity. By studying the terrain, as indicated on the map, it was often possible to guess just about where that battery would be. Then, when the S2 was satisfied, from this information, that he had a good chance of drawing blood, he could take the matter to his own commander and ask for a counterbattery mission. If approved, the big 155's would reach out and search the selected area. Sometimes they were lucky. Sometimes they weren't, but every shell that burst in enemy territory was money in the bank to the infantrymen who heard it going over, so it was never a complete waste.

Martin was puzzled. He kept a rough record of the shell reps for his own information and by the middle of the afternoon he had enough data to make him want to talk to his boss. He called Lieutenant Colonel Cooper, the commander of the 110th Field Artillery Battalion.

"Sir," said Martin, "I believe the Germans have moved some more artillery in opposite us. The way these reports are coming in makes me think they are registering on us. What worries me is how they could be getting any observation on some of the targets they shoot at."

"We think the same thing," Cooper replied, "and I'm asking General Sands for some corps artillery to give us a hand with counterbattery today. Call me again if you get any definite ideas."

Some of the enemy fire falling that day was on targets that had never been hit before, and which couldn't possibly be observed from the enemy lines. The Germans had no equivalent of the American light observation plane that provided the artillery with a bird's-eye view of any front. Therefore there seemed to be only one answer to the accuracy of the fire—the Germans must have infiltrated artillery observers into the battalion lines for the express purpose of registering on vital new targets.

Major Johns ordered out several search parties. They beat through every wooded area and combed every hillock or bush-covered hedgerow. They examined every tall tree and even prodded into suspicious-looking ground that might have covered trapdoor-type holes. They found no observers. After two men were hurt by incoming shell fragments, the Major ordered them back to their holes, none the wiser.*

Martin was defeated. He said it was impossible for artillery to fire with such consistent accuracy from a map. If his first "only" answer had been wrong then all that was left to

---

*Many times during the campaign in Europe did American units suspect that the Germans had observers concealed behind our lines. This probably did occur in some instances. However, the answer usually comes from a less mysterious source. The Germans told us after the war that our radio security was consistently poor, that by monitoring our transmissions they were generally able to keep themselves well informed as to our movements, and that by goniometric intersection on our transmitters they were able to locate most of our command posts as well as other installations. Our people never seemed to realize that in many German units were men who had lived in the States and

believe was that the German artillery had registered on all those targets while the area was still in their hands. Nobody could answer that question, but it didn't stop the accurate fire from coming in steadily.

The mortars were the worst, though. They were even more effective than the 88's there in that position at Dufayel, because the rolling terrain produced many dead spaces which the 88's with their flat trajectory could not reach. It was later that the men came to fear the 88's more than the silently falling mortar shells.

The German mortar gunners must have registered, too, because they had the exact range of every foot of hedgerow held by the battalion. On the 10th of July they covered almost every foot of every hedgerow. That sort of gunnery was rough on the men. They never knew when the first round would fall. But once it had splattered with its flat crash, they all knew that six or maybe a dozen more were coming, each one a little farther up or down the hedgerow. When you heard that first one you pulled the bottom of your foxhole right up into your belly and prayed. When you heard the second one you knew whether or not they were coming your way. If they were coming toward you it got right rough. Each round was a little closer, and they were so damned deliberate about it that the waiting was worse than the crash of the shell itself. You lay there and counted the seconds between the shells until you knew that the next one was YOURS.

The twenty seconds or so was the longest in the world

understood American slang perfectly, and that the so-called double talk which we indulged in rarely fooled them. Even more interesting is the fact that our supposed short-range transmissions during the Louisiana and Tennessee maneuvers were picked up in Germany owing to a phenomenon involving reflection from the Heaviside Layer of ionized particles in the stratosphere. A study of these intercepts often told the enemy when our units were preparing for oversea movement. The German artillery was also skilled in sound- and flash-ranging, but this method did not, of course, locate for them anything except active artillery positions.—Editor.

322

because you'd never know if you were safe until the shell hit. It could hit anywhere outside your hole, even a matter of inches, yet you were okay. If it hit in the hole with you you'd never know it, of course. Actually, only a few shells ever made direct hits on foxholes, but some did and nearly every man had seen a foxhole that had been hit. There was always the little tail-fin section left on the surface, and after the litter bearers had come and gone there was only a pool of dark muck to show that somebody had been in the hole.

It happened twice that day.

A little after 1700 General Gerhardt came striding through the trees behind the command post hole. His manner was neither light nor gay. He came on serious business, that of giving orders for an attack. If he carried them himself they were important.

He wanted to brief all the company commanders but he didn't have time to wait for Able and Baker to worm their way out. Consequently he talked to Kenney; and to McCarthy, who had succeeded Captain Nabb in command of Dog Company; and to Mentzer, together with Major Johns and the staff. All crowded into The Hole.

"Gentlemen," he said, with an edge to his voice that was impressive, "the division attacks tomorrow morning at 0600. All along the line. This is the drive for St.-Lô."

He stopped to consult a notebook. "Your objective will be the town of Belle Fontaine. Of course you will get details from Ordway. But I want to tell you that this is the beginning of a very big and very important operation. I can't tell you more now, but I expect every one of you to do your best tomorrow."

With that he was gone, Weddle and Grimsehl scurrying to get off the steps to make room for his passage, and his aide scrambling to get out of the phone hole and catch up.

Before he got well into the woods, the General stopped suddenly and called, "Oh, Johns."

Major Johns was on his heels. "Yes, sir?"

"Look, boy, you're the sole survivor of the three volunteers who wanted to come with me. Did you know that?"

He didn't wait for an answer. "Whitehead caught an 88 the other day while you were back in those woods." He paused and looked sharply at the Major. "I don't know if it's lucky to ask to get into a war or not. But you stay in there and pitch. I'm counting on you."

He waved and was gone again before Johns could reply.

The staff ate their C-ration supper in thoughtful silence, waiting for the CO and Weddle to be called back to Regiment for particulars concerning the attack. They were called soon enough.

There were few details. The battalions would attack, as the General had said, at 0600. The 1st Battalion would advance in the southwesterly direction, with the village of Belle Fontaine as its initial objective. It was hardlly a thousand yards, across country, but every man in the battalion knew it would be a long thousand. It was just as well that they didn't know just *how* tough that thousand yards was to be.

The 2d Battalion would move on La Forge and the 3d would be in reserve.

That was about all there was to it, except for the usual information concerning artillery support, supplies, location of the regimental command post, and that sort of thing.

Johns and Weddle got back just at dark. Though it was very quiet, the company commanders who were waiting in The Hole were uneasy. None of them wanted to attack from that position. It was too screwy a setup. But there was nothing they could do about it now. The Major had no choice in his order of attack. From the direction of the objective he could do only one thing, let Able and Baker take off from right where they were, with Charlie, in reserve, protecting what would become the exposed and dangerous left flank.

Johns expected trouble on that left flank because they would be moving slantwise across the Charlie front, at least at first. Even in that difficult terrain it was too much to expect that they could get clear without trouble. He told Kenney to try to protect the flank with one platoon while holding two platoons free for him to use to shove through a soft spot, if one was found, or to bolster a weak place if they were hit hard with a counterattack.

By the time the order got down to the platoon leaders their part was pretty simple; all they, in turn, had to say was "All right, gang, let's take that next hedgerow."

When the company commanders had gone, the staff discussed the plan of attack. The question bothering Johns most of all was where to put the advance command post group. He wanted to hold casualties to the barest minimum, yet he wanted to be as far forward as possible. There were a number of good reasons for this. In the first place, keeping the command group close to the companies made a lot of difference in communications, particularly in this close, wooded country. A clump of heavy trees or a high hedgerow could spell the margin between having contact and not having it. That was of supreme importance. Second, if he had to move to a bogged-down company or to any trouble spot, he wanted to have the shortest possible distance to go. Third, the group couldn't afford to stay far behind, in any event, because they fully expected the German paratroopers to close in around them as soon as they started to advance. If the command post group were too far from the rifle companies it would have a good chance of getting cut off and destroyed or captured. Then there was always the consideration that the men liked to know that the Old Man was not far behind, and to see him once in a while when the stuff was flying around. Major Johns was acutely aware of this, but he'd already suffered losses in his command post group by getting them up front and he didn't want that to happen again. There wasn't a good route of advance in the center so he decided to move along close behind Able. That would put the command post on the open flank, away from the known threat to the left but exposed to anything that might come from the right. If danger did materialize, the command post group could always help defend the flank then shift toward the center as soon as they could conveniently disengage.

At midnight the whole staff, less only the S4, was still in The Hole talking about the attack. The night was almost eerily still. Only a quiet voice or two and the occasional passage of heavy shells, high overhead, disturbed the silence.

There was no mortar fire, largely because mortar men don't like to fire at night. The flash of their guns, so comparatively close to the lines, looms bright and clear in the darkness and sometimes a little trail of fire follows a shell for several hundred feet up into the air, making it plain as a tracer and spelling out, "Here I am. Why don't you shell me back?"

There was a rare rifle shot or brief burst of machine-gun fire as some gunner on one side or the other fancied he saw a target. But the stillness between was so heavy that these puny outbursts hardly made a ripple on the great pond of silence.

By 0100 the last patrol was in safely. Only two had been sent out, just to make sure the enemy was still in the same positions and to listen for signs of movement behind his lines. Nothing was stirring.

The radiomen turned on their sets and checked with each other as they did every half hour throughout the day and night, so they would never be completely out of touch for more than 30 minutes if the wires should go out.

The staff was uneasy. They didn't want to turn in. They couldn't say why; there had been other nights like this. They all sensed that everyone shared their own nameless fears.

Mentzer broke the spell. They had all come out of The Hole for a breath of air and were standing by the hedgerow, looking at the few stars that showed through a light overcast that had drifted in since dark. Mentzer was a light-hearted individual, not usually concerned with thinking deeply about abstract matters. He had been a cab driver back in Frederick, Maryland, home of his Headquarters Company. "Ah," he said, "them bastards are just tired after throwin' all that heavy stuff in here all day. They've shot their wad. I'm gonna hit the sack."

He turned and disappeared into the extreme darkness of the woods, headed for his nearby hole.

Down in The Hole the phone rang softly. Weddle went

down to answer it, staying nearly two full minutes before he came back up, saying, "That was the Doc. He says one of his men saw a German out by the medics' latrine. I asked him how could he know it was a Kraut in this dark and he said because the guy crawled over a hedgerow not ten feet from him and he got a good look at his little paratrooper helmet silhouetted against some stars that happened to be in the clear just then. He said the guy grunted when he slid off the hedgerow and he didn't sound like any of our people. The Doc checked but couldn't find anybody else who had been out there. Nobody uses that latrine but the medics."

Major Johns snapped to full alert. "Doc's man was probably seeing things. Nevertheless get Mentzer to grab some of his people who are off duty right now and beat out the area. Get the whole A and P Platoon if you want to, but have a good look around. We can't take any chances."

He wouldn't have admitted that he was nervous. He just believed in playing it safe.

Weddle went after Mentzer while the Major turned to Grimsehl. "George, wake everybody up and check the CP close-in defense. Get the Commando Platoon on their toes. See that there is an alert, tight ring around here tonight—all night."

Grimsehl lost no time in moving out to look for Sergeant Turner, who had charge of the so-called Commando Platoon, which was a group of 10 or 12 men specially picked and trained for tough patrol work. They were kept around the command post for its defense when they were not out on a mission. In a quiet position a double guard at each entrance was usually enough, as all the others slept nearby in holes dug in a circle around the command post. Tonight the battalion commander wanted every man in every hole to be awake and ready for business. He proposed to take no chances on a quick rush by a few determined paratroopers overrunning the guard and tossing grenades into all the holes, including The Hole.

Suddenly a terrific firing broke out.

Every German cannon, mortar, rifle, and machine gun that had fired a round that day cut loose simultaneously.

The sound of mortars coughing on the German side blended with the scream of incoming shells. Grimsehl and Hoffman slid down the steps of The Hole before the first round hit.

It was Ryan's war all over again on a broader front. The sharp roar of artillery shells overrode the flatter crunching of the mortars, while the vicious, snarling, still sharper crack of 88's stood out above both, and the ripping of German machine guns filled in the tiny intervals between explosions. Although the fire was concentrated chiefly on the edges of the gap between the two companies at the orchard, it was hitting all along the front. Some rounds tore into the field and hedgerow near the command post while others rushed overhead to burst in the trees as they searched for the mortar positions.

The phone rang. Major Johns grabbed it. "Red 6."

"Charlie 6, sir. We're catching hell down here with mortars and artillery. I think there is enemy infantry coming in under the fire."

Stoen broke in, the operator having wisely sensed a crisis and cut him into the circuit, "Same here, Major. Only I KNOW there's infantry coming in. They're already in the road with us."

His voice and manner were normally extremely quiet and easy-going. Now his tone was strident with urgency. Had it been anyone but Julian Stoen, the Major might have thought it showed near-panic. "Okay to both of you," he answered as calmly as he could. "Stuff's coming in up here too. Fight 'em and keep me informed."

He spun the crank and said to the operator, "Give me Regiment."

Nothing happened. You can tell when a field wire is dead because it is so very dead. The operator's voice was rising now, too. "Sir," he shouted, "that line is out. I'll get a crew on it right away."

Before Johns could lay the phone down it rang again. It was Stoen. "Sir, for God's sake put all the artillery we got down in front of the lines . . . you know my concentrations . . . call for all of 'em . . . . the bastards are all over us." The phone went dead.

Martin was frantically spinning the artillery phone crank

but there was no answer and the crank spun easily. There was no resistance in the circuit, indicating that the line had been cut. Martin stuck his head out the entrance and called to the radio operator. "Call for concentrations 175 through 183 as fast as they can fire 'em. Tell 'em it's an attack. We need all they can give us."

The operator turned on his set and started calling. He called and called, but he got no answer. They all knew that the set at the Fire Direction Center was not on because they had checked in exactly 8 minutes before, and it would not come on again until 0200. That meant that for 22 minutes the battalion would be cut off from outside support of any kind. A lot could happen in 22 minutes.

The mortar observers, up with the companies, found their lines were out too; but they had radios, and the men at the mortar positions did not need orders to start firing anyway. They could hear what was going on. The mortars started pouring out shells before the first message came back. So, at least, the battalion had its own support working.

"That Kraut back by the aid station!" cried Weddle, suddenly. "He must have been part of a patrol that came through and cut all our wires! Hell, there haven't been enough shells falling to cut 'em ALL. The smart bastards! They even knew when we checked the radios, too."

Major Johns nodded. He was calling Able Company. No answer. That wire was out. They were all out, front and rear. He took the 300 handset from Bein, his new radio operator, and tried to get Charlie Company. Kenney answered, reporting that his whole line was heavily engaged. There was no reply from Baker.

Johns cursed his impotence. His communications, with which he had been so satisfied, were shot to hell. For all the influence he was having on this battle he might as well be back at Division. It was up to the men on the front line now. He had no reserves and no way of getting any. He knew the radiomen were trying to get through to Regiment and the Fire Direction Center. There was absolutely nothing he could do but wait.

The enemy fire was still heavy. The German gunners pounded every company, then searched every position that might hold reserves. The command post was shaken up again and again. Bein's radio lost an aerial, which he replaced in seconds. One of the commando gang took a fragment in his leg. Tracers flew overhead in all directions, ricochets screamed and yowled, and the tearing crackle of German machine gun bullets never stopped.

Only minutes after the barrage hit, the hollow, clumping roar of grenades came from the direction of the Able Company command post. Major Johns rushed into the open to listen more carefully. The sound of the grenades kept coming, punctuated with the short high-pitched burrrrp, burrrrp, burrrrp of the MP 38.* The center of the noise was moving slowly but steadily toward the rear, right through the center of A Company. Johns' stomach crawled up in his chest again, so that nothing but a cold vacuum was left in his belly. His defensive line was broken! The paratroopers were running over Able Company! He took two running steps in that direction, then stopped. It would be pretty silly for him to go tearing off into the dark in the middle of this melee, thus virtually surrendering control.

He turned to Grimsehl. "George! Send a runner to A Company to find out what's happened down there."

Grimsehl went to get the man, who in a few seconds trotted off down the hedgerow, his M1 ready in his hands.

Twenty age-long minutes crept by. The fury of the attack did not diminish. Johns stayed outside to listen, as he could learn more from the nature and location of the firing than he could from his useless radios and telephones. Twice he had to duck back inside, once when a battery volley struck along the other side of the hedgerow, and once when the enemy mortar fire started its orderly march down the near side. The German mortar gunners were, as usual, deadly accurate in their location of the hedgerow, but they were not so effective in the spacing of the rounds.

---

*Maschinen Pistole Model 38 (Schmeisser), a "Tommy" gun issued to parachute troops. Americans called them burp guns, from the sound of their high cyclic rate.

One shell hit between the old phone hole and The Hole and the next struck harmlessly on the far side.

At last came the sound of still more artillery. But this was the good kind—the going-out kind. It was hard to distinguish it from the rest of the din. Nevertheless there are always lulls in any battle, no matter how fierce, and in these intervals the familiar outgoing whine came through clearly. But the volley went out much too far; the first few rounds would have no effect on the Germans, who were storming through the battalion defensive lines.

The artillery fire kept going out, way out, until both Martin and Johns were almost beside themselves with frustration. Suddenly the monotonous calling of Martin's artillery radio operator changed to sharp attention. He had got an answer!

"Fire mission. Concentrations 175 through 183 at once! Request all available fire. Enemy attacking strongly all along front!"

Thank God! breathed the Major. Then he yelled in Martin's ear, "Tell the FDC to tell Regiment what's going on and that if they have any reserves to rack 'em up behind us, we may need 'em."

The message went out quickly.

"On the wa-a-a-ay" came back as an answer.

This time the artillery hit much nearer. It had that authoritative crack to it which told that it was close in, almost as close as the German stuff. And it kept coming.

Somehow the wires to Charlie and Baker were re-spliced time and again. They always went out, but after that first 30 minutes or so they were in most of the time. When they were not, the 300's did the job. The companies had settled down a bit after the first shock and the operators did whatever was necessary to reestablish their communications. Kenny and Stoen both asked for reinforcements, both getting the same answer, "Sorry. There aren't any. Do the best you can."

There was no contact with Able. No runners came in to report, no fire missions were requested. Nothing! There was no longer any heavy firing in the direction of the line originally held by A Company, but there was plenty from an area to the rear of that line. Oddly enough, there was an occasional flurry of fire from well in front of the center. It looked very much as if the company lines had been completely overrun and were falling back.

Martin called for the A Company defensive concentration anyway.

Around 0300 the runner came back. His eyes were very big. "Sir," he reported, "there are Krauts in the A Company CP."

"Nuts," said the Major."

"Yes, sir, there really are."

"How do you know?"

"Well, I had a little trouble, running into people on the way. Some were Krauts, some our own men, so when I got close I crept up sort of easy-like. 'Fore I saw anybody in the road a Kraut challenged me and when I didn't answer he cut loose at me with a burp gun. Missed me, though."

"Nuts," repeated the Major. He didn't want to believe Able had been overrun. He turned to look for Grimsehl but saw instead the man he really wanted. It was Private First Class Gay, Silver Star hero of a lone patrol back at the Bois de Bretel. Gay was sitting very calmly on a corner of The Hole, chewing gum. Johns snapped at him, "Gay! Get the hell down to Able and see for sure if there are Germans in the CP and what the situation is generally."

Gay looked at the Major. His jaw motion slowed to a halt. Then he remembered that he had a reputation to maintain. He rose, checked his carbine, gently detached a grenade from his belt, and started down the hedgerow fiddling with the pin on the grenade.

The German artillery and mortars began to let up some. They seemed more uncertain, as if they weren't too sure just where their own people were. They kept beating the flanks of the salient they had driven into the battalion line, but the rolling barrage under which the paratroopers had first come in had slackened materially. The savage ferocity of the small-arms battle was either increasing, or the lessening of the artillery and mortar fire let the sounds of the rifles, machine guns, submachine guns, and grenades come through more clearly. The indefinite center of the fire was coming from a point that moved farther and farther to the right rear of the command post. Major Johns could not be sure, but the sounds seemed to indicate that A Company was pulling back from in front of the enemy, fighting as it went.

Stoen had managed to report that his right was holding but he had had trouble on his left at the orchard. His whole line had been in action ever since the first shells fell. Germans had gone through his company, he said, on through the orchard in rear, but they had not driven him out of his position. There had even been two grenades thrown into his command post.

The center of the battle surged in close, no more than a hundred yards to the right of the battalion command post. Bullets cracked through the trees, chunked solidly into wood or earth, or snapped overhead in the clear. One long burst, flashing straight down the hedgerow, bored into the top of The Hole between the Major and radio operator Bein. It was beginning to look as if the command post were going to get into the fight. Johns ordered every man into a foxhole. There would be no moving around and no shooting unless the enemy attacked in force. There was no use starting a fight with the little handful of people near the command post. If they had to shoot they would, but there was no point in asking for trouble.

Grimsehl loomed up out of nowhere, prodding a prisoner ahead of him with a bayonet. Some instinct led him to the Major who rose from his hole to see what the S2 had got from the prisoner. "Sir!" Grimsehl said excitedly, "I got this bird from a couple of A Company men. He says they are hitting us with four companies, three infantry companies in the assault and one engineer outfit fighting as infantry in reserve—all paratroopers and about 110 men per company."

"Four companies! And on a narrow front! Wait till Regiment hears this. Maybe we'll get some help now!"

The paratrooper, his hands locked behind his head, must have understood a little. He smiled as if confident that he would not be a prisoner for long.

Grimsehl faded into the dark returning a moment later

without the prisoner, whom he had given to a commando for safekeeping.

"He says they had committed the reserve just before he was grabbed, which was about 0215 or 0230. They were already through the A Company center and right flank by then and they shoved the reserves on through to keep going. But I don't know where they could have got to, because the fighting still isn't much past our line here."

While he was speaking, the center of the battle surged toward the rear, as if it had just gotten free of snag. There was a beating of feet up the hedgerow a few yards toward A Company and the sounds that men make scrambling over a hedgerow. Johns and Grimsehl sank to the ground. The safety on Hoffman's M1 clicked loudly as he pushed it forward into the "Off" position.

But the rushing sounds went straight to the rear, punctuated by brrrrps from German guns. They did not pause at Mentzer's domain or at the aid station. They were headed for the mortar positions.

Major Johns whispered to Bein, "Call Dog and tell them some Krauts are coming toward them from the direction of Battalion."

Bein called, but the only answer he got was the sound of firing from the direction of the nearest mortar position.

The telephone operator, taking the Major by the arm, whispered in his ear, "Phone, sir. It's Regiment. Colonel Ordway."

"Johns? What's going on up there?" The Colonel was excited too.

"Full-scale counterattack, sir. Prisoner says four companies, 440 men, hitting us. Didn't you get my message through the artillery?"

"Yes, but they just said an attack."

"I asked for help. Able was overrun and maybe part of Baker. I think you better . . . ." Realizing that he was talking into a dead line, Johns rang for the operator. "Send the wire crew out again, and ring Message Center for me."

Sergeant Wilson answered the Message Center phone himself, "Yes sir?"

"Sergeant, haven't you got that radio working yet?"

"Yes sir, it's working, but we can't get an answer from Regiment." The sergeant sounded completely unperturbed about the whole business.

"If you ever get through, tell 'em they're going to have Krauts back there very shortly if they don't send me some help to restore these lines."

"Yes, sir. I'll write a message and bring it to you later for signature."

"Oh for Pete's sake! All right." Johns dropped the phone to look for Martin. He found him at a post on the hedgerow, watching the dark field beyond.

"Martin! Get your people to tell Regiment that we have been hit by an enemy force of 440 men, that our line has been broken, and that we are requesting reinforcement."

"Okay, Major, but I'll have to encode that, which will take a while."

"Encode hell. The Jerries know about it. Send it in the clear." The Major was having "security" trouble again.

"If you say so . . . ." The artilleryman repeated the message to his radio operator who reluctantly put it on the air.

The Artillery Fire Direction Center was horrified at the breach of security. They lectured the operator briefly but thoroughly. He replied with a rude sound that was not in the Signal Operating Instructions, adding, "The Major said send it. We need help and the Krauts know it. Now get it for us!"

Kenney called for artillery fire at a new point. Instantly Martin, his operator, and the Fire Direction Center became coldly precise again. They had been firing concentrations on every spot where the paratroopers could possibly form up or through which they would have to move to reinforce the attacking force. Most of the Division artillery and some from Corps must have been supporting, because the whine, scream, crash, roar, crack, and rumble of the shells going overhead and thundering down into enemy territory was almost constant. The sound was extremely comforting, even though the small-arms fight was still raging behind the command post.

A man staggered up to the command post and nearly fell

into Martin's arms. Only some instinct had prevented the CP guards from shooting him, as he had made no attempt to answer their low challenge or to halt. It was an officer, a forward observer who had been with Able Company.

He was pantng, incoherent. Martin and Johns half carried him down the steps into the command post, where they sat him on an ammunition box that served as a chair. In the light of the single candle he made a horrible sight. Blood was smeared over his face, his hands, and his shirt. But Martin could find no wound. The man was dazed, dumb. He sat with his head down, still panting, paying no attention to questions. He stared at the blade of a hunting knife in his right hand. It was still sticky with blood, as he raised and lowered it. He seemed almost to be weighing the knife. He opened and clenched his fingers around the handle, never taking his eyes from the red-stained blade.

Martin heated some coffee over a K-ration box and forced it gently on the forward observer, who was a close friend. The young officer took the coffee and began to settle down. The wild look went out of his eyes. His trembling lessened until it nearly ceased. Finally he began to talk, the words falling out in chunks, sometimes incoherent, "We were out on Able OP 2 . . . . I was asleep . . . . the stuff started falling all around us . . . . Before I knew what was going on . . . . the Krauts were in there with us . . . . They killed two Able boys—right in front of me . . . . I held up my hands and my radioman did too. . . . They took my pistol belt . . . . then the others went on and one Kraut pushed us toward the rear, his rear. . . . We walked a long time . . . . I don't know how far . . . . or where we were . . . . then some of our own mortars came in close. We stopped and the Kraut looked around for cover. There wasn't any so we ran a ways . . . . then the artillery started . . . . it was hitting in front of us. We stopped again . . . . and found some old German fox holes. They had tops on. The guard turned his back on me. He was kicking at a hole to see if he could get in it . . . . and my radioman jumped him. My man jerked off his helmet, hit the Kraut in the back of the neck with it. . . . Then I remembered I still had my knife." He pushed the bloody blade forward and looked at it for a long time, his fingers still closing and opening around the hilt.

"I jerked it out." He stopped talking and put his head down almost to his knees, still holding the knife at an awkward angle in front of him. He didn't move for a full minute—then, with an effort, he sat up again and went on. "I jumped him just as he turned around . . . I hit him with the knife and it went into him . . . then I hit him again and again and again. I couldn't stop hitting him even after . . . after I knew he was dead. My radioman pulled me off him, finally . . . We started back."

Major Johns was bouncing with impatience to ask questions but something held him in restraint until the man stopped. "Where were you? How did you come back? Did you see any more Krauts?"

The lieutenant looked at him dully, as if he didn't understand. But he answered. "I don't know. We didn't see anybody until we got here. I don't know where we were, or how we came back. I didn't know where we were until . . . until I recognized the battalion hedgerow."

It was obvious they were going to get no useful information out of this man. He was another combat exhaustion case, shocked more by the awful experience of killing a man with his own hands than by the fire he had been under and the fact that he had been captured. The Major motioned to Martin, who led the still-dazed man away, and sent him to the aid station.

Gay came back from A Company. He answered the challenge flippantly and slouched into The Hole. There were no grenades hanging from his belt. He reported.

"That runner was right, Major. There WAS some Jerries in the CP."

"What do you mean, 'was'?"

"Just that. There ain't so many now as there was before I got there, least not so many live ones."

"What happened?" The Major was impatient. It was obvious that Gay was enjoying the spotlight again and wanted to draw it out.

"I crawled up to the edge of the sunken road right over

the CP, coming in from around on one side. I couldn't make out who was there, so I made a noise and some bastard challenges me in Dutch. I answers him in Dutch, too, but it don't sound right to him and he asks for the password. I gives it to him with grenades, and hightails it out of there. The stupid bastard never even got a shot at me."

Johns couldn't help smiling. "What about the rest of the line? Could you tell anything about it?"

"Naw, Major, it was too dark to see anything, but there was some shootin' out on the left front and a helluva lot in the right rear. None at all along the road where most of the line used to be."

"All right, Gay, thank you very much. Stick around close, I may need you again."

Gay went out and took his place on the corner of The Hole. He treated himself to a fresh stick of gum.

No battle goes on for hours without lulls. This one, fierce as it was, was no exception. After the flurry of fire back at the mortar positions there was a long pause in the small-arms firing although the artillery was still going over, mostly outward bound now. As Gay went up the steps of The Hole the firing started again, back by the mortars. It grew until it was a first class row, with grenades, burp guns, and rifles all mixed together.

It lacked the size of the earlier fighting, but not ferocity. Nor did it rise and fall in volume quite so much. It gave the impression of determined, plugging fire, kept up by a comparatively few men on both sides, men who weren't going to quit. From the mortar positions it began to move slowly back toward the front again.

As soon as the direction of the sound was definite, the Major began to exult although he could not be sure that the battle had turned. He was puzzled because the sound of German burp guns stood out clearly and dominated the other firing.

The sounds came closer and closer, then died out completely for a few seconds. In the near silence the sound of running feet came not far from the aid station. Then an M1 rifle cracked sharply 8 times from a point no more than a hundred yards back of the command post hedgerow. A burp gun answered. More M1's fired. Two or three other burp guns opened up. Then a light machine gun joined in, its tracers flying toward the enemy lines, a few ricocheting off the hedgerow.

The running feet pounded nearer. In another momentary lull there came again the sound of men scrambling over a hedgerow. Then a burp gun and several rifles fired from the far side of the hedgerow. The machine gun and other burp guns answered them. A rifle grenade burst on the hedgerow itself. More running feet, then grenades and scuffling noises, more grenades. Then came the clear cry, "Goddammit, somebody kill that sonuvabitch before he gets away again."

Every man in the command post group laughed aloud at that. They knew the show was about over. The battalion's lines would be restored before morning.

The firing, with more bloodthirsty yelling, receded toward the A Company line.

Kenney called from C Company to report that the attacks on his line had let up and they were now free from any flanking threat. Stoen, his line out and the radio not working at the moment, sent a messenger to say that they were holding. He had picked up about a squad of A Company men who had been wandering around in the rear. They were using the squad to bolster their own right flank.

There was still no word from Able Company.

It was after 0400. The dawn would soon help clear things up one way or another. If it showed most of four companies of paratroopers in the lines formerly held by Able there might be some trouble. On the other hand if the Krauts were scattered and had not been able to consolidate a position during the darkness, it might be possible to pull some men away from Charlie and Baker, to clean up such enemy as were left.

It occurred to Johns that if the enemy were still around, the command post group might find itself with a fight on its hands as soon as people could see. He again ordered everyone to stay out of sight until he could tell what the score was. There had never been a thought in anyone's mind of withdrawing, even though the attack had carried well to their rear.

The line to Regiment was in again and Colonel Ordway was on the phone. Major Johns gave him a brief report. "Sir, things are getting quiet up here again, but I can't tell yet who owns the area. I don't have the faintest idea where any part of Able is. Baker may have lost some of its left platoon by the orchard, although Stoen tells me they are still in most of their original positions. The Germans got clean through our middle and went as far back as the mortar positions but I think we've got everything in hand now." He waited while a long burst of machine-gun fire snapped overhead, then added, "But you never know."

Colonel Ordway was impatient. "Some sergeant from A Company rushed in here about 3 o'clock with a wild disaster story. Said the whole battalion was destroyed and he was the sole survivor."

"One of MY men said that?"

"Yes, one of YOUR heroes. That was bad enough but he put the wind up for a battalion of 4.2 mortars that are digging in behind you. That whole gang took off." The Colonel paused a moment, then went on. "He picked up about half of my Cannon Company as he went through the woods, too."

Johns was nearly speechless—a man from the Red Battalion—a sergeant too—running away from the enemy! He sputtered into the phone, "Why . . . . why that dirty . . . . ! I'll court-martial him for cowardice if it's the last thing I do!"

The Regimental Commander ignored him. "Can you attack at 0600?"

That stopped Johns cold. It was the first time he had even thought of the attack and, if he had, he would of course have assumed that another outfit would be put in their place. People don't attack too well after fighting for their lives half the night.

"Colonel," he answered, "we couldn't attack a hot breakfast at 0600. I've got most of one company, at least half of another, all of my headquarters, and Lord knows how much of my Weapons outfit. I don't know anything about Able Company yet, nor do I know that we aren't going to be fighting Krauts out of the CP in the next ten minutes. What about the reinforcements I asked for?"

"Nothing doing. Division wouldn't let me send you anything. They still won't believe you had anything but a combat patrol up there. They know about your prisoner's report and I told them about the runaway sergeant. But they still wouldn't let me turn loose anything. They wouldn't even believe what I told them about the 4.2 battalion running off. Had to send their own man down to check, but he'll be until noon getting back with a report."

"Very well, sir, I think we can handle the situation alone now anyway, but I repeat that I can't guarantee ANYthing. You may have a good part of our hostile paratroopers in your lap by the time it gets light, because I believe a lot of them just kept right on going after they got through us. I don't have any idea where they could have got to, but it's quiet now. Stoen and Kenney have even stopped calling for artillery for the first time in more than 3 hours."

That ended the conversation. Johns swung around on Weddle and Hoffman, cursing fervently. "That goddam Division! The ornery SOB's wouldn't believe what we told 'em! I hope that bunch of Krauts gets clean through to where they are, if they can walk that far! Maybe they'll believe us then!"

Stoen called in. The wires had been restored again. He reported that his position was secure and that he was sending a patrol out to the left to see what he could find in the Able Company line. He also said that his 60-mm mortar people, whom he had directed to pull back one hedgerow in order to keep them out of the fight, had found all three of Able's 60's, abandoned. They had picked them up, together with their ammo, and had fired all 6 guns all night long until they were now down to only a few rounds per gun.

Johns looked toward the spot in the darkness that he

thought was occupied by Weddle. He did not often call the S3 by his first name, but this was a special occasion. "Leroy," he said, "I want you to take about six of the commando boys and go down to Able to see if you can tell what happened and what the situation is. I figure it's better to do it in the dark, taking it easy, than it is to wait till it gets light and maybe run into something and get into a fight. Don't get involved in anything unless you have to. If you find it advisable, stay down there and get things straightened out, but send me a message so I'll know what you're doing. Watch out for that Baker patrol, although I don't think you're apt to run into it."

Captain Weddle groped for his helmet and M1, said "Okay," and was gone up the steps.

Once more there was nothing for Johns to do but wait.

It wasn't long until the sky began to lighten. There was no word, of course, from either Weddle or Stoen. It was too soon to expect anything. But the Germans started to throw 88's into the area, which was encouraging. They wouldn't be doing that if they had any reason to believe their own troops were occupying the lines. Johns went outside to look around. As he did so an 88 smashed viciously into a tree just behind The Hole. He grinned as he sniffed the acrid smoke. Dallas and his German paratroopers, hunh!

It was a little past 0500, light enough to see clearly, when the first runner came from Weddle. He was grinning broadly as he trotted up, rifle in hand. "Sir," he said, "Captain Weddle says tell you he has found what is left of two whole platoons of A Company and that Sergeant Shaff has the old CP back again."

He saluted and turned to go back to Weddle. The Major returned his salute, calling after him, "Tell the Captain that makes me very happy."

A little later Stoen called in to say that he was occupying every foot of his old line and that his patrol had returned to tell him about the two Able platoons that were still in position. He had lost a lot of people but didn't know how many more were being found all the time. He had also lost the two .50 caliber machine guns that Regiment had ordered them to use in the attack that morning. Neither Stoen nor Major Johns was concerned about the guns as they had thought all along that it was silly to try to use such heavy guns in an attack in that kind of country.

Weddle got back about 0630 with a strange story. He came into The Hole, demanded a breakfast ration, and sat down on the shelf before he would tell it. Finally he got started.

"Here's what happened to A Company, as near as I can tell now: The mortars and artillery hit them sudden and hard. They hit the outposts at the same time they did the main line. Every SOB in the company put his head down. The Krauts come in under that fire like they loved it. Shaff said they weren't thirty yards back of it. They run plumb over the outposts before the sentries knew there's a Kraut within a hundred yards, so the main line got no warning. One sergeant looked up and saw the shine of a shell burst on a box of machine gun ammunition a Kraut is carrying and he hollers, 'Krauts,' but by then it's too late in most places. The Germans poured right over the edge of the road and run up and down it throwing grenades into the holes where the guys were still hiding from the artillery, shooting anything that moved.

"That bird you got running the company says he was stunned by a grenade in the first assault. He wasn't able to get out of his hole, or to give an order. He seems to be okay now, except a little shaky. He's trying to get things together. He's damn lucky he isn't dead.

"Anyway, the Germans ran through the company CP in nothing flat. Everybody that isn't killed takes off for the rear. That's where our sergeant hero that went back to Regiment come from, I think. But the two platoons in the middle are cut off. You know they aren't all in the road. They can't run if they want to, 'cause they know by now that there're Krauts behind 'em, probably more than in front. So they stayed right there, fighting like good little boys all night long. That was the shooting we heard out front from time to time and couldn't figure. Kee-rist! There's dead Krauts and our dead people all over the place.

"Those of Able that take off, about a platoon plus, altogether, I reckon, hit for the battalion mortar positions. They join up with a few guys from Baker and beat the Krauts back there by quite some time. Then the noncoms and a couple of officers who are around—I still don't know who—rally the whole gang, put them in some sort of position along with the mortar crews. By the time the Krauts get back there they're ready for 'em and kick hell out of 'em. I heard about one bird who waited for a Kraut to come right alongside of him, then raises up, grabs the Kraut's burp pistol, kicks the guy in the crotch, and shoots him with his own gun. That was why we heard so many burp guns. Our guys were taking 'em away from the Krauts and using them against 'em. Our boys like the Schmeissers better'n anything we got, for this kind of fighting.

"This took most of the night. It didn't go quick, mostly because the Heinies were taking it pretty easy after they get through the line, like they don't want to lose contact with one another. Then they had that scrap down by the mortars. Some of the Germans pulled back, just as slow." The S3 stopped, took his helmet off, and scratched his head seriously.

"You know," he went on, "I just can't figure out what happened to all those paratroopers. The boys from Able said there must a been at least two hundred went through the orchard. But I don't believe there was more'n about 40 or 50, maybe 60 at the outside, ever got as far as the mortars."

Johns interrupted, "Could be a lot of 'em got separated in the dark and decided it was no good so they filtered out around the flanks, or went back the way they came."

"Yeah, could be. Then we got to remember that Kenney and Stoen and the two Able platoons had a quota apiece. From the way the Krauts chewed Baker there must'a been quite a few in that crew.

"And I nearly forgot—the artillery knocked hell out of a lot of Germans before they ever got going. That was probably what saved our tails, really. The Able boys said that first concentration, the one that hit so far out, went right into the middle of something, because they heard all kinds of yelling and screaming and carrying on out there. Could of been their reserves, I guess.

"Well, however it happened, it all boils down to the same old story: they hit us, pushed through, took casualties, and got disorganized. We counterattacked and shoved 'em out again—just like the book says."

Grimsehl came in with more details obtained from his prize prisoner. The man, who was from the headquarters company of the German battalion they were facing, seemed to know all about everything. He claimed that the whole attack was a direct result of the visit of the medical officer two days before, when the truce had been requested and granted. The Major stared hard at Grimsehl when he reported that, and the S2 flushed. If this were true the battalion had paid a terrible price to save the life of that one American they had got out of the orchard alive.

Grimsehl went on, "He said that medic came back and told their commander that he had been in our lines and they were lightly held. Of course, he never was in our main line, only in an outpost. If he thought that was the main line I can see how he would believe it to be pretty thin. But I guess they got a surprise when they hit Baker and Charlie, who wouldn't give. Anyway, the German battalion commander decides to have a try at us, because we are sticking out a little and they wanted to straighten their lines and maybe get back the main road behind us, there. He got some more artillery to come in for the show. They were registering and covering it up by firing so much yesterday. Then he got that company of engineers to fight as infantry and act as a reserve.

"This prisoner says what Weddle guessed about our artillery is about right, because the Germans took one hell of a beating in that first concentration. It knocked the engineers cockeyed while they were forming up and delayed their push through the orchard quite a bit.

"I think they had a couple of platoons worrying Charlie and maybe a couple more trying to get around Baker's right, while the rest hit right in the middle. But by the time they got through they were so shot up that the engineers didn't have what it took to roll us up. So they chickened out when they hit the mortars, and decided to quit."

Major Johns accepted the story without comment. It was probably correct. But at that moment he was more concerned with what was going to happen than with what had already happened. He wanted to know how many casualties he had suffered, to get the companies untangled, bring up more ammunition, and see that the men got a little rest. They hadn't had much sleep lately. It still did not occur to him that the attack order would not be cancelled. As far as he was concerned, the 1st Battalion had had enough fighting for the day.

He called the companies for a strength report, and told them to hurry up the reorganizing process. All companies reported some dead, but none had an accurate count as yet. The Doc reported that the aid stations had treated 42 casualties, with more coming in all the time.*

*The facts concerning the German attack were all verified in a German after-action report which the 29th Division captured later at Brest. Major Johns' estimate of the number of troops involved, the casualties suffered, and the progress of the action were all confirmed exactly, showing that the Battalion's information was accurate. Division, which had exhibited such skepticism, was mildly embarrassed, and the Battalion was ultimately awarded the French Croix de Guerre for the action.

Market Garden

After the Breakout of Saint-Lô, the German disaster at the Falaise Gap, and Patton's "end run" with the 7th Armored Army through France, the Allied armies had suddenly won the Battle of France. Inevitably, time for consolidation of these gains had to be taken, but this allowed the Germans equal time to consolidate their losses.

Chester Wilmot says, "Within three weeks of the fall of Paris and the overwhelming defeat of the German armies in the Battle of France, the Wehrmacht had almost recovered its balance; at all events, it was no longer on the run. The Germans were again holding a coherent line—admittedly thin and taut and with meagre reserves behind it—but a line nevertheless. And, because of their successful defense and demolition of the Channel ports and the approaches to Antwerp, they were denying to Eisenhower the supplies with which to maintain the full momentum of his advance. He, in turn, had unwittingly aided their recovery by his reluctance to concentrate the bulk of his logistic resources behind a single thrust at the Ruhr. Even when he had at last determined upon this course, he had not been able to give his northern armies the priority they required.

"When D-Day came for Operation Market Garden, although Eisenhower now had 52 divisions under his command, his sole chance of retaining the initiative, of recreating conditions of mobile warfare and of dealing a decisive blow at the Wehrmacht in the West that autumn rested with the three airborne divisions waiting at their airfields in England, and with the three divisions of XXX British Corps standing at the Dutch frontier. With them, though they could not know it, lay the last, slender chance of ending the German war in 1944." *

Market Garden would be the biggest airdrop of troops ever made—three airborne divisions at once. Field Marshal Montgomery was to be

* *The Struggle for Europe,* by Chester Wilmot, published by Harper & Bros., p. 497.

given the chance to be first across the Rhine. His plan was to drop the 1st British Airborne division on the north bank of the lower Rhine, to seize the bridge-crossing at Arnhem. Bridges at Nijmegen and Grave would be assaulted by the 82nd Airborne (U.S.) and the 101st Airborne (U.S.) would secure the road from Grave to Eindhoven. Then the XXX British Corps would fight their way up the road to Eindhoven and on to Arnhem along a "carpet of airborne troops, hoping to find the bridges over the three major water obstacles already safely in their hands." *

Heavy risks were being taken: surprise was essential—the weather *had* to be good for a successful drop, and for later drops since there were not enough planes and gliders to make the operation all at once.

Unfortunately, surprise was the first element to be lost.

THE ROAD TO ARNHEM

by Chester Wilmot

Sunday, September 17, was fine but overcast. There was little wind and the clouds were high, ideal weather for an airborne drop. By noon more than 1000 troop-carriers and nearly 500 gliders were heading for Holland, for the greatest airborne operation ever undertaken. This aerial armada carried the best part of three divisions which were to be dropped along the line Eindhoven-Nijmegen-Arnhem with the task of capturing the road bridges over the Maas, the Waal and the Neder Rijn and over five other waterways, thus clearing a corridor for the armoured and motorised columns that were to drive north from the Meuse-Escaut Canal to the Zuider Zee. With this one sabre-stroke Montgomery intended to cut Holland in two, outflank the Siegfried Line and establish Second Army beyond the Rhine on the northern threshold of the Ruhr. If all were to go well, the armour would reach the

* *Tide of Victory,* by Winston Churchill, p. 196.

Zuider Zee on the fourth or fifth day, but the hazards were great—especially for the airborne forces.

Because they were to form a corridor fifty miles long, the three divisions had to be landed in depth:

The 101st American (Major-General Maxwell Taylor) between Veghel and Zon, north of Eindhoven;

the 82nd American (Major-General James Gavin) between the Maas and the Waal, south of Nijmegen;

the 1st British (Major-General R. E. Urquhart) beyond the Neder Rijn, west of Arnhem.

The 1st and 82nd Divisions were to operate under command of H.Q. I British Airborne Corps (Lieut.-General F. A. M. Browning), which was also to land south of Nijmegen. A fourth division, 52nd Lowland, was available to be brought in by Dakota as soon as an airfield had been captured.

No such deep penetration, no such mass landing in daylight had ever been attempted. Holland was thick with flak. The Luftwaffe had ample bases within easy range, and its jet-aircraft had recently made their debut. The whole force might be crippled before it even landed. Blown bridges might check the relieving armour, or the slender corridor might be cut behind it, leaving the forward troops stranded. It was a gamble. The dividend could be high but the margin would be narrow.

The greatest danger was the weather, for there were not sufficient transport aircraft to carry the full strength of all three divisions in one "lift." With some 500 aircraft (tugs and troop-carriers) available for each division, it was decided that on the first day both the 82nd and the 101st should land their three parachute regiments,* and that 1st Airborne should bring in one parachute brigade and the bulk of its air-landing brigade. When provision had been made for these, and for essential service troops, there was little room for either field or anti-tank artillery.

*An American parachute regiment was roughly the equivalent in strength of a British parachute brigade.

On D plus 1 and D plus 2 the Americans were to receive their gliderborne artillery and infantry, while two more parachute brigades (one British and one Polish) and the rest of the 1st Airborne Division were to be landed near Arnhem. It was vital, therefore, that there should be fair weather for at least two days so that the airborne divisions could be re-supplied and brought up to full strength.

This was a matter of particular concern to the British division for there was a fundamental weakness in its plan. The outstanding lesson of the Normandy operations was that airborne landings should be made on or hard by the objective, especially when that is a bridge. This had been amply proved by Gale, and the opinion of experienced Allied commanders, such as Gavin, was that "it is in general better to take landing losses and land on the objective than to have to fight after landing in order to reach the objective." *

In making the Arnhem plan this lesson was not observed, because the expert advice which Urquhart received was that heavy losses would be suffered if he attempted to make his initial landings south of the river close to the Arnhem bridge. The flak, it was said, would be intense, and the fenland here too soft for the landing of gliders. It was difficult for Urquhart to overrule this expert opinion, since he had no previous experience of airborne operations. Moreover, he had inherited a division which had suffered heavily in Sicily because its landings had been scattered and strongly opposed. Since then, the doctrine had grown up within the division that it was more important to land accurately and safely than to land close to the objective. Urquhart seems to have been influenced by this doctrine, for he accepted the view that the only feasible dropping and landing areas were north of the river, *six to eight miles west of the Arnhem road bridge which was his principal objective.*

The risk of frustration, inherent in landing so far away, was the greater because the whole division could not arrive in one "lift." Had this been possible, Urquhart could

* James M. Gavin, *Airborne Warfare,* p. 81.

have planned to move against the bridge with his force concentrated and then to seize a dropping-zone for re-supply south of the river. But, because his force was to arrive in three instalments, he decided that he must deploy the air-landing brigade outside Arnhem to protect the DZ-LZ area at least until the second "lift" came in on D plus 1. This meant that during the first critical afternoon he would be able to send to the Arnhem bridge only his lightly-armed parachute battalions and his reconnaissance squadron, and that another twenty-four hours must elapse before the main strength of the division would be available to reinforce the paratroops in the town. Thus the plan appeared to sacrifice the advantage of surprise and to expose Urquhart's divided force to the danger of destruction in detail. Consequently, the success of his operations seemed to rest, even more than did those of the American divisions, on continued fine weather and a slow enemy reaction.

There was a similar, though not so serious, weakness in the plan of the 82nd Division, but in this case it was unavoidable. Gavin had four major objectives: the bridges at Grave, at Nijmegen and over the Maas-Waal Canal, and the Groesbeek Ridge which runs along the German frontier dominating the area between the Maas and the Waal. These objectives were so widely separated that Gavin could not expect to secure them all with the forces which would be available to him in the first twenty-four hours. He decided, therefore, to concentrate his initial landings around Grave and Groesbeek, for Browning, the Corps Commander, had ordered him "not to attempt the seizure of the Nijmegen bridge until all other missions had been accomplished." This was sound, for that bridge would be of little use if Gavin failed to secure the bridges leading to it or the high ground that was essential to its defence.

Next to the weather, the greatest danger was that the relieving forces would not be able to advance rapidly enough to reinforce the airborne troops before they were counterattacked by German units more heavily armed than themselves. Second Army now had three corps along the Meuse-Escaut Canal, but VIII Corps on the right was not yet ready to attack and XII Corps on the left was facing a belt of difficult, marshy country.* Moreover, there were sufficient supplies forward to maintain a deep penetration only by XXX Corps.

The relief of the airborne forces depended, therefore, on Horrocks's three divisions and especially on Guards Armoured. From its bridgehead on the Meuse-Escaut Canal, however, there was only one clear route for the armour and there was every possibility that its advance would be checked, if not stopped, at one of the many water obstacles which lay athwart the road. In case some bridges should be blown, Horrocks had made elaborate preparations to bring forward columns of bridging material, DUKWs and assault-boats, but the task of moving these heavy columns and the necessary infantry and artillery along one road was indeed formidable. Since the Corps plan required the movement through the tenuous "airborne corridor" of some 20,000 vehicles, the success of the whole operation might well turn on the maintenance of the flow of transport by efficient traffic control and good driving.

For Browning, then, the vital questions were: Would the weather hold until his airborne reinforcements arrived? Would XXX Corps get through the corridor faster than the Germans could move against it?

---

*Once the airborne forces had landed, the Order of Battle of Second Army was to be:

VIII CORPS	XXX CORPS	XII CORPS	I AIRBORNE CORPS
11th Armd. Div.	Gds. Armd. Div.	7th Armd. Div.	1st Br. Airborne Div.
3rd Inf. Div.	43rd Inf. Div.	15th Inf. Div.	82nd U.S. Airborne Div.
	50th Inf. Div.	53rd Inf. Div.	
	8th Armd. Bde.	4th Armd. Bde.	52nd Lowland Div. (Air-portable)
	101st U.S. Airborne Div.		

These dangers were fully appreciated by Montgomery, but he hoped that the very violence and magnitude of the assault would leave the Germans so shaken and confused that they would not react with sufficient speed or strength. Second Army Intelligence estimated that the forces immediately opposing XXX Corps amounted to six infantry battalions supported by twenty tanks and twenty-five guns, including a dozen 88s. The crust was expected to be hard but brittle, and behind it, so far as Second Army knew, there were only meagre reserves. Dutch Resistance sources reported that there were a half a dozen low-grade battalions in the Nijmegen area and that some battered Panzer units from France were refitting north of Arnhem. It was suspected by British Intelligence that these might be the survivors of the 9th and 10th SS Panzer Divisions, which had not been identified by contact since the start of the month.* Even if this were so, it appeared to be unlikely that the two divisions together would amount to more than one motor brigade and one armoured brigade. Nevertheless, it was certain that the Germans would strike back with all the forces they could muster, for Southern Holland had to be held if they were to maintain their communications with the forces blocking the approaches to Antwerp and with the launching sites in The Hague, from which V2s were already being fired on London.

The Allied air fleet flew into Holland protected by 1240 fighters. The way was prepared for it by more than 1000 bombers which struck at enemy anti-aircraft batteries along the route and around the dropping-zone. There was little sign of the Luftwaffe, except for fifteen FW-190s encountered over Wesel. Since the previous evening Bomber Com-

*On September 15 the following message was received in London by radio from the Dutch Resistance: "SS Div. Hohenstruffl [sic] along Ijssel, sub-units observed between Arnhem and Zutphen and along Zutphen-Apeldoorn road. . . . Along Ijssel work on field fortifications in progress." This report, however, did not get through to the airborne forces in time to affect the plan.

mand and the Eighth Air Force had attacked the fighter bases from which the Germans could have intervened, but this was not the principal reason for the Luftwaffe's absence. The Allied air offensive against the synthetic oil refineries had been renewed during the past week, and the bulk of the German fighter force was concentrated in Central and Southern Germany. That afternoon not one British troop-carrying aircraft or glider was lost by enemy action, and the casualties suffered by the Americans (35 transports and 13 gliders) were almost entirely due to flak. Altogether, 4600 aircraft of all kinds took part in the airborne operation on this day alone, and of these only 73 were shot down.* Both the Luftwaffe and the ground forces were taken by surprise.

If there was any German commander who should have foreseen this airborne assault, it was Student, whose First Parachute Army was holding the line of the Meuse-Escaut Canal. In his daily report to Model on the 16th, however, he had given no indication that he expected an airborne landing. He had merely said that "increased motor transport activity and confirmed armoured preparations strengthen the appreciation . . . that a heavy attack must be expected very shortly." On the 17th Student's H.Q. was in a cottage at Vught, only eight miles west of one of the American dropping-zones. "About noon," he says, "I was disturbed at my desk by a roaring in the air of such mounting intensity that I left my study and went on to the balcony.

*The forces involved were the following:

COMBAT AIRCRAFT			TRANSPORT AIRCRAFT		
	U.S.	BRITISH		TROOP-CARRIERS	GLIDERS
Bombers	891	222	1st British	155	358
Fighters	869	371	82nd U.S.	482	50
Fighter-Bombers	212	—	101st U.S.	436	70
			Corps H.Q.	—	13

(These figures do not include the aircraft of 2nd T.A.F. which, in support of the breakout by XXX Corps, flew 550 sorties.)

Wherever I looked I saw aircraft; troop-carriers and large aircraft towing gliders. An immense stream passed low over the house. I was greatly impressed but during these minutes I did not think of the danger of the situation." * He was moved more by envy than fear and, as he watched, he said to his Chief of Staff: "Oh, how I wish that I had ever had such powerful means at my disposal!" The wheel had gone full circle since Student himself had planned and led the airborne assault on Rotterdam four years earlier.

Student was not the only German commander who had a "ringside seat" for the airborne landing. Model was even closer, for his Tactical H.Q. was at Oosterbeek on the western edge of Arnhem. As the British parachutists floated down above and around him, Model did not wait to watch. He drove post-haste into Arnhem and there, finding that the local garrison commander had been killed in an air raid, he took command himself, quickly restored order and called in reinforcements from the 9th SS Panzer Division which, as the Dutch had reported, was stationed north of Arnhem.

Thus it was that by a double twist of fortune the two Germans primarily responsible for the defence of Holland found themselves so placed that they could act at once to counter the advantage the Allies had won by gaining surprise. Nor was this all. The German reserves were slender, but Model and Student soon knew exactly where to use them. Early that afternoon an American glider was shot down close to Vught, and, says Student, "a few hours later the orders for the complete airborne operation were on my desk." **

*Interrogation (Liddell Hart). The SS Commander in Holland, Rauter, reports that when he suggested to Model the possibility of an airborne landing the Field-Marshal replied: "Montgomery is a very cautious general, not inclined to plunge into mad adventures." (Netherlands War Ministry Interrogation.)

**It was this series of mischances, not the betrayal of the plan, that accounted for the swift German reaction. In a series of

By half-past one that afternoon the sky over Arnhem, Nijmegen and Veghel was filled with the throb of engines which drowned the soft sigh of gliders swooping in to land. In half a dozen towns and villages eager, grateful people rushed out to greet the airborne troops with flowers, and with food they could ill spare. But in most places the celebrations were cut short by the onset of battle and people fled from gay streets to anxious cellars.

West of Arnhem the paratroops and gliders of the 1st British Airborne Division landed accurately and with little interference from the enemy. Although none of Urquhart's 358 gliders were shot down, 38 failed to arrive. In nearly every case the reason was that the tow-rope broke—a common cause of mishaps in airborne operations—but it was particularly unfortunate that in the missing gliders were most of the armoured jeeps of the Reconnaissance Squadron which was to have rushed the road and rail bridges and seized them by *coup de main*. This was a bad start, but, while the 1st Air-Landing Brigade (Brigadier P. H. W. Hicks) organised the defence of the dropping-zones, the 1st Parachute Brigade (Brigadier G. W. Lathbury) assembled quickly and within an hour of landing was en route for Arnhem.

The drive for the bridges was led by Lt.-Col. J. D. Frost with the 2nd Parachute Battalion which moved smartly

articles in the London *Sunday Dispatch* in April and May 1950, however, Colonel O. Pinto (the wartime head of Dutch counter-espionage at SHAEF) alleged that the Germans were forewarned by a Dutchman, Christian Lindemans, who had been a Resistance Leader until he was suborned by the Abwehr in March 1944. It is true that Lindemans, after returning from Brussels on September 15th, warned the Chief of the Abwehr in Holland (Giskes) that the British were about to attack and would land airborne troops at Eindhoven on the 17th. Giskes has declared, however, that Lindemans "did not mention Arnhem . . . obviously because the objective of the planned air-ground offensive along the road that followed the north bank of the Neder Rijn. Frost sent C Company to seize the railway bridge, but just as his troops got there it was blown, seeming, says one eyewitness, "to curl back on us." The other two companies pressed on, but at Den Brink, less than two miles from the road bridge, they encountered such strong opposition that Frost had to detach B Company to deal with it.

While these operations were in progress, the road bridge lay unguarded. During the afternoon its garrison, some twenty-five men of First War vintage, had fled, and at 7:30 p.m. a Dutch policeman* found the defences deserted. From his post at the northern end of the bridge he looked anxiously westward for the first sign of the paratroops, but, even as they appeared in the September dusk, a party of SS troops drove up from the direction of Nijmegen and secured the southern end. Shortly after eight o'clock Frost —with A Company, his H.Q. and some sappers—took possession of the buildings around the northern approaches, but when he sent a platoon to storm the German positions on the south side, it was thwarted by fire from flak guns and an armoured car. Before long Frost was joined by most of B Company and by part of Brigade H.Q., but, having only 500 men and one anti-tank gun, he could do no more than hold his ground and wait for reinforcements. That night the great steel span was No-Man's-Land.

Meanwhile, the rest of the 1st Parachute Brigade, follow-

was not known to him." Nor did the Germans profit by such information as Lindemans provided, for Student has admitted that he was "completely surprised." The presence of 9th and 10th SS Panzer Divisions in the Arnhem-Nijmegen-Deventer area was the result of orders issued on September 8th, a week before Lindemans reported to Giskes.

*Constable van Kuijk. To him and other members of the Arnhem police force, and to Charles Labouchère of the Dutch Resistance, I am indebted for information about the condition and reaction of the Germans in Arnhem during the battle.

ing on Frost's northern flank, had become heavily engaged within two miles of the DZ. SS Training Battalion Kraft (425 strong) which had arrived in the Oosterbeek-Wolfheze area only the day before, held up the advance of both the 1st and 3rd Parachute Battalions, and gave time for a battlegroup of 9th SS, dispatched by Model, to take up blocking positions north of Oosterbeek, and between that suburb and Arnhem. Since this battlegroup contained half a dozen tanks and some armoured cars, the paratroops could not drive it off. One company managed to slip through to the bridge after dark, but the rest of the brigade made little progress.

During the night Urquhart and Lathbury were stranded at the H.Q. of the 3rd Battalion, and so did not realise that the overall situation was already becoming precarious. The Germans, thanks to Model's personal intervention, had responded more quickly and more strongly than could reasonably have been anticipated. Because of this, the 500 paratroops at the bridge were now isolated. Five miles to the west the other two parachute battalions, fighting separate battles, could not develop a concerted thrust. They were only a mile apart but, owing to a wireless failure, they had no communication with each other. Farther west, the air-landing brigade was widely dispersed in defence of the DZ-LZ area. Here Hicks had his own three battalions (less two companies which were coming with the second "lift") and a battalion of the Glider Pilot Regiment which was to prove in the course of the battle the value of the British policy of training glider crews to fight as infantry. If this brigade could have been committed that night it might have broken through to the bridge before the Germans could establish their blocking force, but Urquhart's plan required Hicks to stay where he was, awaiting the reinforcements that were due to arrive at ten o'clock next morning.

While the British were thus heavily involved at Arnhem, the Americans in the Nijmegen-Eindhoven stretch of the "corridor," finding less opposition, enjoyed more success. They met few Germans near the dropping-zones and most of these fled in panic. By dropping astride the Maas bridge at Grave, one battalion of the 82nd gained this vital objective within an hour of landing. Before dark Gavin's troops had secured the route into Nijmegen by capturing one of the bridges over the Maas-Waal Canal and establishing a cordon across the neck of the rivers along the Groesbeek ridge. Having secured his "air-head," Gavin sent the only battalion he could spare into Nijmegen to test out the defences of the massive bridge that spans the Waal. Four hundred yards from the southern end, however, the paratroops were checked, for the German garrison had already formed a tight perimeter to protect the bridge.

South of the Maas, the 101st Division had a rough passage through the flak defences around Eindhoven but, once on the ground, the Americans had a comparatively clear run. In Veghel they took all four bridges intact, but their southernmost objective, the bridge over the Wilhelmina Canal at Zon, was blown in their faces. Nevertheless, one parachute regiment scrambled across the canal during the night and by dawn was approaching Eindhoven, where it was due to link up with the armour advancing from the south.

At 1330 hours on the afternoon of the 17th, Horrocks was standing on a slag-heap beside the Meuse-Escaut Canal a few yards from "Joe's Bridge." He had just received word that the airborne drop was going "according to plan," and had therefore given orders for the ground attack to begin at 1435 hours. For some time his powerful field-glasses had been sweeping the northern skies but now they were trained along the straight white concrete road that led to Eindhoven. On this one road the success of his whole plan depended. Down this road the entire Corps had to move. Along this road the Guards Armoured Division had to break out.

Five hundred yards north of the Dutch border the Germans had set up a barricade across the road, but Horrocks calculated that because the road was concrete there would be no anti-tank mines embedded in its surface. He planned, therefore, to breach the German defences by the simple ruse of sending an armoured column straight down the road to blast and batter the barricade away and burst into Holland on a one-tank front. Behind the leading squadron were to come two more, carrying infantry on the backs of their tanks and in the wake of this spearhead the rest of the Guards were to follow in close order.

There was no other way north, nor was there any scope for armoured manœuvre, since the ground on either side was soft and swampy. The tanks would have to stay on the road and this would take them through a series of cypress plantations which provided natural cover for anti-tank guns and bazookas. There was no time to send infantry to clear these plantations. They would have to be neutralised by concentrations of fire from artillery and aircraft, concentrations so close and intense that the defenders on either side of the road would be driven from their weapons while the tanks went through. Such was the plan.

Ten minutes before H-Hour the guns of XXX Corps began putting down a rolling barrage one mile wide and five miles deep along the Eindhoven road. From the air a constant stream of Typhoons reinforced the barrage, skimming down to the tops of the trees before firing their rockets and machine-guns. Eight Typhoons from 83 Group arrived every five minutes and as each aircraft made several "strikes" it appeared to the onlooker that the stream was continuous. After the first half-hour a "cab-rank" of eight Typhoons was on call overhead all the time.

As the tanks of the Irish Guards rolled forward up the road, the Typhoon pilots were directed to their targets by radio from an armoured half-track, moving with the column. The white road, standing out against the dark pines, was easily identified, and all the tanks carried fluorescent orange screens which were plainly visible from the air and were soon to be hailed by the Dutch people as banners of liberation. The Typhoons were so efficiently directed that they were able to strike at targets within 200 yards of the tanks.

The Germans were so subdued by this onslaught that the leading squadron of Irish Guards, having shot its way through the barricade, was able to drive on beyond the first belt of woods without mishap. Nevertheless, the enemy (parachutists on one side of the road and SS troops on the other)* recovered quickly and, when the first of the squadrons carrying infantry tried to follow, it came under heavy fire, especially from bazookas. Eight of its tanks were quickly "brewed up," but the infantry jumped clear and began scouring the woods on either flank. After some difficult and confused skirmishing, several "bazooka-parties" were flushed, an anti-tank gun was knocked out and its crew captured. Having no means of sending their prisoners back, the Guards ordered them to climb aboard the surviving tanks, an order which so dismayed the Germans that they promptly revealed the whereabouts of the rest of their battery. This information was relayed at once to the Typhoons and the medium artillery. With their aid the remaining opposition was gradually overcome and by dusk the Irish Guards had reached the day's objective, Valkenswaard, five miles south of Eindhoven.

Horrocks's plan had worked with a remarkable economy of force. One armoured battalion and one infantry battalion, supported by 400 guns and 100 Typhoons, had opened the road for a whole corps. By the afternoon of September 18 (D plus 1) the Guards and the 101st had joined forces in Eindhoven and the way was clear for the armour to drive on through the corridor to Nijmegen, as soon as the bridge at Zon had been rebuilt, a task which would take the sappers no more than twelve hours.

In Rastenburg at midnight on the 17th–18th Hitler conferred with his staff. Although they did not know of the captured orders, they accurately appreciated the scope and objective of the airborne invasion and were clearly taken aback by its imaginative daring. The successful defensive operations of the past ten days had led Hitler to believe that

*The Germans had concentrated five battalions to defend the road: two from the 6th Para. Regiment, one from 9th SS, one from 10th SS, and Penal Battalion No. 6—a unit in which convicts were given the opportunity of regaining their civil rights. Captured documents revealed that these units were organised into an *ad hoc* formation, "Division Walther."

the Western Allies had been halted, and that for the moment he could safely concentrate on repairing the breach in his Eastern Front caused by the collapse of Rumania. He was now faced with a situation which, he admitted, was "much more serious than that in the East," but it is apparent from the record* of this conference that there was not a single field division he could send at once to Holland. Jodl reported that the 59th Division, which had just been withdrawn across the Scheldt Estuary, was moving against the corridor from the west, and that the 107th Panzer Brigade, which was travelling by train from East Prussia to Aachen, had been re-routed to Venlo and would attack from the east. "Emergency units" were being formed throughout Holland and Western Germany; two scratch divisions were already in the Reichswald-Venlo area southeast of Nijmegen; and in the course of a few days the Home Army would be able to provide two depot divisions, though these would be made up of low-grade troops.

The only fresh resources which Hitler could throw into the battle immediately were those of the Luftwaffe. On the 17th his jet-propelled fighter-bombers (Me 262s) had been unable to intervene because their airfields near Rheine had been severely bombed. Hitler was now informed, however, that these bases were being rapidly repaired, and that two fighter *Geschwader* had already been transferred from Berlin to western Germany and would be fit for action over Holland on the day that had just begun, September 18.

That morning the aerial convoys which left England were much more vulnerable than those which had flown in the day before, for this second "lift" was made up almost entirely of tugs and gliders—slow, unwieldy combinations incapable of protecting themselves by violent evasive action. Nevertheless, their fighter screen was so vigilant and strong that of the 1203 gliders which took off from England only 13 were shot down. It was the weather, not the Luftwaffe, that prevented the timely arrival of these reinforcements.

In England thick fog, lying heavy on the airfields, had delayed the departure of the gliders and transports. In

*Führer Conferences, Fragment 42, September 17, 1944.

Holland it was an anxious morning for the airborne troops on the ground. The Germans counter-attacked from the Reichswald and overran the landing-zones of the 82nd Division just before the gliders were due to arrive. There was no opportunity of warning or re-directing the pilots, and Gavin was unaware that his reinforcements had left England two hours late. Expecting the gliders to appear overhead any minute, the Americans counter-attacked in desperate fury and drove the Germans back with half an hour to spare. Even so, the gliders landed under fire and it took all the men Gavin could muster to hold the enemy off. The late arrival of the gliderborne troops saved them from heavy casualties, but it destroyed any chance there had been of capturing the Nijmegen bridge that day.

At Arnhem the delay, and its consequences, were yet more serious. Grounded even longer than the Americans had been, the British troop-carriers and gliders did not arrive until three o'clock, five hours late. By this time the two parachute battalions, which had been checked near Oosterbeek the night before, had forced an entry into Arnhem, but had been cut to pieces in a series of bitter actions around the Elizabeth Hospital, and their combined strength had been reduced to less than 250. They had neither the troops nor the ammunition to break through to the bridge, where Frost with no more than 600 men was still maintaining a gallant but precarious foothold at the northern end.

That morning his troops had effectively blocked the bridge by knocking out six armoured half-tracks which tried to rush through from the south. This road-block was covered by British fire from buildings beside the northern approach to the bridge, but late in the afternoon the Germans counter-attacked with infantry and tanks, and the paratroops had to yield ground when four of the houses they were holding were set alight. By the mere process of burning down the buildings, the Germans were bound to overpower the defenders before long unless substantial reinforcements could get through to them from Nijmegen or from the rest of their own division.

On the evening of this day (Monday, September 18)

the situation north of the Neder Rijn was extremely confused. In Arnhem itself the 1st Parachute Brigade, apart from Frost's battalion, was fast disintegrating. Early that morning Lathbury, the Brigade commander, and Urquhart had tried to reach the troops in the town, but had been cut off and compelled to take cover until the late afternoon. Then, as they sought to make their way back to Oosterbeek, Lathbury was wounded. Urquhart and another officer left him in the care of Dutch civilians, but were themselves forced to hide in the loft of a house. Even after dark, they could not escape, for there were Germans all around and an S.P. gun was stationed in the street outside.

In Urquhart's absence, Hicks (of the air-landing brigade) took command of the division, but he had no contact, even by radio, with Urquhart, Lathbury, Frost or any elements of 1st Parachute Brigade. This was partly due to the use of sets which would not work efficiently in a built-up area, and partly to the fact that a powerful British station was operating on the same frequency that had been allocated to the divisional command net. The frequency had to be changed, but the units isolated in Arnhem could not be advised, nor could they be heard on the old frequency. More serious still was the breakdown of communications with the outside world. Hicks urgently needed air support to deal with German tanks, but he could not call for it, as planned. The wireless link to the R.A.F. was not working, and he could not establish contact either with Airborne Base in England or with Browning's Corps H.Q. only 15 miles away.

For information about events in the town Hicks had to rely on reports from members of the Dutch Resistance who had seized the local telephone exchange. These reports cannot have revealed the full gravity of the situation in Arnhem, for Hicks continued to give prior consideration to the security of the "air-head." Into Arnhem he sent only two of his seven battalions, and he directed the newly-arrived 4th Parachute Brigade (Brigadier J. W. Hackett) to drive the Germans from the high ground north of Oosterbeek and thus strengthen the divisional perimeter. This attack proved to be a costly diversion of effort. The Germans were strongly entrenched in the woods and two parachute battalions lost half their strength in one day's fighting.

The battalions which headed for the bridge suffered even more heavily. It took them thirteen hours to cover three miles and, although they reached the Elizabeth Hospital and the survivors of 1st Parachute Brigade, they could advance no farther. Nor could any reinforcements get through to them. On the following day (Tuesday the 19th) this beleaguered force attacked and attacked in the hope of forcing a passage to the bridge, but German tanks and S.P. guns were covering every approach. When their anti-tank ammunition was exhausted, the airborne troops were driven back street by street through Oosterbeek to Hartenstein, where Urquhart, again in command, was forming a tight perimeter. There he hoped to stand his ground and conserve his strength until the arrival of XXX Corps.

The possibility of 1st Airborne being reinforced, or even re-supplied, by air was now remote, for it was not holding a large enough dropping area and the Germans had greatly increased their flak and fighter defences. That afternoon bad weather, and the appearance of more than five hundred enemy fighters, disrupted the reinforcement plan. Because of thick fog in the Midlands, the Polish Parachute Brigade and the glider infantry regiment of the 82nd Division were not able to leave their airfields. Some 655 troop-carriers and 431 gliders did take off from other bases, but only 60 per cent reached their destinations, and of those that failed to get through 112 gliders and 40 transports were lost. Worst of all, 390 tons of ammunition and food, dropped by parachute for 1st Airborne, fell almost entirely into enemy hands. The prearranged Supply Dropping Point was not located within the original landing area and the division had not been able to capture it. Urquhart had sent a signal suggesting a new dropping area but this had not been received in England.

The non-arrival of the Polish Brigade removed the last chance of any airborne forces coming to the rescue of the paratroops at the bridge in Arnhem. Since the previous morning, when a troop of anti-tank guns had broken through to him, Frost had been completely cut off. Nevertheless, he was still preventing the Germans from using the Arnhem bridge as a route for sending reinforcements to Nijmegen. But now, on the Tuesday evening, his situation was becoming desperate. His men were holding only a dozen houses and a school, and these were being heavily mortared and shelled. The cellars were filled with wounded. The surrounding houses were ablaze. The anti-tank ammunition was almost spent, and the 400 men still fit to fight could no longer drive off the tanks which were systematically demolishing their positions. And yet they fought on, withdrawing only when the buildings they held were set afire; still hoping that help might come from Oosterbeek, and not knowing that this hope was gone, for they had been out of radio communication since the Sunday evening.

On the morning of Wednesday, September 20, they regained contact with Divisional H.Q. through the Arnhem exchange, which was still being operated by Dutch patriots. Only then did Frost learn that there was no hope of rescue or relief unless he could hold out until the ground forces reached him from Nijmegen. There that day a combined attack was to be made upon the Waal bridge by the 82nd and the Guards who had strict instructions that the road to Arnhem must be opened at all costs.

On the morning of Tuesday, the 19th, the Grenadier Guards Group, the spearhead of their division, had driven rapidly through the corridor from Zon to the woods south of Nijmegen. There, however, they had found the Americans so hard pressed by attacks from the Reichswald that no move could be made against the Nijmegen bridges until mid-afternoon. Even then, Gavin could spare only one parachute battalion to operate with the Guards, for, as already mentioned, his glider infantry regiment had not been able to leave England. Since the road and rail bridges were both intact, a column was directed against each, but neither column could penetrate the defences which the Germans had had ample time to prepare.

All the approaches to the road bridge ran through some

gardens, called Huner Park, which the Dutch had fortified before the war and had held for three days in 1940. The Germans in turn had strengthened the defences of the park, especially those of an old mediæval fort and a large wooded knoll, the Valkhof. At the southern edge of the Huner Park the Anglo-American attack was halted. Tanks which tried to rush the bridge were knocked out. Guardsmen and parachutists who tried to infiltrate through the defences were cut off. That night, as Allied troops waited within reach of this great prize, they expected to see it blown to destruction. They did not know that Model himself had given orders that the bridge was not to be blown. "Model," says Student, had "prohibited the demolition of the bridge in the belief that it could be successfully defended."

During the night of the 19th–20th, while a battlegroup of 10th SS was being ferried across the Neder Rijn to stiffen the Nijmegen garrison, Horrocks and Browning made a new plan, designed to give them full possession of the Nijmegen road bridge by simultaneous attacks from north and south. Next day an American parachute regiment (the 504th) was to cross the Waal a mile downstream and seize the northern end of the bridge in concert with an attack on the southern defences by the Grenadier Guards and a battalion of parachutists. First, however, the town of Nijmegen had to be cleared of Germans so that the assault troops could gain access to the south bank of the Waal.

This mopping-up took all the Wednesday morning and it was nearly three o'clock before the 504th were in position to launch their storm-boats into the fast-running river. The combined effect of the current and the severe enemy fire was such that only half the boats carrying the first wave reached the north bank. Undaunted, some 200 men scrambled or swam ashore and established a slender foothold which was gradually reinforced and expanded as the afternoon wore on. This bold assault in clear daylight across a defended river, 400 yards wide, was a most brilliant and courageous feat of arms and was duly rewarded. By 6:30 the Americans had routed the opposition and were advancing towards the road bridge. En route, they secured the northern end of the railway bridge and there they raised the American flag.*

When this signal of success was seen by watchers on the southern bank, the Guards pressed home their attack. Here, in an afternoon of heavy fighting, while an American battalion was clearing the eastern half of Huner Park, the Grenadiers had driven the Germans from the Valkhof and had taken the fort by storm. The capture of these two strongholds opened the way to the bridge. At dusk, shortly before seven o'clock, five British tanks drove through the park, paused to engage some 88s shooting from the far bank, and then raced on with guns alive. Two tanks were hit by bazookas fired from the girders, but two others continued across the 600-yard length of bridge, through the road-block at the northern end and beyond it to link up with the Americans who were just approaching from the west. The Nijmegen bridge was in Allied hands undamaged, and a straight red road ran north to Arnhem.

There by now the staunch defenders of the road bridge had been cut down from 600 to 140 and Frost himself had been wounded. His men were still fighting from half a dozen houses around the northern pylons, but they were no longer holding the school from which for nearly three days they had maintained their road-block, preventing the southward movement of armour and artillery. That afternoon, under point-blank fire from several tanks, the schoolhouse had collapsed in flames and its garrison had been driven into the open streets. Thus it was that three hours before the first British tank crossed the Nijmegen bridge, heading north, the first German tank crossed the Arnhem bridge, heading south.

During the night the Germans made good use of the bridge which had been denied them so long, and on the morning of Thursday, the 21st, R.A.F. reconnaissance reported that twenty tanks were moving south from Arn-

*When Dempsey saw Gavin after this exploit he said: "I am proud to meet the commander of the greatest division in the world to-day." That opinion was endorsed by many another British officer who saw the 82nd in action.

hem and that the Germans appeared to be establishing fresh defences between the Neder Rijn and the Waal astride the Arnhem-Nijmegen road. Nevertheless, Horrocks still hoped to secure a bridgehead over the Neder Rijn, link up with 1st Airborne and drive on to the Zuider Zee in fulfilment of the original plan. Owing to the breakdown of Urquhart's radio communications, however, Horrocks did not know how grave the situation really was.

At nine o'clock that morning, one of Horrocks's artillery units, the 64th Medium Regiment, had established radio contact with the airborne division and had obtained the first direct news from Arnhem since XXX Corps began its attack. Through this channel Urquhart, unaware that Frost's force had at last been overrun, reported:

> Enemy attacking main bridge in strength. Situation critical for slender force [there]. Enemy also attacking divisional position East from HEELSUM vicinity and West from ARNHEM. Situation serious but am forming close perimeter around HARTENSTEIN with remainder of division. Relief essential both areas earliest possible. Still retain control ferry-crossing HEVEADORP.

From this signal Horrocks naturally concluded that Urquhart had some troops at the bridge in Arnhem and had a foothold west of the town large enough to be exploited, if quickly reinforced. He had already ordered the Guards Armoured Division to strike north "as early as possible and at maximum speed" along the main Arnhem road in the hope of breaking through to the bridge before the enemy could organise a new defence line. He now gave orders that, if the direct route were blocked, the Guards should work round west of the main road and head for the Heveadorp ferry. Arrangements had been made for dropping the Polish Parachute Brigade that afternoon near Driel to secure the southern end of the ferry, and it seemed that the Guards and the Poles together should be able to secure a base from which infantry could cross the river into Urquhart's perimeter. Then, with both banks in Allied hands, a bridge could be built at the ferry-site.

The plan was clear but the resources to carry it out were not immediately available. North of the Maas, Horrocks had only two divisions, the Guards and 82nd Airborne. Bad weather had so far prevented the arrival of Gavin's glider infantry regiment, and the rest of the 82nd, with the Coldstream Group in support, was fully engaged in defending the area between the Maas and the Waal, where the Germans were making frequent counter-attacks from the Reichswald flank.* In the Nijmegen bridgehead Horrocks had one parachute regiment and two groups of Guards, but the latter could not resume the offensive until they were relieved by infantry of the 43rd Division which was only just crossing the Maas.

On the one road by which XXX Corps and the American airborne divisions had to be reinforced and maintained traffic was moving slowly. For most of the 45 miles between the Meuse-Escaut Canal and the River Maas the roadway was narrow, and it passed through Eindhoven and half a dozen villages and over two rebuilt bridges. Because this single road was extremely vulnerable to air attack and artillery fire, the columns were ordered to move with vehicles well spaced and, accordingly, it had not been thought that they would be able to average more than ten miles in the hour. This might have been adequate if a steady flow could have been kept up, but an unexpected brake was imposed at the very start of the corridor.

On the first evening two three-tonners, following the armour, had been destroyed by mines which the Germans had laid in the grass verges immediately beside their road-block. In passing through this, the two trucks had gone off the concrete on to the grass and had been blown up. Next morning the wreckage of these vehicles was seen by all drivers moving north and, lest the warning should be dis-

---

*Gavin was also handicapped by shortage of artillery ammunition, for the four U.S. truck companies sent up from France to maintain the American airborne divisions did not reach the Meuse-Escaut Canal until the 20th. It was then found that they were loaded with the wrong type of 105 mm ammunition, and that some trucks had come up empty!

regarded, some overconscientious sapper had set up a notice: DON'T LET THIS HAPPEN TO YOU. KEEP ON THE ROAD. VERGES NOT CLEARED OF MINES.

By this time, in fact, all the mines at the road-block had been lifted, and it was most unlikely that the Germans would have been able to mine the verges of the road ahead since this had been their own supply line until the previous afternoon. Necessary or not, the warning was there, and British drivers, ever cautious, took due note of it. Over the next five miles to Valkenswaard the concrete road was only just wide enough for two vehicles. There were ample grass verges, but whenever convoys were halted to let more urgent columns through, the drivers clung to the concrete, creating a succession of traffic blocks which took hours to clear. The stretch of road between the frontier and Valkenswaard became a bottleneck which governed and constricted the northward flow of convoys.* Another bottleneck soon developed in Eindhoven which was heavily attacked by the Luftwaffe on the evening of the 19th. Here the Germans bombed an ammunition column of the Guards Armoured Division and for the next twenty-four hours the main streets of the town were blocked with wreckage.

The movement of traffic was further delayed by German activity on the flanks of the corridor, for the other two corps of Second Army, compelled to advance across an almost trackless wasteland of heath and swamp, made slow progress. By September 21 they had drawn level with Eindhoven but here they were checked. For the next thirty miles to Grave the corridor was little wider than the road itself, and bottlenecks, such as the Zon bridge and the tortuous streets of St. Oedenrode, were frequently shelled. On the 19th and 20th the Germans attacked this sector of the road from both sides. These attacks were driven off, but the passage of the road continued to be hazardous. The

---

*On the afternoon of the 18th, returning to file a dispatch, I found a traffic jam, two vehicles wide, almost the whole way from the Valkenswaard bridge to the Meuse-Escaut Canal. I was able to move south only by driving along the verge of the road.

advance had been made on such a narrow front that the line of communication was almost the front line; indeed, it had a front on either side. The result was that it took three days to transport the 43rd Division from the Albert Canal to the Maas, a distance of 60 miles, which the troops might have covered almost as quickly on foot.

It was, therefore, the afternoon of the 21st before the Irish Guards were able to attack from the Nijmegen bridgehead, and then they were halted almost at once by the anti-tank screen which the enemy had set up south of Elst. The terrain between the Waal and the Neder Rijn was reclaimed land, laced with innumerable small dykes and drainage channels which made cross-country movement impossible. The Guards had to advance along a road which was raised well above the surrounding polder and was flanked by deep ditches which the armour could not negotiate. On the road the tanks were "sitting shots" for the guns the Germans had sited in orchards and farmyards on either side. A direct attack with infantry and an outflanking movement by the Welsh Guards were equally unsuccessful, primarily because there was so little supporting fire. Owing to the shortage of ammunition, only one battery of artillery was available, and the Guards could not enlist the aid of the Typhoons as they had done so successfully on the first day. The aircraft were on call—in fact, they were overhead—but they could not be directed against the anti-tank guns, because the radio sets in the R.A.F. "contact car" failed to work. This was a grave misfortune. Without the help of the Typhoons there was no chance of the tanks breaking through that afternoon to Arnhem.

While the Guards were halted in front of Elst, the Polish Parachute Brigade was dropped between Elst and Driel in the face of heavy opposition from flak and fighters. But, by the time the Poles reached the south bank of the Neder Rijn, the Heveadorp ferry had been sunk and the northern end of the ferry-sight was in German hands. Urquhart's troops had been driven from it only two hours earlier.

On the previous day when Urquhart ordered his scattered and weakened battalions to withdraw inside the Hartenstein perimeter, some units, finding themselves cut off, had to fight their way in and lost heavily in the process. This was particularly the case with the 10th and 156th Parachute Battalions which had been trying to clear the woods north of Oosterbeek. When they reached the perimeter their combined strength was 135 men, fewer than ten per cent of those who had landed. Moreover, the Germans followed up so strongly that the 3500 survivors of the division were compressed into an area 1000 yards wide and 2000 yards deep. This area was brought under heavy and continuous fire from three sides and was repeatedly attacked by infantry and armour. Thus, although some of the supplies dropped on the 21st fell inside the perimeter, it was almost impossible for the troops to collect them.

The only help that XXX Corps could give the airborne troops on this day came from the guns of the 64th Medium Regiment. Having established radio contact, the regiment was able to bring down considerable and accurate fire on German positions around the Hartenstein perimeter. This relieved the pressure, but that evening, with stocks of food and water almost exhausted and ammunition running low, Urquhart reported: "No knowledge elements of division in ARNHEM for twenty-four hours. Balance of division in very tight perimeter . . . our casualties heavy. Resources stretched to utmost. Relief within twenty-four hours vital."

Early on the morning of the 22nd Horrocks signalled, "43 Div. ordered to take all risks to effect relief today and are directed on ferry. It situation warrants you should withdraw to or cross ferry." Urquhart replied, "We shall be glad to see you."

Horrocks now abandoned the idea of breaking through to the Zuider Zee, but he still retained the hope that he might secure an adequate bridgehead beyond the Neder Rijn for subsequent exploitation when the corridor had been widened and fresh forces had been brought forward. The plan for Friday, the 22nd, therefore, was that the 43rd Division (Major-General G. I. Thomas) should attack from the Nijmegen bridgehead at dawn with two brigades:

one striking along the main road through Elst to Arnhem, and another, on its left, following a side road through Oosterhout to the Heveadorp ferry. As both these brigades had reached Nijmegen on the 21st, Horrocks assumed that, in execution of these orders, Thomas would move his troops across the Waal during the night so that they would be deployed to attack in strength at first light. This, however, was not done and the opportunity of surprising the enemy under cover of the early morning mist was lost. Taking advantage of that mist, armoured cars of the Household Cavalry drove through Oosterhout soon after seven o'clock and made contact with the Poles before Thomas's infantry had even begun their attack.

The mist had cleared when, at 8:30 a.m. on the 22nd, the 7th Somersets advanced towards Oosterhout supported by a squadron of tanks, a troop of 17-pounders, mortar and machine-gun platoons, a battery of self-propelled 25-pounders and a field regiment. An hour later, however, on reaching the outskirts of Oosterhout, the leading platoon was "held up by fire from a tank and some infantry"—to quote the battalion's own history.* The operation then proceeded according to the book, for Thomas had not told the C.O. "to take all risks." The platoon that had been halted was extricated under cover of smoke. Another company with a troop of tanks endeavoured to work round the village but was "held up by heavy mortar fire." These manœuvres occupied most of the morning.

In mid-afternoon, when a battalion attack was made, "resistance was not heavy and was quickly overcome. . . . By 1700 hours the village was clear." This was not surprising. The attack was supported by more than a hundred guns, and the garrison can hardly have been formidable, for Oosterhout yielded only "139 prisoners, one quartermaster's store completely equipped, one Mark III tank, one 88 mm gun and five small A.A. guns." In the entire day's fighting, when the fate of the 1st Airborne Division

*The Story of the Seventh Battalion, the Somerset Light Infantry, by Captain J. L. J. Meredith, p. 73.

and the saving of the whole operaton were at stake, the Somerset's casualties amounted to "nineteen wounded." *

In fairness to the battalion, however, it must be said that they did no more than they had been trained to do. By nature Thomas was cautious and methodical and his troops followed his example. He was extremely thorough in the organisation of his attacks—so thorough that his battalions, like most of the infantry in Second Army, had come to believe that they could not advance without overwhelming fire support.** There was considerable truth in the criticism the Germans had made in Normandy that British infantry sought "to occupy ground rather than to fight over it." The consequences of that policy were never more apparent than on this day at Oosterhout.

Near Driel that morning the Household Cavalry had picked up two officers sent back by Urquhart and had relayed the following message from him: "We are short of ammunition, men, food and medical supplies. DUKWs are essential, two or three would be sufficient. If supplies do not arrive tonight it may be too late." To this signal Horrocks replied, "Everything possible will be done to get the essentials through." Consequently, when he discovered that neither of Thomas's brigades had made any real progress, and that Elst was strongly held, he ordered him to concentrate on opening the road through Oosterhout. The moment the village was clear, Thomas was to dispatch to Heveadorp a strong mobile column carrying supplies for 1st Airborne. At 6 p.m. the column, made up of two infantry companies riding on tanks, carriers and DUKWs, drove through Oosterhout and went on to join the Poles in Driel. Moving nose to tail, the vehicles covered the ten miles in an hour, but darkness had fallen before they

* *The Story of the Seventh Battalion, the Somerset Light Infantry,* by Captain J. L. J. Meridith, p. 75.

** That evening, when I saw General Horrocks, he was inclined to excuse the 43rd's slowness, for he did not know how little opposition there had really been at Oosterhout. Thomas's chief of staff (Lt.-Col. David Meynell), however, said to me, "I rather think it is our fault. We have been slow."

reached the river. It was then found that the banks were so steep and soft that the much-needed DUKWs could not be launched, and it was too late and too dark to reconnoitre firmer crossing places. No assault-boats were available and, although the troops toiled all night with improvised rafts, they were able to ferry across only fifty men of the Polish Brigade and a few small loads of food and ammunition.

It was now clear that a bridgehead could be established west of Arnhem only by a large-scale assault across the Neder Rijn, but the necessary troops and craft could not be brought forward immediately. Early that afternoon German tanks and infantry had cut the corridor between Veghel and Uden, thus isolating all forces north of the Maas. In consequence Horrocks was compelled to send the 32nd Guards Brigade back to reopen the road, a task which they, and American parachutists attacking from the south, were not able to accomplish until the following afternoon. This diversion of half the Guards Armoured Division to clear the corridor weakened the attack towards Arnhem. The direct road from Nijmegen was still blocked by the Germans in Elst and the minor route by which Thomas's troops had reached the Neder Rijn was under fire from Elst and was, in any case, unsuitable for heavy traffic.

On the evening of September 23, after "aerial re-supply" had again been thwarted by bad weather and enemy intervention, Urquhart signalled: "Morale still adequate but continued heavy mortaring and shelling is having obvious effects. We shall hold out but . . . hope for a brighter twenty-four hours ahead." That night, however, no major crossing of the Neder Rijn could be attempted; for 1st Airborne was so desperately in need of ammunition that the relieving forces had to concentrate on the ferrying of supplies. Between dusk and dawn only 250 Poles were able to cross the river and of these barely 150 reached the Hartenstein perimeter.

On Sunday the 24th—for the first time in the eight days since the start of MARKET GARDEN—the R.A.F. was able to provide strong air support for Urquhart's troops. Throughout the afternoon Typhoons struck at German positions around the perimeter and at enemy reinforcements moving towards it. This was the prelude to the assault-crossing, planned for that night, by Polish paratroops and the 4th Dorset. Inside the perimeter the writer of 1st Airborne's war diary noted, "Never was darkness more eagerly awaited." But darkness brought only disappointment. The attack was to have been launched at 10:30 p.m. but when the time came there were no assault boats available for the Poles and only four for the Dorsets. This was a direct consequence of the cutting of the road. After midnight, with these boats and five others that came up later, some 250 men crossed the river, a platoon at a time; but the swiftness of the current and the blackness of the night caused such disorganisation that the landings were widely spread and, before the Dorsets could find the airborne perimeter, the Germans closed in around them.

As dawn was breaking on the ninth day, Urquhart received a letter from Thomas advising him that Second Army had been obliged to abandon the attempt to establish a bridgehead and that 1st Airborne would have to be withdrawn. Urquhart replied that, if this was the plan, his troops must be withdrawn that night.

On the afternoon of the previous day (September 24) Dempsey and Horrocks, meeting at St. Oedenrode, had decided that on the night of the 25–26th, they would make a final attempt to gain a bridgehead north of the Neder Rijn. Their ability to do this, however, depended on the road remaining open for the northward movement of ammunition, assault boats and bridging equipment. Horrocks left St. Oedenrode at 4:30 p.m., but, even as he was driving through Veghel a few minutes later, the Germans came in from the west behind him and cut the corridor again: this time in such strength that it was to remain closed for forty-eight hours. This counter-stroke, combined with information from air reconnaissance that German infantry were digging in on the north bank of the Neder Rijn and that panzer reinforcements were moving towards the only sector of the river where a crossing could be made, forced upon Horrocks and Dempsey the reluctant decision to withdraw the 1st Airborne Division.

Within the shrunken perimeter Urquhart now had only

2500 men. For them, for the past five days, it had been, in the words of the division's own report, "a question of withstanding continuous attacks, mortaring and shelling. The force was dwindling steadily in numbers and strength . . . and was becoming increasingly short of ammunition. Much patching by small parties and frequent minor adjustments of the perimeter were necessary but, except for the deliberate closing-in of the northern face of the perimeter, little or no ground was lost." That, in itself, is a measure of the steadfast endurance and abiding courage of Urquhart's men, for the enemy pressure against the perimeter had been relentless and sustained ever since the paratroops at the bridge had been overwhelmed. From the 22nd onwards, the survivors of the division were heavily outnumbered and heavily out-gunned, but they maintained such a resolute defence, even under attack by tanks and assault guns, that, by the afternoon of the 25th, the Germans were content to contain them.

During this afternoon the airborne troops prepared to make their withdrawal and, at Divisional H.Q. in the Hartenstein Hotel, a signals officer, Lieut. J. Hardy, set free the last of the carrier-pigeons they had brought from England. One of these pigeons reached the H.Q. of VIII British Corps in Belgium, carrying this message:

1. Have to release birds owing to shortage of food and water.

2. About eight tanks lying about in sub-unit areas, very untidy but not otherwise causing us any trouble.

3. Now using as many German weapons as we have British. MGs most effective when aiming towards Germany.

4. Dutch people grand but Dutch tobacco rather stringy.

5. Great beard growing competition on in our unit, but no time to check up on the winner.

They left that night in heavy rain and high wind. A barrage from the guns of XXX Corps screened their departure and kept the enemy quieter than usual. Through woods and gardens, streets and houses which had been their battle-ground for so many days, they slipped away silently in small parties, each man clinging to the hand or the jacket of the man ahead. At the river's edge boats were waiting for them, manned by British and Canadian sappers. All night the ferrying continued under spasmodic fire from mortars and artillery, but the Germans made no direct attempt to prevent the withdrawal, for they did not realise what was happening. The heavy shelling from the south bank, and a gallant diversion by the Dorsets from the narrow foothold they had gained downstream, kept the Germans standing to in anticipation of another assault. Throughout the night the perimeter appeared to be manned, for wounded who could not be moved lay beside weapons and wireless sets and maintained the usual pattern of radio traffic and defensive fire. At daybreak on September 26 the evacuation had to stop, for German machine-guns began sweeping the river. By then 2163 men of the 1st Airborne Division and the Glider Pilot Regiment (together with 160 Poles and 75 Dorsets), had reached the safety of the south bank. Of the ten thousand who had landed north of the Neder Rijn only these few were rescued, and, as near as can be told, 1130 airborne troops remained at Arnhem for ever. Three hundred wounded inside the perimeter, and another two hundred men of the 4th Dorset, were taken prisoner, bringing the total of those captured in and around Arnhem to more than 6000, of whom nearly half were wounded before they fell into enemy hands.* Several hundred more remained at large, succoured and befriended by the Dutch. These were mostly men who had been cut off in the confused fighting of the past ten days or who, like Lathbury and Hackett, escaped from hospitals which the Germans captured. The majority eventually found their way back across the river, but another seven months were to elapse before British troops again set foot in Arnhem.

*The Germans, in a signal sent out by OKW on September 27 and recorded in the diary of the Naval War Staff, claimed that "6,450 prisoners were taken," and gave their own losses as "3,300 men," killed or wounded.

Aftermath

War is an exciting tonic to many men. Combat itself seems to release an exhilaration which can surely be felt in some of the narratives in this volume—in the daring raids, airdrops, and even in the destruction of the *Scharnhorst* in the frigid Arctic waters.

Yet in the aftermath of war the "taste of courage" that drives men in battle loses a certain essence, and is exchanged for a mood of melancholy. This restores a necessary balance and objectivity with which men may then reexperience the trauma of combat.

This awareness of "the passage over" is beautifully evoked in the next selection by Captain Laurence Critchell.

THE DISTANT DRUM WAS STILL*

by Capt. Laurence Critchell

From the small mountain stream at the bottom of the valley it is a climb to the main level of the town. Where the air is quiet there is a fragrance of wild flowers, and up to the very last turn of the road the climber can hear the slip and chuckle of the stream below. Set under the bushes along the way is a very old shrine to Mary and the Christ Child. Moss has grown over the wood.

At the top of the hill the road forks. One way leads past a four-story hotel of white stone and glass. If you are

*From *Four Stars of Hell.*

thirsty after the climb you can stop there for a stein of beer or a glass of cold *Liebfraumilch*. The drinks are served on a terrace, under beach umbrellas, where, in the evening, there are piano and violin concertos by starlight, and one can watch the moon rise over the snowy peak of the Vatzmann, twenty miles across the valley.

Follow the road to the right. It dips, like a slack rope, by a small park. There are scores of children. Like the young women, they are almost all blond. The girls are tanned a rich gold-brown which makes you think of wheat fields in the summertime. They wear flowered skirts and loose blouses, and if you look at them directly they will meet your eye.

There are art shops on the main street of town. Where there are no art shops, the walls themselves are painted. Above the archways on the square by the old palace is a fresco of Christ on the Cross, and around Him the heroic figures of the common people: laborers, farmers and soldiers. There is a little memorial to the war dead in the cool, sweet-smelling hallway of the church—a Christian cross supporting a helmet—and beneath it banks of wild flowers.

The houses are tinted pastel. Balconies lean over the narrow, crowded streets. Everywhere there is the clatter of life: of carts bringing families from the country, of bicycle riders, of sandals slip-slopping on the cobblestones. There is a tailor shop; there is a barber shop; there is a camera store; in another park there is a small motion-picture theater.

The hill road leads out of town, past the cemetery and the Catholic church, and overlooks the valley. Below is the other half of the town. It stands by the junction of two mountain streams. The railroad line from the north comes to an end at this point, but you can follow with your eyes where the tracks run out along the valley, adjoining the slate-colored river. The high snow mountains are all around. The clouds which make showers in the valley only make the snows deeper on those peaks. In the morning the mountains are violet and in the evening they are rose; by starlight they are as cool and remote as the firmament itself.

One of the streams that meet in the village is fed from a blue lake, about two miles away. Around the lake the snow mountains drop down in sheer stone cliffs, as they do at the *fjords* of Norway. There are boats for hire. There is also an electric launch which slips noiselessly out to the extreme end of the waterway, while the old boatman, who wears short pants and a hunting vest, blows a tin horn to demonstrate the echoes, and runs his vessel close to the waterfalls. At the far end of the lake there is a spit of land, and on it a small church dedicated to Saint Bartholomew, where the silence by the altar is so deep that one can hear the waterfalls a mile away.

This is where they thought he would be hiding.

This is Berchtesgaden.

For two months after the close of hostilities in Europe our regiment, with the 101st Airborne Division, occupied the area of Berchtesgaden, where we lived in the rich Bavarian living quarters of former SS troops. Towards the end we went to Linzen, in Austria, where we were on the border of Russian-occupied territory. In the latter part of August all the men of the division who were eligible to go home were assigned to the regiment, and, with Colonel Ballard still in command, entrained from Germany to Bar-le-Duc, France, a lonesome yellow town by a milk-white canal. Eventually, we were moved south to Marseilles and on August 8, 1945, we sailed for the United States.

The job was done.

Twice before in this story I have had to admit inability to convey a state of mind. The first of such references was during the long gloomy winter before the invasion of Normandy. The second was the state of mind, or, more strictly speaking, the state of being, of the soldier under fire. The first I attempted to suggest; the second I could only remark. But there was yet a third, of which I have made no mention at all. It was our state of mind when the firing ceased in Europe.

We had hated the war much more deeply than we had expected. Between the days of high spirits at Camp Toccoa to the sunny, quiet, mid-summer warmth of Berchtesgaden there had been, for almost all of us, experiences of horror endurable only if the heart steeled itself against kindliness, against hope, against life itself. There had been moments of bitterness so dark that, to survive, we could do nothing except go on. We had had to shut our minds against all that justified our presence here on earth and exist as the outer shells of human kind, devoid of pride, devoid of love, devoid even of faith and hope. Of modern war, nothing can be said in mitigation.

With the end of the fighting we expected these emotions to subside. And in a sense they did. But they were succeeded for a brief period by a feeling we had never known before.

Let me see if I can put it down:

During the first weeks after the end of the fighting I flew by C-47 from Salzberg to Paris. My plane was piloted by two young Americans whose names I did not ask. They were in their early twenties. Their navigation was casual— it is termed pilotage in the Air Forces—and anyone watching over their shoulders could tell that Europe had become as familiar to them, in terms of bomb-pitted fields and terra-cotta ruins, as the pleasant farmlands, the clean villages and the long white roads of home. The copilot, with a map across his knees, followed the course with his forefinger and only glanced down now and then at the silver Rhine, the shell craters slowly filling with green water, the silent, deserted gun batteries of the enemy.

It was not peace. It was only silence. And in that silence there was something strange. . . .

In Paris the great flags of the United Nations hung, unfurled, beneath the Arc de Triomphe, over the light of the Unknown—and, it sometimes seemed, eternal—Soldier. Overhead roared B-24s and B-17s, their pilots taking the ground crews on tours of the destruction in the Ruhr valley. And while I watched, one pilot, flying low over the Champs Elysées, coming straight as an arrow from the Place de la Concorde, dipped his wings in thunderous salute as he passed the arch.

But the Frenchmen on the streets below did not look up.

The crowds of men and women along the great boulevards walked slowly, silently, as though dazed and going in a dream. The American soldiers talked in subdued voices or did not talk at all. Everywhere there was a strange oppression. And in the occasional skips and hops of the little children, who had not yet recovered from the great excitement of the day of victory, and who still carried tricolors in their hands—in the sight of this childish joy there was something unmistakably obscene.

There it was. . . . That was it.

For this strange state of mind which fell upon us for a little while after the guns had been silenced was a vague sense of obscenity. It was the faint, lingering aftertaste of having achieved something monstrous. We had unleashed powers beyond our comprehension. Entire countries lay in waste beneath our hands—and, in the doing of it, our hands were forever stained. It was of no avail to tell ourselves that what we had done was what we had had to do, the only thing we could have done. It was enough to know that we had done it. We had turned the evil of our enemies back upon them a hundredfold, and, in so doing, something of our own integrity had been shattered, had been irrevocably lost.

We who had fought this war could feel no pride. Victors and vanquished, all were one. We were one with the crowds moving silently along the boulevards of Paris; the old women hunting through the still ruins of Cologne; the bodies piled like yellow cordwood at Dachau; the dreadful vacant eyes of the beaten German soldiers; the white graves and the black crosses and the haunting melancholy of our hearts. All, all, were one, all were the ghastly horror of what we had known, of what we had helped to do. . . .

Face it when you close this book.

We did.